The Illusion of Free Markets

The Illusion of Free Markets

Punishment and the Myth of Natural Order

Bernard E. Harcourt

Harvard University Press
Cambridge, Massachusetts, and London, England

Printed in the United States of America

First Harvard University Press paperback edition, 2012

Library of Congress Cataloging-in-Publication Data

Harcourt, Bernard E., 1963–
The illusion of free markets : punishment and the myth of natural order / Bernard E. Harcourt.
p. cm.
Includes bibliographical references and index.
ISBN 978-0-674-05726-5 (cloth : alk. paper)
ISBN 978-0-674-06616-8 (pbk.)
1. Punishment—United States. 2. Free enterprise—United States. 3. Chicago school of economics. 4. Chicago Board of Trade. I. Title.
HV9950.H393 2011
330.15'53—dc22 2010027060

To my colleagues
Gary Becker, Ronald Coase,
Richard Epstein, and Richard Posner

Contents

The Paris *Marais* and the Chicago Board of Trade

Commissioner Emmanuel Nicolas Parisot was conducting his rounds in the Saint-Paul market in the *Marais* in Paris. It was early May 1739. As the investigator, examiner, and royal counselor responsible for the Saint-Antoine district, Parisot reported to René Hérault, *lieutenant général de police* at the Châtelet of Paris, the royal palace of justice. Parisot was going from baker to baker, weighing their bread, when he discovered at Jean Thyou's stand "four three-pound breads each light one-and-a-half ounces."[1] At about the same time, Commissioner Charles, also doing his market rounds, discovered at Courtois's bakery on rue de Chantre "one bread labeled eight pounds in weight, light two ounces, two others marked the same weight one ounce light each, six labeled four pounds in weight each one ounce off, another six pound bread light one ounce and a half, two others labeled six pounds in weight, eight others marked four pounds in weight, all a half ounce light."[2] Another commissioner, Delespinay, found a cache of underweight breads in a small room hidden in the back of Aublay's bakery shop on the vieille rue du Temple. Delespinay immediately seized the bread and had it sent to the Sisters of the Charity of the Saint-Gervais parish.[3] (Commissioner Charles had sent his confiscated bread to the Capuchin friars on the rue Saint Honoré and to the poor at the parish of Saint-Germain l'Auxerrois.[4]) When the *lieutenant de police* held court the following May 5, 1739, Hérault condemned the bakers but showed mercy and, "this time only," sentenced each to only fifty livres in fines.[5]

Later the same month, on May 29, master baker Amand, an elected syndic in charge of his community of master bakers, found himself accused of selling a loaf of bread in his shop—specifically, "one white bread weighing four pounds, at eleven sols"—at a higher price than market—to be exact, "three deniers for each pound above the common market price."[6] Hérault declared Amand guilty, fined him three hundred livres, and stripped him of his elected office. In the sentencing order, Hérault ordered the other syndics to assemble within three days of the publication of his sentence and to proceed in their office to the election of a new syndic.[7] A week earlier, Hérault had convicted Marie-Hebert Heguin of buying grain at market for resale and fined her a thousand livres.[8] A royal ordinance prohibited buying grain with the intention of reselling it: "It is permitted to purchase grain at market for one's use; however, it is not permitted to buy grain for resale: the reason, very simply, is that he who buys for purposes of resale must necessarily gain from the transaction and, as a result, will sell it at a higher price than market rate, which constitutes a punishable monopoly."[9]

It is in these terms that M. Edme de la Poix de Fréminville described the Parisian grain markets in his 1758 *Dictionnaire ou traité de la police générale,* in which he collected, assembled, organized, classified, reported, and reprinted a myriad of these sentences and royal ordinances. A manual of policing, a compendium of disciplinary practices, Fréminville's dictionary codified alphabetically a gamut of rules and prescriptions covering not only subsistence—grains, bread, meats, fish, poultry, oysters, and legumes—but also gaming, sanitation, religious practice, guilds, sexual mores, even the charivari. Advertised as a "work necessary to all officers of the police and officers of justice, where they will find each and every one of their obligations and functions classified by each term, necessary as well to all prosecutors and practicing attorneys; & equally useful to priests, churchwardens . . . merchants . . . & others," the dictionary contained 564 pages of the most minute regulation of, well, practically everything.[10]

Fréminville was intimately familiar with these ordinances. Himself a *bailli* for the village and surroundings of Lapalisse in the Auvergne region of central France, Fréminville had magisterial powers in his countryside similar to those that a *lieutenant général de police* would have had in Paris.[11] Fréminville published his dictionary more than fifty years after the first volume of Nicolas Delamare's famous *Traité de la police* had appeared in 1705—the first of four massive *in-folio* tomes documenting and tracing in intricate detail the history of the police of Paris. Fréminville, though, targeted a wider audience with his dictionary. Whereas Delamare had written for the urban police officer—especially the Parisian police administrator—Fréminville pitched his treatise to the far more numerous country magistrates and prosecutors—the many *procureurs fiscaux* who resided in each village in France and administered the police function, meting out justice and regulating all aspects of daily life. By alphabetizing the rules and making them available in a more concise, single volume, *in-quarto,* Fréminville sought to disseminate the disciplinary rules further, to publicize them, to make them known in their finest detail.[12]

"Transgression of laws and ordinances are crimes both large and small, but however slight they may be, the ministry of the *procureur fiscal* must not tolerate them," Fréminville observed. "To despise but ignore small mistakes is to allow larger ones, and impunity throws villains into new infidelities."[13] Quoting Saint-Bernard from book 3 of *De Consideratione,* Fréminville declared that impunity is the "daughter of negligence, mother of insolence, source of impudence, nurse of iniquity and of transgressions of law."[14] He concluded: "The officer whose role is to suppress anything that deviates from what is prescribed as orderly must not neglect, even with respect to minor things, to punish those who contravene."[15]

Oddly, or perhaps not, Fréminville himself was deeply skeptical of these ordinances and opposed the restrictions on commerce associated with the regulation of the grain and bread markets. Fréminville was a partisan of "free trade," he professed. "It is indeed a delicate matter to tinker with the price of grain and its commerce, because he who regulates with an eye to reducing the market price often discovers that, as a result of unforeseen circumstances, the very regulations that he crafted, far from reducing it, raise the price and reduce the supply of the goods in question."[16] To Fréminville, the little-known author of the well-known *Essai sur la police générale des grains, sur leurs prix, &c.,* published anonymously in London in 1753, was entirely right when he declared that "by far the wisest and best policy to adopt is to grant merchants who commerce in grain absolute liberty, and to allow them to transport grain from one province to another, which is most fortunately what is now currently allowed under the King's declaration of September 17, 1754."[17]

Fréminville was a free trader and believed that self-interest would ensure an abundant supply of wheat and barley. This, he thought, was self-evident and demonstrated every day: whereas, for instance, the grain reserves maintained by the state and provinces had to be thrown in the river, rotten and infested, private individuals preserved their stock well in their granaries. "Such waste would never happen with an individual," Fréminville observed, "because it is their own property."[18] Private property and personal interest would help forestall such sordid outcomes and prevent the recurring grain shortages—*les disettes,* as they were called—that plagued France.

Many other historians of the Parisian grain and bread markets would share Fréminville's curious, almost morbid fascination with the intricate details of the ordinances, royal declarations, and sentences of the day. Though they too often favored free commerce, they were seduced by the maze of market regulations—as if they couldn't not look, as if they couldn't not dissect, count, and classify. The leading historical treatment on the *police des grains* from the nineteenth century—the treatise most often cited in later works—is itself the product of an arch-opponent of market regulation. Georges Afanassiev, a *privat-docent* at the University of Odessa in Russia, was a scholar of Anne Robert Jacques Turgot who later turned his attention to the commerce of grain. Afanassiev spent two years conducting archival research at the Bibliothèque and Archives Nationale in Paris in the early 1890s and produced a thorough and well-documented text, *Le Commerce des céréales en France au dix-huitième siècle,* originally printed in Russian, but translated into French and published in Paris in 1894. Afanassiev opposed market regulations, yet studied them in an equally obsessive manner; he was captivated by their pervasive and invasive omnipresence. The leading contemporary treatment of the *police des grains,* Steven Kaplan's magisterial two-volume dissertation turned monograph, *Bread, Politics, and Political Economy in the Reign of Louis XV,* also discloses a slight preference for liberalization. Though remarkably balanced and erudite, the text lets escape a tender glance toward reform. "In many of its particulars," Kaplan's text admits, "the liberal bill of indictment [of the *police des grains*] was well founded," and the later liberal grain reforms "were a devastating critique of the police practices we have discussed."[19]

Despite his free-trade ideology, then, Fréminville dissected and catalogued, reported, cried—much like the sentences from the Paris Châtelet were themselves cried at market—and decried the intricate details of myriad rules and regulations. Of Fréminville's lengthy book, ninety pages concern the cultivation and commerce of grain, the sale of bread, the regulation of the *boulangers* and *meuniers.* A full sixth of the entire dictionary covered everything from prohibiting the purchase of grain on the stalk to prohibiting anyone from walking in fields that have been sown (especially to pick flowers); from fixing the hours of sale to fixing the dates for harvesting; from prohibiting speech that would tend to raise grain prices to requiring seminaries and colleges to warehouse three years' worth of grain at all times.

All sales, naturally, were to take place at market. "It is forbidden, first, to sell or buy grains outside the market. The age-old prohibitions on this question, which dated back to the fourteenth century, had never been repealed, and since 1709 had been taken up again and applied more or less strictly."[20] Fréminville reported that the police of the Châtelet, by sentence dated February 20, 1728, had convicted a man named Lorillard for having sold "two *muids* [a measure] of quality flour . . . outside of the market square."[21] Another police sentence, dated May 27, 1729, had condemned several merchants—Petit, Chateaudun, and the son, René Petit—for having sold sixteen *muids* of wheat elsewhere than at market, and fined them each a thousand livres.[22] There are similar sentences recorded for February 29, 1731; January 31, 1738; and August 3, 1742—all for selling grain or flour off market.[23] In the police sentence dated January 11, 1737, the *lieutenant général* "renewed the prohibitions applicable to all bakers, millers, brewers, and the like, against buying any grain or flour, and to all farmers, farm laborers, and the like, against selling the same, by specimen or sample," anywhere but at the properly designated market.[24]

To ensure that all sales were conducted at market, other regulations imposed an obligation to certify market sales. A sentence issued in the police tribunal of the old Châtelet, dated October 10, 1681, confirms the confiscation of a "*muid* of flour in fifteen bags" for not having obtained a "certificate from where such merchandise was bought," and for failing to turn over the goods "to the measurers upon arrival at the doors and barriers" of the city.[25] It is interesting to note that the inspection here had been conducted by "Marie Claude Croisette, the elder, agent of the guild (Communauté) of the elected syndics of measurers of grain and flour of the city, *fauxbourgs,* and *banlieus* of Paris."[26] The police were not the only investigators, but instead were assisted by the syndics of the merchant communities—and often, it was the other way round.

Once at market, producers were forbidden to sell their grain and flour before a specified hour—an hour that varied according to the season. The eighteenth-century regulations followed daylight saving time. "The opening of trading in the markets and ports of Paris was fixed by a series of ordinances," Afanassiev tells us. "From Easter to Saint-Rémy, sales began at eight o'clock in the morning; from Saint-Rémy to Easter, at nine o'clock. In the provincial markets, market days and opening hours were determined the same way."[27] There were also rules about who could buy first at market. "Typically, the opening [of the market] was reserved for private individuals," Afanassiev writes, "that is to say, those who were neither bakers nor traders. Members of this latter group were not admitted until later. In Paris, they did not have the right to come to the market or be represented there before noon, nor could they even talk with vendors near the perimeter of the market."[28] Fréminville adds: "It is forbidden for all innkeepers, hoteliers, and tavern owners to buy on days of markets and fairs . . . before eight o'clock in the morning from Easter to the first of October, and before nine o'clock from the first of October to Easter."[29]

Other ordinances punished speech that could tend to increase the price of grain: "It is not permitted to hold, spread, or publish any speech that could prevent [the sale of grain] at the fixed price, nor to suggest that the cost of grain will increase, that there isn't any grain at such and such place, or that it is worth a lot more elsewhere; speech of this nature tends to cause the price to increase," Fréminville explained.[30] A police sentence of the Châtelet dated July 22, 1740, fined a man named Fieffé 2,000 livres for having "held in the Gonesse market speech that tended to alarm the public and to raise the price of grain."[31] What, exactly, was the nature of his speech? The squire Martin Rulhier, sheriff of the Île-de-France and commander of the brigade of Saint

Denis, had gone to the Gonesse market to "investigate any violations that could have been committed against the spirit of the king's declarations, the judgments of parliament, and the regulations and sentences of the police."[32] The widow Bethemont, baker at Gonesse, told him that a certain Fieffé, a farmer, had refused to sell her his nine *septiers* of wheat at the common market price. "He would only sell the wheat for thirty livres, whereas the highest price that day had been twenty-six livres; she [the widow Bethemont] had offered twenty-seven, at which he replied that for that price he would prefer to pack it up, especially since he had gotten thirty-three livres at Pont, twenty-eight at Dammartin, and thirty-two at Nanteuil-le-Hardouin. He said he would sell it at the next market, and in effect packed up his nine *septiers* of wheat."[33] The police lieutenant characterized this speech as "tending to alarm the public, cause sedition, increase the price of grain, and consequently that of bread."[34]

According to Fréminville, the grain trade had to be one of the main concerns of the county prosecutor. Fréminville repeatedly underscored the importance of the market regulations: grain and grain markets, he affirmed, "should constitute the largest and principal responsibility of the *Procureur Fiscal*."[35] "We are dealing here with the lives of our fellow humans, and it is imperative that they not be sacrificed to the monopolists who meddle in selling and reselling grain."[36] Fréminville's dictionary covered the grain industry exhaustively, and there were in fact so many regulations of the market that, for the dictionary entry on "Marchés"—the entry on *markets*—Fréminville merely refers the reader, by cross-reference, to another entry.[37] His dictionary reads:

MARKETS. *SEE* POLICE.

To our modern eyes, the Parisian *police des grains*—the intricate and extensive web of royal decrees and ordinances that governed absolutely every aspect of the commerce of grain under the ancien régime, the tangled snare of regulations that gave rise to the very "grain wars of the eighteenth century"—has come to symbolize excessive government control and intervention.[38] The policing of the grain trade, with its tangled lattice of edicts intended to keep down the price of bread in Paris and the provinces, stands today as a labyrinth, a morass of regulations that led to government tinkering in even the most infinitesimal details of each commercial exchange.

Codes, dictionaries, and treatises of the police would proliferate. The codification itself had begun at least as early as the sixteenth century and the important dates were well known: the *réglements* of 1567 and 1577, the *déclaration* of August 31, 1699, or April 19, 1723. The edicts and decrees had spanned several centuries. But the mid-eighteenth century was an important period for the dissemination of the rules, for cataloguing and publishing them in dictionaries and treatises as a way of publicizing them. The year 1758 marked the publication not only of Fréminville's *Dictionnaire,* but also of M. Duchesne's augmented and authoritative second edition of *Code de la police, ou analyse des réglemens de police, divisé en douze titres.* Originally published in Paris in 1757, Duchesne's popular treatise was supplemented and reprinted just twelve months later. It compiled, in over 480 pages, all the police rules and regulations pertaining to religion, customs, health, science and liberal arts, commerce, manufacture, mechanical arts, servants, domestics, and the poor. Within the policing of commerce alone, Duchesne had chapters on weights and measures, on fairs and markets, on commerce in grain, wine, livestock, candles, wood, and wool—to name a few—and on merchants, their agents, currency exchanges, and banks. The year 1758 was also when the first volumes of *Code Louis XV: Recueil des principaux edits, déclarations, ordonnances, arrêts, sentences et réglemens concernant la justice, police et finances depuis 1722 jusqu'en 1740* were published. The *Recueil* would assemble in one place all the important ordinances and sentences on policing and grow to a twelve-volume set.[39] Numerous other codes, including Deslandes's 1767 *Code de la police, ou analyse des réglemens de police, divisé en douze titres,* would also be published and reprinted in Paris during the period.[40]

It was precisely this maze of ordinances that Adam Smith, in *The Wealth of Nations,* castigated as "such absurd regulations, as frequently aggravate the unavoidable misfortune of a dearth, into the dreadful calamity of a famine" or as "the folly of human laws."[41] It was an economic approach, Smith would famously suggest, that "embraced all the prejudices of the mercantile system, in its nature and essence a system of restraint and regulation."[42] Smith's view would shape generations of readers, and even today, most commentators and historians continue to characterize the ancien régime administration as excessive, overregulated, and frenzied in its minute management of even the most trivial infractions. Even Michel Foucault, a careful and subtle reader of the eighteenth century, would characterize the *police des grains* as regulated through and through. In his 1978 lectures at the Collège de France, Foucault specifically deployed the term "discipline" in its most pristine form to describe the administration of the grain trade. In his view, the Parisian *police des grains* of the eighteenth century served as the archetypal example of "discipline" and displayed the three key elements of that seminal concept: *la police des grains* was centripetal; it focused on the smallest of minor details and sought to eradicate all disorder; and it categorized acts and practices as either permissible or impermissible. Foucault went so far as to rename the *police des grains* "la police *disciplinaire* des grains"—the disciplinary policing of the grain trade. "If we take again the example of the *disciplinary* police of grain as it existed until the middle of the eighteenth century, as set out in hundreds of pages in Delamare's *Traité de la police*," Foucault would lecture to his overflowing auditoriums, "we see that the *disciplinary* police of grain is in fact centripetal."[43] To many today, the *police des grains* has become the example of pure discipline.

Our Modern Free Markets

The contrast with our contemporary perception of modern American markets—whether in grain or more broadly—could not be sharper. Today, it seems, commerce has been liberalized, the forces of the free market unleashed, and the constraints of the past lifted. Self-regulating mechanisms have replaced the rigid *police des grains* and brought about, in a more efficient manner, reasonable prices and more abundant supplies. Our contemporary markets and commodity exchanges are far freer—certainly more so than the Parisian markets were in the eighteenth century. And although globalization and population growth loom on the horizon as potential threats to the adequacy of the supply of food, water, and other necessary goods, voluntary and free exchange at home is decidedly the model of choice.

"The close of the twentieth century saw a virtual canonization of market organization as the best, indeed the only effective, way to structure an economic system," observes professor Richard Nelson at Columbia University.[44] As J. Rogers Hollingsworth and Robert Boyer add, "Throughout Eastern and Western Europe as well as in North America during the 1980s, there was a dramatic shift toward a popular belief in the efficacy of self-adjusting market mechanisms. Indeed, the apparent failure of Keynesian economic policies, the strains faced by the Swedish social democratic model, and the collapse of Eastern bloc economies led many journalistic observers to argue that capitalism is a system of free markets that has finally triumphed."[45] Nelson captures the more dominant, orthodox view succinctly:

> For-profit firms are the vehicles of production. They decide what to produce and how, on the basis of their assessments about what is most profitable. . . . Competition among firms assures that production is efficient and tailored to what users want, and prices are kept in line with costs. The role of government is limited to establishing and maintaining a body of law to set the rules for the market game and assuring the availability of basic infrastructure needed for the economy to operate.[46]

Nelson concedes that this is a simplified version of "the standard textbook model in economics," perhaps even a bit of "folk theory."[47] But it is, in broad outline, an accurate description of a dominant view that has had a powerful influence, especially during the latter part of the twentieth century and the beginning of the twenty-first. As Boyer suggests, accurately I believe, "The market is now considered by a majority of managers and politicians as the co-ordinating mechanism 'par excellence.'"[48]

The Great Recession of 2008 shook these beliefs, but by no means displaced them. There is today, at least in the United States, a remarkably persistent force to free-market ideas and an equally strong resistance to government regulation and nationalization. This is reflected well in the debates in 2009 over the partial nationalization of commercial banks that were teetering on the brink of bankruptcy. Even in the deepest hours of the financial collapse—at a time when most economists believed that several of the largest banks, such as Citibank or Bank of America, might go bankrupt—it was not possible to suggest nationalization without also mentioning that the measure would be temporary. In fact, one of the preferred terms for temporary nationalization became "preprivatization"—the idea that the U.S. Treasury needed to nationalize financial institutions in order quickly to clean them out and better privatize them.[49] And as soon as the darkest moments of the financial crisis receded from view, the specter of Keynesianism similarly ebbed and became, once again, a fleeting shadow in public discourse.

The standard view of market superiority in the economic domain traces, naturally, to classical economics and, in its more recent, forceful, and technical iteration, to the Chicago School of economics. The central tenets of the Chicago School can be summarized in these nontechnical terms: "The Chicago School believes that markets—that is, millions of individuals making separate decisions—almost always function better than economies that are managed by governments. In a market system, prices adjust whenever there is a shortage or a glut, and the problem soon resolves itself. Just as important, companies constantly compete with each other, which helps bring down prices, improves the quality of goods and ultimately lifts living standards."[50]

To be sure, many commentators today, especially legal scholars and administrative lawyers who toil in the regulatory domain, consider the original Chicago School position to be extreme. And even some of the staunchest Chicago School adherents have themselves softened their claims to allow for slightly more governmental intervention in cases of market failure associated with externalities, monopolies, collective action, or other coordination problems. One of the most ardent Chicago libertarians, Richard Epstein, for instance, has moderated his view over time and embraced a slightly more collectivist position. "My ideal government is not quite as small as [I suggested in the 1970s], but it is still much smaller than the massive government in place today," Epstein states. "Thus it is not sufficient to assume that the only forms of conduct accompanied by undesirable social consequences are those involving the use of force or fraud. . . . [A] more comprehensive social statement seeks to maximize social welfare, embracing the libertarian prohibitions, but going beyond them to allow certain forms of regulation and taxation to overcome these otherwise intractable coordination problems."[51]

Nevertheless, the Chicago School's initial free-market position has helped shape a more moderate view that tends to dominate public discourse in the United States today: that government intervention in the economic domain *tends to be* inefficient and should therefore be avoided. This view is characterized by a set of gentler a priori assumptions: that market mechanisms tend to work better and government agencies tend to be less efficient because private market participants are better information gatherers and tend to be more invested in the ultimate outcome; that government agencies suffer from greater principal-agent problems, are less nimble at adjusting to changing market conditions, and become more entrenched and subject to interest-group capture; and that, especially when transaction costs are low, market mechanisms are far more likely to result in allocations of rights and resources that optimize the overall size of the economic pie. These familiar arguments together promote a loose default position in favor of "free-market" mechanisms over "regulation." They reflect a more popular and common, albeit softer, tilt toward less regulation—a general view that David Harvey, a perceptive critic, identifies in these terms: "the role of the state is to create and preserve an institutional framework [characterized by strong private property rights, free markets, and free trade]. . . . State interventions in markets (once created) must be kept to a bare minimum because . . . the state cannot possibly possess enough information to second-guess market signals (prices) and because powerful interest groups will inevitably distort and bias state interventions . . . for their own benefit."[52] These are recurring arguments that, in combination, tend to favor less, rather than more, government intervention.

During the 1970s and early 1980s, this view helped bring about a wave of privatization in the United States.[53] The momentum has continued since that time and the effects of privatization have been significant in a wide range of industries, from airlines and communications to what were often viewed as more traditional state and local services. The embrace of privatization strengthened in the 1990s with the collapse of the former Soviet Union and of its political and economic influence over Eastern Europe. Today the call for privatization is no longer limited to Reagan Republicans, but can be heard across the political spectrum—even among younger Democrats. President Bill Clinton's administration supported a large number of alternatives to standard governmental delivery services—thirty-six, in fact—in its "Reinventing Government" strategy.[54] As a Democratic presidential candidate, Barack Obama partially embraced Reaganomics in his book *The Audacity of*

Hope, writing that "Reagan's central insight—that the liberal welfare state had grown complacent and overly bureaucratic, with Democratic policy makers more obsessed with slicing the economic pie than with growing the pie—contained a good deal of truth."[55]

This moderate view has infiltrated the public imagination and shapes contemporary public opinion. Careful scholars of public perceptions—institutional sociologists, economic historians, and economic sociologists—have studied the rise of these beliefs from a range of perspectives and traced, over the latter part of the twentieth century, "a time of market deregulation, state decentralization, and reduced state intervention in economic affairs in general."[56] As the critics of the trend suggest—accurately, but in somewhat provocative terms—these beliefs have become "hegemonic," the "new planetary vulgate," a "thought virus."[57] There has emerged what Jean Comaroff and John Comaroff identify as the "impulse to displace political sovereignty with the sovereignty of '*the* market,' as if the latter had a mind and a morality of its own."[58]

The evidence from public opinion polls confirms the dominance of free-market ideals. In an opinion poll conducted by the *Financial Times* and the Harris Poll on September 6 and 17, 2007, 49 percent of respondents in the United States answered affirmatively to the question "Do you think a free-market, capitalist economy (an economic system in which prices and wages are determined by unrestricted competition between businesses, with limited government regulation or fear of monopolies) is the best economic system or not?"; only 17 percent responded negatively.[59] In another poll, a twenty-nation survey conducted by the Program on International Policy Attitudes (PIPA) at the University of Maryland, researchers found that, on average, 71 percent of respondents in the United States agree with the statement "The free enterprise system and free market economy is the best system on which to base the future of the world"; only 24 percent of respondents disagreed with that statement.[60] Although those polling results preceded the Great Recession, it seems that any temporary shift in the polling numbers receded as rapidly as the fears of imminent collapse. In August and September 2009, a Gallup Poll survey found that a majority of Americans "believed that there was either too much regulation, or about the right amount," whereas only a quarter of Americans felt there was "too little government regulation of business and industry." In another poll conducted in January 2010, Gallup found that 57 percent of Americans were "worried that there will be too much government regulation of business," with only 37 percent of Americans worrying that there will not be enough. On a related question, Gallup discovered that "half of Americans believe the government should become less involved in regulating and controlling business, with 24% saying the government should become more involved and 23% saying things are about right."[61] America's faith in the free-market system is remarkably robust.

This dominant view in favor of free markets is reinforced daily in leading newspapers, other media, and by national leaders on both ends of the political spectrum, right and left—often in unexpected places.[62] In contrast to the disciplinary regimentation characterized by the Parisian *police des grains* at mid-eighteenth century, the contemporary period has seen the virtues of self-adjusting and self-regulated markets. As a result, today's exchanges and marketplaces tend to be far less regulated. At least, that's what we like to tell ourselves.

In the Wheat Pits

Loud buzzers drowned out the trading activity and signaled the close of the market for March 1996 wheat futures at the Chicago Board of Trade at 12:01 P.M. on March 20, 1996. The closing period—which spanned just one minute, from 12:00 P.M. to 12:01 P.M.—had just expired, following a period of tight supplies in the wheat market. There were sixty-one buy order contracts that were still unfilled, and the last contracts had traded at $5.30 to $5.35 a bushel, in line with the morning's trades. Two traders who held market-on-close orders, George F. Frey and John C. Bedore, bid up the price through closing to approximately $6.00 per bushel, but they were met with no responses from other members of the pit.

At 12:02 P.M., one minute past the close, J. Brian Schaer, a local in the pit, offered to sell contracts at $7.00, and approximately twelve seconds later, at 12:02:12 P.M., sold thirty-one contracts at that price to Frey and Bedore—who had been bidding up the price hoping to close their open orders. Donald W. Scheck, another local, then offered contracts at $7.50, with Brian Schaer matching that offer. In the next half a minute, Scheck sold fourteen contracts to a broker, Jay P. Ieronimo, and Schaer sold another sixteen contracts to Frey and Ieronimo, with the final trades taking place at 12:02:50 P.M.—one minute and fifty seconds past closing.

Rule 1007.00 of the Chicago Board of Trade provides that the pit committee—in this case, the "Wheat Pit Committee" chaired by Jay Ieronimo, who had just traded after closing—could authorize an extension of the closing period, for one minute only, in the case of an extraordinary expiration. That never happened, but even if it had, it would only have extended the trading period to 12:02 P.M., which would not have covered the trades contracted after that.[63] A number of board officials, including the Chicago Board of Trade chairman, Patrick Arbor, and the Exchange Pit Reporter floor supervisor, Patrick Sgaraglino, gathered to discuss whether any trades after

12:02 P.M. should be honored and cleared through the house. They decided the trades would stand because of "special circumstances" surrounding the March wheat futures.

Ieronimo, in his capacity as chair of the Wheat Pit Committee, then began asking around to find out if any of the traders were interested in holding a modified closing call—known in the trade as an "MCC" and consisting of "a two-minute post-close trading session which may occur after the end of a trading session and allows market users to close out unliquidated positions. Pit committees schedule MCC sessions only when there is an expression of interest. The MCC settlement price, which serves as the basis for the trading range during the MCC session, is selected by the pit committee."[64] Brian Schaer, who had sold contracts past 12:02 P.M., was apparently the only trader who expressed interest in an MCC.

Ieronimo decided to hold the MCC. "A bull horn was used to announce that an MCC would be held from 12:14 P.M. to 12:16 P.M. A few seconds before the start of the MCC, an Exchange official announced that the MCC price range would be $5.30 to $5.32 per bushel."[65] Ray Czupek, the floor manager and broker for Louis Dreyfus Corporation—which still held a significant long position in March wheat—offered contracts at $5.32 per bushel—thus entering the market for new business in violation of the board rule against entering new orders during an MCC. Brian Schaer and Donald Scheck, who had both sold contracts ranging between $7.00 and $7.50 after the one-minute extension to closing, were the only ones to bite. Schaer and Scheck both bought contracts sufficient to offset the entire positions that they had just created post-closing, and made profits on their trades of, respectively, $434,800 and $152,600. There were no other trades made during the MCC. Others involved in the earlier trading saw large losses, some as high as $300,000.

The Office of Investigations and Audits of the Chicago Board of Trade conducted a quick review of the March futures expiration, and about a month later the Business Conduct Committee of the board issued charges against Schaer, Scheck, Ieronimo, Frey, Bedore, and Czupek, as well as Dreyfus and two other firms. They were charged with violations of Chicago Board Rules 1007.00, 350.05(h), 1007.02, and 425.02, proscribing after-hours trading, as well as violations of MCC conventions and hedging rules. Board Rules 1007.00 and 1007.02, for instance, set forth the following restrictions on trading:

> On the last day of trading in an expiring future, a bell shall be rung at 12 o'clock noon designating the beginning of the close of the expiring future. Trading shall be permitted thereafter for a period not to exceed

> one minute and quotations made during this time period shall constitute the close. When in the opinion of the relevant Pit Committee extraordinary conditions prevail any such one minute period may be extended to two minutes by special authorization of the relevant Pit Committee . . .
>
> Immediately following the prescribed closing procedure for all contracts, there shall be a two (2) minute trading period (the "modified closing call"). All trades which may occur during regularly prescribed trading hours may occur during the call at prices within the lesser of the actual closing range or a range of three (3) official trading increments, i.e., one (1) increment above and below the settlement price, or at prices within the lesser of the actual closing range or a range of nine (9) official trading increments, i.e., four (4) increments above and below the settlement price, as the Regulatory Compliance Committee shall prescribe; (ii) no new orders may be entered into the call; (iii) cancellations may be entered into the call; (iv) stop, limit and other resting orders elected by prices during the close may be executed during the call; and (v) individual members may trade as a principal and/or agent during the call. In accordance with the determination of the Regulatory Compliance Committee, CBOT contracts shall be traded during the Modified Closing Call as follows: Lesser of actual closing range or nine trading increments [for] Wheat Futures and Options.[66]

During the summer of 1996, the board entered into settlement negotiations with Schaer, Scheck, and the other individuals and firms. Settlements reached with Schaer, Scheck, Ieronimo, Frey, and Bedore involved the board's issuing letters of reprimand against each of them; the Dreyfus Corporation was required to admit wrongdoing and pay a $10,000 fine.

The issue was far from resolved, however. The divisions of enforcement and of trading and markets of the Commodity Futures Trading Commission recommended that the commission review the six settlements because they did not believe that the written sanctions were "commensurate with the gravity of the alleged violation and otherwise failed to conform to Commission guidance on sanctions."[67] In light of the commission's decision to review, the Chicago Board of Trade conducted additional investigations and interviewed thirty-eight persons. The interviews were transcribed and then reviewed by the staff of the Commodity Futures Trading Commission, which oversees the board; afterward the board prepared follow-up questions for nineteen persons at the request of the commission staff, and resubmitted the second round of interviews to the commission. The board also submitted documentary evidence: trading cards, order tickets, and other reports.

The commission conducted an additional investigation of its own. In addition to the board documents, the record of the disciplinary proceedings, and written argument by the parties, it reviewed "observations of Commission floor surveillance staff during the expiration" and "information independently obtained by the Commission staff."[68] The latter included "interviews with commercial participants, market analyses, trading profiles of the two locals [Schaer and Scheck] involved in the expiration, a trade practice investigation, review of data to determine compliance with speculative position limits, and a review of the 'gap' function in the CBOT's price reporting system."[69]

The commission set aside the sanctions and remanded the cases back to the board of trade because the penalties had not been severe enough. "In order to protect the integrity of the markets, the exchanges must vigorously enforce their rules concerning trading hours and impose meaningful sanctions in disciplinary proceedings alleging trading after the close," three commissioners declared. "We believe that imposing reprimands for misconduct as serious as that alleged here, even in the context of settled proceedings, reflects an apparent unwillingness on the part of the CBOT to enforce its rules in the manner necessary to ensure an effective self-regulatory disciplinary program."[70]

The notion of "self-regulation" is critical in the commission's written opinion. The very term "self-regulatory" is used seven times in the main text, another five times in the margin, and twice in the dissenting opinion: strict sanctions are "necessary to ensure an effective self-regulatory disciplinary program," reflect the board's "critical self-regulatory responsibilities" and whether the board "adequately fulfilled its self-regulatory responsibilities," indicate "the seriousness with which the self-regulatory organization views its rules," and are crucial for such "self-regulatory organizations."[71] In this case, the commission concludes, "the sanctions chosen by the CBOT are inadequate in light of . . . their reflection of an apparent failure in the self-regulatory system."[72] "In exercising their self-regulatory responsibilities," the commission emphasizes, "exchanges should take vigorous action against those who engage in activities which violate their rules."[73] In conclusion, the commission notes, "The CBOT's approach in these cases could seriously undermine its ability to operate effectively as a self-regulatory organization."[74]

The commissioners justify their concern with the following statement:

> Any disregard of established trading hours should be viewed as a significant violation. Rules governing the time, place, and manner of trading help to ensure a fair and open market. No one of these requirements is less important than the others, and noncompliance with any one of them may be as damaging to the market as noncompliance with all of

> them. Even when done in the pit by "open outcry," post-close trading threatens an open and competitive market because a large segment of the market—those who obey the rules governing trading hours—are excluded from participating. As former Commission Chairman Philip Johnson has observed, the rationale for prohibiting trading other than during official trading hours is that "true competition is only present in the marketplace during normal hours of trading." The absence of "true competition" calls into question the price discovery role of the exchange and could result in loss of confidence in CBOT prices. As we recently stated, "open and competitive execution is the bedrock underlying public confidence in the objectivity and fairness of futures trading."[75]

Trading-hour infractions are extremely significant, the commission emphasized. In fact, "Congress has determined that activities like [these] are *malum in se*, and it is our duty to assure that this legislative determination is effectuated."[76]

The U.S. Attorney's office in Chicago began investigating trading-hour infractions on the Chicago Board of Trade. In order to preempt further federal intervention, the board revised its rules regarding the possible extension of the closing period. "Most notably, the CBOT deleted the provision under which the close of an expiring contract could be extended from one minute to two minutes, thus eliminating potential confusion among floor members about the appropriate duration for a close in an expiring contract. The CBOT also now precludes the pit reporters from accepting price quotations more than 30 seconds after the close for futures in order to assure that trading is halted on time."[77]

Framing the Inquiry

More than two centuries divide the Parisian *police des grains* from these enforcement proceedings at the Chicago Board of Trade. The two periods bear important similarities and differences. Yet the general perception of the two moments could not be more radically divergent. The Paris markets of the mid-eighteenth century signify the epitome of excessive regulation—of government intervention gone awry, of authoritarian control of the economy, of pure discipline. In contrast, the Chicago Board of Trade is, to our modern eyes at least, the epitome of the free market in the Western world, the pinnacle of liberalized exchange, the zenith of late-modern capitalism. Simply put, the Chicago Board of Trade *is* the free market. And when we look at the Chicago Board or the New York Stock Exchange, we do not see the intricate web of regulations regarding closing periods and trading hours, price control, surveillance, and computer monitoring. We do not see Chicago Board Rules 1007.00, 350.05(h), 1007.02, and 425.02, which proscribe after-hours trading and explain MCC conventions, trading ranges, and hedging rules. Instead, we see the free market at work.

How did that come about? How did we come to see these spaces as so markedly different, especially given that, in both epochs, these markets were the exclusive venue to exchange commodities and both of them were so fully administered? Who, when, where, how—the hours of opening and closing, the identity of the merchants, traders, and buyers, the means of delivery, controls on variations in pricing—all aspects of trading on the markets were regulated. Even the price of commodity futures is set during an MCC, and today the very price of money—the most important commodity of all—is fixed by the government. Truth is, our contemporary markets are shot through with layers of overlapping governmental supervision, of exchange rules and regulations, of federal and state criminal oversight, of policing and self-policing, and self-regulatory mechanisms—as is evident in a case such as that of Schaer and Scheck. Our contemporary markets, much like the Parisian markets of the eighteenth century, are thoroughly policed.

Naturally, there are differences. No police prefect or *procureur fiscal* has the authority to set the right price of a loaf of bread or a stack of wheat today—though even this difference is less sharp than at first glance. Recall again that Board Rules 1007.00 and 1007.02 fix the price ahead of time for the commodity at an MCC. Moreover, the commission for trading, in other words the price of the transaction, is generally fixed, and the price of money is set by the central bank. (A close inspection of the eighteenth-century records reveals, in addition, that the fixing of prices then was actually haphazard, irregularly enforced, and more of a guideline than a rule.) True, no *huissard* patrols the exchange floor conducting inspections and ferreting out fraud or deception today—although here too, computer algorithms, federal investigators, and the exchanges themselves monitor each and every trade to detect suspicious activity, often on "a customer-by-customer basis."[78] True, contemporary enforcement proceedings are more likely to involve self-regulatory mechanisms, such as self-monitoring by the exchange itself, though here again the eighteenth-century markets were also heavily self-policed under a guild system that used elected syndics to monitor the commercial activities of guild members and enforce the rules.[79] In both cases, there was also a mix of self-regulation by market players—Parisian syndics and oversight committees at the Chicago Board—and government regulators—the *lieutenant général de police* as well as the Futures Trading Commission and U.S. attorneys.

There are indeed differences and similarities, but they are both vastly more complicated than those simple labels of "over-regulated" and "free" would suggest. How is it, then, that so many of us have come to perceive the first economic regime—the Paris markets circa 1758—as governed by, to borrow Adam Smith's words, "such absurd regulations," and yet view the second regime, today's Chicago Board of Trade, as "free"? What has shaped our perception so profoundly that we would label one "discipline" and the other "liberty"?

Public Economy, Police, and Liberty

And let's be clear. In answering this question, let's not be too simplistic, nor risk bias. The issue is not simply that we read "freedom" onto a contemporary landscape that is shot through with regulatory mechanisms. It is not just that our free markets are far from free—not just that our modern American administrative state resembles, in so many ways, the disciplinary apparatus of eighteenth-century Parisian policing, or that the Commodity Futures Trading Commission bears a strong family resemblance to the *lieutenant général de police* at the Paris Châtelet. Nor is it that we care a lot about liberty today, whereas the eighteenth-century Parisians did not value freedom. No, that would be far too naïve, a mere caricature. The problem is also that we read "discipline," or rather "excessive regulation," onto the Parisian *police des grains*. Indeed, we impose the category of discipline too easily, too reflexively, on the eighteenth century, forgetting that, in the early decades of that century, the *police des grains* was perceived by many, if not most (and certainly by the dominant political elite at the time), as liberty enhancing.

It was only by means of these detailed regulations, it was believed, that it would be possible to reduce the price of commodities and thereby enhance the liberty of ordinary citizens. Nicolas Delamare, throughout his *Traité de la police*, specifically emphasized this link between police administration and liberty.[80] In 1693 and 1700, by order of the Parlement of Paris, Delamare had been sent to several provinces that were suffering from shortages—from *disettes*. A few years later, in 1709 and 1710, he would again be sent to areas afflicted by scarcity.[81] He had seen the horrors of famine up close and, we are told, he knew how to solve the crises. As the historian Musart would write: "Very quickly, he calmed the popular emotions by reestablishing plenty in the markets and by making the price of bread go down. To the great satisfaction of the people, he severely punished the fraudulent schemes of the land owners and merchants that had, to a great extent, provoked the grain shortage. Finally, after having left these provinces with the wheat that they needed, he had the surplus rushed to Paris, whose supply was not assured."[82] It is during this period that Delamare wrote his now famous treatise—publishing the first volume in 1705, the second in 1710, and the third in 1719.[83]

Delamare declared himself in favor of free commerce in theory, but leaned toward regulation in practice as a way to promote liberty of commerce and fair competition. Throughout, the ideal was liberty—in theory and practice. Delamare believed, in theory, that free commerce was the best solution: that the needs of one province could be resolved by an overabundance in another province—or so he argued in 1710. But the reality, Delamare maintained, is that merchants are avaricious and conniving, and the only practical solution was to "police"—to administer, to intervene. The bad motives of the merchant class made the regulations necessary.[84] And those very regulations were what ensured freedom in practice. The discourse was always about liberty: large segments of the political and intellectual leadership believed that these administrative decrees and edicts were necessary to ensure abundance and plenty, to ward off the risk of a *disette*, to provide sustenance to the masses, and thereby guarantee their liberty and lives. Although today we may perceive the regulation of Parisian markets as excessively disciplinary and repressive, at an earlier time these same regulations formed part of a coherent vision of public administration—under the earlier rubric of "police"—that was an integral part of the field of public economy. And the central task of public economy, in the eyes of its earliest exponents, was precisely to ensure the abundance and cheapness of food and consumable goods at market in order to guarantee freedom—to provide for what was called, at the time, *"bon marché,"* good and plentiful markets at reasonable prices.

The younger Adam Smith understood this well and in fact used the discourse of "police" and *"bon marché"* in his lectures on moral philosophy and jurisprudence in the early 1760s. It was precisely under the rubric of "police" that Smith lectured on public economy, on the regulation of markets, on monopolies, money, and trade: on how best to regulate agricultural production and manufacturing; on how to encourage the division of labor; on what to do with foreign trade; on how to manage currency, banking, and interest rates—in sum, on how to increase the wealth of a nation, or, which was the same thing for Smith, on how to enable citizens to obtain needed and desired necessities of life: food, clothes, and lodging. In fact, Smith placed his entire discussion of public economy under the rubric of "police" and he identified the principal task of "police" as facilitating *bon marché*.

In his *Lectures on Jurisprudence*, which he delivered at Glasgow University during the period 1762 to 1764—after the publication of *The Theory of Moral Sentiments* in 1759 but before *The Wealth of Nations* in 1776—the young Adam Smith used exclusively the rubric of "police" to discuss public economy. Once the internal security of a nation had been ensured and subjects could benefit from their private property, Smith reportedly lectured in 1762–1763, the state's attention should turn to the task of promoting the state's wealth. "This produces what we call police," Smith said. "Whatever regulations are made with respect to the trade, commerce, agriculture, manufactures of the country are considered as belonging to the police."[85] The young Smith traced the notion of police to French administration, citing the folklore that the king of France demanded three services from his *lieutenant général de police*—namely, that he assure the cleanliness and security of the nation and the abundance and cheapness of goods at market. Smith referred specifically to the famous Marquis d'Argenson, chief of police in Paris from 1697 to 1718, who was reportedly told, upon acceding to the post, that the king of France expected three things of him: "1st, the clean[lin]ess or *neteté;* 2nd, the *aisance*, ease or security; and 3rd, *bon marché* or cheapness of provisions."[86] Smith lectured that the goal of police is "the means proper to produce opulence," and that "the objects of Police are the cheapness of commodities, public security, and cleanliness."[87] Under the heading of "police," Smith stated in his 1763–1764 lectures, "we will consider the opulence of a state," or, more specifically, "the consideration of cheapness or plenty, or, which is the same thing, the most proper way of procuring wealth and abundance."[88]

To the early public economists—including the young Adam Smith—"police" was precisely what ensured the abundant provision of necessary foods and commodities. The term "police" conveyed a number of meanings—not just the enforcement function associated with the *lieutenant général de police* that, at least in some respects, resembles more closely our contemporary understanding of law enforcement, blue uniforms, and order maintenance.[89] The expression "police" also captured, in broader terms, what we could call today "administration," but administration limited to the subdivisions of the state; the term *gouvernement* or governing, in contrast, covered the administration of *l'État* or the state.[90] But the different meanings were imbricated: the administration of subsistence and markets fell under the jurisdiction of policing functions and were perceived as calling for surveillance. As the early Smith lectures demonstrate, public economy and "police" were continuous. And thus, among the champions of the *police des grains*—for instance, Commissioner Delamare himself—the policing of markets was perceived as the only mechanism to reduce the price of bread and ensure *bon marché*. True liberty required government organization. In order to achieve cheapness and plenty—the central goals of public economy—it was necessary to calibrate the market. According to this view, police and liberty formed a coherent whole: policing was the prerequisite of *bon marché*, and *bon marché* the prerequisite of liberty. The historian Judith Miller fleshes out this idea masterfully in her 1999 book *Mastering the Market,* where she demonstrates how administration ensured, or was viewed as ensuring, economic well-being.

It would take but a small step to extend this logic of administration to the larger field of crime and punishment. The young Milanese aristocrat Cesare Beccaria would do just this in his concise yet seminal tract *Dei delitti e delle pene* (On crimes and punishments), published anonymously in 1764. The new field of public economy—which rested on the detailed administration and policing of rules and regulations—had tamed and civilized nations, Beccaria boasted. European nations had been civilized through commercial exchange and economic regimentation. "We have discovered the true relations between sovereign and subjects," Beccaria declared, "and there is waged among nations a silent war by trade, which is the most humane sort of war and more worthy of reasonable men."[91]

The same lessons and techniques, Beccaria maintained, could tame and civilize Europe's punishment practices, and in the process, eliminate the brutal excesses of seventeenth-century penality. Administration, regulation, proportionality—these would free men from the shackles of the past, from barbarity, torture, and capital punishment. Under Beccaria's influence, the field of public economy would colonize the penal domain and impose the same logic of measured and proportional responses to the problem of man's natural tendency toward deviance. In Beccaria's eyes, men had always behaved the same in economic and in social exchange: they privileged their own self-interest and always tended toward deviance. In the penal sphere—just as in the economic domain—the solution Beccaria proposed was to properly administer a rational framework of tariffs and prices—in essence, to set the right price for deviance in order to minimize its occurrence. For Beccaria, policing and public economy were coterminous. In his lectures on public economy delivered in Milan in 1769—the notes of which were published posthumously—Beccaria covered five areas: agriculture, arts and manufacturing, commerce, finance, and police. "Of Police" constituted an integral part of the study of economics—an entire section alongside commerce and finance —because it shared the same rationality, namely that of strict public administration.

A common thread tied many thinkers in this period, from the young Adam Smith in Scotland to the young Cesare Beccaria in Milan: a continuity between the police domain and public economy, between administration and the wealth of nations, all in furtherance of liberty. For both Smith and Beccaria, the two spheres overlapped. To Smith, the umbrella category was police, and that category subsumed the discussion of public economy and the wealth of a nation. To Beccaria—and other cameralists of his time—the overarching category was public economy, within which police formed one important sector alongside commerce and finance. But in both, the two domains were seamless and continuous. The two fields overlapped.

The Secrets of the Police Archives

Yet that's not all. To make matters even more complicated, it is not just that eighteenth-century thinkers *perceived* the *police des grains* as liberty enhancing. In point of fact, the Parisian grain and bread markets were far more "free" in the eighteenth century than we acknowledge today—which explains in large part why it was so easy for the defenders of the system, for Commissioner Delamare or Cesare Beccaria (at least on one reading), to portray the regime as freedom enhancing. The sheer multiplicity of regulations meant that they were essentially ineffective and could hardly be enforced. "The *police* regulations were innumerable under the *ancien régime*," professor Olivier-Martin would explain in his magisterial lectures at the University of Paris, "and as a result, the relative impotence of the police is well established."[92] The rules concerning the trade in grain fit within a larger context of innumerable regulations about everything else. There were, after all, 564 pages in Fréminville's *Dictionnaire* listing prohibitions on practically everything, from the charivari to flying kites in public spaces, to leaving artichoke leaves or pea shells in the marketplace.[93] Even a cursory review of the *Collection officielle des ordonnances de police* at midcentury reveals a myriad of regulations prohibiting everything from butcher boys using their dogs to pull a chair or cart (no. 88) to confectioners using vermilion in their marzipan (no. 72); property owners were ordered to empty any water from their cellars (no. 70) and wine merchant salesclerks were required to wear small brass badges with the city's coat-of-arms on one side and the words "commis courtiers de vins" etched on the other.[94] Moreover, in the specific context of grain and markets, there was a maze of regulations, including prohibitions on harvesting with scythes to rules preventing millers and brewers from bringing dogs ("des chiens ou dogues") to the marketplace.[95] In Duchesne's *Code de la police,* a book 507 pages long, there were indeed twenty-six pages dedicated to the *police des grains,* but that left 481 other pages dedicated to, well, anything and everything.[96]

More important, the police regulations concerned trivial matters. The violations themselves were trifling and involved fines only, and mostly petty fines at that. Accusations triggered minimal process. The punishments were minor. As Duchesne explained in *Des sentences:* "The intervention of prosecutors is not necessary in *police* matters, everything there should be treated summarily and judged immediately"; "fines and other punishments imposed in *police* matters are not accompanied by disgrace"; and "the punishments [meted out by the police] ordinarily should be moderate and serve only to prevent the repetition of the offense."[97] The police jurisdiction was essentially a civil, not criminal, matter, and for most of the seventeenth and eighteenth centuries was part of the civil chamber. At various times, such as during the reforms of the Bureau de Police of 1572, the police functions were reduced to street cleaning; and at other times, as we will see, it appears that street cleaning was practically all the police cared about.[98]

A close examination of the archives from the police of the Châtelet of Paris maintained at the National Archives of France, the famous *Série Y*, reveals the trivial and sporadic nature of the policing. The leading recurring violation that the police commissioners noted on their rounds was the failure to sweep one's storefront—the entry read "non balayé," or "NB" for short, in other words "not swept." The next most common violation involved fecal matter on the sidewalk—here, the commissioners would abbreviate as "MF" for "matières fécales." The papers, reports, and records of the police chamber read like those of a small claims court, offering details of predominantly trivial matters. For instance, the carton of papers for the first six months of 1758—the carton labeled Y-9459A—contains month-by-month reports of the daily activity of the police commissioners and lists all the violations that the commissioners observed. Most of the list is devoted to sidewalk-sweeping violations: "Police des 8 et 9 février 1758: Le devant de la porte du cabaret au merle blanc *non balayé*. Rue des francs Bourgeois: Le devant du cabaret de tardif aux fontaines de bourgogne *non balayé*," with the occasional entry for individuals found gaming or drinking in taverns past the closing hour. The report of Commissioner Dubuisson, submitted on July 21, 1758, and archived in carton Y-9459B, is typical:

8 July 1758—no violations
10 said month—no violations
11 said month—no violations
12 s.m.—3 cases of failure to sweep the street
13—nothing
14—nothing
15—nothing
17—nothing
18 said month of July—4 cases of failure to sweep
19 s.m.—8 cases of failure to sweep
20 s.m.—nothing

The same commissioner's report for the following week, July 28, 1758, is similarly focused on trivial matters:

21 July—no violations
22 same month—vehicle without plates or a number blocking public access; stones left in disarray by a master mason blocking the gutter; neglected mound of gravel; 2 cases of failure to sweep
24—nothing
25—nothing
26—wood and stones blocking the public way; 4 cases of failure to sweep
28 s.m.—3 cases of neglected gravel; manure causing bad odors; garbage thrown in our presence from the window of the second floor of the house occupied by the baker near the rue de la tinerandrie; failure to sweep

The contrast between these reports and the records of the criminal jurisdiction of the Châtelet of Paris is striking. A review of criminal-jurisdiction records for January and February 1760—carton Y-9650—discloses serious cases, with extensive investigations and evidence reports, and long indictments with numerous witnesses. The process and types of cases in the criminal files make the activities of the police chamber look like child's play.

The trivial nature of the commissioners' beat reports reflects, in part, that these commissioners had a large number of other functions, both civil and criminal, beyond merely identifying petty violations of police ordinances. The commissioners—whose full title was "commissaires enquêteurs examinateurs, conseiller du roi," or commissioner, investigator, examiner, and royal counselor—had multiple jobs and were available twenty-four hours a day. They served as notary publics and registrars of police complaints (in cases ranging from rape and theft to traffic accidents); made inventories, sealed property, and took testimony; and were responsible for maintaining the peace and investigating serious crimes, including capital cases.[99] The commissioners purchased their office from the king at a hefty price (as much as 100,000 livres by the late eighteenth century).[100] In addition, several of their functions were remunerated on a commission basis—and as a result happened to take a lot more of their time.[101] In 1759, for instance, a commissioner was allowed to ask for three livres per hour, with a minimum fee of nine livres, for taking down complaints and declarations; eight livres per one hundred lines (each thirteen syllables long) of an inventory; and half a livre per page (with twenty-two lines of twelve syllables considered a page) for copying any and all documents.[102] In other words, the commissioners were busy with other, often more remunerative tasks.[103]

And they too—like so many of us—were drawn more to the high-profile cases than to the pedestrian tasks of policing fine-only ordinances and the removal of fecal matter. So when one examines their papers at the National Archives, it becomes clear that they were far more interested in the verbal testimonials of witnesses in capital cases or the more intriguing cases of *pédérastes* (homosexuals) and *femmes du monde* (prostitutes).[104] Even in the day-to-day policing, they were far more exercised when they discovered illicit card games and other gambling establishments. When cases involving grain did come to their attention, they generally involved alleged theft or fraud, not simply trivial deviations from market regulations.[105] A careful review of the sentences meted out by the police chamber of the Châtelet reveals that the *police des grains* constituted a minor function of the chamber's jurisdiction. Our perceptions of the importance of grain regulation may well be distorted by the personal biases of the historians and narrators of the field, either because they were ideologically opposed to the *police des grains* and had an interest in inflating the appearance of excessive regulation, or because they were themselves commissioners or lieutenants of the police—such as Delamare and Fréminville—and so were invested in the importance of their own functions. In both theory and practice, though, there was far more freedom in the eighteenth-century regime of "police" than we tend to acknowledge today. In sum, the level of enforcement in the Parisian markets does not justify the simple assessment of "discipline" as opposed to today's "free" markets.

Liberty and Discipline

Let's take stock, then. The eighteenth-century police regimen was far more free than we tend to characterize it today; by the same token, our modern free markets—the Chicago Board of Trade, for instance—are far more disciplined than we tend to admit. There is more freedom in discipline, and more discipline in freedom, than meets the eye. And what is puzzling is not just the veneer of "freedom" that is imposed on our practices today, but first that our predecessors imposed that same veneer on the practices that dominated their time, and second that we are so quick to recharacterize earlier models of market and social organization as oppressive, overly regulated, and excessively disciplined.

One way to paper over this complexity would be to suggest that there were disciplinary forms of organization in the eighteenth century, and that there are liberal forms of market administration today, but that in both cases we are simply dealing with the larger category of governance. In other words, there are two different techniques of governing, the first through disciplinary mechanisms and regulation, the second through liberalized exchange and self-correcting mechanisms, and they operate in different ways. Not better or worse, just different. But such an explanation seems to miss the central point, namely that the *categories* themselves are misleading and empty. The categories of "discipline" or "overregulation" on the one hand, and of "liberalized" or "free markets" on the other, are impossible to properly quantify or measure. It is simply impossible to know whether the *police des grains* in the Parisian markets was more or less "free" or "liberty enhancing" than the policing of the Chicago Board of Trade. As a practical matter, it is infeasible to measure with exactitude whether the differences—with all the attendant technological transformations—outweigh the similarities. It is impossible to quantify objectively the uniform and gaze of the *huissard*—the enforcer who accompanied the commissioners—and measure it against the electronic impulse that reads every single stock trade on a high volume alert. It is impracticable to weigh the effect of prohibiting *la vente par échantillons*—the sale by samples—against that of shutting down a thriving secondary market in mutual fund shares. How do we weigh the requirement that all grain be sold at the Paris markets against the contemporary requirement that all grain futures be traded at the Chicago Board of Trade? These questions do not seem to have an answer that is honest and not merely ideological. There is a problem, it seems, with the categories themselves.

Which brings us back, then, to square one: How did the eighteenth-century model of police administration become the epitome of that particular category of "discipline," and the Chicago Board of Trade the bastion of that other category of "freedom"? What made possible this particular vision of the world? And at what price? That is, what are the implications of seeing the world through these categories?

The Birth of Natural Order

The answer to the first question turns on the introduction of the idea of "natural order" into the field of political economy in the mid-eighteenth century—the notion that economic exchange constitutes a system that autonomously can achieve equilibrium without government intervention or outside interference—and the eventual metamorphosis of this idea, over the nineteenth and twentieth centuries, into the concept of the inherent efficiency of markets. This idea of natural order makes possible the belief in self-adjusting and self-sustaining markets that, in turn, creates the very possibility of displacing governance mechanisms, and is precisely what allowed eighteenth-century thinkers to reimagine their social reality. It is what made possible the shift from viewing the *police des grains* as liberty enhancing to considering it an oppressive and misguided policy. It has also enabled our contemporary perception of modern markets as free.

In order to understand that pivotal shift, it is necessary to return to the historical moment when the model of the *police des grains* would be felt, legitimately and by the political elite, to be oppressive and unnecessary. We must trace back to the moment of resistance to the "discipline" of the *police des grains* and move forward to the present, identifying one of the first critical concerted oppositions that would eventually blossom into the belief and faith in liberalized exchange—a far different ideal that would fundamentally reshape the way we think about markets and punishment. We must return, then, to the mid-eighteenth century.

From Physiocracy to Market Efficiency

If cheapness and plenty, *bon marché,* was the goal of public economy and of the *police des grains* in the early decades of the eighteenth century, things could hardly have been more different only a few decades later among the increasingly important and influential circles of economists in France and England. The contrast is striking and captured best by the newer dogma of François Quesnay:

> Abondance et non-valeur n'est pas richesse.
> Disette et cherté est misère.
> Abondance et cherté est opulence.[106]

In other words, abundance and plenty do not translate into the wealth of a nation. Scarcity and high prices, of course, are misery. It is the combination of abundance and high prices that produces "opulence" (wealth) and well-being.

The momentous shift reflected in this simple maxim would radically transform the meaning and role of "police." Quesnay, a highly accomplished physician at Versailles—he was the first doctor to Madame de Pompadour and an ordinary to Louis XV—and a prolific writer in the medical field, turned his attention to economics in 1756 and founded an intellectual circle that included notable thinkers and prolific writers such as the Marquis de Mirabeau, Pierre Samuel Du Pont de Nemours, and Le Mercier de la Rivière, among others. From Quesnay's first published contribution to the field of political economy, his encyclopedia entry on *Fermiers* (farmers) in volume 6 of the *Encyclopédie,* published in 1756, to his final contributions to economics collected and published in Du Pont de Nemours's *Physiocratie* in 1767, Quesnay would fundamentally reorient the relationship between public economy and police. Governmental intervention in the markets would become portrayed as oppressive and interfering with the autonomous functioning of an economic system governed by natural laws and natural order; and police would be relegated to a realm outside the market, where those who did not comply with the natural order would be punished, and punished severely.

According to Quesnay and his disciples, natural order reigned in the economic domain—in agriculture and commerce—and thereby obviated the need for police. In their writings, the sphere of economic exchange would be viewed as an autonomous self-adjusting system regulated by natural laws, which, when left to its own devices, would alone produce a net product.[107] The only way for the state to participate in the wealth of the nation, in their view, was not to administer, but instead to pull out of the sphere of agricultural production and stop intervening in commerce and trade. The logic severed the police function from the economic domain and relegated it to the margin—and this logic rested entirely on the notion of "natural order." Within a short decade, Quesnay and his disciples would become known around the world as the "Physiocrats," a neologism meant to designate "the rule of nature."

François Quesnay presented the idea of natural order to his contemporaries in his *Tableau économique,* first in draft form in 1758–1759 and then in 1760 in an augmented published volume of the Marquis de Mirabeau's *L'Ami des hommes.* The *Tableau* was a graphic depiction of cash and commodity flows between the three principal classes of society—the cultivators, the property owners, and the manufacturers. By means of a zigzag line graph, Quesnay sought to illustrate his main theses, namely that agricultural production is the sole source of all societal wealth, that wealth can only be produced by means of an autonomous system of exchange, and therefore that the state must stop intervening with tariffs, creating restrictions on the flow of trade, and imposing other regulations.

Quesnay's *Tableau économique* received a lot of attention because it attempted to graphically and systematically represent an economic system—what Louis Dumont would refer to as "an ordered whole."[108] This is precisely what Marx found so brilliant in Quesnay.[109] But what was even more important and influential on future liberal thought than the notion of an economic system was the idea of natural order. Systems can function well with external calibration and intervention, much like an engine may function as a perfect whole so long as one adds fuel. What was remarkable about Quesnay's *Tableau* is that his system was governed by natural order and was entirely autonomous of external inputs. What Quesnay contributed was not merely the idea of system, but that of natural orderliness—an idea that would eventually receive its most elaborate articulation in Le Mercier de la Rivière's 1767 book *L'ordre naturel et essentiel des sociétés politiques.*

To be sure, the idea of natural order was not new and the Physiocrats were not the first to elaborate the concept, nor to introduce it in economic thinking. Simone Meyssonnier, in her detailed history of the origins of French liberal thought in the eighteenth century, *La balance et l'horloge* (1989), traces the idea back to Pierre Le Pesant de Boisguilbert, who wrote almost a hundred years earlier, in the period 1695 to 1707.[110] Joseph Schumpeter, in his magisterial *History of Economic Analysis* (1954), traced the notion back to the Scholastics—the theologians of the fourteenth and fifteenth centuries.[111] Schumpeter placed Quesnay firmly among the "philosophers of natural law" influenced by Aquinas and the medieval natural order theorists.[112] Friedrich Hayek and Louis Dumont, as many others would, traced the origins back to Bernard Mandeville's *Fable of the Bees; or, Private Vices, Publick Benefits* (1714). And Du Pont de Nemours himself—the chief publicist and greatest admirer and disciple of Quesnay—traced the Physiocratic doctrine to, among others, the Marquis d'Argenson, who is credited with having invented the maxim "Pas trop gouverner" (not to govern too much).[113]

But even if Quesnay was not truly original, his persistence, his relentlessness, his obsession with natural order caused the idea to be perceived as new—and radical. Many believed that it inaugurated, in the words of Du Pont de Nemours, "a new science in Europe," and many championed Quesnay as the founding father of that new science.[114] As Emma Rothschild suggests, "In an epoch of almost obsessive preoccupation with newness—new sciences, new systems of trade, new music, objects wholly new in the world—the revolution in economic thought was genuinely innovative. Quesnay and his followers conceived of national economies, for the first time, as vast systems of interdependent flows; Turgot described them as constituted by the interconnected transactions of millions of individual agents. All individuals, the poor as well as the rich, the agricultural labourers as well as the great merchants, were identified as part of a single economic system."[115]

The birth—or, perhaps to be fair, the emergence and maturation—of the idea of natural order helped shape a vision of the economic sphere as an autonomous, self-adjusting, and self-regulated system that could achieve a natural equilibrium spontaneously and produce increased wealth. No doubt material shifts in technology, transformations in agricultural and industrial production, and larger changes in demographics and international relations played important roles in the perceptual change. But what made the notion of a "naturally ordered market" comprehensible, coherent, and convincing was precisely the insertion of the idea of natural order into the economic domain. This intervention fundamentally altered the discourse and the dominant way of reasoning and understanding the world—especially the relationship between "public economy" and "police."

The idea of natural order was highly influential in France, England, and abroad, and a similar notion of orderliness leached into nineteenth-century liberal thought. Although Adam Smith and Jeremy Bentham explicitly would reject the Physiocratic approach—primarily because of Quesnay's devotion to agriculture as the sole means of creating national wealth—Smith especially, but Bentham as well, would embrace a similar notion of orderliness in their economic writings. By 1776, the year *The Wealth of Nations* was published, Smith no longer used the term "police" to discuss public economy. In fact, the word "police" appears rarely in the text of *The Wealth of Nations* and never as the overarching rubric for political economy.[116]

Through Smith predominantly, notions of harmony of interests and orderliness would make their way across the Atlantic into early republican thought and eventually into modern economic and political writings. Physiocratic ideas would also travel to the United States during the Revolutionary period, though the influence was more attenuated. Benjamin Franklin, for one, was greatly influenced by his personal encounter with the Physiocrats and with their writings, and he adopted "almost without reservation" the central tenets of Quesnay, including the central idea "that political interference with this natural order of economic life was pernicious."[117] Franklin even published some of his writings in the Physiocrats' journal, the *Éphémérides*.[118] But the main channel of influence would be through the English-language texts of Adam Smith and, as we will see, Jeremy Bentham.

The evolution of the idea of natural order is a fascinating story with some unexpected turns. Bentham, surely, is one of them. Bentham plays an absolutely pivotal role, especially by way of his influence on the welfarist strand of law and economics that developed at the University of Chicago in the 1960s and 1970s. Although Bentham expressly rejected notions of natural rights, famously calling them "nonsense on stilts," he nevertheless privileged individual information and self-interest to such an extent that he introduced into his economic writings a default in favor of government quietism—effectively reproducing an element of harmony of self-interests. To be sure, Bentham's opus has been subjected to wildly different readings over the past two centuries. He has been portrayed by some as individualist, by others as collectivist; by some as naturalist, by others as constructivist; by some as laissez-faire, and by still others as the father of the welfare state. Bentham inspired both nineteenth-century British laissez-faire theorists and collectivist thinkers who would eventually evolve into Keynesians. But regardless of this wide range of readings—or rather, *because* of the wide range—Bentham's legacy contains a sharp contrast between the ambiguity in his economic views and his unbending interventionism in the field of crime and punishment. It is in the comparison of Bentham's economics with his punishment writings that we can identify a notion of orderliness in the economic sphere.

Primarily through the intermediary of Smith and Bentham, the initial insertion of an idea of orderliness in economic exchange gradually metamorphosed, over time, into the contemporary belief in the inherent efficiency of markets or, in more popular parlance, the preference for free markets. A technical, more scientific version of this popular belief in free markets would be developed by the Chicago School of economics—and Bentham plays a pivotal role here, not only as an inspiration for Gary Becker's famous 1968 article on crime and punishment, but also as the foil against which Friedrich Hayek developed the notion of "spontaneous order." Through the intermediary of the Chicago economist Ronald Coase, and what became known as the Coase Theorem, the Benthamite welfarist strand of law and economics, and the Hayekian strand of libertarian economics, would converge on an idea of market efficiency that would have important implications for punishment. The convergence would allow the more libertarian Richard Epstein and the more pragmatic Richard Posner—both staunch adherents of law and economics—to focus on the idea of orderly markets and embrace the principle that "when transaction costs are low, the market is, virtually by definition, the most efficient method of allocating resources."[119] Today's embrace of the free market traces back precisely to the severing of "police" from "public economy" that the Physiocrats performed. And it is the resulting dichotomy that makes possible our perception both that the Parisian markets of the eighteenth century were overly regimented and that our existing markets and exchanges are substantially free.

At What Price?

To understand how these perceptions became dominant, then, it is crucial to trace the birth of natural order and explore how it developed into its current market-efficiency manifestation.[120] And the place to begin is not with Friedrich Hayek, Milton Friedman, and the founding of the Mont Pèlerin Society in 1947, nor with the rise of Reagan Republicanism in the 1970s, nor for that matter with the emergence of a Washington Consensus in the 1990s—though they each have an important role in the development of the ideas. Instead, the place to begin is at that contested moment in the eighteenth century when notions of natural order were beginning to take shape.

It is equally important to ask the correlative: at what price have so many of us come to believe that the economy is the realm of natural order and that the legitimate and competent sphere of policing—of administration and government—lies elsewhere? What flows from that sharp dichotomy between orderliness in the market and ordering in the penal sphere? At what price do we embrace these categories? And here, the answer is equally clear: at the price, first, of naturalizing the market and thereby effectively shielding from normative assessment the regulatory mechanisms in our contemporary markets and the wealth distributions that occur daily; and at the price, second, of easing, facilitating, and enabling the massive expansion of our penal sphere, or, to be more provocative, of making possible mass incarceration today.

Naturalizing Wealth Distributions

Let's explore each of these claims. First, the ideas of natural order and market efficiency have helped naturalize the market itself and thereby shield from normative assessment the massive wealth distributions that take place there. Those distributions come to be seen as the natural consequence of an orderly market, and as such are less open to normative evaluation. They become more normal, somewhat necessary, and assessing them becomes practically futile. And the result is that those very distributional consequences get shielded from political, social, and moral debates: the naturalness of the market depoliticizes the distributional outcomes.

Nietzsche made this point far more elegantly in his *Genealogy of Morals*, in discussing the value of truth. So long as we held the thesis that truth was divine, Nietzsche suggested, assessing the value of truth was not fully permitted. It is only once we let go of that idea of divine truth that we opened the door to the assessment of truth, in other words, to raising the question of the value of truth. "From the moment faith in the God of the ascetic ideal is denied," Nietzsche wrote, "a *new problem arises:* that of the *value* of truth."[121] In parallel fashion, faith in natural order and market efficiency forecloses a full normative assessment of market outcomes. It closes the door on the very condition of possibility. It effectively depoliticizes the market itself and its outcomes. It is only when the illusion of natural order is lifted that a real problem arises: that of the justice of the organizational rules and their distributional consequences.

The idea of natural order, in effect, masks the state's role, the government's ties to nonstate organizations—such as the Chicago Board of Trade—and the extensive legal and regulatory framework that embeds these associations. Robert Hale and other legal realists in the early twentieth century demonstrated the extent to which the distribution of income and wealth is the product of the legal rules we choose to impose.[122] Hale trained our attention on the foundational rules of property and contract law, showing how free, voluntary, compensated exchange is in fact the product of the legal coercion that the government establishes through its role in defining property rights.[123]

But Hale's insight applies with even greater force to the rules and regulations that we see at the Chicago Board of Trade. The truth is, every action of the broker, buyer, seller, investment bank, brokerage firm, exchange member—or even nonmember—is scrutinized and manipulated. Rules, oversight committees, advisory letters, investigations, and legal actions abound. The list of do's and don'ts is extensive. Brokerage firms may combine and use blacklists to restrict retail buyers from reselling their publicly offered stock during a "retail restricted period" of between thirty and ninety days following their purchase of newly offered stock, but the same brokerage firms may allow large institutions to dump their stock in the aftermarket at any time.[124] Exchange members on the New York Stock Exchange may get together and fix the commission rate on stock transactions of less than $500,000—that is, they may set the price of buying and selling stock—but freely negotiate commissions for larger stock transactions.[125] The National Association of Securities Dealers may agree to restrict the sale and fix the resale price of securities of open-ended management companies—"mutual funds"—in the secondary market between dealers, between dealers and investors, and between investors, thereby eliminating the secondary market in mutual funds—a market that was significant prior to 1940.[126] And competing bidders in a corporate takeover may join together and make joint takeover offers to stockholders, even if it means that together they reduce the offering price for the stock purchase.[127] But exchange members may not get together and forbid other members from sharing commissions earned from the purchase or sale of stock with nonmember broker-dealers; and an exchange may not order its members to remove private telephone connections to the offices of nonmember brokers—unless the Securities and Exchange Commission reviews and approves such a policy.[128] The rules and regulations surrounding our modern markets are intricate and arcane, and they belie the simplistic idea that our markets are "free." The reality today is far more complex.

It is equally true that the practices of the Physiocrats were also more complex than they might appear at first glance: they too were far more constrained in their actions than they were in their rhetoric. Le Mercier de la Rivière served as *intendant*—administrative governor—of Martinique on two occasions during the early 1760s, and during his second tour of duty in 1763, after he had been fully converted to Physiocracy, he himself set the price of bread and meats. That is, at a time when he was preaching the merits of free markets, he was enacting a most stringent *police des grains* and himself fixing prices:

> No 271. Ordinance of MM., the General and Intendant, increasing the price of bread. September 24, 1763.
>
> The current price of wheat flour making it impossible for bakers to provide bread to the public at the specified price of 7 sols 6 deniers per pound, at the ordinary weight of 16 ounces, we order that from this day

forward, bakers will be held to furnish their bread at the weight of 14 ounces for 7 sols 6 deniers, and this shall continue until otherwise ordered by us . . .

We promulgate this to the king's prosecutors, etc.
Rendered at Martinique, September 24, 1763.

Signed, Marquis de Fenelon, and De La Rivière[129]

That's right, signed Le Mercier De La Rivière. Like Mercier, we today want to see freedom even when there is nothing but constraint before us. That desire, that urge is precisely what masks the distributions that accompany the administration of contemporary markets. Because we want to believe that the markets are operating on their own, we fail to properly scrutinize how the administration of the markets actually distributes wealth. Because we want to believe in self-adjusting markets, we do not adequately investigate the consequences of our choices. It is not that difficult, after all, to identify the distributional outcomes; but when they are mischaracterized as the natural consequence of a natural order, making normative assessments becomes entirely beside the point. It makes little sense to raise questions about natural phenomena. In this sense, the idea of natural order or, today, of market efficiency effectively obfuscates the massive distribution of wealth and resources that occur through the market. Natural order essentially depoliticizes the market.

Expanding the Penal Sphere

Second, the belief in market orderliness facilitates the expansion of the penal sphere. Here too, it is crucial to return to the eighteenth century. Surprisingly, the birth of natural order in the writings of the Physiocrats led seamlessly to the expansion of the penal sphere as the legitimate space for governmental administration and intervention. The idea of economic orderliness matured into a political theory that combined laissez-faire in commercial matters with centralized, authoritarian policing elsewhere—what the Physiocrats referred to as the doctrine of "legal despotism." Under this rubric, François Quesnay and Mercier de la Rivière formulated a political ideal of complete governmental inactivity in all but the penal sphere. Indeed, given the existence of natural laws governing commerce, the *économistes* envisaged no role for the legislature except to criminalize and punish severely those who deviate from the natural order.

Natural order in the universe implied legal despotism in human affairs, and the Physiocrats embraced this doctrine in 1767 with the publication of both Quesnay's essay "Despotisme de la Chine" and Le Mercier's book *L'ordre naturel et essentiel des sociétés politiques.* Their economic writings led them, in a syllogistic manner, to the political conclusion that natural order in an autonomous economic sphere demands both that there be no human intervention (in terms of positive law) in the economic realm and that positive law limit itself to punishing deviance from the natural order, in other words, theft and violence. The logic was, well, syllogistic:

1. The economic, agricultural, and commercial realm is governed by fundamental natural laws that best promote the interests of mankind.
2. As a result, positive human-made laws can do no more than merely instantiate the fundamental natural laws. At best, positive law would simply mirror the natural order; any deviation would produce disorder rather than order.
3. Therefore, positive law should not extend to the domain of natural laws, or, as Quesnay stated, "Positive legislation should therefore not reach the domain of physical laws."[130]
4. For this reason there is no need for a separate legislature. All law-making power should be centralized in a unified executive—an enlightened legal despot—who learns and implements the laws of nature.
5. Only those men whose passions are out of alignment with the natural order—those whose passions are "*déréglées,*" as Quesnay wrote—will fail to see and appreciate the fundamental laws as natural.[131]
6. The only object of positive manmade laws, then, should be to severely punish those whose passions are out of order, as a way to protect society from these thieves and derelicts—"*des voleurs et des méchans,*" as Quesnay would say.[132]

The idea of natural order does all the work in this logical argument, and it leads inexorably to a penal sphere that is, on the one hand, marginalized from the economic realm, but on the other hand, unleashed and allowed to expand without any limitation. Those men whose passions are out of order cannot appreciate the natural order, so the legal despot should have full and unlimited discretion to repress and punish. Manmade, positive law thus serves only one legitimate function: to punish those who violate the natural order.

Notice that the penal sphere is portrayed in this view as exceptional. It is the only domain where natural order does not autonomously produce the best result for mankind. It is the only place where order does not reign. It is the space outside the dominant realm of natural orderliness, the extremity where one finds, in Quesnay's words, the *passions déréglées* and the *hommes pervers.*[133] The contrast with Beccaria and other cameralists could not be more pronounced: their seamless web of police and public economy gives way, in the Physiocrats' paradigm, to a sharp distinction between a realm of economic order where laissez-faire must govern, and a realm for positive laws and penal sanctions where the government must intervene—harshly. As we will see, a strict and severe police is necessary to deal firmly with those who are out of order. The Physiocrats insert natural order in the economic domain but, in the process, establish the penal sphere as the outer limit of the system, as the only legitimate realm for administration and repression, as the zone of policing.

This new penal paradigm significantly influenced nineteenth-century liberal thought. By an odd amalgam of liberal economic theory and Beccaria on punishment, nineteenth-century thinkers would replicate this exceptional relationship between markets and punishment: natural orderliness in the economic sphere, but government intervention in the penal realm. This is most evident in Jeremy Bentham's work. The contrast between Bentham's presumption of quietism in economic matters and his arch-interventionism in the penal domain effectively reproduced and reiterated the Physiocratic duality of economy and police. On the public economy side, Bentham tended toward Adam Smith's liberalism. His *Manual of Political Economy,* written in the mid-1790s, rehearsed a presumption of governmental quietism based on his stringent belief in the superiority of individuals' information and self-interest. But on the punishment side, Bentham embraced Beccaria's philosophy whole cloth—especially Beccaria's notion that policing is a sphere of human activity that must be shot through with government intervention. In fact, the criminal code, for Bentham, was precisely a "grand catalogue of prices" by means of which the government set the value of deviance. The penal code was a menu of fixed prices—the polar opposite of laissez-faire.

Beccaria's influence on Bentham was formative. Beccaria's small tract *On Crimes and Punishments* had been translated into English in 1767—when Bentham was nineteen years old. Bentham wrote the main manuscript of his first work on the topic, *Rationale for Punishment,* in 1775 when he was, in H. L. A. Hart's words, "fresh from the study of Beccaria's already famous book."[134] Bentham agreed with Beccaria on all major aspects of his theory of punishment: they both viewed deviance and rule-breaking in this domain as natural and universal—as the basic condition of man; they both critiqued the brutalizing effect of excessive punishment and endorsed marginal deterrence as a limiting principle on punishment; they both favored speedy and certain punishments as a way to reinforce the associations of punishment with crime; and more generally, they agreed on the need for formal law and legality as the source of legitimacy for the criminal justice system and the sovereign.

Naturally, Bentham did have some reservations about Beccaria; but on the whole, those pale in comparison to the debt that Bentham properly acknowledged.[135] In fact, Bentham took pains to express how much Beccaria had contributed to his own intellectual development. Speaking of Beccaria, Bentham exclaimed: "Oh my master, first evangelist of Reason, you who have raised your Italy so far above England. . . . [Y]ou who have made so many useful excursions into the path of utility, what is there left for us to do?—Never to turn aside from that path."[136]

Despite this praise, in Bentham's work the relationship between police and political economy had radically changed. Bentham's rule of thumb, in the narrowly economic domain, was to do nothing barring "some special reason": "*Be quiet* ought on those occasions to be the motto, or watch word, of government."[137] The penal sphere, by contrast, demanded government ordering through and through—from the panopticon prison to the criminal code as a grand menu of prices.

This distinction between the economic and penal spheres helped shape the contours of British nineteenth-century conceptions of laissez-faire. Putting aside for the moment the rich historical debates over whether there ever was an age of laissez-faire in Britain during the mid-nineteenth century or, for that matter, whether Bentham's writings and Benthamites more generally contributed to or undermined laissez-faire policies—to which we will return—the reigning definition of laissez-faire at the time itself encapsulated this Benthamite contrast. The doctrine of laissez-faire in the mid-nineteenth century essentially allowed three functions for the government: first, maintaining the external defense of the country; second, providing for the internal order and security of persons; and third, possibly, providing for minimal public amenities—and the third was certainly tenuous at best.[138] To be sure, the fifth book of Smith's *Wealth of Nations* contained extensive discussions of public works and education; and many have read Bentham as the precursor to the welfare state. But the contrast nevertheless remains and is still determinative: criminalization and punishment became, undisputedly, the most legitimate and competent task of the government. There, for sure, government intervention was proper, necessary, legitimate, and competent. There, natural orderliness had to be replaced by governmental ordering.

Through a serpentine road leading from Smith and Bentham to collectivist welfare economists such as Henry Sidgwick and Arthur Pigou, to Friedrich Hayek's notion of "spontaneous order" and the emergence of the Chicago School of law and economics, this view of an exceptional penal sphere where government is fully legitimate has influenced the public imagination today. This outlook is reflected—even among the staunchest libertarians—in the pervasive idea that fraud and coercion are the major exception to unregulated markets. It is also reflected, in an updated, more technical vocabulary, in this succinct passage by Richard Posner in an article in 1985:

> The major function of criminal law in a capitalist society is to prevent people from bypassing the system of voluntary, compensated exchange—the "market," explicit or implicit—in situations where, because transaction costs are low, the market is a more efficient method of allocating resources than forced exchange. . . . When transaction costs are low, the market is, virtually by definition, the most efficient method of allocating resources. Attempts to bypass the market will therefore be discouraged by a legal system bent on promoting efficiency.[139]

In other words, the market is efficient, and within that space there is no need for government intervention. What is criminalized and punished is behavior outside the space of the orderly market that seeks to circumvent free, voluntary, compensated exchange. There, government intervention is necessary, legitimate, and competent.

Although Posner here uses a more technical and scientific approach to the question, and contemporary jargon, he nevertheless advances the very same idea: in the economic domain, there exists a space that is governed by a certain inherent orderliness that should make us cautious about government interference; by contrast, the state has free rein outside that space to punish bypassers, the disorderly, those who don't play by the game of the market, those who don't respect the order of economic exchange.

In this sense, the idea of natural order has led today to an understanding of the criminal sanction that replicates closely the legal despotism of the eighteenth century: the legitimate sphere for state intervention is the space outside the market, the zone of market bypassing. This rehearses, eerily, François Quesnay's idea that the *homme pervers*—the perverted man—is perverted precisely because he does not abide by the natural order of free exchange. Being "out of order" or "déréglé" translates, today, into this idea of bypassing an orderly market. The modern view replicates the logic of the Physiocrats.

But this contemporary approach is not a mere reiteration. There is a new vocabulary, new metaphors, new models, and a far more scientific approach. The theme of natural order has been replaced by equilibrium theory, Pareto improvements, and Kaldor-Hicks efficiency—to which I will return later. The natural-law metaphor from physics or hydraulics has been supplanted by concepts of orderliness from information technology and computational sciences. Agriculture and economic exchange have been refined and relegated to the "competitive" market. The idea of natural order has been transposed into the Coase Theorem. And the royal crowning of Physiocracy—recall that Louis XV amused himself printing the first edition of Quesnay's *Tableau économique* on the private royal printing press at Versailles—has been replaced by the Sveriges Riksbank Prize in Economic Sciences in Memory of Alfred Nobel, colloquially referred to as the Nobel Prize in Economics.[140]

These differences in metaphor and vocabulary have important implications. The new scientific models are far more convincing today. Rhetorically, they are far more powerful. After all, the idea of "natural order" today sounds somewhat naïve—a bit too metaphysical or quasi-religious. A throwback to some earlier time. Hydraulic metaphors are passé. By contrast, as we shall see, Pareto improvements do much more efficient work today. And we value a Nobel Prize far more than the opinion of a monarch.

Each new iteration of these ideas also changes, however slightly, the relationship between economy and punishment. For the Physiocrats, there was a sharp demarcation between the economic realm, governed by natural order, and the disorderly people who would be governed through punishment. The two arenas were entirely distinct, as different as night and day—or as order and disorder. By contrast, when Bentham refers to the penal code as a grand menu of prices, he is speaking the language of pricing, of rational choice, of economics. Economic rationality is now seeping into the penal sphere, into the zone of government intervention (though recall that a preference for quietism, entirely absent in the penal sphere, still controls the economic domain). The line has thus become blurrier, at least in one direction. And when Gary Becker further extends economic rationality into nonmarket behaviors, such as crime and punishment, but also marriage or racial discrimination—for which he received the Nobel Prize—there is even greater encroachment of economics into the penal arena. In these more modern iterations, then, government intervention is increasingly modeled on economic rationality. But—and this is most important—not vice versa. Voluntary, free, compensated exchange inside the market remains inoculated, shielded from the government's hands. Once we pass the boundary into the market, there is no longer a legitimate role for state intervention.

The subtle shifts in this narrative of distinct economic and penal spheres have made each iteration more palatable and persuasive. They respond to historical and institutional changes, and to practices on the ground. They are situated in conversation with earlier political initiatives and resistance. Gary Becker's extension of rational choice to crime and punishment, for example, came at a timely historical moment in 1968, amid a growing critique of the excesses of penal welfarism, of rehabilitation, of the asylum, of cultural and genetic theories of crime. It offered a simplicity and equality that many—including Michel Foucault—came to admire.[141] It told us that we are all potential criminals. That each one of us will commit crime if the price is right. Becker's reasoning did away with problematic theories of genetic predisposition, of dangerousness, of anomie, and of poverty and culture, theories that were often laced with racist or classist assumptions. "Some persons become 'criminals,'" Becker explained, "not because their basic motivation differs from that of other persons, but because their benefits and costs differ. I cannot pause to discuss the many general implications of this approach, except to remark that criminal behavior becomes part of a much more general theory and does not require ad hoc concepts of differential association, anomie, and the like, nor does it assume perfect knowledge, lightning-fast calculations, or any of the other caricatures of economic theory."[142] At the same time, Becker's approach was a clear alternative to conservative get-tough-on-crime rhetoric. It was progressive, both as a reaction against penal welfarism and against the conservative backlash, and in this sense, it was appealing to everyone—which makes it all the more paradoxical that it would ultimately facilitate the massive expansion of the penal sphere. But there were a few critical steps along the way—or, as I will suggest, missteps—that reinserted an idea of natural order into the reasoning and ultimately fueled the carceral expansion.

Neoliberal Penality

This modern view—let's call it "neoliberal penality"—facilitates the expansion of the penal sphere in direct and indirect ways. Most directly, it fuels prison growth by giving politicians a powerful rhetorical tool to enact severe law-and-order government policies that pack prisons. This was made clear during President Ronald Reagan's administration in the 1980s, which explicitly exploited the paradoxical logic of neoliberal penality to justify its punitive policies—as Katherine Beckett has brilliantly shown in *Making Crime Pay* (1997). Beckett reveals the direct link there, demonstrating how President Reagan advocated that "public assistance is an 'illegitimate' state function, whereas policing and social control constitute its real 'constitutional' obligation."[143] Here is Ronald Reagan, in his own words, rallying his base at a fundraising event:

> This is precisely what we're trying to do to the bloated Federal Government today: remove it from interfering in areas where it doesn't belong, but at the same time strengthen its ability to perform its constitutional and legitimate functions. . . . In the area of public order and law enforcement, for example, we're reversing a dangerous trend of the last decade.

While crime was steadily increasing, the Federal commitment in terms of personnel was steadily shrinking.[144]

President Reagan articulated here the core idea in neoliberal penality, namely that the government does not belong in the economic sphere, which has its own orderliness, but it has a legitimate role to play outside that sphere, especially in law enforcement. Notice how Reagan even used the term "legitimate." That is the core of neoliberal penality, and it is made possible by belief in the inherent efficiency of the free market. The logic of neoliberal penality played directly into Ronald Reagan's hands.

But this logic also facilitates the expansion of the penal sphere in less direct ways, most of all by reducing resistance to the tough-on-crime political strategies that have led to mass incarceration. Our punitive appetite has been fed, since the 1960s, by politicians who have strategically deployed concerns about crime, drugs, and race for political votes, as well as by news coverage of the issues surrounding crime and race. What has allowed these political strategies to achieve their fullest fruition is precisely the lack of resistance that accompanies neoliberal penality—that accompanies the belief that the government's legitimate role is virtually limited to the punishment arena. The punitive society we now live in has been made possible by—not caused by, but made possible by—this belief that there is a categorical difference between the free market, where intervention is inappropriate, and the penal sphere, where it is necessary and legitimate. This way of thinking makes it easier both to resist government intervention in the marketplace, as well as to embrace the criminalization and punishment of any "disorder." In Quesnay's original writings, the retributive punitiveness against the "perverted" men who did not abide by natural order was severe, and we have witnessed this same severity in mass incarceration. Neoliberal penality facilitates passing new criminal statutes and wielding the penal sanction more liberally because that is where government is necessary, that is where the state can legitimately act, that is the proper and competent sphere of politics. By creating and reinforcing this categorical division between a space of free self-regulation and an arena where coercion is necessary, appropriate, and effective, neoliberal penality has fertilized the growth of the penal domain.

There is another indirect way in which this discourse has led to a dramatic expansion in our prisons that I will mention only briefly here. As noted earlier, neoliberal penality naturalizes the market and thereby obscures the actual regulation of the marketplace. By obscuring the rules and making the outcomes seem natural and deserved, neoliberal penality makes it easier for certain market players to reorganize economic exchanges in such a way as to maximize their take, a move that ultimately increases social inequality; and there is strong evidence of sharply increased inequality in the United States since the 1970s.[145] Increased social inequality, in turn, has its own dynamic that tends to produce heightened punitive repression to maintain social order.[146]

Modern penal outcomes in the United States bear this out, especially from 1973 to 2008—a period of massive expansion of the carceral sphere during which free-market ideas and privatization flourished. During this thirty-five-year span, the United States experienced skyrocketing rates of incarceration and exorbitant institutionalization costs.[147] A study by the PEW Center on States published in March 2008 reported that prison spending outpaced all other comparable spending budgets, with the single exception of Medicaid.[148] With about 1 percent of the adult population in the United States behind bars, the size and cost of our penal sphere is undoubtedly greater than it has ever been. The costs and human capital associated with the criminal sanction are, today, exceedingly large. This is entirely consistent with a neoliberal penal vision: across the country, state legislatures are far more willing to spend dollars and to intervene in the penal sphere than they are in education or elsewhere, because that is where the government is perceived to have a legitimate and effective role. That is where the government is, relatively speaking, believed to be competent.

The other period of massive carceral expansion in United States history—the birth of the penitentiary system in the 1820s—also coincided with the twin phenomena of expanding markets and an ideal of limited government intervention. The birth of the penitentiary system occurred during a period that contemporary historians now refer to as the "Market Revolution," and earlier historians called "laissez-faire."[149] It was a tipping point in American history during which people came to believe "that the market should be the universal arbiter of interests."[150] It was also a time when notions of natural order dominated the most popular economic writings, for instance, the work of William Gouge, who used the expression "the natural order of things" consistently in his discussion of money and banking.[151] As all leading historians of the penitentiary have demonstrated, the Jacksonian era gave birth to our modern prison system. It is fair to say, with David Rothman, that "one can properly label the Jacksonian years 'the age of the asylum.'"[152]

Neoliberal penality and its earlier iterations have fertilized the carceral sphere. They have made possible, by resolving any possible cognitive dissonance, a world in which 71 percent of American respondents could favor the free-market economy as the very best system on which to base the future of the world and, at the very same time, live in a place that operates the world's biggest, most expensive, government-run, interventionist, prison system that incarcerates more than one out of every hundred adults in the country. A world in which a majority of Americans are worried about excessive regulation by the government, yet seemingly turn a blind eye to mass incarceration.

Let me emphasize that I am not making a causal argument. I do not contend that the discourse of natural order, nor the rationality of liberal or neoliberal penality, *caused* either the birth of the penitentiary in the 1820s or mass incarceration at the turn of the twenty-first century. There are direct material and political explanations for these punitive turns. In the modern era, the War on Drugs, the Southern backlash against the civil rights movement, conservative law-and-order and New Democrat tough-on-crime presidential and gubernatorial politics, racial conflicts, specific racial discrimination in crack-cocaine sentencing and profiling, as well as the embrace of actuarial methods, selective incapacitation, mandatory minimum sentences, and three-strikes laws, among other factors, played a direct role and are immediately responsible for the exponential growth of our prison populations. A number of superb books explore in fascinating detail the direct, material causes that have gorged our prisons, escalated social control, and distorted our politics, especially Katherine Beckett's *Making Crime Pay* (1997), David Garland's *Culture of Control* (2001), Jonathan Simon's *Governing through Crime* (2008), and Loïc Wacquant's *Punishing the Poor* (2009). A number of other talented scholars have explored the tragic consequences of mass incarceration in the United States, including Angela Davis, Marie Gottschalk, Douglas Massey, Marc Mauer, Tracey Meares, Lorna Rhodes, Michael Tonry, Bruce Western, and Franklin Zimring.[153]

This book is a companion to this remarkable literature on America's experience with punishment and massive incarceration. I seek not to displace these accounts, but to enrich them by tracing the genealogy of a form of rationality that has helped Americans paper over the cognitive dissonance of living in a society that is marked by fear of big government and skepticism of government efficiency, a resounding embrace of free-market ideals, and paradoxically, the largest government-run prison bureaucracy in the world—in raw numbers or per capita.

The focus on neoliberal penality helps account for why the penal sphere took the brunt of the political shifts during the Market Revolution and during the late twentieth century. The link to punishment was already embedded in eighteenth-century Physiocratic thought—and would permeate Bentham's writings on the panopticon and inspire neoliberal work on crime and punishment. The original logic in Quesnay's theory of legal despotism helps explain why the shift occurred in the penal sphere and not elsewhere—why, as Loïc Wacquant shows, the hyper ghetto evolved, in a symbiotic relationship, with the prison; why, as David Garland explains, the culture of control would express itself through the penal sphere; why, as Jonathan Simon demonstrates, governmentality would operate through crime. Neoliberal penality explains why it is the carceral sphere and not the welfare state (which can also be punitive and oppressive) that has massively expanded: because that is the space where government intervention is considered necessary, appropriate, legitimate, and effective.

Moreover, this account ties the post-1970s neoliberal turn back to earlier iterations, affording a longer view of the relationship between economy and punishment. It sheds light on earlier punitive turns, such as the birth of the penitentiary system in the 1820s, and in that sense does not limit the analysis to contemporary neoliberalism. It speaks both to liberal *and* neoliberal penality. To be sure, the term "neoliberalism" is deeply contested—like most "ism" terms—even among those who carefully study the concept such as David Harvey, Jean and John Comaroff, Michael Dawson, Nikolas Rose, or Lisa Wedeen.[154] Nevertheless, much of the critical writing on neoliberalism tends to focus on the period following 1970—referring to the period before that as "embedded liberalism"—and especially on the rise of Ronald Reagan and Margaret Thatcher, on the wave of privatizations that ensued, and on the "Washington Consensus" of the 1990s.[155] Many critical punishment theorists, such as David Garland, Jonathan Simon, and Loïc Wacquant, have focused on the recent neoliberal period—or late-modern or advanced liberal period, some prefer to say—and documented the shifts in punitive practices.[156] In *Punishing the Poor*, for instance, Wacquant expressly ties the punitive turn to the evisceration of the welfare state since the 1970s and its replacement with workfare. The account in this book is intended to *extend* the historical horizon. Our contemporary faith in the free markets does not date to the 1970s, but precedes it by several centuries. In this sense, it is important to tie the modern neoliberal period back to its earlier manifestations. The key point is that the very logic of neoliberal penality was embedded in the first articulations of liberal economic theory. Here I trace the genealogy of our contemporary rationality back to the birth of natural order—and offer a way out.

A Word on Method

The categories of "free market" and "regulated," it turns out, hinder rather than help. They are, in effect, illusory and distort rather than advance our knowledge. Ultimately, the categories themselves—of "free markets" and "excessive regulation," of "natural order" and "discipline"—need to be discarded. In this sense, this project continues in the furrow of a lengthy nominalist tradition—a strain of thought that runs through the work of thinkers as far back as the medieval Franciscan friar William of Ockham, to the sixteenth-century Renaissance essays of Michel de Montaigne, to the nineteenth-century polemics of Friedrich Nietzsche.[157] It starts by conceptualizing "free markets" and "excessive regulation," or "natural order" and "administration," or "policing"—or, more simply, "freedom" and "discipline"—as what William of Ockham would have called universals, and then explores what work those universals are accomplishing. It challenges the very existence of those universal categories in order to discover, first, how the designations work, but second, what they hide regarding the unique aspects of individual entities—in this case, individual forms of social, political, and economic organization. And it develops what could be described as a nominalist thesis: that we have developed and deployed these universals to make sense of what are in fact irreducibly individual phenomena, to place discrete and divergent practices into a coherent framework, to deploy simple heuristic devices or stereotypes to expedite our evaluation and judgment, and that, in so doing, we have created structures of meaning that do work for us—at a steep price.

Nominalist Readings

The historian Paul Veyne, in his book *Foucault: Sa pensée, sa personne* (2008), excavated a similar nominalist influence in the work of Michel Foucault, drawing particular attention to the opening passage of Foucault's 1979 lectures at the Collège de France, *Naissance de la biopolitique*.[158] In that opening lecture, Foucault stepped back to explain and reframe his larger intellectual project—as he so often did—and to place his writings within a methodological framework. The method in all his work, Foucault explained, had always been to start by doing away with the central explanatory concept, as a way to reexamine the work that the concept accomplished. Foucault lectured:

> I start from the decision, both theoretical and methodological, which consists in saying: suppose that the universals do not exist, and then I ask the question to history and historians: how can you write the history if you do not admit *a priori* that something like the state, society, the sovereign, subjects exist? It is the same question that I posed when I asked: . . . suppose that madness does not exist.[159]

The use of the term "universals" is revealing and, as Paul Veyne suggested, the passage links Foucault back to the tradition of nominalism.[160] Foucault's method was to critically examine the very conceptions that we construct in order to learn something about ourselves.[161] Foucault's nominalism was fed, in part, by a large dose of skepticism—especially, skepticism of the constructs of others, of those many universals. It is in this sense that Veyne correctly characterized Foucault as a skeptic—although it is important to keep nominalism and skepticism distinct and separate.[162]

In a similar vein, this project asks: suppose that "free markets" or "excessive regulation" do not exist. What does that tell us about the way that we now interpret and perceive our social organization? What work do those concepts perform? These questions too are nominalist and build on a centuries-old tradition of thought. But although this project shares a methodological sensibility with Foucault, it breaks sharply from his analysis. More than anyone, Foucault reified the idea that the *police des grains* under the ancien régime was regulated excessively, and he strongly intimated that the modern economic sphere had been liberalized. Even though Foucault's overarching project was to show that both were forms of governance, he nevertheless created and deployed categories in a manner that is completely antithetical to this project.

In his 1978 lectures *Sécurité, Territoire, Population,* Foucault specifically defined "discipline" in its purest, most pristine form, using as his chief illustration the *police des grains* of eighteenth-century France. In fact, as noted earlier, he even substituted the expression or cleverly inserted the term in the expression itself, "la police *disciplinaire* des grains."[163] This project specifically seeks to demystify both that claim and the work being done there by the term "discipline." Similarly, in his analysis of liberalized markets, Foucault again reified the difference by means of his contrast with discipline. To describe more modern market practices, Foucault abandoned the older paradigm and fashioned a new category: *sécurité.* In his 1979 lectures, *Naissance de la biopolitique,* Foucault analyzed the "liberal" mode of rationality under the rubric of *sécurité*—what he later called "gouvernementalité"—tracing liberalism to the idea of a self-limitation on governance.[164] Liberal practice is the project of "not governing too much," in the words of Benjamin Franklin and the Marquis d'Argenson, and had its roots at the birth of political economy: "Political economy," Foucault lectured, "is fundamentally what has ensured the auto-limitation of governmental reason."[165] Listen closely: "l'autolimitation de la raison gouvernementale." Even for Foucault, one of the sharpest critics of neoliberalism, there is a tangible substratum of liberty at play. There are new practices of liberalization. There are free movements and processes of free circulation of goods: "Liberalism—not interfering, allowing free movement, letting things follow their course; *laisser faire, passer et aller*—basically and fundamentally means acting so that reality develops, goes its way, and follows its own course according to the laws, principles, and mechanism of reality itself."[166]

It is this "auto-limitation" that led Foucault to name and deploy the new category of *sécurité,* which is different precisely in those three ways from discipline. First, whereas discipline confines, concentrates, and encloses its space of operation, *sécurité* is centrifugal: "The apparatuses of security . . . have the constant tendency to expand; they are centrifugal. . . . Security therefore involves organizing, or anyway allowing the development of ever-wider circuits."[167] Second, whereas discipline focuses on even the smallest infractions, *sécurité* lets the small things go. "The apparatus of security . . . lets things happen . . . allowing prices to rise, allowing scarcity to develop, and letting people go hungry."[168] Third, whereas discipline seeks to eliminate and eradicate completely, *sécurité* in contrast tries only to minimize—to seek an optimal level of the targeted behavior, to achieve a certain equilibrium. Not to eliminate, but to regulate to an optimal degree. *Sécurité* is pragmatic. It tries to figure out how to optimize. In sum, *sécurité* differs dramatically from *discipline* in its modes of functioning. For Foucault, the practices differ in fact. As Foucault explained: "An apparatus of security . . . cannot operate well except on condition that it is given freedom, in the modern sense that it acquires in the eighteenth century: no longer the exemptions and privileges attached to a person, but the possibility of movement, change of place, and processes of circulation of both people and things."[169]

This project is markedly different. The point here is not to show that both the *police des grains* and modern market organization are forms of governmentality—which is certainly true—but rather that neither can be categorized in the ways they tend to be perceived and that the categories themselves of overly disciplined—of the "disciplinary" *police des grains*—and of liberalized markets, that those categories themselves are meaningless and obfuscate the real work that needs to be done. In this project, it is crucial to distinguish and carefully delineate practice from rhetoric—though they may well both constitute discourse—and to make sure we know exactly which one we are describing and comparing.

The fundamental problem is that the foundational categories of, on the one hand, "market efficiency" or "free markets," and on the other hand, "excessive regulation," "governmental inefficiency," or "discipline," are illusory and misleading categories that fail to capture the irreducibly individual phenomena of different forms of market organization. In all markets, the state is present. Naturally, it is present when it fixes the price of a commodity such as wheat or bread. But it is also present when it subsidizes the cultivation or production of wheat, when it grants a charter to the Chicago Board of Trade, when it permits trading of an instrument like a futures contract, when it protects the property interests of wheat wholesalers, when it facilitates the river transport of wheat, when it criminalizes the coordination of prices, when it allows the merger of grain companies, when it polices the timing of trades, and so on. In addition, whenever the government is not itself regulating a market, it implicitly or explicitly delegates that authority to another entity. All markets are highly regulated. At the same time, in all markets, there is freedom. Even in a controlled economy where the price is fixed, there are variations in the quality of the goods sold and along other dimensions that create product differentiation. These produce lines at certain stores and not at others. Even in a highly criminalized economy where certain goods are outlawed, robust black markets emerge and develop that facilitate the sale and purchase of illegal goods.

In the economic sphere, there is freedom and there is constraint. What we see is a reflection on us, not of the market. In the end, it makes little sense to describe one regime as "free" and another as "regulated." All systems have complicated regulatory mechanisms that make the market function and dysfunction. What is most important is to remember that the categories we use to organize, understand, discuss, categorize, and compare the different organizing principles are just that—labels. They do not capture the true individuality of the objects described. And they have the unfortunate effect of obscuring rather than enlightening. They obscure by making one set of objects seem natural and necessary, and the other naturally unnecessary.

The central error is that we use these categories for purposes of evaluation and practice—for purposes of policy making. We classify forms of market organization into "free" and "regulated" in order to embrace or reject those forms of economic organization. Even today, politicians and commentators continue to argue for more "regulation" as if "regulation" were a solution. The issue is not more or less regulation; the issue is how regulatory mechanisms and regimes distribute wealth. And the categories of "free" and "regulated" are simply not useful when evaluating different forms of economic organization and their distributional consequences. The idea that "government tends to be inefficient" or that "markets are naturally efficient" is not helpful—no more so than their opposites, that "government is a more efficient regulator" or that "market failure is pervasive." There are examples of remarkably efficient government projects (high-speed rail and mass transport in certain countries), just as there are dramatic examples of waste in private enterprises (consider the recently disclosed overpriced office and bathroom renovations for CEOs at private investment banks). When it comes to evaluating how resources are distributed, these categories simply do not help. And that is the only important goal: to determine how resources are allocated and distributed, and whether those distributions correspond to our political values.

Frames of Reference

I am by no means the first to toil in these fields.[170] Yet the precise objective of this project may well differ from earlier interventions. This study seeks to explore how a certain mode of rationality rendered natural a conception of the penal sphere as lying outside the free market and as being the repository for necessary, legitimate, and competent government intervention. The goal is not to offer a historical explanation of what caused this mode of rationality, nor to propose a material explanation as to how the idea of natural order emerged. It is, instead, to trace a genealogy of how this rationality became believable. How it became so obvious and natural, and at what price.

Let me emphasize the last question—at what price—in part by drawing a contrast to Albert Hirschman's remarkable essay "The Passions and the Interests: Political Arguments for Capitalism before Its Triumph." Hirschman demonstrated there how ideas evolve over time and argued that the "spirit of capitalism" grew and changed from within. The process, Hirschman suggested, was endogenous to the reasoning and rationality of the period. In contrast to Marxist analyses, which trace the emergence of capitalism to changes in material processes and class structures—to the end of feudal land relations and the rise of new modes of production—and in contrast to Weber, who traced the rise of capitalism in part to a new ethic of Protestantism, Hirschman offered a more seamless history of ideas, wherein self-interest came to be perceived as the useful passion that could be counted on to rein in the less productive passions. The theory of interests—and especially, the theories of self-interest represented in the private vices and public virtues of Mandeville, or the hidden hand of Adam Smith—evolved as one conceivable and more auspicious way of dealing with excessive cultures of glory and with passions such as lust. The other means that had been developed—such as repression or rehabilitation of the passions—seemed less likely to succeed than pitting one passion against the others.

Hirschman's story traces the history of how an idea became popular, and I embrace that method in one sense—insofar as this project too explores how the idea of natural order became dominant in our contemporary neoliberal imagination. At the same time, however, this project seeks to push the analysis further; to explore how the acceptance of those beliefs—beliefs in natural order and legal despotism—affects our contemporary social distributions. In other words, at what price? Ways of reasoning and seeing the world, I contend, facilitate certain material developments—sometimes inadvertently, many times knowingly. They make possible, and can ease, certain types of distribution. We come to believe certain ideas, as Hirschman demonstrated well, but those beliefs then have significant consequences.

At the same time, however, there are limitations to rarefied idealism: I do not contend that ideas have such real effects on the world that they themselves or they alone necessarily transform our practices. I do not believe that a new idea can necessarily change the way we produce, the way we work, the amount of work we do. I am not Weberian in the stylized sense of *The Protes-*

tant Ethic and the Spirit of Capitalism. Although this project focuses predominantly on the development of the ideas of natural order and legal despotism, and on their potential influence on our social distributions, this is not to deny the causal influence of material changes, economic and technological shifts, and political transformation: how the Southern resistance and backlash against the civil rights movement encouraged and strengthened a law-and-order response to crime in the 1970s, as Katherine Beckett has ably shown; how the withering of the welfare state has fed the concentration of ghettoization and fueled a hypertrophic prison population, as Loïc Wacquant has documented well; or how the technological development of actuarial tools promoted the use of racial profiling.[171] This project does not address those material and political transformations. That would be another project—equally important, but calling for another book-length treatment. In this sense, this project is neither merely a history of ideas, nor an intellectual history, but it is also not a material explanation of how these ideas evolve over time. It is instead a tracing—or genealogy—of how a certain set of beliefs became common and an analysis of how those beliefs influence our practices.

Luc Boltanski and Ève Chiapello's *The New Spirit of Capitalism* is enlightening in this respect. Boltanski and Chiapello's work focuses precisely on the intersection of how new ideas—in their case, 1960s critiques of Fordist capitalist principles of hierarchical organization—reshaped work practices into more fluid networks with greater roles for individual initiative, creativity, and autonomy, and thereby helped neutralize the thrust of the original critiques themselves. Boltanski and Chiapello take seriously how new ideas translate into practices, conducting a close reading of modern business-management manuals to demonstrate how the ideas permeated the reasoning of management and influenced institutional organization. Michel Foucault's lectures at the Collège de France in 1978 and 1979 are also enlightening. Not only did Foucault specifically address the Parisian bread markets of the eighteenth century, the birth of Physiocratic thought, and postwar American neoliberalism—including the seminal work on crime and punishment that Gary Becker penned in 1968—but he also related neoliberal thought back to the early development of public economy.

A Prolegomenon

But let me not confuse matters more as I draw family resemblances, clarify differences, and acknowledge debts. Instead let me be as specific as possible about my own project. To summarize: In the short period from 1756 to 1767, François Quesnay and the Physiocrats injected the notion of natural order into the economic domain and argued that commerce constituted an autonomous, self-regulating system that required no external intervention. This conception of natural order grounded their theories of economic production and of the wealth of nations. The natural order that reigned in the economic domain demanded that there be no interference with the laws of nature. It also gave rise to a political theory that Quesnay and Le Mercier would call "legal despotism." In their writings from 1767, Quesnay and Le Mercier argued for a unitary executive—an absolute, hereditary monarch—who would recognize and thereby instantiate the laws of nature without the benefit of a legislative body. Precisely because the natural laws were perfect and most advantageous to mankind, Quesnay and Mercier argued, there was nothing for a legislator to do in the economic sphere. Manmade laws and government intervention could only disrupt the natural laws governing economic production. Positive manmade law, then, was relegated to one and only one area: to criminalize and severely punish those men who did not recognize and abide by the natural order, those men who were unregulated—"*déréglés*"—and disorderly, those who stole and were wicked.

The Physiocrats' idea of natural order and the theory of legal despotism fundamentally reshaped the relationship between, on the one hand, commerce, trade, and economic relations, and on the other hand, punishment practices and theory. In the previous period, a dominant view held that the criminal sanction was a form of governmental intervention no different from the general administration of commerce and trade. Punishments formed part of a larger administrative framework intended to set prices and regulate all domains of human behavior, whether economic, social, or penal. That earlier framework was captured best by the famous tract of Cesare Beccaria, *On Crimes and Punishments,* published in 1764. In the period after the Physiocrats, a different vision took hold, one in which the criminal sanction—by contrast to economic administration—would serve as the exclusive device for the state to legitimately intervene, but in the penal area only. By means of this fundamental transformation, the criminal sanction changed from an ordinary form of regulation no different than tariffs and levies, to an exceptional mechanism of state intervention in situations lying beyond or outside the market model. By pushing the state outside the market and giving it free rein there, the Physiocratic ideal of natural order would eventually facilitate the expansion of the penal sphere.

These ideas of natural order and legal despotism would be rehearsed in history, resurfacing in different guises, and ultimately would shape the contemporary public imagination in the United States. Jeremy Bentham in the nineteenth century would curiously replicate this rationality by means of a unique alchemy that blended Cesare Beccaria on punishment with a naturalist reading of Adam Smith on economic liberty. Modern economically minded thinkers would reformulate, in more technical and scientific jargon, a notion of orderliness in commerce under the rubric of the inherent efficiency of markets. Precisely because of this notion of efficiency, the government would be relegated outside the market to the realm of "market bypassing," where it could legitimately intervene and punish effectively.

In this sense, this project asks: What work do the categories of "natural order" and "market efficiency," of "excess regulation" and "discipline," do for us? What do we achieve when we distribute mechanisms of market organization into the two categories—the free and the constrained—and then judge them on that basis? The answer I propose is that we have deployed these categories in a seemingly obvious and natural way, but that they are in fact misleading and incoherent and have had detrimental consequences. First, they naturalize and thereby mask the rules and regulations that do exist. This, in turn, effectively keeps us from making the connection between the different methods of organizing markets and their distributive consequences, and from fully assessing the justice of the resulting outcomes. Second, they facilitate the expansion of our penal sphere in both direct and indirect ways, predominantly by resolving the paradox of limited government and mass incarceration. Let me emphasize: it is not just that the categories are not useful. They have been affirmatively detrimental. The logic of neoliberal penality has made possible our contemporary punishment practices by fueling the belief that the legitimate and competent space for government intervention is the penal sphere. The logic of neoliberal penality has facilitated our punishment practices by weakening any resistance to governmental initiatives in the penal domain because that is where the state may legitimately, competently, and effectively govern.

This book is a prolegomenon, a necessary first step in the direction of properly assessing modern forms of social and economic organization. Why necessary? Because of the deafening and dominant discourse of natural order and market efficiency. The very idea that we would use the term "free" to describe our current market system—a system that is regulated through and through—is a testament to the work that needs to be done. It may be fair to say that the idea of natural order has so deeply and fundamentally warped our understanding of economic systems that it will take a lot of effort to reach the point where we can properly assess different alternatives for the administration of markets and punishment, and dismantle our carceral state.

1

Beccaria on Crime and Punishment

The place to begin is at that contested moment when the idea of natural order began to take hold in the field of public economy and allowed eighteenth-century thinkers to separate economic exchange from the penal sphere. One text, more than any other, galvanized the controversy: Cesare Beccaria's tract *On Crimes and Punishments,* which is surely today the most famous eighteenth-century text on punishment. Beccaria's short tract arrived precisely at the moment of contestation and became, through selective readings and appropriations, a mirror of what his contemporaries wanted to read into the relationship between markets and punishment.

To the *philosophes* of the *Encyclopédie,* Beccaria's work represented the epitome of Enlightenment reasoning on punishment and a guarantee of freedom. To the Physiocrats, Beccaria's writings served as the prime example of a disciplinary paradigm of government intervention, the foil against which they would develop their notion of natural order. Surprisingly—or perhaps not—the struggle over Beccaria's legacy continues to the present. Today, Chicago School thinkers such as Gary Becker and Richard Posner appropriate Beccaria as the founder, with Jeremy Bentham, of the economic approach to crime and punishment, while poststructuralist thinkers like Michel Foucault interpret Beccaria as the pivotal theorist of discipline and regimentation.

"Perhaps not," I suggest, because the competition over readings, interpretations, and appropriations of texts is, in truth, no different than the struggle over the categories themselves. Finding discipline in the *police des grains* is hardly different than reading discipline into Beccaria's tract. Categorizing those police practices under the rubric of regimentation rather than freedom, as Fréminville would, is no different than appropriating Beccaria as the symbol of discipline, or, for that matter, as the icon of Enlightenment reasoning, or the founder of rational choice theory. Just like the categories themselves, we deploy readings of texts to help shape, to confirm, to argue for our understanding of practices: to demonstrate the oppressiveness of government interventions at an earlier time—or to praise them. To highlight the liberating and emancipatory potential of free markets—or to mythologize them. Whether we are reading Beccaria's *On Crimes and Punishments,* or for that matter Quesnay's *Tableau économique,* our appropriations and readings of texts are productive. They do a lot of work.

The competition over Beccaria's text has been particularly productive, allowing many generations of thinkers to mold the history of intellectual thought and promote their views in the struggle over natural order and the *police des grains*—over liberty and discipline. And gradually, over two centuries, these competing appropriations of Beccaria have given way to a clear demarcation between the market and the penal sphere. But let's not start at the end. Let's begin with the first who appropriated Beccaria, the *philosophes* of the *Encyclopédie,* who saw in his short tract everything they wanted to see about the Enlightenment and civilization. Truth be told, were it not for them, neither the liberal French Physiocrats, nor the proponents of law and economics today, would have had any material to play with. Let us begin the story, then, with Beccaria in Paris.

Beccaria, the *Philosophe*

Cesare Beccaria's short tract *On Crimes and Punishments* met with mixed reviews when it first appeared in Italian in April 1764. Published anonymously in Livorno for fear of repercussions (the tract was strongly secular and egalitarian), it was panned in the Parisian *Gazette littéraire de l'Europe* as a simple restatement of Rousseau's *Social Contract* and attacked in Italy as the work of a "socialista" (some historians contend that this was the first use of the term "socialist").[1] But it soon caught the eye and admiration of that small circle of French *philosophes* known as the Encyclopédistes. André Morellet, an abbé of the Sorbonne, recalls in his *Mémoires* that it was the statesman Guillaume-Chrétien de Lamoignon de Malesherbes who first became interested in Beccaria's essay. Malesherbes had a few guests over for dinner—Turgot, at the time *intendant* of Limoges; Jean le Rond d'Alembert, the philosopher and co-editor with Denis Diderot of the *Encyclopédie;* Morellet; and a few others—and, having just received Beccaria's tract from Italy, discussed the new work with his guests. "He was troubled by the length and obscurity of the introduction, and was trying to rephrase the first sentence," Morellet recalls. "'Try to translate this,' de Malesherbes told me. I went to his library and returned with the phrase as it is today. Everyone was satisfied and pressed me to continue. I took the book with me and published it in French six weeks later."[2]

Morellet's recollection may have been somewhat fanciful, but his translation, *Traité des délits et des peines,* was made public at the end of December 1765.[3] In a letter to Beccaria a few days later, dated January 3, 1766, Morellet sent the young author the compliments of Diderot and d'Alembert; the philosopher Claude Adrien Helvétius; the naturalist Georges-Louis Leclerc, count de Buffon; Paul-Henri Thiry, baron d'Holbach; as well as David Hume who was at the time living in Paris—all of whom, Morellet wrote, had read and greatly enjoyed the translation. Hume, in fact, had read both the original and the translation in detail.[4] Morellet informed Beccaria that he had also delivered a copy of the book to Rousseau, and, in that January 3 letter, invited Beccaria to Paris.[5] D'Alembert, Diderot, Helvétius, d'Holbach, Malesherbes, and Morellet all wanted to meet and converse with the Italian, who was only twenty-eight years old at the time.[6]

Beccaria arrived in Paris in October 1766 and in short order met them all, as well as other notable thinkers and courtesans, such as Jean-Charles Philibert Trudaine de Montigny, the Marquis de Chastellux, Suzanne Churchod Necker (the wife of Jacques Necker, the future finance minister), and Marie Thérèse Rodet Geoffrin.[7] Beccaria had an abbreviated stay in Paris—he fled Parisian society earlier than expected in December 1766, leaving behind some skeptics—but his visit caught the attention of Voltaire, who wrote an anonymous pamphlet commenting on and praising his work.[8] Voltaire's "Commentaire sur le livre des délits et des peines" was printed regularly as a preface to Morellet's translation in all subsequent French editions, propelling Beccaria's tract to fame.[9]

"I am ashamed to write about these matters after what has been said by the author of *On Crimes and Punishments,*" Voltaire confessed. "I should limit myself to hope that we all and often reread this great work by this lover of humanity."[10] In a letter attributed to Voltaire, dated May 30, 1768, Voltaire thanked Beccaria "with all my heart. These sentiments are those of the entire Europe. . . . You toil on behalf of reason and humanity, both of which have been quashed for so long. You revive those two sisters, beaten for over sixteen hundred years. They are finally beginning to walk and talk; but as soon as they do, fanaticism again rears its ugly head."[11]

In a time of brutal corporal punishment, Beccaria's tract advocated for the abolition of the death penalty, for measured and proportional punishments, for the end of torture, and for equal treatment regardless of nobility or wealth—and within several years, as Franco Venturi, a leading historian of the Italian Enlightenment, notes, "the triumph of Beccaria's work could not have been more complete in Parisian intellectual circles."[12] Its influence extended swiftly well beyond Europe. Beccaria's work was lauded by the Empress Catherine II of Russia, who invited him to rewrite the Russian penal code. Thomas Jefferson copied whole pages of the work into his diary and drew on it in his effort to abolish the death penalty.[13] John Adams was quoting Beccaria's text as early as 1770 in his defense of those implicated in the Boston Massacre.[14] In short order, Beccaria's tract became known as *the* Enlightenment text on punishment—the epitome of Enlightenment reason in the field of crime and punishment.[15]

In this reading, *On Crimes and Punishments* became the very symbol of the Enlightenment—an impassioned critique of the excessively brutal, arbitrary, and unequal punishment practices of the seventeenth and eighteenth centuries, and a manifesto for legal reform centered on the Enlightenment values of lenience, rationality, justice, and the rule of law, in the tradition of the French *philosophes* of the *Encyclopédie.* The text offers a passionate plea against the use of judicial torture to extract confessions from the accused, as well as to exonerate guilt; against the use of secret evidence and accusations; against sentencing inequalities based on wealth and social status; and against excessively brutal corporal punishments and the death penalty. Beccaria closes the book with this sentence, which captures well this reading of his tract: "In order that punishment should not be an act of violence perpetrated by one or many upon a private citizen, it is essential that it should be public, speedy, necessary, the minimum possible in the given circumstances, proportionate to the crime, and determined by the law."[16]

Beccaria, the Rational Action Theorist

Today, in the United States at least, Beccaria's short tract receives a quite different reading. *On Crimes and Punishments* is celebrated as the first economic analysis of crime and Beccaria is revered as the first economist to have applied rational choice theory to the field of crime and punishment. Beccaria is portrayed as the first to have rigorously applied the tools and logic of economics to criminal justice issues.

In part, this was Jeremy Bentham's doing. Bentham traced many of his greatest insights to Beccaria—including "the sacred truth that the greatest happiness of the greatest number is the foundation of morals and legislation."[17] As H. L. A. Hart recounts, Beccaria's treatise was the cornerstone of Bentham's conception of "moral arithmetic," which was at the heart of the utilitarian philosophy he developed.[18]

It was thus Beccaria as economist who came to the foreground in the nineteenth century and in the Anglo-Saxon world—which is not entirely surprising. After all, after fleeing Parisian society and returning to Milan, Beccaria was appointed to one of only three chairs in public economy established during the eighteenth century—the newly created Professor of Cameral Sciences at the Palatine School in Milan, endowed and bestowed by the Holy Roman

Empress Maria Theresa of Austria in 1768.[19] Beccaria taught public economy for two years before entering public service as an economic adviser and civil servant for the Milanese republic.[20] Joseph Schumpeter, in his magisterial history of economic thought, actually placed Beccaria at the fountainhead of classical economic theory—with Adam Smith and A. R. J. Turgot. Schumpeter in fact called Beccaria "the Italian A. Smith," and Adam Smith "the Scottish Beccaria."[21]

More recently, contemporary scholars of law and economics have embraced Beccaria as one of their own. Richard Posner traces his intellectual genealogy, in the area of penal law, specifically to Beccaria. In introducing his economic model of criminal law in 1985, Posner writes: "The economic analysis of criminal law began on a very high plane in the eighteenth and early nineteenth centuries with the work of Beccaria and Bentham, but its revival in modern times dates only from 1968, when Gary Becker's article on the economics of crime and punishment appeared."[22] Gary Becker too, in his influential 1968 paper "Crime and Punishment: An Economic Approach," appropriates Beccaria: "Lest the reader be repelled by the apparent novelty of an 'economic' framework for illegal behavior, let him recall that two important contributors to criminology during the eighteenth and nineteenth centuries, Beccaria and Bentham, explicitly applied an economic calculus. Unfortunately, such an approach has lost favor during the last hundred years, and my efforts can be viewed as a resurrection, modernization, and thereby I hope improvement on these much earlier pioneering studies."[23]

Much like Becker and Posner, Beccaria sought to extend the logic of economic rationality to the social sphere—to the field of crime and punishment. Beccaria believed that the logic of economics could tame and civilize society, could guide our policies in the social domain, could determine right from wrong, and just from unjust punishment. His project in *On Crimes and Punishments* was precisely to extend economic rationality to the penal sphere, so as to achieve there what had been achieved in the field of commercial exchange. And so he writes in his Introduction:

> We have discovered the true relations between sovereign and subjects and between nation and nation. Commerce has been stimulated by philosophic truths . . . and there is waged among nations a silent war by trade, which is the most humane sort of war and more worthy of reasonable men. Such is the progress we owe to the present enlightened century. But there are very few who have scrutinized and fought against the savagery and the disorderliness of the procedures of criminal justice, a part of legislation which is so prominent and so neglected in almost the whole of Europe.[24]

That was precisely the goal that Cesare Beccaria set for himself: to impose economic rationality on the barbaric sphere of punishment; to civilize and tame punishment the way that commerce had tamed man; to harmonize the economic and penal spheres.

In this reading, Beccaria is one of the first rational choice theorists of crime and punishment and his writings are premised on the very idea that men are self-interested pursuers of pleasure. It is a reading that emphasizes Beccaria's contention that "every man makes himself the centre of all the world's affairs," and that "pleasure and pain are the motive forces of all sentient beings."[25] According to this view, Beccaria's central thesis was simple: if we could understand *homo œconomicus* as a rational calculating individual, we could apply a very similar model to understand *homo scelestus* in the larger social realm.[26]

Beccaria developed theories of marginal deterrence that later became a cornerstone of Becker and Posner's economic model of crime. "If an equal punishment is laid down for two crimes which damage society equally, men will not have a stronger deterrent against committing the greater crime if they find it more advantageous to do so," Beccaria wrote, prefacing later economic analysis of criminal law.[27] Beccaria set forth a number of other rules that strongly influenced Bentham and other utilitarian theorists. For instance, Beccaria suggested in his work that the certainty of punishment is more important than the harshness of the punishment; that the harsher the punishment, the more likely the criminal will commit more crimes to avoid it; and that an attempt should be punished less severely than a completed crime in order to give an incentive to the culprit not to complete the crime—again, a notion of marginal deterrence that was highly influential on subsequent theorists.[28]

As in Bentham, the right to punish for Beccaria was a necessary evil: an evil, in that punishment is necessarily tyrannous and thus bad; but necessary, in the sense that it is the only way to restrain men. Consequently, "any punishment that goes beyond the need to preserve this bond is unjust by its very nature."[29] Given that punishment is viewed as an evil and that the harm of crime is the harm to social welfare, the purpose of punishment becomes simply the prevention of future similar acts. The purpose of punishment is not to look backward, Beccaria emphasized—foreshadowing English utilitarianism. It will not undo a crime already committed. "The wailings of a wretch," Beccaria wrote, cannot "undo what has been done and turn back the clock."[30] The purpose of punishment to Beccaria was "nothing other than to prevent the offender from doing fresh harm to his fellows and to deter others from doing likewise."[31] And insofar as punishment was an evil, there were limiting pressures on its application. Anything more than necessary, Beccaria maintained, was "superfluous and, therefore, tyrannous."[32]

Beccaria was an early proponent of the idea that pleasure and pain are the metrics and motives of human action. "The proximate and efficient cause of actions is the flight from pain, their final cause is the love of pleasure."[33] The notion of maximizing social welfare was central to Beccaria's work.[34] In this regard, Beccaria drew heavily on the work of his compatriot and close colleague Pietro Verri, who articulated in his *Meditazioni sulla felicità* (Meditations on happiness), published a year earlier in 1763, the keystone to their new philosophical approach: happiness.[35] "The end of the social pact," Verri wrote in 1763, "is the well-being of each of the individuals who join together to form society, who do so in order that this well-being becomes absorbed into the public happiness or rather the greatest possible happiness distributed with the greatest equality possible."[36]

Beccaria wrote, in the very introductory pages of his short tract, that the litmus test of state intervention should be whether "they conduce to *the greatest happiness shared among the greater number.*"[37] In this passage, Beccaria endorsed a utilitarian framework that sought to maximize not just social welfare, but more specifically the equal distribution of social welfare. Beccaria's—and Verri's—conception of welfare, in this sense, was somewhat unique in its emphasis on equality.[38] Similarly, in his *Reflections,* Beccaria wrote of achieving as a goal "the greatest possible happiness divided among the greatest number."[39] Societies that approximate this are "social," Beccaria wrote, and those that are farthest away are "savage."[40] This definition of social welfare, which emphasized equality, differed from that of other liberal economists, including Bentham.

Beccaria, the Cameralist

But there were—at least in the eyes of some—even greater differences that set Beccaria apart from his contemporary liberal economists, and for that matter from later members of the law-and-economics movement. The economic rationality that Beccaria intended to impose in the punishment field, it seemed, was not the self-regulated and self-adjusting market system with its natural efficiency. It was instead, at least on one reading, the economic logic of minute governmental administration of every aspect of economics and exchange. It was the economic model of "police" typified by the *police des grains.* Beccaria's idea of "the progress we owe to the present enlightened century" was not the liberalization of trade, but rather the intense administration of markets and commerce.

Beccaria is one of those remarkable authors whose writings form the keystone of important intellectual traditions, and yet who is actually little read, especially in the United States. Most of his economic writings have never been translated into English, nor even into French. Though his ideas captured the spirit of a time, his actual economic texts remain buried, occasionally collected in Italian editions that are not widely distributed.[41] The full flavor of his economics, it turns out, may have escaped his modern disciples.

It did not escape the early French economists, however, especially Pierre Samuel Du Pont de Nemours, the lifelong disciple and principal publicist of François Quesnay and the Physiocrats.[42] In Du Pont's eyes, Beccaria was anchored in an earlier tradition of cameralist public economy, a connection that presented a serious stumbling block for Du Pont and his French economist colleagues. Like Becker and Posner, Du Pont recognized the importance of Beccaria; but unlike them, he saw in Beccaria all the faults of the government interventionist and so was scathing in his critique.

Beccaria, it seems, had not met Du Pont or François Quesnay during his visit to Paris in 1766—in fact, it is not clear whether Beccaria was exposed at all to Physiocratic thought while there. Those who surrounded him and received him in Paris were primarily in the circle of *philosophes*—d'Alembert, Diderot, Morellet, d'Holbach, and Malesherbes. Beccaria attended the salons of Mme. Necker and Mme. Geoffrin, and therefore, in all likelihood, did not cross paths with Quesnay or the Physiocrats.[43] The Physiocrats frequented different salons—those of Louise Elisabeth de La Rochefoucauld and Madame Suard.[44]

From Beccaria's correspondence, it appears that he first came to the attention of the Physiocrats in 1769 as a result of the publication in Italy of his inaugural lecture delivered in Milan on January 9 of that year; the chevalier Louis Claude Bigot de Sainte Croix, secretary to the French embassy in Turin and a disciple of Quesnay, initiated contact with Beccaria in March 1769 and offered to translate the inaugural lecture into French.[45] Du Pont de Nemours first corresponded with Beccaria in 1770, and in his letters, there is every indication that Beccaria had not been exposed to the Physiocrats during his stay in Paris.[46] The French *économistes* seem to have engaged Beccaria much later, through entirely different channels than the *philosophes*.[47] (Incidentally, Beccaria also would not have physically met Turgot, or for that matter Adam Smith, during his short stay in Paris because the dates of his visit did not overlap with their passages through the city.)[48]

As editor-in-chief of the review *Éphémérides du citoyen,* the organ of the Physiocrats, Du Pont proudly announced Beccaria's appointment to one of the first chairs in political economy in the third volume of the journal, published in 1769.[49] Yet although Du Pont praised Beccaria for being one of the first recognized economists, he used the announcement to underscore deep differences between Beccaria and the Physiocrats—differences that could be traced to Beccaria's earlier tract, *On Crimes and Punishments*.[50] Du Pont focused his critique primarily on the question of the right to property, suggesting that Beccaria had not properly recognized the importance of that right: "The *right to property*," Du Pont emphasized, "is not *a terrible right*," and, he added, "*contraband* is not *a theft on the Treasury*."[51]

Beccaria had included a chapter on contraband in his little tract, where he had advocated severe punishment, including the galleys, for smuggling. "Such a crime deserves a fairly heavy punishment," Beccaria wrote, "even up to imprisonment or penal servitude."[52] In the case of a tobacco smuggler, for instance, Beccaria prescribed a prison regime including "toil and exertion in the excise service which [the smuggler] wished to defraud."[53] Du Pont's reaction in the *Éphémérides* was visceral and it centered on the notion of private property. To Du Pont, the real criminals are not those who smuggle contraband, but those who regulate commerce: "If there is, then, a true *offense that deserves prison and penal servitude*, it's not that of the smugglers, but that of the *Regulators* who have proposed and still propose, who have compelled and still compel the adoption of royal edicts that hamper trade, of fiscal inquisitions, and of monopolistic threats to the natural rights of citizens, to their property, to their civil liberty, deterring useful work, and as fearsome for public as for private wealth."[54]

A few months later, Du Pont published a translation of Beccaria's inaugural lecture in the *Éphémérides*, but annotated the text heavily in the margins.[55] His disagreement, in passages, is sharp—at times vitriolic. Du Pont began by criticizing Beccaria's method, which, he suggested, starts with the particular instead of with general principles and first truths. The wrong method, Du Pont declared, "led M. de Beccaria astray" and made him "take very thin consequences for general principles, and very dangerous errors for general truths."[56] Du Pont hoped that, with some guidance, the young Italian economist "would change considerably his opinions on very many points."[57]

Du Pont was extremely critical of Beccaria's other proposals as well. In his lecture, Beccaria had advocated placing tariffs and charges on the importation of value-added products and on the exportation of primary resources. Du Pont took issue: "It is distressing to hear again these alleged maxims that have caused so much harm, especially from a Philosopher, from an illustrious Professor, charged by the state to refute political errors and to substitute them with the knowledge of useful truths."[58] Du Pont dedicated eight long pages to disparaging Beccaria and his policy proposals, suggesting that they inevitably would lead to an impoverished nation that manufactures nothing but luxury goods, and then concluded, "We have already said enough perhaps to show a Philosopher as shrewd as *M. le Marquis de* Beccaria that trying to make a *People* more industrial than liberty and instruction would lead them, amounts to a completely wrongheaded understanding of politics."[59]

Du Pont also attacked Beccaria for suggesting, in *On Crimes and Punishments,* that merchants who engage in evasive measures such as smuggling contraband should be sent *"aux galères"*—to the galleys—and composed a lengthy monologue by one hypothetical such merchant, whom he named "Galérien," that protested his fate and lauded liberty of commerce and the pursuit of self-interest.[60] In his inaugural lecture, Beccaria had praised Colbert—the enemy of free trade—and traced the history of economics to Vauban, Montesquieu, Hume, Genovesi, and a few others, but he left out entirely the Physiocrats. This too caught Du Pont's ire.[61]

For Du Pont, Beccaria was a threatening influence and promoted a markedly different brand of economics. Instead of opposing commercial regulation and the penal sphere—as the Physiocrats had done—Beccaria sought to integrate and harmonize the two: to regulate the penal sphere in the image of economic administration; to infuse the penal with that logic of regulated competition "which is the most humane sort of war and more worthy of reasonable men"; and to inject the criminal sanction within the economic domain; in sum, to simultaneously penalize and economize both fields.[62] Beccaria's position embraced, at its heart, both intense administration and a notion of liberty, which was anathema to Du Pont.

Du Pont was on to something—something that only a careful reader of Beccaria's other texts, largely unknown today, could discover.

2

Policing the Public Economy

Beccaria published two texts in 1764. The one on crime and punishment is known today around the world. The other is practically forgotten. It has never been translated into English and was not translated into French until 2001. It appeared originally on October 20 as a short article in volume 15 of *Il Caffè*—the journal that Beccaria and others, including most notably the brothers Alessandro and Pietro Verri, were publishing in the image of the *Spectator* and in the shadow of the *Encyclopédie*. The article, "Tentativo analitico su i contraband" (A sketch of a formal model on the question of contraband) set forth, with the use of mathematical equations and simple algebra, the expected relationship between the rate of tariffs and the amount of potential contraband.

If the article is remembered today, it is only for its method—for the use of mathematical equations to resolve an economic question at such an early date. Joseph Schumpeter, in his magisterial review of economic thought, recognized only three precursors to modern econometrics: Daniel Bernoulli for a 1731 article on probabilities; Achille Nicolas Isnard for a treatise in 1781; and Beccaria for this article published in 1764.[1] The substantive intervention in Beccaria's short article, however, has been largely ignored by history.

To our detriment. The short article reveals a lot about Beccaria's economic agenda and his vision of the penal sphere. Beccaria's endeavor, in his 1764 article, was to figure out the amount of potential contraband that a merchant had to smuggle in order for the merchant to come out even—to retain the same amount of capital as he originally had in his merchandise—given the different tariff rates imposed by the sovereign authorities and given that he would likely lose some of his contraband. At the same time, Beccaria was trying to figure out, for the sovereign, how to fix the tariff at the most advantageous level to maximize the return to the treasury. "We are trying to determine how much a merchant ought to defraud the king's right, in terms of the value of any given commodity, such that, even if he loses the rest, he ends up with the same amount of capital as before thanks to the profit from smuggling."[2] In order to resolve this question, Beccaria went through a sequence of algebraic equations and drew from them a general theorem—perhaps fanciful, but sounding very scientific: "Given equal spatial capacity, a steady surveillance, and maximum industriousness by the merchants, the *nisus* to offset the tariff with the contraband will be equal to the square of the value of the merchandise, divided by the sum of that value and the tariff."[3]

This research, Beccaria added, should help the authorities set tariffs at the optimal level in order to maximize the prince's revenues and balance trade. "Determining such values in a general sense can elucidate how to design a tariff," Beccaria claimed.[4] And he concluded from his study: "The advantage of this research, for the drafter of tariffs, will be to know how much smuggling to expect from the merchants even after a certain number of seizures."[5]

Clearly—at least, in this text—Beccaria was not in the business of eliminating government tariffs, but rather of mathematically calculating the optimal rate of taxation in order to maximize the sovereign's revenue. This sounded in cameralism—the economics of how to maximize the prince's wealth. Beccaria was demonstrating how to use mathematics to advance the cameral economic sciences, using as his example how best to set a trade tariff. The advantage of his discovery, Beccaria asserted, falls to the "constructor of tariffs"—the administrators who are charged with devising proper tariffs.[6] Beccaria saw himself in the role of adviser to the prince with respect to the setting of taxes and charges on commerce. And he was not yet even working for the Milanese republic; in fact, he would not become a civil servant for another seven years. He was a young intellectual—yet he viewed himself and identified as the prince's counselor, one whose job was to figure out how best to maximize the sovereign's revenues through taxation. This is indeed far from the approach of François Quesnay—or, for that matter, the later Adam Smith.

What is equally remarkable about Beccaria's youthful intervention is his underlying conception of deviance and criminality: Beccaria assumed that everyone engages in criminal activity—especially merchants—and will continue to engage in criminal activity despite sovereign enforcement of the penal code. Merchants adjust their level of criminal activity—the amount of contraband—in order to maximize their revenue. Beccaria formalized the relationship between deviance, enforcement, and tariffs, but at the end of the day, the merchants are still engaged in illegal behavior. This is not a story of minor vices, such as self-interest or greed, promoting the public good. This is not Mandeville's story of private vices and public virtues. Instead, it is a story of widespread criminal behavior that is tolerated—in fact, that is both minimized and maximized to increase the sovereign's wealth—but tolerated because it is viewed as entirely inevitable. The merchant is considered an incorrigible white-collar criminal—not merely a self-interested rational actor.[7]

Beccaria's *Elements of Public Economy*

These early tariff writings have largely been ignored or forgotten outside of Italy—they were never translated into English, and only recently were they translated into French. In fact, Beccaria's economic writings have largely been ignored in the Anglo-Saxon world. As Peter Groenewegen, a historian of eighteenth-century economics, suggests, "Beccaria has been almost totally ignored in the histories of economics," with the notable exception, naturally, of Joseph Schumpeter.[8] Beccaria the cameral economist has been lost and forgotten, buried under the more palatable reading of Beccaria the Enlightenment philosopher of measured punishment or Beccaria the rational choice economist.

But Beccaria's writings as a cameral economist offer a very different picture of his views on punishment—a third reading as it were. In this expanded context, those punishment writings formed only one part of his larger, fully integrated theory of public economy—a more unified, coherent, and systemic view of regulating commerce within which punishment was to operate and according to which punishment theory was modeled.

Beccaria's lectures and writings in public economy mostly have come down to us as fragments. His inaugural lecture, "A Discourse on Public Œconomy and Commerce," delivered on January 9, 1769, when he assumed his chair as professor of cameral sciences at the Palatine School of Milan, was immediately translated into English and published in London in 1769, as well as translated into French and immediately published—as we saw earlier—in the *Éphémérides*. The lecture notes from Beccaria's course in public economy, written during the period 1771 to 1772, were published posthumously in Italian in 1804 under the title "Elementi di economia pubblica" (Elements of public economy), though the notes were never translated into English, or French for that matter. Then there are numerous economic and commerce reports that Beccaria wrote for the Milanese government, for which he worked as a lifelong civil servant after his two years in academia.[9] None of those memoranda have made it to the English world.

Beccaria's lectures on public economy were divided into five major sections: agriculture, arts and manufacturing, commerce, finance, and police—with an introductory part that set out the outline and general principles. The final section, titled "Of Police," formed an integral part of his lectures on public economy—it represented an entire section alongside commerce and finance, and it covered both policing and taxation. It should come as no surprise, then, that Pasquale Pasquino translated Beccaria's appointment at the Palatine School as "chair of political economy and science of the police."[10]

Beccaria understood the science of public economy to include, at its very core, the science of the police. By a curious twist of fate, however, Beccaria's lecture notes on "police"—as well as those on taxation and public finance—are missing. The *Elementi* that have come down to us today contain parts 1, 2, 3, and 4—but go no further. The lectures on "police" have never been found, an accident of history that has proven strangely productive and come to distort our reading of Beccaria's writings on punishment. Nevertheless, despite the absence of the lecture notes, it is possible to piece together a cameralist reading of Beccaria's theory of police from his other economic writings and from his political and historical situation in the Milanese republic.

Beccaria and his closest intellectual allies, the brothers Pietro and Alessandro Verri, positioned themselves politically against the traditional, ecclesiastical power structure of their aristocratic Lombard parents and in favor of reforms, some of which they helped introduce on behalf of the Austrian Habsburg Empire. The Verris and Beccaria endorsed systemic change aimed at a more organized and centralized economic power; greater government intervention as a way to increase state revenues; and more formal legal structures and regulatory mechanisms. "Like Verri," Richard Bellamy explained, Beccaria set as his aim "the substitution of the existing irregular, particularist and custom-bound legal system, based on hereditary rights and the personal rule of the monarch and nobility, by a regular centralized and rational system of justice that was equal for all and grounded in the rule of law."[11]

The key words here are centralized and rational. In this view, the history and development of public economy reflects a trajectory from chaotic self-interest and overly passionate desire first to modes of cooperation and conformity, to the common good, and ultimately to centralized rational governance—that is, to a form of enlightened despotism. The end of economic science is the centralization of power in the hands of a sovereign state pursuing rational policies intended to increase its overall wealth. Public economy becomes a state-centric discipline in which the analysis centers on the "riches of the states" and on the "economic aims of the state"—not simply the wealth of the nation.[12] The ultimate objective is for the state, through its enlightened leaders, to formulate policy to enrich the state. By means of centralization and rationalization, Beccaria espoused a form of enlightened despotism. In his *Reflections,* fragments of a projected work on the *Ripulimento delle nazioni,* Beccaria wrote: "The ruler and governor is required to know what is advantageous to his people and how to secure it for them, and to have a desire to do so. *The people are required simply not to obstruct by their opinions or habits the true benefits they are offered nor the true means employed to render them happy.*"[13]

"Not to obstruct"—that was all that was required, according to Beccaria. But notice that the people were the ones who simply had to refrain from obstructing. The people, not the sovereign. How different this was from François Quesnay, who famously told the King of France, Louis XV, that all Louis XV had to do to improve the economy was nothing—he just had to avoid obstructing the natural order. According to Beccaria, this model of centralized administration would bring about "a new and happy order of things."[14]

Notice too how, according to this vision, order is the product of law and rationality. Orderliness is not the product of spontaneous equilibrium, it is not the default condition that characterizes the state of nature, it does not govern in the absence of state intervention. Rather, orderliness is the product of centralized and rational power. Beccaria's model was France under the centralized royal administration of Louis XIV and his principal adviser, Colbert: "Louis XIV and Colbert raised up France, invigorating every type of industry and all the fine arts almost at a stroke; the arts of luxury and of peace were wonderfully nourished and encouraged in the midst of ambitious enterprises of conquest," Beccaria exclaimed.[15] Again, this view is very different from that of Du Pont de Nemours and the Physiocrats. For Beccaria, the concepts of order and rationality were mapped onto the enlightened lawgiver.[16]

In fact, according to Beccaria, it was precisely private interests that stumped economic growth and science. The advancement of public economy had been impeded, Beccaria wrote, by "resistance put up by private interests and the fantastic illusions of prejudice and error."[17] Rather than leading to ordered equilibrium, private interests held back the progress of reason and economic knowledge. In this view, the task of public economy was to mold self-interest so as to make it conform to the larger interests of society. If the economy were to rein in self-interest—civilize it, socialize it—it would revitalize the individual's sense of common purpose and patriotism, or, as Beccaria put it, it would "unite the individual's own utility with that of the public."[18] Here too Beccaria's view is not that of private vices and public virtues; it is instead a story of molding and tampering this self-interest in order to shape a more public-minded individual.

The task of public economy was to mold individuals into more reciprocal and public-minded actors, to diminish self-interest, to correct human foibles. Men needed to be trained, disciplined, made rational in a public-minded way. Left to their own devices, men were weak, biased, and lazy—and these traits needed to be corrected. "It is characteristic of human beings to throw themselves blindly into their present and immediate concerns, neglecting the future," Beccaria declared in his inaugural lecture; "they wish to do much, but with the least possible effort; they are stimulated and regulated by certainty, as much of good as of evil, and are disheartened by arbitrariness and uncertainty."[19]

Beccaria characterized these human weaknesses as "the universal bias of human nature," but suggested that they could be remedied or corrected by means of proper government intervention, specifically by creating obstacles to nonproductive behaviors. The model, for Beccaria, was price regulation: manipulating the price in this case of behaviors (rather than commodities) in order to channel human action. The universal bias of human nature, Beccaria claimed, "is much more securely regulated by obstacles than by prohibitions."[20] In other words, increasing the price for socially unacceptable behaviors, whether inside or outside the market, is far more effective than prohibition. Beccaria also advocated training "young men" to think in a rational, calculating way—finding ways to "habituate them to that spirit of calculation."[21]

These views on human nature translated, at the macroeconomic level, into mercantilist policies. Beccaria embraced, in his inaugural lecture, "four principal means of promoting trade": "concurrence in the price of things, œconomy in the price of labour, cheapness of carriage, and low interest of money."[22] The expression "concurrence in the price of things" was a term of art that originated with the Scholastics and with the idea of a "just price"—a price determined by "common estimation."[23]

Not surprisingly, Du Pont de Nemours argued in the margins of the French translation of the inaugural lecture published in the *Éphémérides* that this first principle was both misguided and semantically meaningless. The notion of competition between merchants and vendors naturally made sense to Du Pont, but not "concurrence in the price of things." "One simply cannot employ the latter expression," Du Pont stated emphatically. "It has no basis in language and has no meaning at all."[24] One meaning, though, does emerge when the idea is juxtaposed with the other trade principles that Beccaria espoused—keeping down the price of labor, subsidizing transportation costs, and maintaining low rates of interest on credit—as well as with policies that Beccaria proposed to encourage industrial production, namely, increasing duties and tariffs on the export of raw materials and on the import of manufactured goods, and inversely, easing duties on the import of raw materials and the export of manufactured goods.[25] These policy proposals—flagged by Du Pont—trace back to the cameral sciences, not forward to liberal thought.

"Of Police"

This reading of Beccaria corresponds closely to the notion of "police" that formed part of public economy. In the eighteenth century, the term "police" was predominantly used to signify "governing" or "administration."[26] In Germany, by the eighteenth century the term *polizei* had become synonymous with the notion of welfare; in France, it had become synonymous with administration, with the internal management of a city or region. This is reflected, for instance, in the written records of the Parlement de Paris. The Parlement used the term "règlement de police générale" as a way to discuss an administrative regulation, as in the following passage from a *remonstrance* dated June 19, 1718: "We have learned from our fathers that any law that contains a general police regulation [*un règlement de police générale*] for the entire kingdom should be registered at Parliament and it is in this first tribunal of the king's justice that it is published."[27] The use of the term "police" here signified what one might call today, in broad terms, "an administrative rule or policy," although typically the term "police" was limited to the subdivisions of the French state. The term "government," in contrast, would more likely have encompassed the administration of the entire French state—as one can see well in the early sections of Delamare's *Traité de la police*.[28]

In his lectures titled *Security, Territory, Population,* Michel Foucault traced the notion of "police" to the seventeenth century and the emerging concept of preserving the state in good order: "Police will be the calculation and technique that will make it possible to establish a mobile, yet stable and controllable relationship between the state's internal order and the development of its forces."[29] This notion of stability is reflected in the writings of Johann von Justi, one of the leading German theorists of what was known as *Polizeiwissenschaft,* or the science of police, the "laws and regulation that concern the interior of a state and which endeavor to strengthen and increase the power of this state and make good use of its forces."[30] Along these lines, the focus of policing was on ensuring reproduction and the abundance of the population, *bon marché* and the abundance of food and provisions, well-being and the health and safety of the citizens, the orderly professions and proper circulation of goods and traffic—which amounts to practically all social order.[31] As Foucault remarked, "ce dont la police s'occupe, au fond, c'est la société."[32]

Alongside this meaning of "police," there were also the exacting, more practical responsibilities catalogued in the various police manuals of the eighteenth century. Most ancien régime commentators followed Delamare in dividing the business of the police into eleven categories spanning such areas of human activity as religion, customs (in taverns and public baths, and concerning gambling or excessive drinking), health, subsistence (activities related to the markets and the provision of goods), roads, rivers and streets, public order and tranquility, sciences and liberal arts (the work of doctors, surgeons, and apothecaries, as well as of printing establishments and libraries), as well as commerce, manufacturing, and mechanical arts (including the activities of guilds, servants, domestic workers, laborers, and indigents).[33] Beccaria specifically addressed some of these functions in his text, including specific measures to deter public disorder such as "street-lighting at public expense, the posting of guards in the various districts of the city, sober and moral sermons delivered in the silence and sacred peace of churches protected by public authorities, and homilies in defence of public and private interests in the nation's councils, in parliaments or wherever the majesty of the sovereign power resides."[34] As Beccaria explained in his tract, "These make up one of the main branches of the care of the magistrate, which the French call *police*."[35]

In its concrete manifestation, the function of the police was institutionalized in Paris in March 1667 with the creation of the police lieutenant at the Paris Châtelet, who effectively took over the policing responsibilities from the provost of Paris. In the ancien régime, the police had both the executive function of policing and arrest, and the judicial function of condemning and sentencing *(la police judiciaire)*. The edict creating the lieutenancy defined the role of the police as, first, to ensure public order; second, to provide an abundance of necessities; and third, to maintain the condition and well-being of all residents.[36] The actual list of enumerated duties, though, was extensive and ranged from overseeing the cleaning of streets to supervising publishing, printing, and bookselling.[37] During the ancien régime, the police chamber of Paris was organized into five different subdivisions that covered a wide swath of society, including not only the provision of food for Parisians and the lighting and cleaning of the city's streets, but also the oversight of everything from wet nurses to "Jews," lotteries, guilds, hotels, and "foreigners."[38]

The different connotations of "police" tend to blend into each other, though it is important to maintain the distinction that Pasquale Pasquino emphasized between a conception of positive police powers—concerned with promoting happiness, the public good, and order—and the more familiar idea of the police that developed at the turn of the nineteenth century, according to which the police are concerned with the task of averting crime and reducing future danger. The task of policing in the first sense—in the sense of public economy—specifically aimed at "maintaining and augmenting the happiness of the citizens *omnium et singularum*, of all and of each."[39] Pasquino unearthed numerous treatises that address this function of "police" as public economy, and the titles are striking to our modern eyes precisely because of their juxtaposition of the terms "science," "police," and "finance." Joseph von Sonnenfels's *Foundations of the Science of Police, Commerce and Finance,* published in 1765, is a good illustration. Pasquino in fact discovered a bibliography that contained 3,215 titles under the caption "science of police in the strict sense" for German-speaking regions during the seventeenth and eighteenth centuries alone.[40]

These German sources correspond to the conception of policing that Adam Smith discussed in his Glasgow lectures. Under the rubric "police," Smith discussed the entire field of public economy—or what would later make up his writings on *The Wealth of Nations.* Edwin Cannan, the noted historian of economics and editor of the *Wealth of Nations,* remarked on Smith's surprising nomenclature. "To 'consider the opulence of a state' under the head of 'police' seems at first sight a little strange," he observed.[41] Cannan meticulously compared the Glasgow lectures with *The Wealth of Nations* and remarked on how closely related the two texts are.[42] The use of the term "police" gets "dropped," according to Cannan, because it is "not sufficiently indicating the subject."[43] But only to our modern eyes, truly. This conception of public economy as "police" was precisely how Beccaria, the cameralist, understood his own economics—and it was reflected best in the rules and regulations surrounding the Parisian markets.

Eighteenth-Century *Police des Grains*

The rules of policing are set forth in numbing detail in the police manuals of the early to mid-eighteenth century. Delamare's *Traité,* Fréminville's *Dictionnaire,* Duchesne's *Code de la police,* Jacques-Antoine Sallé's *Traité* and his *Esprit des ordonnances,* Nicolas des Essarts's *Dictionnaire universel de police*—these manuals catalogued and alphabetized, listed and reprinted the rules and regulations surrounding commerce and exchange. Although their authors most often favored the liberalization of trade, the manuals belabored the same regimentation of ordinances, and at every possible occasion underscored the convictions and judgments that accompanied these regulations. Wherever possible, the manuals would reproduce, in full, with all the accompanying pomp, circumstance, and signature lines, the fines that were meted out by the police lieutenant. Detail and repetition—numbing detail and tedious repetition—are often powerful mnemonic devices. They can also serve a political objective. Here, it seemed, the catalogues rendered the *police des grains* all the more oppressive.

First and foremost, the *police des grains* prohibited the sale of grain anywhere other than at the markets, *halles,* and ports. This prohibition had ancient customary roots in a series of ordinances running from the customs of

Beauvais in 1238, through two edicts of Philippe-le-Bel in 1304 and 1305, to the laws of François I, the royal ordinances of 1567 and 1577, and the Parliamentary Act of 1662.[44] A whole set of subsidiary regulations then organized the marketplace. Some ordinances prohibited selling by sample and required cultivators to bring all their goods to the marketplace; other rules fixed the hours of markets, the order of sale, and the provision of stalls. There were rules about who could buy first at market.[45] Sellers and bakers were expected to maintain their stalls, be present at the market, and supply sufficient sustenance.[46] Sellers could not employ middlemen, though they could use their wives, children, or domestic servants.[47] And, whatever the weather, they or their proxy had to man their stalls.[48] Bakers could only transport the grain they purchased over land, not by waterway.[49] It was also strictly forbidden for millers to buy flour for resale or as a baker's agent.[50] Seditious words that might cause a panic or scarcity or might contribute to increased prices were also prohibited.[51] There were also, naturally, strict rules about weights and measures intended to protect the consumer from fraud by merchants and innkeepers.[52]

There were some more colorful rules, like the ones prohibiting merchants from bringing their grain into the taverns, or prohibiting carters and transporters from taking their dogs ("mastiffs") with them into the markets.[53] Still other rules prohibited the young from dancing on the day of the market: "It is strictly prohibited for young people to organize dances, called *Baladoires,* on market or fair days," Fréminville explained. "Dancing, according to Saint Thomas and Saint Ambrose, is the partner of sensuality and immodesty; *deliciarum comes atque luxuria saltatio.*"[54] No selling in taverns, no dancing—these were, indeed, the more colorful regulations, but they all fit in the larger framework of limiting wholesale practices.

A second cluster of regulations affected the stock of grain and the timing of sales. Cultivators were required to sell their grains within two years of harvest—another proscription that had ancient roots (Afanassiev traced the practice to as early as 1577).[55] If the seller did not sell at market, he could "entrust the safe storage of his merchandise to the officers of the market and wait for the next market. However, if he did not sell his merchandise in the course of the next two consecutive markets, he was obliged to dispose of it during the third at a reduced price."[56] Parisian bakers and merchants were required to buy their grain outside a certain perimeter of Paris—at first eight *lieues,* and then ten.[57] This limitation on the sale of grain around Paris stayed in effect—with some back and forth—throughout the eighteenth century until the reforms of Turgot.[58]

A third category of rules set out the institutional mechanisms to ensure an effective police. The price of grain at market had to be recorded by a "greffier," and attested to by the merchants. The *greffiers* had to make a report and keep a register where they recorded the price of all the different grains and qualities, and had to have those registers signed by the justice of the peace.[59] The measuring instruments of grain merchants in the markets had to be verified and checked by the "procureur fiscal." There were also "officiers de marché"—officers of the markets—who were charged with overseeing the payment of dues by the sellers in the marketplace, dues that were based on the quantity of commodities sold. In addition to the measurers, there were other officers of the market known as "porteurs jurés" who would do most of the heavy lifting. Whereas the measurer measured the grain and verified its quality, the porters would carry, pour, empty, and so on, the sacks of grain. They had a monopoly on the discharge of grains and their transport; in addition they were charged with keeping any grains that were not sold at market.[60] Their office too traced back to the Middle Ages, though Turgot eliminated it in 1776.[61]

There were additional sets of rules for bakers, merchants, and other tradespeople. Fréminville dedicated twelve pages of his *Dictionnaire de la police* to "boulangers," noting that "bakers practice a trade that the Fiscal Procurer must oversee continually, especially with regard to the making of bread, which is the principal food of mankind: he should carefully pay close attention that the bread is of good quality and properly baked, and of the proper weight; [and should ensure] that the grain is properly milled, that both white and brown bread is made, that the bran is weighed; he should set a reserve price, set aside some leavened dough to start the next batch, and then calculate the price of everything, and total it up."[62]

Similarly, there were rules concerning merchants. In smaller markets, the cultivators could sell their grain themselves, but in the city markets, the commerce of grain was conducted by grain merchants and the rights and duties of these merchants were set forth in the royal ordinances. They essentially had to be licensed by the government and entry was restricted. "No laborers, 'gentilshommes,' or officers associated with the commerce of grains could be a grain merchant; no officers of the market, nor any miller, nor baker could practice the commerce of grain."[63]

Beccaria's *On Crimes and Punishments*

When Beccaria lauds the developments in commerce as the civilizing force of modernity in the opening passages of *On Crimes and Punishments,* it is to these minute regulations of the market that he was referring—or at least, to his imagination of how these regulations were practiced. His model was that of public economy, and his innovation was to extend this rationality to the penal sphere. Beccaria's intervention, in the field of crime and punishment, was precisely to apply the idea of the regulated market to punishment practices: to "administer" punishment in order to make punishments proportional and logical—just like the *police des grains*.

This objective is reflected in his emphasis on proportionality. There were to be no exceptional punishments meted out. Everything was supposed to be rational, graduated, measured. In fact, according to Beccaria's view, it is precisely the proportionality between the severity of the crime and the severity of the punishment that reflects the level of civilization and humanity of a country. "If there were an exact and universal scale of crimes and punishments," Beccaria wrote, "we should have an approximate and common measure of the gradations of tyranny and liberty, and of the basic humanity and evil of the different nations."[64] Rational and proportional punishment is what ensured liberty.

The universe of crime and punishment mirrored perfectly Beccaria's understanding of public economy. Both were grounded on the notion that rational, self-interested men naturally tend to violate social norms and law. "Each individual," Beccaria declared in the opening chapter, "is always seeking to extract from the repository not only his own due but also the portions which are owing to others."[65] This "despotic spirit of every man," Beccaria explained, tends to "resubmerg[e] society's laws into the ancient chaos."[66] Beccaria continued: "The common run of men do not accept stable principles of conduct. . . . Neither eloquence, nor exhortations, not even the most sublime truths have been enough to hold back for long the passions aroused by the immediate impact made by objects which are close at hand."[67] The "self-interested passions," Beccaria emphasized, "are ranged against the universal good," and for that reason, the sovereign needs to intervene in economic and social domains to enforce both commercial and trade policies to regulate exchange, as well as penal sanctions to regulate human interaction.[68] The criminal sanction operated in the same fashion as economic regulation: just as trade restrictions and the regulation of commerce influence the price of goods, the penal sanction influences the price of crime. Regulation was necessary and pervasive—a feature of both public economy and of the regulation of deviant behavior.

Beccaria, the Disciplinarian

It should not come entirely as a surprise, then, that some readers would portray Beccaria as the epitome of discipline. This is a fourth reading, or perhaps appropriation, of Beccaria's famous little tract. In *Discipline and Punish,*

Michel Foucault famously places Beccaria at the heart of what he identifies as the disciplinary turn.

As mentioned earlier, Foucault, in his 1978 lectures *Security, Territory, Population,* used the example of the regulation of the Parisian grain markets as the very prototype of his concept of discipline. The *police des grains,* Foucault explained in his lecture of January 18, 1978, is the quintessential example of discipline and satisfies all three dimensions of the concept. First, as Foucault explained, "discipline concentrates, focuses, and encloses. The first action of discipline is in fact to circumscribe a space in which its power and the mechanisms of its power will function fully and without limit."[69] The *police des grains* was centripetal precisely in this sense, Foucault maintained. It turns inward onto a determined space and seeks to control, to dominate that circumscribed field. "It isolates, it concentrates, it encloses, it is protectionist, and it focuses essentially on action on the market or on the space of the market and what surrounds it."[70]

Second, discipline is exhaustive: it seeks to regulate everything, down to the most minute details. "Discipline allows nothing to escape," Foucault explained. "Not only does it not allow things to run their course, its principle is that things, the smallest things, must not be abandoned to themselves. The smallest infraction of discipline must be taken up with all the more care for it being small."[71] This is the notion of discipline as order maintenance. The *police des grains* is precisely about letting nothing escape the view of regulation, Foucault declared.

Third, discipline is prohibitive. "How basically does discipline, like systems of legality, proceed?" Foucault asked. "Well, they divide everything according to a code of the permitted and the forbidden. Then, within these two fields of the permitted and the forbidden, they specify and precisely define what is forbidden and what is permitted, or rather, what is obligatory."[72] Again, the *police des grains* was the perfect example, Foucault maintained. It sought to define these two spheres and then determine exactly which types of commercial behaviors are allowed and which are prohibited. In sum, the *police des grains* was disciplinary per se, or as Foucault lectured, it was "la police *disciplinaire* des grains."[73]

At the very same time—and not by mere coincidence—Beccaria's short tract formed the keystone to Michel Foucault's genealogy of discipline in his magisterial *Surveiller et punir* (1975). *On Crimes and Punishments* captured perfectly, in Foucault's words, that "new strategy for the exercise of the power to punish" at the heart of eighteenth-century reform: "not to punish less, but to punish better; to punish with a severity perhaps attenuated, but to punish with greater universality and necessity; to insert the power to punish more deeply into the social body."[74] Such a strategy represented the crowning moment of the Enlightenment reform ideal that Foucault described as having led to the birth of the prison and, more generally, the carceral sphere.

Beccaria's tract stands in for the Enlightenment reforms and thus defines the pivotal period between the brutal corporal punishments of the seventeenth century and the perfection of discipline in the twentieth century. Beccaria is portrayed as the central reformer who drew on Enlightenment themes of equality, humanity, lenience, autonomy, and universality, on utilitarian principles of prevention and correction, and on an imagined system of coded penalties that would speak directly to the general public. By way of these reforms, punishments were to represent to the observer, in more muted but powerful ways than the brutal punishments, the lessons to be learned—the associations to be remembered. The humanized spectacle was to serve as a constant morality play, intended to teach a lesson to adults about the consequences of vice. Beccaria plays the pivotal role in this dramatic representation, as one of the leading theoreticians of the Enlightenment reforms—the first of the "grands 'réformateurs,'" Foucault explained, who announced all the "rules that authorised, no, better, required 'leniency' as a calculated economy of the power to punish."[75]

In this reading, Beccaria, the public economist, the cameralist, infused the economic discipline of "police" into the punishment sphere, transforming our brutal corporal practices into regimented and minutely regulated techniques of correction and rehabilitation. Across the economy and society, disciplinary practices displaced freedom and progressive Enlightenment reason. Foucault's reading of Beccaria makes a mockery of Voltaire's and is at odds with that of Jeremy Bentham and contemporary adherents of law and economics like Richard Posner and Gary Becker. But it resonates strongly with Du Pont de Nemours's criticism of the young Italian economist. The paradox is complete: Jeremy Bentham and contemporary liberal economists embrace Beccaria as a founding father, while early French liberal economists and Foucault portray Beccaria as a disciplinarian.

This paradox is due to the chasm between economy and policing—between market administration and penal regulation. Contemporary liberal economists and early British liberals—whether by choice or inadvertently—focused on Beccaria's penality and disregarded his economic writings. They ignored Beccaria the cameralist. The Physiocrats, in contrast, focused primarily on Beccaria's economics and the implications of his work for commerce—even when reading his seminal tract *On Crimes and Punishments*. They strenuously resisted his effort to coordinate economy and society—not seeing or deliberately ignoring the fact that Beccaria's writings on punishment could possibly advance their theory of legal despotism. Becker and Posner, in contrast, have seen the potential of Beccaria's writings on punishment and embraced those—in part because they may not fully realize that those writings went hand in hand with such an interventionist approach in the economic domain.

Foucault, by contrast, reacted against the disciplinarity both of the *police des grains* and of Beccaria's writings on punishment. But Foucault's project was entirely different: to suggest that both the discipline of the *police des grains* and the laissez-faire approach of early liberalism were forms of governmentality, ways of governing. Unlike Beccaria's contemporaries, Foucault did not intend to take sides in the *guerre des blés;* he sought instead to show continuity from the disciplinary practices of the seventeenth and early eighteenth centuries to the liberal discourse of the eighteenth and nineteenth centuries. Yet in the very process, Foucault's writings reified the categories themselves. By turning the *police des grains* into the *police disciplinaire des grains,* Foucault may not have allowed himself to see the underside of enforcement and underenforcement of those eighteenth-century ordinances.

3

The Birth of Natural Order

"The laws that govern societies are the laws of natural order, the most advantageous to humankind."[1] With these words, François Quesnay opened his 1767 essay "The Despotism of China." The essay would be one of Quesnay's last contributions to the field of economics—a discipline he helped establish—and this first sentence captured the organizing principle of his entire economic thought: natural order. The economic domain, Quesnay believed, was governed by a natural order and constituted an autonomous, self-regulating system that required no external intervention—no administration, no "police." The same year, 1767, Quesnay's leading disciple, Pierre Paul Le Mercier de La Rivière, would similarly open his book *The Natural and Essential Order of Political Societies* by declaring: "There exists a natural *order* for the government of men reunited in society."[2]

This concept of natural order grounded the Physiocrats' theories about economic production and the wealth of nations. It was the very foundation of their argument for free commerce and trade. The natural order that reigned in the economic domain demanded that there be no human interference. And so Quesnay would write in his *General Maxims of Political Economy,* also penned in 1767: "*Let us maintain complete liberty of commerce;* for THE POLICY IN DOMESTIC AND FOREIGN TRADE THAT IS THE SUREST, THE MOST APPROPRIATE, THE MOST PROFITABLE TO THE NATION AND TO THE STATE CONSISTS IN COMPLETE FREEDOM OF COMPETITION."[3]

The contrast to Beccaria the cameralist could not be greater—as the Physiocrats themselves emphasized. Today, François Quesnay and the Physiocrats are predominantly read in just this way: as the antithesis to the *police des grains* and to an earlier economic view belonging to the tradition of public œconomy, of *Cameralwissenschaft,* of *Polizeiwissenschaft.* This dominant reading focuses on the element of liberty in Quesnay's economic system—liberty from government intervention in commerce and trade. But it does so at the expense of another interpretation, one that focuses instead on his political theory of legal despotism. The dominant reading tends to ignore—or underplay—Quesnay's argument for absolute hereditary monarchy, with a completely unified executive and legislative power limited exclusively to punishment. Many, even subtle readers, have not allowed themselves to appreciate fully those constraints in early liberalism. Though often keenly aware of the Physiocratic embrace of legal despotism, many readers somehow failed to emphasize how the natural orderliness of the French economists would fuel a desire to rein in the disorder of deviance and exercise the severe right to punish, offering instead a somewhat selective reading of the Physiocrats.[4] Like Beccaria, François Quesnay's writings have been used in different ways by different readers—and these interpretations, in turn, have influenced our attitudes toward markets and punishment. Here too, the appropriations have been productive. Let's begin then with Quesnay's most notable contemporary.

Adam Smith's Reading of Quesnay

"Perfect liberty"—that was how Adam Smith characterized François Quesnay's economic system, with a mixture of praise and criticism. Praise for having championed liberty; criticism for having, if anything, demanded too much perfection. In book 4 of *The Wealth of Nations*—in a passage that is now famous, at least among Quesnay scholars—Smith praised the French economist and his *Tableau économique:* "In representing the wealth of nations as consisting, not in the inconsumable riches of money, but in the consumable goods annually reproduced by the labour of society; and *in representing perfect liberty as the only effectual expedient for rendering this annual reproduction the greatest possible,* its doctrine seems to be in every respect as just as it is generous and liberal."[5] Smith singled out "perfect liberty" as one of the chief contributions of Quesnay's writings.

Some have gone so far as to claim that Adam Smith intended to dedicate *The Wealth of Nations* to François Quesnay.[6] Such a claim, however, is hard to believe, not only because of the caustic criticism that Smith leveled against Quesnay in *The Wealth of Nations,* but also because of the fierce rivalry between the two economists. Smith was sharply critical of Quesnay. Smith's text contained a detailed discussion of the Physiocratic system in book 4, chapter 9, where he argued that Quesnay's was one of those systems that had mistaken agriculture as the primary wealth-producing sector of the economy. Indeed, the Physiocrats' emphasis on agriculture could not have come at a worse time given that the Industrial Revolution was about to occur.[7] Quesnay's single-minded focus during this historical period on agriculture, which Smith characterized as "too narrow and confined," probably explains why today Quesnay's writings remain largely unknown in the Anglo-Saxon world.[8]

There was also passionate rivalry between Smith and the French *économistes*—not only Quesnay and his sect, but others as well, such as Louis XVI's *contrôleur général,* Turgot.[9] (Just as there were, incidentally, sharp internal rivalries between Quesnay and Turgot.[10]) In fact, ever since the publication of *The Wealth of Nations* in 1776—ten years after Smith visited Paris—there have been claims of borrowing, influence, and even plagiarism. Much ink has been spilled, for instance, on the "Smith-Turgot Myth," the allegation that Smith borrowed heavily from Turgot's book *Reflections on the Formation and the Distribution of Riches.* The rumor that Smith may have been the anonymous translator of Turgot's *Reflections* and that Turgot's book heavily influenced Smith is, as economic historian Peter Groenewegen wrote, "the oldest controversy in the history of economic thought."[11] Even today, the questions persist.[12] As recently as 1992, historian Emma Rothschild traced the remarkable and numerous parallels in the expressions and writings of Turgot and Smith (and Condorcet)—finding striking similarities in the language and expressions.[13]

There has also been a lot written about the influence of Quesnay on Smith. Many historians—such as Campbell and Skinner, Groenewegen, and Cartelier—have traced the conceptual similarities and innovations between the two economists, as well as the historical timing of the shifts in Smith's thought and vocabulary.[14] Most seem to suggest that Smith's encounter with the Physiocrats was important to the development of his work. *The Wealth of Nations* tracks pretty closely the *Lectures on Jurisprudence* that Smith delivered at the University of Glasgow before traveling to Paris, with the notable exception of the discussion of Physiocratic thought.[15] Several of the significant additions that appear in *The Wealth of Nations*—especially the conception of annual produce and the theory of unproductive labor—are said to trace to his encounter with the Physiocrats. "They were of course due to the acquaintance with the French *Économistes* which Adam Smith made during his visit to France with the Duke of Buccleugh in 1764–6," Edwin Cannan has suggested.[16] The conclusion, for Cannan, was self-evident: "When we find that there is no trace of these theories in the *Lectures* and a great deal in the *Wealth of Nations,* and that in the meantime Adam Smith had been to France and mixed with all the prominent members of the 'sect,' including their master, Quesnay, it is difficult to understand why we should be asked, without any evidence, to refrain from believing that he came under physiocratic influence after and not before or during his Glasgow period."[17]

It is indeed hard to believe that Smith would have wanted to dedicate *The*

Wealth of Nations to an intellectual rival and someone he criticized so caustically in the very book he would have dedicated. And yet Smith's own biographer, Dugald Stewart, claimed to have heard this from none other than Smith himself.[18]

The Doctor and the Tutor

It turns out, however, that there may have been more to the relationship between Quesnay and Smith than their encounters in Parisian salons, though they certainly did meet there.[19] The clue is buried in Adam Smith's correspondence—and it sheds light on Smith's reading of Quesnay. Surprisingly, it has not been fully appreciated by later readers, perhaps in part because it seems to have nothing to do with economics, agriculture, or the wealth of nations.

Smith and Quesnay spent several very intense days and nights together, not in their capacity as economists, but in their roles as tutor and doctor. The two were together at the sickbed of Smith's charge, the Duke of Buccleugh, and, two months later, at the deathbed of his brother, Hew Campbell Scott. At the time, in 1766, Quesnay was an elderly and accomplished surgeon and physician, the first doctor to the Marquise de Pompadour—the mistress of Louis XV—and an ordinary to the king of France himself. Quesnay lived at Versailles in his famous *entresol* (mezzanine apartment) and had been a prolific writer in the medical field, having published a number of tomes on medical scientific topics—quite an accomplishment for an autodidact from a humble background.[20] For his part, Smith had resigned his professorship in moral philosophy at the University of Glasgow in 1764 to tutor the Duke of Buccleugh, and together they had traveled in France—staying, for the most part, in Toulouse through November 1765. From then on, for the next eleven months, Smith and the Duke of Buccleugh stayed in and around Paris.[21]

When Hew Campbell Scott, the brother of the Duke of Buccleugh, fell ill with a fever while in Paris visiting his brother, Adam Smith—and Quesnay—stayed at his bedside for several days and nights. As Smith explained in a letter dated October 15, 1766:

> On Monday morning [October 13, 1766], Dr. Gem observed some degree of fever in Mr Scott's pulse which he had thought entirely free of it for some days before. Mr Quenay observed the same thing. . . . [T]hey [Gem and Quesnay] gave him, what they had given for two days before, a very gentle opiate to quiet his stomach and to give him a little rest in the night time. . . . The Physicians were both much pleased with his situ-

> ation and imagined that all the violence of his disorder was over. Quenay said that he had been at a loss before but he now knew what to do. I thought I might venture to go to my Bankers. . . . Upon my return I found him quite delirious, and that too with no very violent fever. I immediately sent for Quenai who ordered him instantly to be blooded.[22]

Quesnay and Dr. Gem continued to attend to the young Scott, whose health continued to deteriorate, despite—or perhaps because of—the bleedings. Tragically, the young man passed away six days later on October 19, 1766.

This was not the first time that Smith and Quesnay had shared moments together at the side of a sick patient—though perhaps it was the more intense of the experiences they had. A few months earlier, in August 1766, Smith had accompanied the Duke of Buccleugh to Compiègne to hunt with the king and his court, and the duke fell ill.[23] Smith wrote to his stepfather, Charles Townshend, on August 26, 1766:

> I was sure he had a fever, and begged of him to send for a physician. He refused a long time, but at last, upon seeing me uneasy, consented. I sent for Quenay, first ordinary physician to the King. He sent me word he was ill. . . . I went to Quenay myself to beg that, notwithstanding his illness, which was not dangerous, he would come to see the Duke. He told me he was an old infirm man, whose attendance could not be depended on, and advised me, as his friend, to depend upon De la Saone, first physician to the Queen. I went to De la Saone, who was gone out and was not expected home till late that night. I returned to Quenay, who followed me immediately to the Duke. It was by this time seven at night. The Duke was in the same profuse sweat which he had been in all day and all the preceding night. In this situation Quenay declared that it was improper to do anything till the sweat should be over. He only ordered him some cooling ptisane drink.[24]

These intense encounters left a deep impression on Smith on both a personal and intellectual level, insofar as they helped shape Smith's reading of Quesnay's economic writings. On the personal front, Smith's correspondence is again revealing. "He is my particular and intimate friend," Smith wrote of Quesnay in a letter dated October 15, 1766. "Quênai is one of the worthiest men in France and one of the best Physicians that is to be met with in any country. He was not only the Physician but the friend and confidant of Madame Pompadour a woman who was no contemptible Judge of merit."[25]

More important, for our purposes, these encounters made their way into *The Wealth of Nations*, published ten years later in 1776. Here too, some context regarding chronology will be helpful. By the summer and fall of 1766—

by the time Smith and Quesnay met at Scott's deathbed—it is very likely that Smith was working on, or at the very least, thinking a lot about, *The Wealth of Nations.* Much of the material on which the book draws, the *Lectures on Jurisprudence,* had been delivered in 1762–1764 at Glasgow. The best historical evidence suggests that Smith began writing *The Wealth of Nations* while in Toulouse in 1764. Smith wrote to David Hume, in a letter dated July 5, 1764, "I have begun to write a book in order to pass away the time."[26] According to the editors of Smith's correspondence, this is the "first mention of writing *WN.*"[27]

For his part, Quesnay was practically at the height of his influence in the budding field of economics, which he himself had helped found in France. Quesnay turned his attention to economics and wrote his first two economic texts—the *Encyclopédie* entry for "Fermiers" in 1756 and for "Grains" in 1757—when he was already an elderly man, sixty-four years old, and a highly accomplished doctor.[28] That was only ten years before he met Smith, and Quesnay would pen his last interventions in economics only two years later, in 1768—shortly after Du Pont published the most famous collection of Quesnay's writings under the title *Physiocratie.* (Quesnay would then turn his attention to mathematics.) So in 1766, when the two men met at Scott's bedside, they were both deep in thought—not only about fevers and bleedings, but also about their own well-developed economic systems.

In a fascinating passage in book 4 of *The Wealth of Nations,* Smith brought medicine back into his reading of Quesnay's economics.[29] According to Smith's interpretation, Quesnay required a very strict and precise regimen of diet and exercise for the political body to thrive—and that strict diet was perfect freedom. Smith himself took a less dogmatic position and suggested that Quesnay was perhaps asking for too much, and that societies could still thrive even if they did not have perfect freedom:

> Some speculative physicians seem to have imagined that the health of the human body could be preserved only by a certain precise regimen of diet and exercise, of which every, the smallest, violation necessarily occasioned some degree of disease or disorder proportioned to the degree of the violation. . . . Mr. Quesnai, who was himself a physician, and a very speculative physician, seems to have entertained a notion of the same kind concerning the political body, and to have imagined that it would thrive and prosper only under a certain precise regimen, the exact regimen of perfect liberty and perfect justice. He seems not to have considered that in the political body, the natural effort which every man is continually making to better his own condition, is a principle of preservation capable of preventing and correcting, in many respects, the bad effects

> of a political œconomy, in some degree both partial and oppressive. Such a political œconomy, though it no doubt retards more or less, is not always capable of stopping altogether the natural progress of a nation towards wealth and prosperity, and still less of making it go backwards. . . . In the political body, however, the wisdom of nature has fortunately made ample provision for remedying many of the bad effects of the folly and injustice of man; in the same manner as it has done in the natural body, for remedying those of his sloth and intemperance.[30]

Smith reread Quesnay, the economist and physician, as excessively dogmatic—or perhaps better, as excessively disciplined, too regimented, too demanding of absolute freedom, of perfect diet and exercise. Smith's reading portrayed Quesnay as the polar antithesis to the *police des grains.*

Not surprisingly, this is the Quesnay who became most well-known: he became notorious as the principal advocate of a governmental approach to commerce that allows free internal markets and free external trade, that does not burden industry with regulations, and that leaves citizens with a choice of expenditures. "All trade should be free because it is in the best interest of the merchants to attach themselves to the safest and most profitable branches of foreign trade," Quesnay wrote.[31] "The government need only," Quesnay clarified, "refrain from hampering industry, allow citizens to spend liberally and according to their preferences, . . . abolish the prohibitions and impediments that are prejudicial to domestic trade and to reciprocal foreign trade, abolish or moderate excessive tolls for travelling on rivers and crossing borders," and "eliminate the privileges that the provinces have surreptitiously arrogated."[32]

From his earliest writings, Quesnay espoused free trade in grain. Quesnay's first published contribution to the field of political economy was his encyclopedia entry on "Farmers" in volume 6 of the French *Encyclopédie,* published in 1756. In that first entry, Quesnay underscored the importance of liberty, which at that early stage was a peculiarly class-based idea that favored large property owners. As Ronald Meek suggests, correctly, the entry was in truth "an impressive plea for the introduction into France of large-scale capitalist agriculture on the English model."[33] But the notion of liberty pervaded the entry.[34]

The following year, 1757, Quesnay published another entry, "*Grains* (econ. polit.)" in volume 7 of the *Encyclopédie,* and argued strongly for a free market in the commerce of grains: "If the commerce in *grain* were free, if statute labor [*les corvées*] were abolished, a large number of taxable property-owners currently living in the cities without occupation would return to the countryside to cultivate their lands peacefully and participate in the advantages of agriculture."[35] In some passages, Quesnay was stringently opposed to government intervention aimed at holding down the price of agricultural commodities, and in his entry, he explicitly attacked Colbert.[36] In summarizing the entry, Du Pont emphasized the central idea of liberty at the very heart of Quesnay's intervention: "It's an irrefutable argument in favor of free trade in general and of liberty of commerce in grain in particular."[37]

Quesnay's rhetoric of liberty sounded novel and modern at the time. Tocqueville famously noted, in *L'ancien régime et la Révolution,* that the Physiocrats were the writers who sounded most truly revolutionary toward the end of the ancien régime. "We can already see in their writings that revolutionary and democratic temperament that we know so well," Tocqueville would write.[38]

Without a doubt, Smith's reading of Quesnay as promoting "perfect liberty" was the product of their personal acquaintance, including their encounter at Hew Scott's deathbed, not of a close reading of Quesnay's texts. As the editor of Smith's *Wealth of Nations* notes, "In his exposition of physiocratic doctrine, Smith does not appear to follow any particular book closely. His library contained Du Pont's *Physiocratie, ou constitution naturelle du gouvernement le plus avantageux au genre humain,* 1768 (see Bonar, *Catalogue,* p. 92), and he refers lower down to La Rivière, *L'ordre naturel et essentiel des sociétés politiques,* 1767, but he probably relied largely on his recollection of conversations in Paris."[39] And so, Smith would paint Quesnay as espousing "perfect liberty" in order, all the better, to reject the idea. One does not need perfection, Smith maintained. One does not need absolute liberty. Self-interest and the natural desire of all men to improve their own condition would still provide the engine for economic growth in the absence of perfect liberty. Smith was less extreme than Quesnay, and more pragmatic.

Marx's Reading of Quesnay

Marx read a different Quesnay: a Quesnay who was not focused so much on perfect liberty, but on system and necessity. A Quesnay for whom political economy had its own necessary internal logic with no degrees of freedom: an economic system that functioned on its own, that had a direction of its own, that followed a necessary path—that had no liberty. A form of economic determinism.

In discussing Quesnay's *Tableau* in *Theories of Surplus Value,* volume 4 of his book *Capital,* Marx distinctly focused on the element of "system," on the integrated character of the whole: "This attempt to represent the whole in one table that is composed in fact of only five lines, connecting six points of departure to their endpoints, in the second half of the eighteenth century, at the infancy of public economy, was a stroke of genius, without a doubt the most brilliant in the history of public economy."[40] Marx identified Quesnay's central insight as the attempt to systematize exchange, but did not leave matters there. As Ronald Meek explained, "Marx subjects Quesnay's *Analysis* to an exhaustive study in the early 1860s, labored in the hot July of 1863 to substitute a new *Tableau* for Quesnay's, and later, in 1878, published a detailed critique of some comments on the *Tableau* made by the unfortunate Duhring."[41]

Marx's reading of Quesnay influenced several generations of historians and interpreters of Quesnay, especially the French anthropologist Louis Dumont and the American historian Elizabeth Fox-Genovese—and in part, Joseph Schumpeter.[42] In his seminal work, *Homo aequalis: Genèse et épanouissement de l'idéologie économique* (1977), Dumont traced the genesis of economic ideology to the central idea of the economy as a system—as having the traits of a stable and equilibrated whole. In Dumont's view, the birth of economic rationality as a coherent system is associated with two major shifts that marked the onset of modernity. The first was the advent of movable wealth as opposed to real property wealth: it is only in societies where assets other than land become autonomous and valuable that there can develop a new conception of wealth characteristic of modern societies.[43] The second was the shift from privileging relations between men and men to privileging those between men and things—again, due in large part to the emergence of the notion of an economic system. This was an important theme for Marx, as Dumont himself recognized.[44] Dumont's project was to identify how the idea of the economic system was born and grew, and how it colonized other discourses—which is why Quesnay played such an important role for Dumont. Quesnay was the first to try to systematize economic relations between land and revenue.

Fox-Genovese also read Quesnay in similar terms, focusing on the notions of system and autonomy: "Quesnay transformed economics from the role it had occupied from Aristotle to Rousseau as the management of the social household—first the city, then the state—to its modern role as the science of wealth. In so doing," Fox-Genovese explained, "he disengaged economic process from its anthropological role as servant of the sociopolitical order, and established its claim to be the direct manifestation of the natural order. In other words, he argued that the economic process itself embodied natural law and should thus dictate the sociopolitical order."[45] These readings emphasize economic system at the expense, to some degree, of liberty. In this view, the economic domain is governed by laws. It is regimented. It is shot through with necessity.

This reading is reflected in many passages of Quesnay's, but most importantly, in his famous *Tableau économique*, developed in 1758 and 1759, and first published in Mirabeau's *L'Ami des hommes* in 1760.[46] Quesnay's *Tableau économique* contains one of the first mathematical expressions of the notion of system equilibrium. It also represents one of the first attempts to work out an economic system mathematically, and as Schumpeter explained, it was "the first method ever devised in order to convey an *explicit* conception of the nature of economic equilibrium."[47]

In his *Tableau,* Quesnay posits that the economic life of a nation consists fundamentally of the relations between three classes within economic society: *la classe productive,* which consists of those who work the land; *la classe des propriétaires,* which consists of those who own the land, and thus receive its revenue; and *la classe sterile,* which comprises artisans and manufacturers.[48] Quesnay depicts, in his *Tableau,* how goods and payments flow among the various classes. The resulting web of relations is confusing—and has often been referred to as a "zigzag"—but the central insight is that the class of agricultural producers *("la classe productive")* is the only class that is able to generate wealth, since it is only from the earth that wealth can be created. In contrast, arts and manufacture can only reproduce the value invested into them, and so, while they produce the things necessary, for example, to till the earth, they are not able to actually generate value in the way that *la classe productive* can. Given the interdependent equilibrium that emerges between the classes, a disruption of *la classe productive* entails disruption and impoverishment for the others, while what adds to the prosperity of *la classe productive* contributes to the wealth and prosperity of the nation as a whole.[49]

As Fox-Genovese and others have noted, "The vast literature devoted by modern economists to Physiocracy demonstrates conclusively that the *Tableau* does not work. In 1766, three years after his adherence to the *Secte,* Du Pont still encountered difficulties in explaining it to his own satisfaction. Although since this time, numerous economists have succeeded in explaining it to their own satisfaction, none of their reconstructions has convinced a majority of their peers. . . . [N]o physiocrat other than Quesnay himself appears to have understood the mechanism."[50] Marx himself spent a great amount of time trying to reconstruct and correct the *Tableau*—as many others have after him. But what matters is not whether the representation of the system worked; what matters is that a visual representation of the system was created that caught the eye and imagination of a great many of Quesnay's contemporaries.

The Natural Law Reading of Quesnay

The freedom inherent in "perfect liberty" could hardly be more opposed to the necessity inherent in "economic system." The two readings of Quesnay were deeply at odds: either economic determinism is entirely unmoored from individual behavior, in which case a theory of economic system has no implications for individual liberty (a seemingly unlikely possibility here); or the theory of economic determinism depends on specific kinds of human behavior, in which case individual behavior cannot be left free. In the latter case, only one form of individual liberty corresponds with economic determinism; all other forms have to be constrained, defined, cabined—straight-jacketed.

Natural law solved the puzzle—and led to a third reading of Quesnay: the one conception of liberty that makes the economic system work rests on the notion of natural laws that make individuals pursue their self-interest and thereby produce natural order. On November 29, 1935, Charles Bourthoumieux defended his doctoral thesis to the University of Paris law faculty. His thesis, "Le Mythe de l'ordre naturel en économie politique depuis Quesnay" (The myth of natural order in political economy since Quesnay), was that Quesnay's central insight had shaped the field of economics to the present. "The idea of natural order, which the Physiocrats drew from the natural law tradition and from religious thought," Bourthoumieux wrote, "combined with the intellectual movement in scientific thought which originated with Bacon, has dominated all the writings of the economists and sociologists who have followed and can be considered, because of this, the legacy of Quesnay's thought and of his disciples."[51]

Bourthoumieux's doctoral dissertation has been forgotten by most, but remains very insightful. The idea of natural order, Bourthoumieux explained, is precisely the belief that "beyond each individual, there exists a sovereign will, a necessity, or an evolution that effectively governs economic and social life following certain rigorous rules."[52] Bourthoumieux added: "This idea, which traversed the entire nineteenth century, has constituted the central thread of the history of economic doctrine. Although it has traversed so many varied and different systems of thought, it is the common thread to all economists, since all of them since Quesnay propose to uncover the 'natural laws of society.'"[53]

Indeed, natural order was a, if not the, central insight that defined the Physiocrats—consider, for instance, the very title of Le Mercier de la Rivière's main work, *L'ordre naturel et essentiel des sociétés politiques* (1767). Many of the principal economic maxims that Quesnay derived from his *Tableau* revolved around the notion of natural order. So, for instance, Quesnay's fourth observation is that the wealth of a nation is inextricably linked to whether economic agents comply with *l'ordre naturel*.[54] Natural order is also directly tied to flourishing commerce and free competition.[55] There are many passages about this in Quesnay, and in all of them, it is the notion of natural order that makes the economic system function autonomously and that resolves the tension with individual liberty.[56] Natural order guides individual behavior and makes liberty possible.

It is interesting that Turgot, too, deployed in his writings a notion of equilibrium that resembled natural order—particularly given Turgot's complicated and ambivalent relationship to Physiocracy. Turgot is best known for liberalizing the grain trade when he was appointed *contrôleur général* in 1774 by Louis XVI. But although his actions as minister were relatively consistent with the economic views of Quesnay, Turgot was fiercely independent and refused to be closely affiliated with Quesnay and his school of thought. In a revealing note written to Du Pont de Nemours—who had been his secretary for several years—Turgot explicitly distanced himself from the Physiocrats.[57] Turgot viewed the Physiocrats as a "sect" and was extremely dismissive of them.[58] (He was not alone in this judgment. David Hume, for one, felt the same way.[59]) Nevertheless, Turgot developed in his writings a central notion of equilibrium that bore strong similarities to Quesnay's idea of natural order. One can see distinct traces of it in his *Reflections on the Formation and the Distribution of Riches,* written in 1766 and published in 1769–1770; in his correspondence with David Hume; and in his *Lettres sur le commerce des blés,* published in 1770.[60] There he would write that "conditions in different markets 'are related to one another by a reciprocal dependence, and arrive at equilibrium themselves.'"[61] Turgot implanted an idea of natural equilibrium at the heart of the relationship between the price and the cost (or what Turgot referred to as the "fundamental price") of a commodity.[62] He used a slightly different vocabulary—the analogy of fluids, hydraulics, and physics—to describe the natural equilibrium, but the idea essentially mirrored Quesnay's concept of the natural order, which lay at the very heart of Physiocratic writings.

Quesnay was by no means the first to discover natural order. The very idea and the use of the concept, even in economic matters, had deep roots in the Scholastic tradition of the fifteenth century—and they go back even further to Aristotle, as Schumpeter emphasized. Simone Meyssonnier traced the idea to Pierre Le Pesant de Boisguilbert, who wrote at the turn of the eighteenth century.[63] But the Physiocrats were the ones who became associated with the idea of natural order—which was vilified by many, defended by others. They became known as the most vocal defenders of natural order. And they shaped the way we think about it today.

The Rule of Nature

Perfect liberty, economic system, natural order—a fragile logic reconciles these different readings of Quesnay, a logic that relies heavily on the concept of Nature. According to this logic, natural law and its orderliness alone can reconcile the perfect liberty of the individual with the determinism of an autonomous economic system.

The very label "Physiocrat" points to the centrality of the notions of natural law and natural order. Du Pont de Nemours was the first to label Quesnay's school of thought "Physiocratie" in the 1767 publication of his edited volume *Physiocratie; ou, Constitution naturelle du gouvernement le plus avantageux au genre humain.*[64] The term "Physiocratie" was a neologism meant to signify the rule ("-crat") of nature ("physio-"). Though the word "nature" had several connotations, including for instance the idea that agriculture alone was the source of all wealth, these different connotations all revolved around the idea of an *ordre naturel.* As the historian Étienne-Charles de Loménie de Brienne explained: "They took on that moniker by combining two Greek words that mean, the first, *nature,* and the second, *rule,* because they claimed to have discovered the governmental and administrative system that conforms best to the laws of nature."[65]

The neologism is telling, and it reflects well how natural law was at the heart of the intellectual movement. On its foundation, François Quesnay would construct, in the decade from 1756 to 1767, an economic and political theory that would allow his disciples to reimagine and reconceive liberty and self-interest, and provide a theoretical structure that legitimated liberty of commerce and trade. There is a famous legend regarding a conversation that Quesnay purportedly had with the dauphin that in many ways captures the centrality of natural laws and its implications:

> —Well what would you do if you were the king? asked the prince.
> —I would do absolutely nothing.
> —And who then would govern?
> —The laws![66]

Nature, in this view, played a self-regulating function. There was a dynamic element to Quesnay's economic system that relied on the internal logic of markets—of natural laws—to self-adjust, a reading that is emphasized by both Albert Hirschman and Michel Foucault. Nature regulated nature, markets regulated markets. The internal logic of both allowed for self-regulation. And in this, there was a striking similarity between Quesnay's views of medicine and his economics. In the medical area, Quesnay argued that doctors should allow the fever to heal the patient. Rather than viewing fever as something that needed to be eradicated, eliminated, immediately addressed by means of bleedings, Quesnay took the position that the fever could possibly help cure the patient. His medical belief was very similar to that of allowing higher prices in the market to self-regulate a grain shortage. An increase in price, like an increase in fever, could actually help the organism.[67]

> Ex natura, jus, ordo, et leges
> Ex homine, arbitrium, regimen, et coercitio.[68]

This was Quesnay's motto, affixed to the title page of Du Pont de Nemours's edition of *Physiocratie*. And this notion of natural order served as the main foil against those earlier conceptions of public economy, of "police," and of *bon marché*—earlier conceptions, admittedly, that Quesnay himself had helped to construct and paint as oppressive, disciplinary, antiquated, and outmoded. The contrast was sharp. Police and *bon marché* may well have been the rallying call of the cameralists, but the writings of the new French *économistes* offered a far different perspective. The contrast is captured best in Quesnay's nineteenth maxim, from his *Maximes générales* of 1767—one of his latest works:

> *Do not believe that the low price of commodities is beneficial to the humble folk;* for the low price of goods reduces the wage of the common people, decreases their wealth, provides them with less work and fewer lucrative jobs, and destroys the nation's revenue.[69]

It was not *bon marché*, but rather its opposite—*cherté* or high prices—that would ensure abundance for the people and prosperity for the nation. The rhetoric had flipped. And the very meaning of liberty would change, as a new logic emerged, one centered around the notions of natural law and natural order.

4

The Rise of Legal Despotism

There was a darker side to these natural laws that many readers ignored. But some others could not. "I beg you, Sir, do not talk to me any more of your *legal despotism*," Jean-Jacques Rousseau declared. It was 1767, and Mirabeau had just sent Rousseau a copy of Le Mercier de la Rivière's newly published book *L'ordre naturel et essentiel des sociétés politiques*. Rousseau wrote back, impassioned: "I can only see here two contradictory terms which, when reunited, mean absolutely nothing to me."[1]

In a separate letter about Mercier's book, Rousseau mocked the very notion of natural order, suggesting that it was entirely empty. Rousseau used a fictionalized conversation between Mercier and Catherine II to ridicule Mercier's ideas. Mercier had been invited and had in fact traveled to Russia to offer advice to Catherine II at the suggestion of Diderot, who had read *L'ordre naturel*.[2] Mercier did not last long, and after a few interviews with Catherine II, returned to France claiming that Catherine II was simply trying to use him to justify her arbitrary despotism.[3] Many, especially Grimm but also Falconet, Voltaire, and here, Rousseau, managed to turn the entire affair into parody and to use it to rail against "legal despotism":

> Just as Corsicans and Poles applied to Rousseau, Catherine of Russia, in consequence of her admiration for La Rivière's book, summoned him to Russia to assist her in making laws. "Sir," said the czarina, "could you point out to me the best means for the good government of a state?" "Madame, there is only one way, and that is being just; in other words, in keeping order and exacting obedience to the laws." "But on what base is it best to make the laws of an empire repose?" "There is only one base, madame: the nature of things and of men." "Just so; but when you wish to give laws to a people, what are the rules which indicate most surely such laws as are most suitable?" "To give or make laws, madame, is a task that God has left to none. Ah, who is the man that should think himself capable of dictating laws for beings that he does not know, or

knows so ill? And by what right can he impose laws on beings whom God has never placed in his hands?" "To what, then, do you reduce the science of government?" "To studying carefully, recognising, and setting forth, the laws which God has graven so manifestly in the very organization of men, when he called them into existence. To wish to go any further would be a great misfortune and a most destructive undertaking." "Sir, I am very pleased to have heard what you have to say; I wish you good day."[4]

Mirabeau responded by letter to Rousseau in an effort to redeem Mercier. The central point of Mercier's book, Mirabeau explained, was the importance of private property and natural law—the keystones to Physiocratic political theory, and to the Physiocrats' ideal of legal despotism. "You don't understand our laws, you say; well, we have none other than *private property,* personal, chattel, and real, from which derive all other liberties that do not harm the property of others. It is on the basis of this general law, which can be applied in any and every case, that we derive our *legal despotism* that scares you so."[5]

Legal despotism, though, did not so much scare Rousseau as it repelled him. And yet it was, according to the Physiocrats, the necessary outcome of the rule of nature. The idea of natural order, Quesnay would explain in 1767, inexorably led to a political theory of despotism. Natural order in the autonomous economic sphere demanded, first, that there be no human intervention in terms of positive law in the economic realm and, second, that positive law limit itself to punishing the deviant.

The Unitary Executive

The logic was impeccable: the political, moral, and economic realms were governed, the Physiocrats believed, by fundamental natural laws established by an almighty being in order to best promote the interests of mankind. In terms of good governance, positive law could do no more than merely instantiate the fundamental natural laws. Positive law could have no governance function beyond that, which is why the Physiocrats saw no need for a separate legislature, but endorsed instead a unified executive—a legal despot—who would merely implement the laws of nature. Anything beyond that would necessarily produce disorder rather than order. Thus the positive law should not extend to the domain of physical laws: "La législation positive ne doit donc pas s'étendre sur le domaine des loix physiques," Quesnay wrote.[6] Only those men whose passions are out of order, who fail to see and abide by the laws of nature, deviate from those laws. Those are the men whose passions are "déréglées."[7] The principal object of the positive law, then, is to severely punish those whose passions are out of order, so as to protect society from those thieves and derelicts.[8]

There is some dispute as to who first came up with the concept of "legal despotism"—whether it was Quesnay or Le Mercier de la Rivière.[9] It is reported that Mercier was working for six months in Quesnay's *entresol* at the palace of Versailles during the critical period before Quesnay's work on despotism in China was published in the *Éphémérides* in March, April, May, and June of 1767; but Mercier's own work, *L'ordre naturel,* a lengthy book, was published in its entirety in July 1767 and, had its distribution not been delayed by the censors, it would surely have predated Quesnay's work on China.[10] One commentator, Paul Dubreuil, contends that the expression likely came from Mercier, but that Mercier and Quesnay had been working in collaboration.[11] The political project of a deeply despotic, centralized political authority, however, traced to earlier Quesnay writings, especially the unpublished joint manuscript of Quesnay and Mirabeau, *Le traité de la monarchie.* As Elizabeth Fox-Genovese has shown, it is there that Quesnay first came to grips with the political implications of their economic ideas and it remained unpublished because it was so threatening—and would have been censured. But it is certainly there that we get the first glimpse of what would become legal despotism.[12]

What is clear is that legal despotism is fully articulated in 1767, also present in Le Trosne's *Ordre social,* and summarized in Du Pont de Nemours's *Origine et les progrès d'une science nouvelle.*[13] In these works, the Physiocrats embrace absolute, hereditary monarchy founded on divine right.[14] Quesnay synthesized the idea neatly in his first *Maxime* from 1767: "The sovereign authority must be *singular,* and set above all the individuals in society and all the unjust undertakings of individual interests; for the goal of domination and obedience is the protection of everyone and the legitimate interest of all. The system of *checks and balances* in a government is a harmful opinion that reveals only the dissension among the powerful and the overburdening of the weak."[15] Why, you may ask? Because only a unitary executive who is co-owner of the net product and of the lands will have an interest that is pure and not in any way in conflict with the interests of the nation.[16] The only way for a ruler to govern well is for the interests to be aligned; and only he who has a property interest in the lands themselves has an interest in increasing the net product and not simply in rent-seeking. "In other words, hereditary, absolute monarchy, since there cannot be checks and balances, nor separation of powers."[17]

Quesnay's article "Despotisme de la Chine" (1767) best articulates the political project. In the "Préliminaire" to the original manuscript, Quesnay set forth his political vision, tying together notions of fundamental natural law, natural order, and legal despotism. It is here that we see the necessary link between natural order and a robust penal sphere: according to Quesnay, the natural laws that govern the economic sphere require that the legal despot not interfere with economic matters and limit his governance to the enforcement of penal sanctions against those who deviate from the natural order. This "Préliminaire" is the most important section of the essay, and the only section that is known to have been written entirely in Quesnay's hand.[18] It is also the only section of the manuscript that is not merely descriptive, but instead proposes a normative political vision. Du Pont moved it into the body of the printed text in the *Éphémérides* and renamed it chapter 8, "Comparison of the Chinese Laws with the Natural Principles of Prosperous States"—this, no doubt, to reduce the likelihood of censorship.[19]

The text itself is remarkable and advances, at its core, a theory of positive law focused entirely on punishing those who deviate from natural law. The central function of positive law, Quesnay tells us, is repressive. The only role for human law is to punish the deviant, such as thieves and the malintentioned: "de préserver la société des voleurs et des méchans," Quesnay wrote.[20] Quesnay placed the penal sanction outside the realm of economic exchange as the proper instrument to deal with deviance from natural law:

> The natural and fundamental laws of societies . . . imprint themselves on men's hearts, they are the light that illuminates and masters their conscience: this light can only be weakened or obscured by their disordered passions [*leurs passions déréglées*]. The principal object of positive laws is this very disorderliness [*dérèglement*], to which they oppose a severe punishment to those perverse men [*une sanction redoubtable aux hommes pervers*]. For, on the whole, what is it that is truly necessary for the prosperity of a nation? *To cultivate the land as successfully as possible and to keep society safe from thieves and evil people* [*des voleurs et des méchans*]. The first part is governed by self-interest, the second is entrusted to the civil government.[21]

According to this view, the purpose of civil government and the function of positive law are to protect the autonomous and self-sustaining economic system from thieves and delinquents. The retributive element is strong. Those who do not play by the natural rules of economic exchange deserve to be treated as criminals and punished severely.

The same year, 1767, Le Mercier de la Rivière published his masterpiece *L'ordre naturel et essentiel des sociétés politiques.* The book was a big success, selling more than three thousand copies in a few months, and it created quite a stir among the *Philosophes.*[22] Adam Smith paid special attention to Mercier in *The Wealth of Nations,* singling him out for praise.[23] The book itself is fascinating and presents the same vision of the need for despotic legal power. Du Pont would place Mercier de la Rivière in a school of his own—too dogmatically "despotic," Du Pont would suggest. But his text, at least on one reading, betrays the same political vision as Quesnay's.

The touchstone for Mercier was that positive law conform to and be guided by natural order. "Positive law [should be] in exact conformity with the natural and essential laws of society," Mercier declared.[24] Given that social order is natural and necessary—and legible to reason—it followed, Mercier held, that natural order should guide all positive laws.[25] In this sense, according to Mercier, men do not make law, they instead discover and come to know, through *évidence,* the existing natural laws.[26] Sovereign power, Mercier argued, is a *pouvoir tutélaire*—a tutelary power, a relationship of trusteeship. It derives from the simple need for coercive force to back up the just and natural laws.[27] The legislative function and the executive power both depend on physical force and the ability to have their will obeyed. Sovereignty is inextricably linked with power.[28]

On these principles, Mercier developed a theory of unitary, absolute power. Legislative power collapses into the executive branch, dictated as it is by natural law.[29] This power, Mercier contended, must be held in the hand of one person, and as a result Mercier espoused hereditary, absolute monarchy. Absolute and unique in order to ensure that the interests of the sovereign line up with those of his subjects—of all different classes.[30] But Mercier advocated not just any kind of despotism, only legal despotism. And he did not consider the abstract notion of "despotism" to be nefarious. To the contrary, all humans and human knowledge are guided by self-evidence—or, as Mercier and his contemporaries would say, by *évidence*—and *évidence* is itself inherently despotic: factual evidence forces us to comply, it commands our actions, it controls our will.[31] Quesnay himself had written the encyclopedia entry on "evidence" and it was the very basis of Mercier's mode of reasoning. Just like the despotism of *évidence,* nature and the natural order dictate despotism in social relations and in the penal sphere.[32]

The notion of legal in "legal despotism" was precisely the idea of natural laws—of laws that are common to all societies. Mercier distinguished between these and the positive laws that were instituted in particular societies, using as his principal example criminal homicide and crimes of violence. Natural law, Mercier argued, embodied a prohibition on homicide; positive law represented the actual punishment that is meted out in any particular case. The two must conform, Mercier maintained: punishment must be severe or it will undermine the natural prohibition. In this respect, positive laws had to conform to the natural law.[33]

The Physiocrats would choose as their motto "proprieté, sûreté, liberté"—property, security, liberty.[34] The slogan captured well the central political implications of their thought. Starting from private property, the Physiocratic system ensured "security" through the penal process and "liberty" in the economic domain, thereby instantiating that fundamental duality between punishment and political economy.

Le Mercier, *Intendant* of Martinique

Mercier was the only member of the inner circle of Physiocrats who would have the opportunity to govern, and his practices would breathe life into the notion of legal despotism even before he came to write *L'ordre naturel*.

The chronology is important here. Le Mercier de la Rivière first entered public service in 1746, at the age of twenty-seven, as an adviser to parliament—specifically as "conseiller à la première chamber des enquêtes du Parlement de Paris."[35] Mercier earned a strong reputation at parliament and was intricately involved in mediating the relationship between the court at Versailles and the Parlement de Paris.[36] In 1758, Mercier came to the attention of Madame de Pompadour who had Louis XV appoint him *intendant* of Martinique, an official administrative position that he would occupy on two separate occasions. (At the time, Martinique, along with the islands of Santo Domingo and Guadeloupe, were the most precious colonial possessions of the ancien régime; in fact, only a few years later Louis XV would cede the Canadian possessions in order to safeguard these valuable islands.) Mercier was *intendant* of Martinique first from March 1759 to February 1762, when he had to capitulate to the British, and then a second time from July 1763 to June 1764, when he returned to France due to severe illness. After his second stint as *intendant*, he returned to France somewhat disgraced and spent the next thirty years in private life. He contributed his first essay to the review of the economists in November 1765, wrote his most famous text in 1767, and later engaged in a highly publicized dispute with the abbé Galiani on the *polices des grains*—known as "la bagarre"—all while advocating Physiocracy.[37]

Mercier's administration in Martinique would instantiate his later writings on legal despotism.[38] During his second term as *intendant* of Martinique, Mercier implemented a quasi-despotic form of government. With Mercier at the helm, Louis XV replaced the governing legislative body in Martinique with a single chamber composed of seven members, all of whom were nominated by the king and chosen by Mercier. Eventually, the royal administration deprived the chamber of its right to speak directly to the authorities and declared that the chamber could only propose measures, but no longer enact them. In short order, the chamber lost all its powers.[39]

In keeping with this despotic approach, Mercier focused his administration on policing and law enforcement. Mercier himself created a police force in Martinique, mainly to protect the proprietors. His lasting legacy on the island, in fact, seems to have been this police administration. As the historian Louis-Philippe May explained, "Le Mercier had demonstrated the necessity of organizing the defense of the island and, to guarantee the protection of the property owners, the need to create a military police [*maréchaussée*] and 'well-paid police commissioners.' . . . Le Mercier himself would give, *proprio motu,* from August 23, 1763 to February 12, 1764, six edicts pertaining to the organization of a strict police force [*une police sévère*] that would extend to the most remote areas."[40]

The first ordinance establishing the police, dated August 23, 1763, created what were called "Commissaires de la Paroisse" (village, or parish, commissioners). The preamble is interesting: "[We have] decided that it would best serve the King, in this colony, to establish Commissioners [*Commissaires*] in each parish [who would be] responsible for keeping the peace, and for executing the various orders that we address to them."[41] These commissioners were given the authority "to arrest wrongdoers and other disturbers of the peace, to have them taken to the closest royal prisons, on the condition that they report back to us within twenty-four hours."[42]

A second ordinance, dated October 18, 1763, set out the functions and duties of the *maréchaussée.* The focus of their functions was to assure public order regarding four specific domains: gaming, taverns, public markets, and "Negroes." They were in charge of the regulations concerning these domains—including the public markets. Their task was to ensure that in their neighborhood "nothing happened that disturbed the peace or violated police regulations regarding gambling, taverns, public markets and slaves."[43] Most of the regulation, it turns out, was about slaves. Here is a sampling:

> VII. Every archer of the military police [*maréchaussée*] who knows of a brown slave [*un Esclave marron*] denounced by his master can arrest him, and, if need be, take him to prison; in which case he will be paid for the capture, and will receive the money for his own profit alone.
>
> VIII. The capture of brown slaves arrested in the cities . . . will be paid 6 livres; that of said slaves in the countryside or in the cities far from their residence will be paid 12 livres; and 24 livres when the capture is made in

> the big woods; this regulation hereby supersedes all contrary regulations.[44]

In fact, Mercier de la Rivière himself was setting the price of capture for slaves: for example, twelve livres for slaves arrested at night in towns or boroughs a certain distance from their masters' homes.[45]

In a third order, this one dated October 19, 1763, Mercier and the governor, Fenelon, set out the functions of the *commissaires des paroisses.* Here is their charge:

> First Article. In each parish of this island, there will be a Commissioner who will have under his authority a Lieutenant; he will be responsible for seeing to the maintenance of order and to general policing [*la police publique*]; for preventing acts of vigilante justice; for arresting wrongdoers, vagrants, disreputable people, and peddlers of whatever state, color or condition . . . ; in a word, for stopping anything and everything that contravenes the regulations regarding the police, commerce, and the King's rights.[46]

Mercier and Fenelon also established lieutenant commissioners in order to assist in all police functions, namely "to see to the maintenance of law and order, to have wrongdoers and other disturbers of the peace arrested, to see to the execution of our orders and our edicts and regulations concerning *police,* commerce, and navigation, and generally to do everything that regards the service of the aforementioned Commissioners."[47] In another order dated December 14, 1763, Mercier and Fenelon refined the responsibilities of the *maréchaussée,* fixing the exact price of their functions related to the arrest of "Negroes," the distribution of funds, and the prohibition of physically abusing arrested persons of color. "We hereby bar and prohibit most unequivocally any officer or archer from striking or insulting anyone that they are commanded to arrest, under penalty of *cassation* in the event that they strike anyone, and in addition, for the archers, under penalty of being sent to a court of ordinary jurisdiction."[48]

In a final order dated February 12, 1764, perhaps one of Mercier's last acts before leaving Martinique, he and Fenelon regulated the policing of vagabonds and of persons without papers. These regulations required all white persons to register with the police and punished both those who did not have registration papers as well as their hosts or employers. The regulations were intended to prevent sailors, soldiers, or criminals from taking refuge in the homes of legitimate residents of Martinique and from seeking employment as a way of escaping the consequences of their acts.[49] Steep penalties, including the threat of *galère* (transportation), were attached to these ordinances.[50]

A "severe police"—that is how the historian May would remember Mercier's legacy in Martinique. How fitting for a man who would embrace legal despotism only three years later in his *L'ordre naturel.* In this regard at least, Mercier's praxis corresponded well with his writings, especially because these police functions were intimately related to the maintenance of slavery—the ultimate form of private property on the island. Policing the slave population was a—if not the—key component of these penal initiatives.[51]

History, ultimately, would not look favorably on Mercier's policing. As May shows, the creation of the police force was itself a political intervention that redistributed power on the island—and that ultimately backfired against Mercier. In creating the police, Mercier was concentrating the power to police in the king's hands—an unwelcome development for the local masters and proprietors who had previously held this authority.

The fact is, Martinique society had been heavily militarized since its European inception in the early seventeenth century and the *milice*—the local militia—had always played a very important role in policing the population. From at least 1627 onward, the Martinique colonists and whites had acted as soldier peasants—armed and somewhat trained to defend the island—and an institutionalized militia was well in place by the time of French colonization in 1635.[52] In his memoirs from 1660, Father Brunetti wrote that "all the inhabitants of Martinique carry arms and there isn't one who, going off his property, would not wear at least a sword on his side."[53] The *milice* had also become a means for ordinary colonists to acquire titles of nobility and a source of hope for *miliciens de couleur* who longed for official freedom.[54] After years of internecine struggles against other military units, the *milice* had achieved formal status in the early eighteenth century and had become central to the organization of Martiniquais society.[55] Mercier, then, was taking on an important institution and his intervention was met by indignation from the local aristocracy and landowners. In fact, in 1776, after Mercier's departure, the *milice* would be reestablished.[56]

Looking back, Mercier's creation of a police force was certainly not an effort to liberalize a traditional government function, to reduce the amount of government intervention, or to promote the liberty of all. On the contrary, Mercier's political initiatives concentrated state power and increased government intervention. In contrast to his stated economic beliefs, in Martinique under his stewardship, state control grew through the police function. This would be in keeping with Mercier's embrace of legal despotism three years later in *L'ordre naturel.*

Natural Order and Inequality

Mercier's emphasis on private property went hand in hand with a robust justification of inequality—and some *philosophes,* especially Rousseau, would have none of this.[57] The formation of society, Mercier argued, was intended to protect the right to private property, and therefore to protect the inequalities associated with that right, or as he put it: "the law of property, that fundamental law of society, that law which is the basic reason for all other laws, *necessarily* excludes equality."[58] Mercier would write:

> I will conclude this [second] chapter with an observation on the inequality of man: those who complain about it, fail to recognize that inequality is in the very essence of order and justice: once I have acquired the *exclusive* ownership of property, no one else can be its owner like me at the same moment. . . . Therefore, one must not interpret the inequality of human conditions as an abuse that originates with society; even if you were able to dissolve societies, I would defy you to make the inequalities disappear; they have their source in the inequality of physical powers and in a multitude of chance events that are entirely independent of our will.[59]

For Mercier, inequality was natural and inevitable. The social condition would never overcome inequality—it was inscribed in the natural order prior to civil society and inextricably woven into organized society. Mercier recognized that, at certain times, gross inequalities could cause disorder. "But what should we conclude from that?" he asked. "Should we set out to equalize conditions?" No, he answered. "No, because we would have to destroy all private property, and consequently society itself. Nevertheless, we should redress the disorders that cause the problems insofar as they forcibly arrange things so that all the rights are on one side and all the duties on the other."[60]

The contrast with Rousseau could not have been sharper. Whereas for Rousseau inequality was the product of civilization and civil society, for Mercier it predated the social condition. It was inscribed in nature.[61] And along many other dimensions as well, the conflict was stark and sharply worded. The conventional wisdom in political philosophy was that man gave up many of his natural liberties to join civil society. The Physiocrats, by contrast, maintained that those very liberties originated in the state of nature and came to full fruition in society. Whereas Montesquieu had shown that political liberty depended on separation of powers, the Physiocrats counseled a unified executive. Along with their ideas about individual liberty and the economic system, they embraced legal despotism in politics. Embedded in the very idea of natural orderliness—at the very heart of their enterprise—lay an absolute, hereditary, unified monarch who declared positive laws to punish those who did not recognize the force of natural law.

The debate between Rousseau and Mercier ultimately reveals a deep tension in Physiocratic doctrine—at least, to our modern eyes—between the liberty of economic exchange and the despotism of governance. For while the Physiocrats' discourse of liberty sounded practically revolutionary at the time, their embrace of legal despotism was resoundingly reactionary. The Martiniquais police, after all, served as the principal enforcement mechanism of chattel slavery—a dramatic illustration of this central paradox. This key tension would recur in both early liberal and twentieth-century neoliberal writings. Each reiteration, slightly more technical than the last, would have embedded in it this paradox of natural order and strict policing. From Jeremy Bentham's writings on punishment to more contemporary neoliberal works, each generation would reconstitute, however oddly, Quesnay's juxtaposition of liberty in economics and legal despotism in the penal sphere.

5

Bentham's Strange Alchemy

In a series of letters he wrote from White Russia in the year 1787, collected in his *Panopticon; or, The Inspection-House,* Bentham outlined an imaginative plan for a panoptic prison that would reunite discipline and market efficiency. The former, discipline, permeated the *Panopticon*—as Michel Foucault so forcefully reminded us in *Discipline and Punish,* where he appropriated the very concept to define one extremity of the disciplinary project, the space of generalized surveillance.[1] Writing of the "Advantages of the Plan" in his sixth letter, Bentham highlighted the disciplinary reach: "I flatter myself there can now be little doubt of the plan's possessing the fundamental advantages I have been attributing to it: I mean, the *apparent omnipresence* of the inspector (if divines will allow me the expression) combined with the extreme facility of his *real presence.*"[2]

But Bentham's interest in market efficiency also drove his invention. The panopticon aimed to mete out surveillance *"at the lowest possible cost,"* as Foucault also reminded us, emphasizing: "economically, by the low expenditure it involves; politically, by its discretion, its low exteriorization, its relative invisibility, the little resistance it arouses."[3] Efficiency was indeed a key selling point. In his sixth letter, Bentham immediately followed up the idea of omnipresence with a claim regarding the economic savings to be reaped. "A collateral advantage it possesses, and on the score of frugality a very material one," Bentham wrote, "is that which respects the *number* of the inspectors requisite. . . . [F]or the trouble of inspection is diminished in no less proportion than the strictness of inspection is increased."[4] Efficiency was a central concern of Bentham's. In this regard, Philip Smith is undoubtedly right: "An admirer of much in Adam Smith, he envisaged the penal institution as a profitable enterprise."[5] Philip Smith adds:

> When Bentham famously wrote that the panopticon had untied the Gordian knot of the Poor Laws he was referring to the fact that such in-

> stitutions could become attractive to the private sector and thus run without cost to the public. The panoptical principle would allow fewer staff to be employed, thinner walls to be built, and better work rates to be accomplished. . . . Here was an institution primarily designed to make money rather than remake souls, one in which the governor would be an industrial Gradgrind, not a philosopher, and one who would not burden the unwilling taxpayer.[6]

Bentham's letters on the panopticon crystallize the peculiar alchemy that only Bentham could achieve and achieved seemingly first: a combination of Beccaria on punishment with a concern for Adam Smith on the economy, or, more precisely, a mixture of a cameralist reading of Beccaria on crime and punishment with a moderate, naturalist reading of Adam Smith. By means of his peculiar alchemy, Bentham would ultimately replicate—however unintentionally—the Physiocratic paradox, namely an element of natural orderliness in the economic realm and legal despotism in the penal sphere. Bentham's alchemy would prove terribly productive and help shape modern American conceptions of the criminal sanction. In this way, Bentham inadvertently provided the link from the nineteenth century to the present, in large part due to his significant influence on modern legal, economic, and political thought—that is, he provided both inspiration to contemporary consequentialist thinkers and a productive foil to believers in natural rights.

Creative readings of Bentham's economic views have proliferated wildly over the past two centuries, and, in the process, Bentham's work has been bent in every possible direction, from individualist to collectivist, from naturalist to constructivist, from laissez-faire zealot to founder of the welfare state. Bentham's writings on education, public health, and women's suffrage have buoyed many progressives, including John Dewey; his consequentialist, cost-benefit approach has been embraced by many modern conservatives; and his quietist tendencies have infuriated many on the left, most notably Marx, who referred to Bentham as "an insipid, pedantic, leather-tongued oracle of the ordinary bourgeois intelligence of the 19th century."[7]

Navigating this landscape of Bentham readings is no easy task. The burden of this chapter is to show that, although Bentham expressly rejected notions of natural rights, he nevertheless introduced an element of natural harmony back into his economic theory. But the argument here does not stand or fall on that proposition alone, because the more crucial point is that, regardless of one's reading of Bentham's economics, there is no question that his views on punishment were unbendingly interventionist.

It is the *contrast* between Bentham's economics and his views on punishment that reiterates the duality of the Physiocrats. In a modified way, to be sure, since Bentham extends the economic rationality of pricing to the field of crime and punishment. But at its heart, the contrast between the element of quietism in Bentham's economics and his embrace of full intervention in penality clearly echoes the Physiocratic approach. Bentham may well have regarded punishment as "in itself evil"—just like Beccaria before him—but he viewed the penal sphere as the domain of pure state intervention. From Bentham's design of the panopticon to his view of the penal code as a grand menu of prices, there is no doubting his pure constructivism in the punishment field. In this sense, it is the comparison to his economic views that solves the puzzle. It is in the tension that we can most clearly see Bentham's curious alchemy.

Jeremy Bentham on Punishment and Political Economy

Bentham embraced Beccaria on punishment. Not the humanitarian Beccaria of the *philosophes*, but the utilitarian Beccaria, the Beccaria of pain and pleasure, of marginal utility. The Beccaria of calculated and proportional sanctions intended to signal the price of crime and the fine gradations of punishment. Bentham espoused the ideas of Beccaria the cameralist, Beccaria the interventionist, Beccaria the price fixer—but only as these ideas applied to the penal sphere. Neither Bentham, nor later scholars of law and economics, would embrace Beccaria's cameralism in the economic domain. But more on that later.

In the penal sphere, Beccaria's influence on Bentham was paramount, not only with regard to the central utilitarian assumption that individuals rationally pursue pleasure and avoid pain, but also for the central insight regarding the measurement of pain and pleasure. "It was from Beccaria's little treatise on crimes and punishments," Bentham wrote, "that I drew, as I well remember, the first hint of this principle [that monetary values can be used as an instrument to measure the quantity of pain or pleasure], by which the precision and clearness and incontestableness of mathematical calculation are introduced for the first time into the field of morals."[8] Bentham also drew on Beccaria regarding the "fundamental axiom" that the measure of right and wrong is the greatest happiness of the greatest number. That formulation, as has been shown, "appears word for word in the English translation of Beccaria (in the original it is '*la massima felicita divisa nel maggior numero*')."[9] Bentham traced these insights specifically to the one he called his "master."

With a few minor exceptions, then, Bentham on crime and punishment mirrors Beccaria's short tract. Bentham agreed with Beccaria on most criminal law issues, including the death penalty. Regarding capital punishment,

Bentham went so far as to write that Beccaria had covered the topic so well, there was little anyone could add: "the more attention one gives to the punishment of death the more he will be inclined to adopt the opinion of Beccaria—that it ought to be disused. This subject is so ably discussed in his book that to treat it after him is a work that may well be dispensed with."[10]

Bentham explicitly acknowledged his debt to Beccaria on a wide range of penal issues, but the parallel is clearly apparent from the text itself. Most of the penal theories that Bentham articulated, including his central insight of marginal deterrence, can be identified in Beccaria's short tract *On Crimes and Punishments*. For instance, Bentham's key idea that the lower the probability of apprehension, the higher the optimal punishment—an idea that is central to modern economic analyses of crime and punishment—had already been examined by Beccaria, who wrote: "One of the most effective brakes on crime is not the harshness of its punishment, but the unerringness of punishment. . . . The certainty of even a mild punishment will make a bigger impression than the fear of a more awful one which is united to a hope of not being punished at all."[11] Similarly, on Bentham's insight that fines are preferable to imprisonment if the convict can pay—which would be rehearsed by later proponents of law and economics—Beccaria again had already surveyed the territory, writing, "Thefts without violence should be punished with fines. . . . [But] since this is generally the crime of poverty and desperation, the crime of that unhappy section of men to whom the perhaps 'terrible' and 'unnecessary' right to property has allowed nothing but a bare existence . . . the most fitting punishment shall be the only sort of slavery which can be called just, namely the temporary enslavement of the labour and person of the criminal to society."[12] In these passages, Beccaria was working out the precise theorems that Bentham and members of the law-and-economics movement would later reinvent.

In his economics, however, Bentham ignored Beccaria the price-setting cameralist and turned instead to Adam Smith, albeit an interpretation of Smith that would be considered moderate by some today. Bentham turned in earnest to the study of political economy in 1786 at the age of thirty-eight and dedicated eighteen years to the enterprise.[13] And when he did so, he turned almost unbendingly to Smith's *Wealth of Nations*. Werner Stark, the editor of Bentham's economic writings, would go so far as to say that "the *Wealth of Nations* was Bentham's economic bible and he assimilated it until he thought its terms and spoke its tongue."[14] This is not to suggest that Bentham never departed from Smith's economics. He did so famously in his *Defence of Usury*, which was diametrically opposed to Smith's view, and he kept a running tab of "problematic points" in Smith's work.[15] But in the main, Bentham treated Smith as his guide.

Nowhere is this more evident than in Bentham's *Manual of Political Economy,* written in the period 1793 to 1795, in which he intended to succinctly and comprehensively present his economic view as a guide to action. Bentham's *Manual* reflects a clear debt to Smith. Bentham recognized on the very first page that his own *Manual* tracked Smith's thought closely—that "the principles here laid down concur with those laid down by that illustrious writer."[16] Bentham distinguished and justified his *Manual,* in relation to *The Wealth of Nations,* as the practical guide to implement the theoretical view. "His object was the science," Bentham wrote; "my object is the art." Or, as Bentham would explain, "This work is to Dr. Smith's, what a book on the art of medicine is to a book of anatomy or physiology."[17] Bentham's emphasis was not on theory, but on practice. It was not on pure knowledge, but on governing: "The great object, the great *desideratum,* is to know what ought and what ought not to be done by government."[18] And on that vital question, the *Manual* reveals a distinct bias in favor of quietism—but let me not get ahead of myself.

Readings of Adam Smith

To suggest that Bentham was influenced by Adam Smith actually raises more questions than it answers. Of all authors, Smith has received perhaps the widest possible range of readings—from Smith the laissez-faire purist to Smith the incipient socialist. Reading Adam Smith is undoubtedly the most telling Rorschach test in the discipline: how readers interpret Adam Smith, along both dimensions that matter most here—the theoretical underpinnings and the policy recommendations—tells us far more about the reader than it does about Smith.

On the theoretical side, some readers emphasize a naturalist reading of Smith, others an element of utility developed by Smith's close friend, David Hume. In the first camp, Jacob Viner believed that Smith's most insightful and original contribution was the introduction into economics of the idea of a harmonious order of nature—essentially, the idea of natural order. In a lecture delivered in 1927 at the University of Chicago, Viner would declare that "Smith's major claim to originality, in English economic thought at least" was his introduction of the idea of natural order into economics, an idea that "philosophers and theologians had already applied to the world in general." Viner continued: "Smith's further doctrine that this underlying natural order required, for its most beneficent operation, a system of natural liberty, and that in the main public regulation and private monopoly were corruptions of that natural order, at once gave to economics a bond of union with the prevailing philosophy and theology, and to economists and statesmen a program of practical reform."[19] The parallel to certain readings of François Quesnay is striking.

Historians such as J. Bartlet Brebner and Colin Holmes would similarly underscore the naturalist foundations of Smith's thought, often emphasizing Smith's earlier work *The Theory of Moral Sentiments*, where Smith applied the doctrine of harmonious order to the field of ethics. Brebner would write, for instance, that "Smith, as his *Theory of Moral Sentiments* had to some degree foreshadowed, argued that the identification or unification [necessary to secure the common good] would be a *natural* one, that is, that if each individual was left free to pursue what he regarded as his own interest he would be 'led by an invisible hand' and by 'more familiar causes' to collaborate in the achievement of the general good."[20]

Other economic historians, however, such as Lionel Robbins, traced Smith's sensibilities to Humean utilitarianism. Robbins argued that the philosophical origin of eighteenth-century economic theory was the principle of utility "according to which all laws and rights were to be regarded as essentially man-made and to be evaluated according to their effects on the general happiness, long term and short."[21] To be sure, influences are often overlapping. "Life is not consistent and influences are mixed," Robbins would concede. "This can well be seen in Adam Smith, who so frequently uses the terminology of the *Naturrecht,* but whose arguments are so consistently utilitarian in character."[22] In fact, Robbins would go so far as to recast Smith's notion of the "invisible hand" not as a phenomenon of natural order, but rather as an accoutrement of the legislator: "The invisible hand which guides men to promote ends which were no part of their intention, is not the hand of some god or some natural agency independent of human effort; it is the hand of the lawgiver, the hand which withdraws from the sphere of the pursuit of self-interest those possibilities which do not harmonize with the public good."[23]

Along the dimension of policy, there are, if possible, even wider disagreements. At one extreme, George Stigler, one of the founders of the Chicago School of economics, presents Smith as a purist who placed rational self-interest and free markets at the very center of his enterprise. The central insight of Adam Smith, whom Stigler referred to as "our venerable master," is that "the conduct of economic affairs is best left to private citizens." What Smith demonstrated was "the incapacity of the state in economic affairs."[24] On Stigler's reading, Smith had two main bases: he believed "in the efficiency of the system of natural liberty," and "he deeply distrusted the state." These bases, in Stigler's view, led to one policy recommendation: Smith "wishe[d] most economic life to be free of state regulation."[25] Naturally, Smith recognized departures from these working principles in the case of externalities, but overall his was the "case for *laissez faire*."[26] In his 1976 preface to the authoritative University of Chicago 1976 reprint of *The Wealth of Nations,* Stigler pointed to the famous butcher, brewer, and baker passage and added: "This drive of self-interest, which the modern economist has relabeled 'utility-maximizing behavior,' is always present in *The Wealth of Nations:* Smith uses it to explain how men choose occupations, how farmers till their lands, even how the leaders of the American Revolution (which was just beginning) are led by it to rebellion."[27] This is, to a certain extent, the reading of Smith that would be pilloried under the oft-quoted catchphrase of Thomas Carlyle, "anarchy plus the constable," or Ferdinand Lassalle's analogy of the state as mere "night watchman."

Further along the spectrum, Emma Rothschild and Amartya Sen emphasize a kinder, gentler Smith. They portray Smith as an anticolonialist thinker who opposed monopolies granted to the Indies trading companies because of the nefarious mixing of sovereignty and commerce. This is the Smith opposed to the American colonial enterprise because of the extraordinary expense it imposed on Great Britain. This is the Smith who objected to imperialism. The Smith with a soft touch in his policy recommendations, always caring about the "lower ranks." The Smith who conceived of wealth—of the wealth of nations—as the general living condition of all members of society: not just the large property owner, not just the wealthy farmer, but "a workman, even of the lowest and poorest order" who "if he is frugal and industrious," can "enjoy a greater share of the necessaries and conveniences of life than it is possible for any savage to acquire."[28] The Smith who argued for taxation of commerce (rather than prohibition, for instance in the case of the exportation of wool).[29] The Smith who opposed the unfettered self-interest of merchants (mostly to keep them from obtaining monopolies). In sum, the Smith who was far more sympathetic to Turgot and Condorcet than to Quesnay and "perfect liberty."

At the far end of the extreme, there is the Smith who did not believe in laissez-faire, nor for that matter in the "invisible hand." In 1952, Lionel Robbins would notoriously write that "to identify such doctrines with the declared and easily accessible views of the Classical Economists is a sure sign of ignorance or malice."[30] Numerous historians have tracked the instances of government intervention that Smith favored and drawn long lists of his interventionist policies.[31] Even a partial list, we are told, "would suffice to provide ammunition for several socialist orations."[32] "Clearly," Colin Holmes concludes, "Adam Smith was not a doctrinaire advocate of *laissez-faire;* he envisaged a wide and flexible range of economic activities for government."[33]

According to scholars at this extreme, Smith used the metaphor of the invisible hand in jest. "The image of the invisible hand was a minor, and even, it has been suggested, an ironic element in Smith's own economic thought," it is said; the principle itself, "in its twentieth-century sense, was quite un-Smithian."[34] According to this view, Smith was more a historian of the market economy than an advocate of laissez-faire economics. Smith traced the emergence of market exchange and advocated less government intervention—taxing rather than prohibiting the exportation of wool—but he was by no means a free marketer.[35] "The more imposing idea of a general competitive equilibrium, in which the outcome of the self-interested actions of individuals is a system or order of maximal efficiency, is far less close to Smith's own conceptions," Rothschild and Sen note.[36] According to Rothschild, "the invisible hand is in conflict with other parts of Smith's work" and "it is the *sort* of idea he would not have liked."[37] Much earlier in 1883, Carl Menger too had expressed caution about Smith's use of the term, suggesting that Smith had an idiosyncratic understanding of the concept.[38]

Have I mentioned that readings of texts are often no different than the categories we fight over? Anyone who remains skeptical should read William Grampp's marvelous catalogue of the ten most common readings of what Smith meant by the "invisible hand."[39] Surely, the range of appropriations of Smith's writings is one of the more impressive illustrations of this point.

Bentham's Reading of Smith

Bentham's reading of Smith lies, along the theoretical dimension, closer to the side of natural order, though Bentham himself would strenuously resist the language of natural rights. Along the policy dimension, Bentham ultimately embraced a more moderate Smith.

To be sure, Bentham himself explicitly rejected naturalism. He is, as you will recall, the one who described the concept of natural rights as "simple nonsense . . . rhetorical nonsense,—nonsense upon stilts."[40] At the explicit, rhetorical level, there is no question that Bentham rejected the idea of natural order. Here Jacob Viner is undoubtedly right when he concluded that "of explicit formulation by Bentham of a doctrine of natural harmony I can find not the slightest trace in his writings."[41]

But in the process of drawing on Adam Smith, Bentham replicated a certain naturalism in his economics. Bentham's *Manual of Political Economy* reflects this clearly. Chapter 2, titled "Fundamental Principles," essentially articulates why it would be unwise for a statesman or for the government to intervene in economic matters. The chapter is a manifesto for government inaction—offering arguments that still resonate loudly in contemporary discourse. First, private individuals know their interests far better than the government does: "The chance there is of a man's possessing in his superior degree the faculties of knowledge and judgment depends itself in great measure on the degree of interest he has in the concern," Bentham wrote. The private farmer, miller, merchant, or manufacturer simply knows more than the government expert. As a result, Bentham argued, "A first Lord of the Treasury for instance, or other Member of Parliament, or a first Lord of Trade, is not likely to have had so many opportunities of acquiring knowledge relative to farming as a farmer, relative to distilling as a distiller, relative to manufacturing of stuffs as a manufacturer of stuffs, relative to the selling of the produce of any of those trades at home or abroad as one who has made the selling of them the business of his life."[42] Second, private individuals will pursue their personal interests more effectively than the government would on their behalf: "The interest which a man takes in the affairs of another, a member of the sovereignty for example in those of a subject, is not likely to be so great as the interest which either of them takes in his own: still less where that other is a perfect stranger to him."[43]

The combination of these two first reasons leads, syllogistically, to Bentham's presumption against intervention. "In not one of these particulars is the statesman likely to be more than upon a par with the individual whose choice relative to the subjects in question he is so ready to control: in almost all of them he is constantly and necessarily inferior beyond all measure," Bentham would add. Bentham then goes on to repeat, in a style like that of a Baptist preacher, the handicaps of the lord of the treasury, of the member of Parliament, of the first lord of trade: not likely to have bestowed attention to the business, not likely to bestow attention with equal energy, not likely to possess so much knowledge, not likely to form the best mode of carrying on the trade, still less likely to make a better choice—a veritable litany of inferiorities. To top it off, even if the statesman "by any accident" happened to have the knowledge, "yet even this would not afford them any sufficient warrant for endeavoring to employ the power of government in inducing any individual or individuals to embark in such branch of trade, unless the statesman had also a stronger regard for the interest of the trader than the trader himself, in other words, loved every man better than any man loves himself."[44] In short, even if the government had the information and self-interest, it would not use it as well as would the individual. Bentham was blunt: "so sure it is that the information is true, so sure is it that the exercise of power would be unnecessary, and to no use."[45]

Now, you may agree or disagree with Bentham about the probability that a government official will know more or less than the private individual. Many agree with Bentham, which is why the argument from expertise and self-interest remains so vibrant today, as it has over the ages. But many also disagree, which is why administrative agencies today are often staffed by experts from within the industries that they supervise. The administrative movement of the New Deal rested precisely on the promise of enlisting the most talented insiders as experts to better capture all this information and self-interest. Again, you may agree or disagree; this debate is seemingly eternal. But what is clear and indisputable is that, first, Bentham himself sided with the government skeptics, and, second, that his position was not necessary or dictated, that it represented a choice. Bentham chose to take a strong position on the matter ex ante. Instead of keeping an open mind, instead of deciding to empirically evaluate each and every situation, instead of performing a case-by-case analysis—which is what a true empiricist would do—Bentham staked out an extreme position in the debate and sided strongly with the skeptics. Readers of Bentham can point to instances where Bentham argued for government intervention—to an agenda for government—but the underlying default, the presumption, the thumb on the scale, was a bias toward nonintervention. The superiority of the individual's information and self-interest fundamentally underlay Bentham's economics.

Bentham did not hide this bias in his *Manual of Political Economy.* Government there is viewed as essentially "incompetent" and as having been, in economic affairs, not only "perfectly useless" but "always more or less pernicious."[46] Bentham tirelessly writes of the "absurdity" of government measures and of their great "mischief."[47] The *Manual* is essentially an effort to minimize the damage of government intervention by critiquing most of the existing measures and delineating a few proper measures that the government should engage in—essentially the granting of patents and the stockpiling of subsistence goods.

Bentham telegraphed this view even more succinctly in the opening pages of his *Institute of Political Economy,* written a few years later (between 1800 and 1804). "Without some special reason," Bentham declared, the state should not interfere in economic matters. He also famously wrote as the opening paragraphs of his *Agenda* for government—yes, that's right, his "agenda" for the state, not his "non-agenda":

> General rule: nothing ought to be done or attempted by government for the purpose of causing an augmentation to take place in the national mass of wealth, with a view to encrease of the means of either subsistence or enjoyment, without some special reason. *Be quiet* ought on those occasions to be the motto, or watch word, of government.
>
> For this quietism there are two main reasons.
>
> 1. Generally speaking, any interposition for this purpose on the part of government is *needless.* . . . Generally speaking, [there is] no one who knows what it is for your interest to do, as you yourself: no one who is disposed with so much ardour and constancy to pursue it.

2. Generally speaking, it is moreover likely to be *pernicious,* viz. by being unconducive, or even obstructive, with reference to the attainment of the end in view. Each individual bestowing more time and attention upon the means of preserving and encreasing his portion of wealth than is or can be bestowed by government, is likely to take a more effectual course than what in his instance and on his behalf would be taken by government.[48]

Bentham then went on for multiple pages defending a laissez-faire presumption, concluding that "with few exceptions, and those not very considerable ones, the attainment [of] the maximum of enjoyment will be most effectually secured by leaving to each individual to pursue the attainment of his own particular maximum of enjoyment in proportion as he is in possession of the means."[49] Because human wisdom is tied to self-interest, Bentham wrote, governmental interference could only result in less wealth being created.[50] To help explain this, Bentham drew analogies to nature: "Nature gives a premium for the application of industry to the most advantageous branch, a premium which is sure to be disposed of to the best advantage."[51] Bentham completed the argument, suggesting that giving individuals the greatest freedom to pursue their own self-interest will not only result in the greatest advantage for themselves, but will also produce the greatest happiness and advantage for society as a whole.[52]

Note that this is not simply a tie-breaking device. Bentham is not merely stating that, if in equipoise, do nothing. This is a theory of a harmony of self-interests that imposes a heavy burden of proof on anyone advocating for state intervention. It rests on resolute predictions about the high likelihood of individuals having more information about, and interest in, outcomes, and of government being incompetent. Note also that if Bentham had been a purist, whether in his empiricism or in his utilitarianism, there would have been no need for such a strong presumption. From a purely neutral perspective, there would have been no need to presume any harmony of interests; he would need only to conduct an empirical utility analysis to see where the chips fell, that is, he would need only to determine whether statist intervention would increase or decrease overall social welfare.

Bentham was prepared to override his own presumption—as we saw in the *Manual*—in the case of patents and stockpiles of subsistence goods. And in his political and legal writings, particularly his later *Constitutional Code,* Bentham proposed governmental reforms that proved to be significant in scope.[53] But if one reads closely his *Manual* and *Institute,* and compares the proposed governmental non-agenda to the agenda, the message is clear: government is incompetent in economic matters and its authority must be limited to the greatest extent possible. In practice, the default position is nonintervention. In theory, too, there is a certain harmony of self-interest: the private pursuit of self-interest is generally a better guide than state intervention.

In the end, although Bentham was vocally opposed to a natural rights framework, he ultimately reproduced a notion of natural harmony in his economics. This reading of Bentham was advanced early on, in 1901, by Élie Halévy, and taken up again in the mid-twentieth century by Gunnar Myrdal.[54] Myrdal was right about a lot—particularly his social analyses of American race relations—and I would say he was right here too: although Bentham explicitly disavowed a natural law framework, by embracing Adam Smith as he did, he ultimately reverted to a certain naturalism in his economics. Myrdal hit the nail on the head when he wrote:

> Bentham, unlike the physiocrats, started out with strong condemnation of the aprioristic metaphysics implied in the assumption of natural laws and conceived of his own philosophical exertions as the working out, on the basis of empirically ascertained sensations, of general rules for public morals and legislation, i.e. interferences by the state. In the economic field, the result of this—as of any other attempt at founding moral and political views solely upon an observation of facts—was . . . a relapse into the doctrine of a natural harmony of individual interests which, in its turn, carries an inextricable anti-state and anti-organisation bias.[55]

Bentham's economic writings, as a whole, support this view. This is not to deny that Bentham supported and was in fact responsible for significant statist reforms that expanded the scope of the governmental function. Nor is this to suggest that Bentham was a purist on laissez-faire. No, Bentham's economics are a rich and complex bricolage of utilitarianism, spontaneous harmony, and laissez-faire intuitions in theory, and welfare reforms in practice. But as Myrdal concluded, correctly I believe, "In the end, even in the economic thinking based on utilitarianism, the notion of a harmony of interests inserted itself in the practical and political conclusions as a major predilection."[56]

There are, as we will see momentarily, practically as many readings of Bentham as there are of Smith—which only compounds the interpretive puzzles. To say that Bentham was influenced by Smith hardly resolves the matter. To offer another reading of Bentham's economic views also barely advances the debate—however firmly one believes that reading, as I do. What does conclusively resolve the controversy, though, is the contrast between Bentham's views on punishment and his economic sensibilities, between the pervasive panopticism of his punishment writings and the quietist default in his economics. An element of spontaneous harmony made its way into his economics, in very sharp contrast with his views in the punishment field. It is precisely the contrast, the opposition, the presence of spontaneous harmony in one space and not in the other, that reproduced the doctrine of legal despotism from the Physiocrats—that mirrors Quesnay and Le Mercier's stark opposition between economy and society.

Readings of Bentham

Like Smith's, Bentham's opus is subject to widely divergent readings.[57] The field of Bentham studies is a veritable minefield—whether the topic is interpretations of Bentham, the influence of Bentham on British laissez-faire, the emergence of a British welfare state in the nineteenth century, or even the very existence of nineteenth-century laissez-faire. As the historian Gertrude Himmelfarb wrote at the height of the controversy:

> There are those who, interpreting Bentham as a laissez-faireist, have ascribed to him the largest influence in determining the laissez-faire character of mid-Victorian society. Others, interpreting him as a collectivist, have ascribed to him the largest influence in introducing collectivism into mid-Victorian society. Still others have interpreted him as a laissez-faireist who could not, for that reason, have had any influence on the growing collectivism of the century. And still others have interpreted him as a collectivist whose particular ideology had little influence on the emerging institutions, agencies, administrative techniques, and structures.[58]

John Maynard Keynes was one of those who placed Bentham in the category of extreme partisans of laissez-faire—in line with the Manchester School; other historians, similarly, would argue of Bentham that "under his influence *laissez-faire* held the field in English industry and commerce for the greater part of a century."[59] In this vein, Bentham has been described as individualist, laissez-faireist, and liberal.[60]

Other scholars read a completely different Bentham, essentially a modern big-government administrator. Robbins would go so far as to opine, in his important 1953 monograph *The Theory of Economic Policy in English Classical Political Economy,* that after rereading Bentham's *Constitutional Code* (Bentham's project for a practical utopia), "I feel that, in some respects at any rate, modern practice has yet some little distance to go before it catches up with Jeremy Bentham."[61] The legal scholar Julius Stone would write of Bentham and Benthamites that "They cried 'Hands on!' as much as, if not more than, 'Hands off!'"[62] Similarly, Ellen Paul would refer to Bentham as "a meliorist social engineer if there ever was one [who] laid the theoretical groundwork for the enervation of the 'let alone' principle."[63] "By the time Bentham was finished enumerating various 'agenda' for government, his 'be quiet' dictum for government lay mortally wounded," Paul writes.[64] Paul compiles the list of government tasks that Bentham approved—as others have done for Smith—and finds the list quite long.[65] As Colin Holmes writes, "Clearly, Jeremy Bentham was not the supporter of an inflexible *laissez-faire* ideal."[66] Or, even more strenuously, as Charles Rowley would write, "Bentham did not believe in the invisible hand. Self-interest would only lead to the greatest happiness if the law was correctly devised."[67]

The historian J. Bartlet Brebner is the one who would spark much of the revisionist interpretation of Bentham, writing in 1948 that "Jeremy Bentham and John Stuart Mill, who have been commonly represented as typical, almost fundamental, formulators of laissez faire, were in fact the exact opposite, that is, the formulator of state intervention for collectivist ends and his devout apostle."[68] Referring to the British constitutional scholar Albert Venn Dicey, who was identified with the opposite view, Brebner would declare: "In using Bentham as the archetype of British individualism he was conveying the exact opposite of the truth. Jeremy Bentham was the archetype of British collectivism."[69] Numerous historians would line up behind this position.[70] Henry Parris would characterize Dicey's view as "a mere travesty of Benthamism."[71] Jennifer Hart as well would portray the Benthamites as central to the statist interventions.[72] In support of these readings, many cite Bentham's notorious statement that "I have not, I never had, nor ever shall have, any horror, sentimental or anarchical, of the hand of government."[73] Along these lines, Bentham has been called, among other things, "authoritarian, . . . despotic, totalitarian, collectivist, behaviouralist ('a cold-blooded, empirical social engineer'), constructivist, panopticist and paternalist."[74]

And this is only the tip of the iceberg. There is substantial controversy over Bentham's influence on British practice. Everyone agrees that the Benthamites played a key role in staffing royal commissions that ultimately led to interventionist legislation, but they disagree as to whether the results were intended by Bentham, whether the results were inherent in Bentham's thought, and even whether the Benthamites themselves acted intentionally or unwittingly to help bring about statist policies.

There is controversy as well over whether Benthamites preserved or undermined a minimalist state. Some, like Jacob Viner, trace the welfare reforms directly to Bentham. According to Viner, "Bentham was the first person to propose birth-control as a measure of economic reform, and this *before* Malthus had published his first *Essay on the Principle of Population*. The Ministry of Health which he proposed would be made responsible not only for general sanitation and routine public health work, but also for smoke prevention, local health-museums, and the policing of the medical profession to prevent their formation of monopolies."[75] Many, like Ellen Paul, argue that the successors to Bentham, because of their reliance on the principle of utility, ended up eviscerating the laissez-faire doctrine: "in the hands of John Stuart Mill and his successors little was left of noninterventionism but a hollow shell."[76]

Earlier scholars, such as Dicey himself, argued that Benthamites brought about the demise of laissez-faire because of both the logic of utilitarianism, which could be marshaled in favor of government regulation, and the fact that these very Benthamites had replaced a corrupt state with an efficient one. "Faith in laissez-faire suffered an eclipse; hence the principle of utility became an argument in favour, not of individual freedom, but of the absolutism of the State. . . . English administrative mechanism was reformed and strengthened. The machinery was thus provided for the practical extension of the activity of the State. . . . Benthamites, it was then seen, had forged the arms most needed by socialists," Dicey wrote.[77] Still other historians contend that Benthamism had little influence. One historian, Oliver MacDonagh, goes so far in the other direction as to suggest that, in this area, "Benthamism had no influence upon opinion at large or, for that matter, upon the overwhelming majority of public servants."[78]

There are raging controversies over whether laissez-faire actually prevailed in nineteenth-century Britain or instead was merely a myth. For many decades in the early twentieth century, the dominant interpretation was that during the mid-nineteenth century in Britain, there was a zenith of laissez-faire inspired by Bentham's influence in economics. That at least was the thesis of Albert Venn Dicey, which reigned for many years and was shared by many important historians in the early twentieth century.[79] Dicey would write, for instance, that "though *laissez-faire* is not an essential part of Utilitarianism it was practically the most vital part of Bentham's legislative doctrine, and in England gave to the movement for reform of the law, both its power and its character."[80] This reading of English history had many adherents.[81] In 1968 Eric Hobsbawm would write, "By the middle of the nineteenth century government policy in Britain came as near *laissez-faire* as has ever been practicable in a modern state. Government was small and comparatively cheap, and as time went on it became even cheaper by comparison with other states."[82]

Starting in the 1940s, however, this view was challenged by a number of historians, who argued that Britain did not experience much in the way of laissez-faire and that Bentham himself was not much of an individualist in economic matters—or, as Brebner would write, that "Jeremy Bentham was the archetype of British collectivism."[83] Brebner led the charge here too, essentially arguing that the "age of *laissez-faire*" was largely a myth: "laissez faire never prevailed in Great Britain or in any other modern state," Brebner declared.[84] Karl Polanyi, in his seminal work *The Great Transformation,* argued that the fiction of laissez-faire at midcentury was only made possible by "an enormous increase in continuous, centrally organized and controlled interventionism" or, as he famously wrote there, "laissez-faire was planned."[85] Numerous historians, such as Colin Holmes and David Roberts, joined the fray in support of this reappraisal of the earlier period and concluded that there was, contra Dicey, pervasive and growing interventionism in the nineteenth century.[86]

Such revisionism extended into the area of free trade as well. John Nye would demonstrate empirically that "Britain was not as much of a free trader in the nineteenth century as has been previously perceived, especially in comparison to France."[87] Overall, as Roberts would suggest, the Victorian era was not the heyday of laissez-faire, but rather a time of social reform and bureaucratic growth, as well as the starting point for British collectivism.[88] Much of the literature attributed the growing interventionism not to ideology or the force of collectivist ideas, but instead to current events: publicized abuses, accidents, and scandals called for political responses, and that ultimately led to a far larger administrative state than had been envisioned.[89]

There were, naturally, voices on both sides of the debate. In response to the skeptics, other historians and scholars argued that, though perhaps more tempered than originally suggested, a strong laissez-faire attitude had nevertheless moderated much of the movement toward state interventionism.[90] Ellen Paul, for instance, concluded from a review of all the historical evidence that "by comparison with the England of earlier and later centuries, the nineteenth century was a 'high tide' of laissez faire."[91] Arthur Taylor, too, concluded that laissez-faire was "until at least 1870, and arguably for a further twenty-five years beyond that, the strongest impulse influencing the shape and character of governmental economic policy."[92] Paul also marshaled Joseph Spengler's insightful argument that, as a historiographical matter, government interventionism may leave more traces in the historical record than laissez-faire ideas and practices, especially if the latter are more dominant and require less justification.[93]

There are additional controversies over whether David Ricardo, Thomas Malthus, John Stuart Mill, Henry Sidgwick, and J. E. Cairnes gradually transitioned from more laissez-faire beliefs to a more state-interventionist point of view.[94] The proponents of free trade and laissez-faire in the nineteenth century were well identified: the theorists of the Manchester School, Richard Cobden and John Bright; academics such as Herbert Spencer; and journalists and popular writers such as James Wilson, Harriet Martineau, and Jane Marcet.[95] According to some, though, Mill would "extrude the collectivistic tendencies in Benthamism and drive the principle of utility to its statist denouement."[96] Though highly individualist in some ways, Mill had sympathetic evaluations of the socialist Henri de St. Simon, Charles Fourier, and Robert Owen. Mill's disciples, J. E. Cairnes and Henry Sidgwick, would continue in a more collectivist direction. In "Political Economy and Laissez-faire," Cairnes wrote that the principle of laissez-faire was "totally destitute of all scientific authority."[97] Sidgwick too would write that "the general presumption derived from abstract economic reasoning is not in favor of leaving industry altogether to private enterprise, in any community that can usefully be taken as an ideal for the guidance of practical statesmanship; but is on the contrary in favour of supplementing and controlling such enterprise in various ways by the collective action of the community."[98]

One reading of the British historical record is that later Benthamites and Bentham's influence on utilitarians, not Bentham himself, were responsible for the gradual wandering away from laissez-faire. By shifting the intellectual ground from its naturalistic antecedents—from the notion of natural law—to a more utilitarian framework grounded on principles of utility, Bentham paved the way for a gradual evisceration of the laissez-faire ideal. As Josh Cohen reminds us, this is precisely the view that Dewey would take in *Liberalism and Social Action*.[99]

A Final Word

A lot of ink has been spilled trying to reconcile Bentham's economic views and influence. By contrast, practically no one is stretching Bentham's punishment writings in a similar way. No one is quarreling over whether he advocated a "hands-off" or a "hands-on" approach there, because on the punishment side, it was all hands on deck. It was the panopticon prison. It was the grand menu of prices. It was all about fixing the price of crime—about price setting—and in this project, the state was given full throttle, placed front and center. The difference between Bentham's views in the two domains of economics and punishment is overwhelming—regardless of how you read his economics—and it is this difference that reiterates the duality of punishment and economy found in the Physiocratic doctrine.

Yet although there was reiteration, the exact relationship between economy and punishment had changed slightly. Bentham applied economic reasoning to the penal domain. He cared about the efficiency of the panopticon prison, as we saw in the opening of this chapter. He deployed the pleasure and pain calculus to *homo criminalis*. He viewed the criminal sanction as a price mechanism. In this sense, his economic rationality extended into the punishment field. But the bleeding was one way only. *Be quiet* was not, by any means, "the motto, or watch word, of government" in the penal sphere.[100] Instead, in the realm of punishment the government was pulling all the levers.

By a strange twist of fate, Bentham wrote his *Manual of Political Economy* in 1794, the same year that Cesare Beccaria, who at age fifty-six was still a relatively young public servant, passed away in Milan. And with Beccaria, it seems, there also passed away his distinct cameral view of punishment and public economy—his vision of a fully integrated web of commercial, social, and penal intervention. By the early nineteenth century, the space of public economy had been displaced by the liberal turn in economics, by the Revolutionary embrace of Turgot's economic policies in France, and by the long shadow of Adam Smith's *Wealth of Nations* and Bentham's economic writings in the Anglo-Saxon world. In the process, the penal sanction was pushed outside the economic sphere, where an element of natural orderliness would reign. This vision of a spontaneously ordered economic sphere would recur in the mid- to late twentieth century in the more technical vocabulary and stylized manner of the Chicago School.

6

The Chicago School

"From Bentham to Becker": that is the title of Richard Posner's genealogy of the law-and-economics movement in his 2001 book *Frontiers of Legal Theory*.[1] Posner traces the intellectual lineage back to Jeremy Bentham, whom he describes as one of the movement's "most illustrious progenitors."[2] "If one year must be picked for the beginning of the movement, it would be 1968," Posner writes.[3] Why 1968? Because, Posner explains, "in 1968 Gary Becker published his article on crime, reviving and refining Bentham."[4] The article, "Crime and Punishment: An Economic Approach," demonstrated the reach of economic analysis. According to Posner, it proved that "no field of law could not be placed under the lens of economics with illuminating results."[5] According to this first genealogy, Bentham is the precursor and inspiration for Chicago School law and economics—even though, as in the case of Becker, the inspiration may have been inadvertent. "Becker performed an important service for law and economics simply by reviving Bentham's theory of crime," Posner maintains, "and dressing it in the language of modern economics."[6] In this account, Bentham's theory of punishment had lain dormant for 150 years until Becker breathed life back into it.

Posner's account is, naturally, part folktale. Other economists had explored the economic analysis of crime in Bentham's early footsteps, but they tended to be collectivists, such as Henry Sidgwick, one of the intellectual fathers of welfare economics.[7] In Posner's story, Becker was the first to extend Bentham to nonmarket areas like crime and punishment: "The handful of economists between Bentham and Becker who claimed that utility maximization was a universal feature of human psychology . . . did not cite Bentham for this proposition, and, more important, did very little with his insight into the possibility of applying economics to nonmarket behavior."[8]

Richard Epstein, another stalwart of the law-and-economics movement and a professor at the University of Chicago Law School as well, traces the genealogy of law and economics elsewhere. Epstein draws the lineage back to Friedrich Hayek, who had a much less favorable view of Bentham. Epstein's own economic views come out of the Hayekian tradition of natural law theory.[9] Epstein acknowledges the tension and confesses that "the equivocation between natural law theories and consequentialist ones continued in a limited way" throughout his book *Takings: Private Property and the Power of Eminent Domain* (1985).[10] Nevertheless, Epstein became a convert to the law-and-economics approach, in his words "an adherent and practitioner of the art," despite his concerns about the collectivist tendencies of utilitarianism.[11]

Hayek as well was concerned about Bentham, whom he portrayed as a constructivist. Hayek maintained that Bentham's utilitarianism was only superficially individualist, that it ultimately led to collectivism. He argued that "*Benthamite constructivism* has been a major threat to individual liberty and a precursor of totalitarian social control."[12] According to this account, Bentham brought to its knees the traditional liberal principles of English freedom that traversed the writings of Adam Smith and David Hume. "Bentham and his Utilitarians did much to destroy the beliefs which England had in part preserved from the Middle Ages, by their scornful treatment of most of what until then had been the most admired features of the British constitution," Hayek wrote in 1959 in *The Constitution of Liberty*. "And they introduced into Britain what had so far been entirely absent—the desire to remake the whole of the law and institutions on rational principles."[13]

Bentham and Hayek: two starkly different progenitors of the modern economic analysis of law. They are strange bedfellows indeed—and other strange bedfellows followed. One can hardly imagine how both Richard Epstein and Richard Posner became leading members of the same intellectual movement—Epstein as director of the Law and Economics Program at the University of Chicago Law School, Posner as author of the foundational text *Economic Analysis of Law,* and both as dominant figures in law and economics. Equally puzzling is how they would both converge, ultimately, on a similar vision of punishment and political economy—a vision that essentially replicates that curious alchemy of orderliness in the economic realm and state intervention in the penal sphere. How could it be that in both the Benthamite and the Hayekian strands of law and economics, there would remain today this paradox of punishment and political economy?

To see why and how these two different intellectual traditions would ultimately converge, it is crucial to understand how and where their paths crossed. The intersection occurred in October 1960 with the publication of Ronald Coase's article "The Problem of Social Cost." Everyone—whether they are Hayekian or Benthamite, staunch supporters or vocal critics of the economic theory of law—agrees that law and economics grew on the shoulders of the "Coase Theorem." Consider Richard Posner, who wrote: "The proposal of what might grandly be called *the* economic theory of law builds on a pioneering article by Ronald Coase."[14] It is true as well for Richard Epstein, who writes that "Coase's insight of the basic importance of transaction costs in shaping the analysis of legal rules and institutions was clearly correct and . . . offered greater power and clarity of exposition than the simpler models of individual autonomy that I had adopted in my earlier work."[15] In fact, Epstein himself attributes his own conversion and adherence to law and economics between the years 1975 and 1980 to Ronald Coase's work.[16] The centrality of Coase to these different strands of law and economics is also acknowledged in both the authorized biographies and the critical histories of the law-and-economics movement.[17]

Ronald Coase on Welfare Economics

The "Coase Theorem" was distilled from Ronald Coase's research on the political economy of broadcasting, in particular on the allocation of broadcast frequency waves. Coase's research was primarily aimed at the welfare economic program developed by Arthur Pigou in his famous and influential 1920 treatise, *The Economics of Welfare*.[18] Since at least John Stuart Mill and Henry Sidgwick, much of the discipline of economics had focused on the concept of "market failure," especially on "externalities" (situations where a producer does not internalize all the costs of production, but allows some to be borne by neighbors or the larger society, so that the commercial activity is beneficial, on net, to him but imposes social costs on society).[19] Arthur Pigou, the successor to Alfred Marshall as chair of political economy at the University of Cambridge, had argued in his classic 1920 text that the proper way to address externalities was through government-imposed taxes and subsidies. Much of the discipline, thus, had normalized the "Pigovian solution" of tax and transfer. During the postwar period, too, the problem of externalities and other market failures, such as monopolization, dominated the discipline of economics, resulting in policies that expanded significantly the scope of government intervention.

Coase was swimming against this tide and understood his central insight as a reaction against Pigou's system. Coase himself framed his theory as a rejection of Pigou: "The significance to me of the Coase Theorem is that it undermines the Pigovian system," Coase emphasized in 1991.[20] In 1959 Coase had published an article called "The Federal Communications Commission," in which he argued that broadcast frequencies should be allocated in a manner that takes into account economic efficiency—specifically, that frequencies should be assigned to higher-value users. Coase observed that, in a world with no transaction costs, market negotiations tended to produce that very result. The following year, in "The Problem of Social Cost," Coase demonstrated, using hypothetical utility calculations, how firms and individuals could negotiate to find efficient outcomes that would allocate resources to the highest-value users. Coase recognized that such outcomes would only occur in a situation where the transaction costs of negotiation were null or minimal. But he argued that even when transaction costs are non-negligible, courts could try to implement the efficient outcome by determining how rights would be assigned if there were no transaction costs.

This, Coase argued, represented a rejection of Pigovian welfare economics, because it meant that in a world of low transaction costs, there is no need for government to intervene: free-market bargaining would achieve the optimal result. As he explained:

> Pigou's conclusion and that of most economists using standard economic theory was, and perhaps still is, that some kind of government action (usually the imposition of taxes) was required to restrain those whose actions had harmful effects on others, often termed negative externalities. What I showed in that article, as I thought, was that in a regime of zero transaction costs, an assumption of standard economic theory, negotiations between the parties would lead to those arrangements being made which would maximise wealth and this irrespective of the initial assignment of rights. . . . Since standard economic theory assumes transaction costs to be zero, the Coase Theorem demonstrates that the Pigovian solutions are unnecessary in these circumstances.[21]

Coase recognized, naturally, that the assumption of zero costs was somewhat misleading, and therefore he viewed the Coase Theorem as a preliminary step to further research. "I tend to regard the Coase Theorem as a stepping stone on the way to an analysis of an economy with positive transaction costs," he explained. He added: "Of course, it does not imply, when transaction costs are positive, that government actions (such as government operation, regulation or taxation, including subsidies) could not produce a better result than relying on negotiations between individuals in the market. Whether this would be so could be discovered not by studying imaginary governments but what real governments actually do. My conclusion: Let us study the world of positive transaction costs."[22]

But on that matter, Coase himself had some priors—priors that lined up neatly with free-market assumptions. In his 1960 article, Coase expressly stated that "commonly" the benefits of government regulation are outweighed by their costs, that economists have "over-estimate[d] the advantages which come from governmental regulation," and that overall, "government regulation should be curtailed."[23] Coase rehearsed the traditional objections to government regulation, writing that they are "made by a fallible administration subject to political pressures and operating without any competitive check," and "enforced in some cases in which they are clearly inappropriate."[24] Coase intimated, too, that the facts necessary to defend regulation were impossible to obtain. "I am unable to imagine how the data needed for such a taxation system could be assembled," Coase remarked. "Indeed, the proposal to solve the [externality] problems by the use of taxes bristles with difficulties: the problem of calculation, the difference between average and marginal damage, the interrelations between the damage suffered on different properties, etc."[25] And after discussing government regulation to solve the problem of externalities, Coase wrote, "There is, of course, a further alternative, which is to do nothing about the problem at all. And given that the costs involved in solving the problem by regulations issued by the governmental administrative machine will often be heavy . . . , it will no doubt be commonly the case that the gain which would come from regulating the actions which give rise to the harmful effects will be less than the costs involved in Government regulation."[26]

Coase believed that there was too much government regulation and he expressly stated in his famous 1960 article that governmental intervention should be "curtailed"—despite the fact that, as he himself emphasized repeatedly, there was not yet any empirical evidence on the matter:

> All solutions have costs and there is no reason to suppose that government regulation is called for simply because the problem is not well handled by the market or the firm. . . . It is my belief that economists, and policy-makers generally, have tended to over-estimate the advantages, which come from governmental regulation. But this belief, even if justified, does not do more than suggest that government regulation should be curtailed. It does not tell us where the boundary line should be drawn.[27]

Coase's overall message to government administration was clear: if transaction costs are low, do nothing because free-market transactions will produce the most efficient outcome; and if transaction costs are high, "commonly" do nothing and "curtail" your interventionist tendencies because it is too hard to assemble the necessary data, the calculations are intractable, and government tends to be inefficient.[28]

The Rebirth of Natural Order

Let's stop here for a moment and freeze this frame. For it is precisely here that Coase introduced an idea of orderliness: a presumption, a bias, a prejudice that favors the natural mechanisms of market exchange over state intervention. Right here. Of course, Coase used a different vocabulary; his jargon was more technical, his lexicon more scientific, and these differences in language matter because they made his argument more persuasive. Rhetorically, a mathematical model, even a hypothetical mathematical model, does much more work today than mere talk of "natural order." But beneath the new veneer lies the same basic intuition as the Physiocrats: that a hands-off approach in economics will serve us better than government intervention; that markets and exchange will produce a higher net product, if left to their own devices. François Quesnay would undoubtedly have been amused at this reframing of an "ordre naturel."

It is important to emphasize that there was absolutely no good reason, nor any need, to introduce this bias here. Coase sincerely believed that there was not enough empirical evidence on these matters, and he would spend most of his life encouraging more empirical research, including case-by-case, fact-intensive analyses where transaction costs were present. This was not a situation where Coase could say, "I have looked at all the evidence, and I have discovered that regulation is inefficient." In fact, there was no empirical research at the time and there still is very little today. As George Stigler observed in his *Memoirs,* "We now have begun to study the nature and size of transaction costs—something we did not do before—but I confess that surprisingly little of this work has been done in the nearly three decades that have passed since the Coase Theorem was published."[29] So this was a situation, instead, where Coase was essentially saying: "We need to do a lot more empirical research because we don't know much about these complex cases, and, by the way, I really favor the free market."

Note the parallel to Bentham (at least, one reading of Bentham): as an empiricist, there was no reason for Bentham, in his *Manual of Political Economy,* to state a preference for quietism. If he had been faithful to his empiricist priors, Bentham would simply have called for utility calculations without presuming who had better information, who had more self-interest, and where the chips would land. In both cases, Coase and Bentham could have remained entirely agnostic and left the whole domain to the empiricists. Instead, they both injected an idea of natural order. This is important, as we will see later. For now, though, let's move to the next frame.

Both the Hayekian and the Benthamite law-and-economics traditions fully embraced the Coase Theorem. This is clear in Richard Epstein's writings, for instance, where he declares, "The object of the law is to develop a set of rules that promotes the closest possible approximation to the world of zero transaction costs."[30] Or, as Epstein writes elsewhere, "a concern with transactions costs plays the central organizing role in formulating the legal responses to many classic private law problems."[31] Posner's embrace of the Coase Theorem is also obvious in his writings summarizing the central insight of law and economics: "Where, despite the law's best efforts, market transaction costs remain high, the law should simulate the market's allocation of resources by assigning property rights to the highest-valued users."[32]

Converging on Coase

The question is, why? Why did two very different intellectual traditions converge on the Coase Theorem and ultimately embrace that tension between orderliness in economics and the need for ordering through punishment—what I have called "neoliberal penality"? Let me telegraph the response first, before offering a detailed explanation.

First, the Hayekian pathway is entirely logical. The link back from Hayek's notion of "spontaneous order" to Smith's naturalism is plain, even though the new iteration speaks a new language and draws on new models from computer science. The link forward to the Coasian bias against regulation is also logical in many ways, both institutional and intellectual. Hayek was in part responsible for bringing Ronald Coase to the University of Chicago and was "very influential," as Coase himself acknowledged, on his intellectual development. "Hayek was terribly important at the London School of Economics in ways that perhaps people wouldn't realize," Coase emphasized in 1983. "He helped to make our theory more precise. . . . Really he was very important. Our theory was very sloppy, and Hayek did a lot to improve things."[33] Here, the genealogical enterprise is made easy.

The second, the Benthamite welfarist link, is less obvious. In some ways, it is somewhat counterintuitive—particularly from within a strong collectivist reading of Bentham. One could well imagine a Benthamite welfarist view of the criminal sanction that eschewed all notion of natural order. It would go something like this: all human behavior should be subject to a welfare calculus in order to determine which behaviors can be regulated by means of punishment so as to achieve a level of that behavior and of associated social expenditures that minimizes overall social costs. In this view, crime would be defined as any behavior that should be subject to the criminal sanction, and criminal law would apply to any and all behaviors that could be efficiently regulated by means of the penal sanction—whether fines, shaming, imprisonment, or other punishments. According to this perspective, there is no natural order; all behaviors are potentially subject to regulation, regardless of whether they are market transactions or market bypassing. The "free market" plays no role in the analysis and confers no immunities. Further, there is no division of punishment and economy. There is no sacrosanct sphere of the competitive market that is immune from our penal gaze. There are just individual behaviors, each of which triggers a punishment/welfare calculus. Such a vision would be entirely consistent with a purely constructivist reading of Bentham, that is, a reading of Bentham that deemphasizes the Smithian influence of harmonious self-interest.

Gary Becker almost achieved that genuinely welfarist position. He missed the mark, though, because of a simple error: instead of defining crime through the welfare calculus, he took for granted the statutory definition of crime. It is precisely that move—taking the definition of crime as given—that then allowed Richard Posner to inject a "free market" tilt into Becker's theory.[34] It is precisely what allowed Posner to define crime as "market bypassing" and to insert the Coasian bias against intervention in the economic domain. More important, it is what allowed him to enlist Bentham and Becker in a project that naturalizes market efficiency and pushes punishment outside the market. And it is what ultimately replicates the duality of legal despotism: order in the market and state intervention outside. Now on to the details.

Hayek and the Road to Spontaneous Order

"Spontaneous order" lies at the heart of Friedrich Hayek's thought and writings.[35] Hayek himself italicized the term for emphasis and elaborated on it at length as a "grown order," a "self-generating or endogenous order," what the Greeks called a "kosmos" meaning originally, Hayek explained, "a right order in a state or a community."[36] This order is the social theoretic insight that founds Hayek's worldview and his economic understanding. "It would be no exaggeration to say," Hayek declared in 1973, "that social theory begins with—and has an object only because of—the discovery that there exist orderly structures which are the product of the action of many men but are not the result of human design."[37]

It is hard to communicate fully the importance of this notion of spontaneous order without physically imposing the full text on the reader. Hayek opens his three-volume work *Law, Legislation and Liberty*—after an epigraph from Adam Smith's discussion of the invisible hand "in the great chessboard of human society"—with the following statement: "The central concept around which the discussion of this book will turn is that of order, and particularly the distinction between two kinds of order which we will provisionally call 'made' and 'grown' orders."[38] Order simply is the organizing principle of Hayek's thought, as he explained in a lecture in 1967:

> The achievement of human purposes is possible only because we recognize the world we live in as orderly. . . . Without the knowledge of such an order of the world in which we live, purposive action would be impossible. . . . While we have the terms "arrangement" or "organisation" to describe a *made* order, we have no single distinctive word to describe an order which has formed *spontaneously.* The ancient Greeks were more fortunate in this respect. . . . [A]n order which existed or formed itself independently of any human will directed to that end they called *cosmos*. . . . Only a *cosmos* can thus constitute an open society, while a political order conceived as an organization must remain closed or tribal.[39]

This central social theoretic insight led Hayek to his interest, as an economist, in "the spontaneously formed order of the market."[40] The spontaneously formed order occurs precisely "because in the course of millennia men develop rules of conduct which lead to the formation of such an order of the separate spontaneous activities of individuals."[41] Hayek traced the notion of spontaneous order to the work of Bernard Mandeville, David Hume, and Adam Smith. Mandeville was the originator, the one who inaugurated "the definite breakthrough in modern thought of the twin ideas of evolution and of the spontaneous formation of an order."[42] Mandeville, "a mastermind" for this very insight, is the one who inspired Hume: "I do not intend to pitch my claim on behalf of Mandeville higher than to say that he made Hume possible."[43] And Mandeville and Hume, in turn, provided the material that made Adam Smith's idea of the "invisible hand" possible—the very idea that, combined with a notion of cultural evolution, was at the core of Hayek's notion of spontaneous order.[44]

Hayek wrote that Smith's idea of the "invisible hand" was Smith's most significant contribution to social theory.[45] Indeed, Smith's "recognition that a man's efforts will benefit more people" was precisely at the root of Hayek's notion of spontaneous order.[46] Hayek borrowed Smith's expression of the invisible hand to correct and improve on Smith himself: the successful entrepreneur, Hayek wrote, "is led by the invisible hand of the market to bring the succor of modern conveniences to the poorest homes he does not even know."[47] Elaborating on this point in the introductory passages of *The Fatal Conceit* in 1988, Hayek wrote:

> Economics has from its origins been concerned with how an extended order of human interaction comes into existence through a process of variation, winnowing and sifting far surpassing our vision or our capacity to design. Adam Smith was the first to perceive that we have stumbled upon methods of ordering human economic cooperation that exceed the limits of our knowledge and perception. His "invisible hand"

> had perhaps better have been described as an invisible or unsurveyable pattern. We are led—for example by the pricing system in market exchange—to do things by circumstances of which we are largely unaware and which produce results that we do not intend. In our economic activities we do not know the needs which we satisfy nor the sources of the things which we get. Almost all of us serve people whom we do not know, and even of whose existence we are ignorant; and we in turn constantly live on the services of other people of whom we know nothing. . . . Modern economics explains how such an extended order can come into being.[48]

Hayek updated Smith's metaphor, turning to the more modern sciences—computation, computer science, and information technology—to give greater resonance to the idea of orderliness. Here again, the new iteration would differ in important respects, displacing an older and more staid image of hydraulics and simplistic physics with a far more updated and contemporary figure of speech. Hayek would promote the notion of information processing, in a computational sense, as a central component of market coordination. The historian and philosopher of economic thought, Philip Mirowski, has demonstrated the metaphorical transformation of the notion of orderliness into something more akin to what he calls "cyborg science," especially in Hayek's work.[49] (A cyborg is a cybernetic organism that mixes natural and artificial systems and intelligence.) Mirowski in fact refers to Hayek as "the pivotal agent provocateur in disseminating the germs of these cyborg themes" and to Hayek's *Use of Knowledge in Society* as "the manifesto (in retrospect) of the Cyborg Revolution."[50] Hayek's updating would reinvigorate the idea of natural order.

It is also important to recognize that Hayek positioned his defense of liberty to counter a conception of liberalism that he associated with Jeremy Bentham and English utilitarianism. The latter, according to Hayek, stemmed from a Continental European tradition, from the work of "Voltaire, Rousseau, Condorcet and the French Revolution which became the ancestor of modern socialism."[51] Hayek placed Benthamite utilitarianism in this lineage: "English utilitarianism has taken over much of this Continental tradition."[52] And so it is Bentham who essentially represents the break from the more enlightened version of liberalism (Hume, Smith, Burke) that Hayek espoused. As Hayek explained, "Bentham and his followers replaced the English legal tradition by a constructivist utilitarianism derived more from Continental rationalism."[53]

In this sense, Bentham was the constructivist foil against which Hayek developed his social theory—an interplay that is, historically, fascinating. Because of the ideological drift of Benthamism during the late nineteenth century, Hayek's reaction against market interference could not fall back on the utility principle, but instead had to draw on notions of naturalism—on Smith and spontaneous order. As a historical matter, Bentham had come to stand for the slide toward interventionism. At least, that is the story among contemporary libertarian theorists.[54]

Hayek and the Chicago School of Economics

Hayek had a strong influence on the economic vision of Milton Friedman and George Stigler, the leading economists who shaped the Chicago School of economics.[55] Hayek galvanized these young economists with his book *The Road to Serfdom* in 1944, brought them together at the Mont Pèlerin Hotel in 1947, and helped establish, with the Volker Fund, the institutional framework at the University of Chicago Law School that would give birth to the law-and-economics movement.[56]

At the first Mont Pèlerin gathering, Hayek proposed two basic principles for the assembled group: individualism and private property.[57] Milton Friedman would make those his calling, as would the Chicago School more generally. As George Stigler recounts in his *Memoirs*, Friedman was "the primary architect of the Chicago School" and specifically identified, as one of the main aspects or "fundamental contributions to the formation of the Chicago School," Friedman's "strong defenses of laissez-faire policies."[58] In his own words, Milton Friedman would describe the Chicago School as "stand[ing] for belief in the efficacy of the free market as a means of organizing resources, for skepticism about government intervention into economic affairs, and for emphasis on the quantity theory of money as a key factor in producing inflation."[59]

The relationship between these free-market tenets and punishment, however, would be left to the lawyers, especially to Richard Epstein. Epstein was himself significantly influenced by Hayek, whom he considered one of the most, if not the most, important voice for individual liberty, private property, and limited government in the twentieth century. In the preface to his *Simple Rules for a Complex World* (1995), Epstein singles out Hayek as his source of inspiration regarding "strong private rights and limited government." "In reaching this conclusion," Epstein writes, "I have been heavily influenced by the work of Friedrich Hayek, in particular his important manifesto, *The Road to Serfdom*."[60]

According to Epstein, it is punishment that delimits the free market. "I do not believe that a just society is one that has no coercive laws," Epstein explains. "I do think that the prohibition against force and fraud is the central component of a just order."[61] The criminal sanction polices the market in the case of fraud and coercion, especially where civil remedies are inadequate due to the insolvency of the culprit.[62] Aside from this legitimate form of criminal intervention, the state must avoid as much as possible interfering in voluntary market exchange: "Government must avoid the excesses of regulation that have become part and parcel of the modern legal order," Epstein emphasizes. "We must not pass laws that disrupt the operation of normal competitive markets. We must minimize the level of progressive and special taxes."[63]

The view of spontaneous order in the economic domain, bordered by the criminal sanction for fraud and violence, reproduces closely the Physiocratic model of legal despotism. Recall that the Physiocrats believed in positive legal intervention only in the case of fraud and violence, or for *les voleurs et les méchans*, as Quesnay would say.[64] In sum, within the Hayekian tradition of law and economics, the link back to the Physiocrats is hardly controversial. *"Spontaneous order"* takes the place of natural order—updated by means of computer science metaphors, but clearly connected to the earlier notion nonetheless.

The link forward to efficiency is also clear. It was present in Hayek's thought from the beginning. Spontaneous order was beneficial to everyone in society, Hayek argued, in part because it was maximally efficient; it represented the most advantageous utilization of resources. The market, Hayek wrote, represents a "more efficient allocation of resources than any design could achieve."[65] This view would be demonstrated and made scientific by the Coase Theorem, and today it represents Hayek's legacy. As the economist and presidential adviser Larry Summers reportedly stated: "What's the single most important thing to learn from an economics course today? What I tried to leave my students with is the view that the invisible hand is more powerful than the hidden hand. Things will happen in well-organized efforts without direction, controls, plans. That's the consensus among economists. That's the Hayek legacy."[66]

The Benthamite Tradition

Richard Posner once wrote, "It would be extremely difficult to establish a causal relation between Bentham and an event—the birth of the law and economics movement—that occurred almost a century and a half after his death. But I think he can be shown to be one of the inspirers."[67] In Posner's view, it is Bentham, not Hayek, who is the proximate cause of the economic analysis of law. Posner's attachment to this intellectual lineage has been consistent. In a notable (and somewhat remarkable) roundtable discussion among members of the Chicago School held in 1981—a discussion that included, among others, Gary Becker, Walter Blum, Robert Bork, Ronald Coase, Harold Demsetz, Aaron Director, Milton Friedman, Edmund Kitch, William Landes, Jesse Markham, George Priest, and George Stigler—Posner was the first to declare Jeremy Bentham a progenitor of law and economics.[68]

Bentham's central contribution, according to Posner, was twofold: he advanced the psychological theory that individuals seek to maximize pleasure or happiness over pain, and he suggested that all men calculate their welfare. This combination of psychological and cognitive insights led to the theory of rational utility maximization, from which the field of economics has drawn.

The "clearest evidence" of Bentham's influence on the modern economic analysis of law, according to Posner, is Gary Becker's analysis of crime and punishment, which Posner notes "has turned out to be a fount of economic writing on crime and its control."[69] The inspiration was simple: to apply economic rationality—the utilitarian calculus of pain and pleasure, or the simple analysis of costs and benefits—outside the narrow field of macroeconomics. That was Bentham's key insight. "Bentham may be taken to have invented nonmarket economics," Posner notes.[70] "His invention lay fallow for almost as long as his theory of crime and punishment."[71] Until Gary Becker.[72]

To understand how the Benthamite branch of law and economics would converge with the Hayekian, it is important to discuss two developments: the evolution of the central idea of "efficiency," and the development of their theory of criminal law. This time, let's start with crime and punishment.

Becker on Crime and Punishment

Gary Becker's economic approach, in his 1968 paper, was anchored on a social welfare model. Here Becker shied away from broad statements of market efficiency, preferring to engage in technical analyses of social costs. The key mechanism in Becker's model is that the demand curve for crime, like most demand curves, is downward sloping: as crime becomes more expensive, fewer and fewer people are willing to engage in criminal conduct. This is the foundation of the economic approach to crime and the central egalitarian insight of Becker's model.

In this sense, Becker's approach did away with other troubling criminological theories. Becker's intervention was a rejection of the psychological and criminological theories of the twentieth century that had produced the excesses of both social defense and penal welfarism. As Becker emphasized in his paper, "A useful theory of criminal behavior can dispense with special theories of anomie, psychological inadequacies, or inheritance of special traits, and simply extend the economist's usual analysis of choice."[73] The economic model assumes only that an individual—any one of us—would engage in illegal activity as long as the benefits outweigh the costs, that is, as long as the price is right. As a result, a form of equality underlay the economic approach, an ideal of equality that would pull the rug from under the dominant discourse of rehabilitation. Becker's approach tapped into the critique of the asylum that was brewing in the work of David Rothman, Michel Foucault, Thomas Szasz, and others. It represented a highly progressive move toward doing away with the types of psychological, genetic, or behavioral theories that had "gone wrong"—that had led to hyperinstitutionalization in asylums, excessive forms of social control or social defense, even sterilization and eugenics. The rational-choice assumption was effectively the great equalizer. Precisely for this reason, many, including Foucault himself, would come to admire this aspect of Becker's theory. The paradox, it seems, would reveal itself only later.

At the same time, Becker's approach was a clear alternative to the conservative law-and-order movement. The timing is important here. As Katherine Beckett reminds us, in 1964, the Republican presidential candidate, Barry Goldwater, had announced that "the abuse of law and order in this country is going to be an issue [in this election]—at least I'm going to make it one because I think the responsibility has to start some place."[74] George Wallace in Alabama, at the time, campaigned on the refrain that the Supreme Court was "bending over backwards to help criminals."[75] Goldwater's new priority helped to inaugurate a law-and-order platform that would come to engulf much of the country over the next several decades. Jonathan Simon traces this history exquisitely in his *Governing through Crime* (2007), as does David Garland in *The Culture of Control* (2001).

In this historical context, Becker's approach constituted a progressive move that countered the race baiting and culture bashing of the conservatives. We are all potential criminals, Becker would tell us. Each and every one of us would commit a crime if the price were right. Becker's model emphasized marginal analysis. It focused on changes in behavior associated with a marginal change in incentives. Consequently criminal law enforcement would, in Becker's model, hinge on social cost and welfare maximization. That is, the ideal amount of law enforcement would be tied to the calculation of both crime and policing (and corrections). The optimal level of enforcement of any particular crime would be that which minimized both the costs associated with the crime and the costs of repressing that crime through prevention and punishment.

The central contribution of Becker's model is to pinpoint, given a certain definition of crime, what level of policing and punishment minimizes total social costs—or as Becker provocatively wrote, "How many offenses *should* be permitted and how many offenders *should* go unpunished?"[76] It is clear that there are tradeoffs in this paradigm. Some crimes may be better cost-reducers than others: costly crimes that cost little to deter may be more efficient to prosecute, in contrast to low-cost crimes that are expensive to deter. But the determination of which crimes to enforce and the value that we put on particular crimes ultimately turns on the penal code, and in that sense, crime is defined outside the model. And because crime is defined outside the model, Becker offered no indication of what should be criminalized—leaving it to the lawyers to define crimes. It is here that the trouble began.

Becker's model could have led to a definition of crime based on welfare maximization: in this view, crime could have been defined as any human behavior that can be most efficiently regulated by means of the criminal sanction. Or, more robustly, any human behavior that, when criminalized properly, maximizes social welfare. In other words, Becker could have applied his model to behavior writ large, rather than to criminal behavior narrowly defined by the penal code. And it would have been possible, according to the Beckerian model, to determine for each behavior whether it contributes to social welfare or whether instead it would maximize welfare to criminalize and enforce prohibitions on such behavior. Such an analysis would have identified as "crimes" those behaviors that both have a net cost to society and can be deterred most effectively by the criminal sanction.

This more radical approach would have meant that all domains of economic, social, and political life would have been subject to potential criminal supervision. It would have meant that the penal sanction, at least theoretically, could have extended throughout economy and society. In this sense, it would have replicated in a more modern vocabulary the cameralist reading of Beccaria, insofar as all aspects of social life could have been regulated through and through. Becker, however, did not take this path. He noted, for instance, that "the concept of harm and the function relating its amount to the activity level are familiar to economists from their many discussions of activities causing external diseconomies. From this perspective, criminal activities *are an important subset* of the class of activities that cause diseconomies, with the level of criminal activities measured by the number of offenses."[77] Becker did not broaden the scope of the analysis to treat all "diseconomies." Instead, he merely acknowledged that the penal sphere forms part of a larger and growing regulatory web:

> Since the turn of the century, legislation in Western countries has expanded rapidly to reverse the brief dominance of laissez-faire during the nineteenth century. The state no longer merely protects against violations of person and property through murder, rape, or burglary but also restricts "discrimination" against certain minorities, collusive busi-

> ness arrangements, "jaywalking," travel, the materials used in construction, and thousands of other activities. The activities restricted not only are numerous but also range widely, affecting persons in very different pursuits and of diverse social backgrounds, education levels, ages, races, etc.[78]

Despite his recognition of the potential seamlessness of the criminal sanction and other forms of regulation, Becker confined his analysis to positive statutory law—a limitation that allowed the lawyer-economists to define crime, and that ultimately oriented Becker's model back in the direction of the Physiocrats. The resulting model was modified to be sure by a welfare calculus that extended into the penal domain; but it nonetheless assumed orderliness in one arena and not in the other.

The Lawyer Defines Crime

It fell on Richard Posner to define the notion of "crime." The trouble is, he did not define crime based on a welfare analysis, but instead on a presumption of market efficiency. Posner relied, essentially, on the Coase Theorem, with its natural-order bias. In this sense, Posner embedded the free-market presumption right into the very conception of crime—in the very delineation of legal rights. Posner writes: "I argue that what is forbidden is a class of inefficient acts."[79]

In this framework, crime becomes "market bypassing." The conventional criminal act—theft, robbery, burglary, even murder—represents an attempt, in Posner's view, to go around the free market. Not just the market for the goods in question—the television that is stolen, the automobile that is carjacked—but also the market for labor. It represents an express bypassing of the traditional means of obtaining money, namely, working. "The market transaction that [the criminal] bypasses is the exchange of his labor for money in a lawful occupation. But it is still market bypassing," Posner emphasizes.[80]

This is true, Posner tells us, even for crimes of passion—for rape and passionate murder. "Crimes of passion," Posner writes, "often bypass implicit markets—for example, in friendship, love, respect."[81] Rape represents, for Posner, an attempt to avoid a regular market—where the market is understood as a system where agents voluntarily transfer benefits to one another for compensation. Rape bypasses the market for sex and the market for marriage: of the rapist, Posner writes, "If he spent his time raping rather than dating women he would be bypassing an implicit market."[82] Rape is inefficient, Posner contends, for society as a whole—even if not, necessarily, for the rapist—because it violates the central mechanism of markets, namely, determining exchangeable value. "The essential characteristic of a market, and the source of the ethical appeal of market systems," Posner explains, "is that in a market people have to be compensated for parting with the things that have value to them, unless transaction costs are prohibitive. Someone who gets his satisfactions in life from beating up other people, without compensating them, rather than from engaging in trade with them is thus bypassing explicit markets."[83]

In Posner's view, the criminal law maps onto a simple formula: it prescribes acts that are inefficient in the sense in which they are not governed by the laws of the free market. It is in this sense that "the prohibition against rape is to the marriage and sex 'markets' as the prohibition against theft is to explicit markets in goods and services."[84] These acts, because they are inefficient, do not increase the welfare of society. For Posner, the criminal sanction has an economic function, not only because all human activity can be analyzed as market activity, but also because the criminal sanction is intended to deter behaviors that are not economically efficient. It is precisely for these reasons that Posner is at a loss why certain categories of purportedly efficient behavior are criminalized, such as voluntary exchanges that are incidental to criminal acts (such as pimping, dealing in pornography, or selling babies for adoption).[85] These categories of efficient behavior "create obvious difficulties for a positive economic analysis of law," Posner acknowledges.[86] He adds: "It is hard for an economist to understand why the voluntary exchange of valuable goods should be criminal. Such exchange, prima facie at least, promotes rather than reduces efficiency—whether it concerns hard-core or soft-core pornography, cocaine or cigarettes, common carriage or contract carriage."[87]

Notice the striking parallel with Du Pont de Nemours's critique of Beccaria: recall how Du Pont vehemently criticized Beccaria for arguing that persons who evade tariffs should be dealt with harshly by the criminal authorities. Beccaria had been arguing for a more egalitarian enforcement of the criminal law that would not shield the wealthy, and Du Pont had criticized him from an efficiency perspective, arguing that the merchant's resistance to tariffs and transportation of contraband was economically efficient and proper, and therefore morally justified. Posner makes exactly the same move here: the penal code should not criminalize behavior that is economically efficient and that increases, rather than decreases, social welfare.

The bottom line, according to Posner, is that human transactions that operate through a market—a market writ large in the sense that it includes sex and pleasure—are normally efficient and therefore should not be criminalized. The penal sanction should be reserved for behaviors that avoid or bypass the market. This view has both a positive and a normative aspect. As a positive claim, it describes and explains the reach of the criminal law. As

Posner observes, "the major criminal prohibitions seem explicable as measures for discouraging inefficient behavior rather than for achieving moral objectives that economics may not be able to explain—the major exception being the prohibition of victimless crimes."[88] From this positivist perspective, it also explains the need for criminal sanctions rather than civil sanctions—at least among the poor. In Posner's view, penal sanctions are necessary because they alone will deter inefficient behavior. "Much of this market bypassing cannot be deterred by tort law—that is, by privately enforced damage suits. The optimal damages that would be required for deterrence would so frequently exceed the offender's ability to pay that public enforcement and nonmonetary sanctions such as imprisonment are required."[89] But it also, naturally, has an important normative dimension: it sets the contours of what the criminal law should punish.

This explains, then, the passage quoted in the Introduction, whose reference to the market will probably make far more sense now:

> The major function of criminal law in a capitalist society is to prevent people from bypassing the system of voluntary, compensated exchange—the "market," explicit or implicit—in situations where, because transaction costs are low, the market is a more efficient method of allocating resources than forced exchange. . . . When transaction costs are low, the market is, virtually by definition, the most efficient method of allocating resources. Attempts to bypass the market will therefore be discouraged by a legal system bent on promoting efficiency.[90]

Let's stop again and now freeze this frame. It is precisely here that Posner inserts into Becker's model the assumption of market efficiency—and with it a notion of natural order and the resulting tension of neoliberal penality. Right here is where Posner embeds the Coase Theorem into Becker's model: "When transaction costs are low, the market is, virtually by definition, the most efficient method of allocating resources." The Coase Theorem, then, is what allows Posner to take the next step and assert that in a market society, we should criminalize market bypassing.

Now Posner would try to intuit the claim of efficiency, render it obvious, practically tautological. He would argue that traditional crimes are, by their very definition, obviously inefficient. Traditional crimes are inefficient because they are socially expensive: they involve far greater costs, in terms of policing and judging, than would an ordinary market exchange. "If I covet my neighbor's car," Posner explains, "it is more efficient to force me to negotiate with my neighbor—to pay him his price—than it is to allow me to take his car subject to being required by a court to pay the neighbor whatever the court decides the car is worth."[91] Theft is inefficient, in this view, because it involves courts, police, judges, lawyers, and so on. As Posner explained originally in 1973 in the first edition of *Economic Analysis of Law:*

> Theft is punished because it is inefficient to permit the market to be bypassed in this way. Only two parties are involved; if the automobile is really worth more to the thief, a sale can readily be arranged. We prefer this to his taking the car without the owner's consent. The taking substitutes for an inexpensive market transaction a costly legal transaction, in which a court must measure the relative values of the automobile to the parties.[92]

This is obvious, right? Unfortunately not. The theft and the contract—both the traditional crime and the voluntary, compensated exchange—are embedded in complex and expensive legal regimes that require enforcement, courts, lawyers and judges, remedies, liens, marshals and constables, title companies, and large government agencies (from the Department of Motor Vehicles to the Department of Corrections). To focus on the micro-exchange—the handshake and a check, if you will—in the case of a "voluntary market transaction" but on the institutional framework built around a property offense in the case of theft is to commit a sleight of hand. Sales of cars are embedded in equally complex and costly legal regimes, practices, and institutions. To claim that the theft is by definition inefficient is to simply ignore Becker's economic approach to crime and punishment, in which the question of efficiency also involves which *kind* of sanction, criminal or civil, minimizes social costs. It also ignores Becker's central point that allowing *some* thefts in all likelihood maximizes social welfare. Instead of conducting a Beckerian analysis, Posner asserts a simplistic and incorrect definition of crime. And in that very act, Posner injects the free-market bias into the analysis of crime and punishment, producing convergence with the Hayekians on the earlier Physiocratic duality of economy and society.

The Efficiency of the Market

Ultimately, in these writings, the Physiocratic belief in natural order metamorphoses into a faith in the efficiency of "free" exchange. The earlier, more nebulous concept of an "economic system" is refined and narrowed to the "market." To unpack this claim, a few observations are necessary. First, it is crucial to properly understand how the contemporary use of the term "efficiency" itself becomes refined and improved—and in the process, so much more persuasive. As a result of the work of economists like Vilfredo Pareto, Nicholas Kaldor, and John Hicks, the field of welfare analysis developed a far more workable definition of efficiency. Earlier versions of the concept of welfare maximization had aggregated individual welfare without always paying attention to particular individuals whose welfare might decline. This was true, to a certain extent, of Bentham himself. In his *Introduction to the Principles of Morals and Legislation,* where he clearly defined all his terms, Bentham wrote, "An action then may be said to be conformable to the principle of utility, or, for shortness' sake, to utility, (meaning with respect to the community at large) when the tendency it has to augment the happiness of the community is greater than any it has to diminish it."[93] The interest of the community, in this formulation, represents the sum of the interests of the individuals, but increasing the total utility of the community may still mean that some individuals end up worse off. The utility principle, which Bentham would also discuss under the rubric of "the *greatest happiness* or *greatest felicity* principle," might still allow for decreased utility of some individuals.[94]

In the twentieth century, this collective notion of welfare would give way to more refined definitions of "efficiency." The first, associated with Pareto, provides that an improvement in collective welfare requires that absolutely no individual be made worse off. In other words, a Pareto improvement is possible if some people are made better off, but none worse off. This gives rise to the notion of a Pareto efficient (or Pareto optimal) outcome, which is one in which no further Pareto improvements can be made. It also gave rise to another definition of efficiency, the Kaldor-Hicks efficient outcome, where persons who would be made better off by a Pareto improvement could hypothetically compensate those who are made worse off, so that a Pareto efficient result would have obtained at least in theory. These crisper definitions of efficiency are now used instead of the earlier, looser notion of welfare maximization.[95]

Once the Pareto and Kaldor-Hicks refinements are in place, it becomes far easier to argue that "efficient" outcomes are in fact neutral, objective, or nonnormative, since no one should be opposed to a Pareto improvement in the distribution of resources (unless, of course, equity matters). Some view these Pareto and Kaldor-Hicks refinements as "a much weaker form of utilitarianism," since they narrow the category of welfare improvements and eviscerate the possibility of collective welfare debates.[96] Some argue that they render the entire economic analysis trivial and marginal, something everyone could agree about and that therefore functions only at the margins.[97] I think otherwise. Making the term "efficiency" so much less controversial has in fact empowered the welfarist argument, at least in the legal domain. This is especially true since, as Coase admitted, it is generally impossible to imagine assembling the empirical data to support any of these complex welfare calculations. Being able to claim that a legal rule or allocation of resources is Pareto efficient is far more persuasive than to say that it maximizes collective welfare. It facilitates a myth of neutrality. It allows proponents of law and economics to argue, as Posner does, that efficiency "offers a neutral standpoint on politically controversial legal topics."[98] In most legal controversies, we are told, lawyers tend to favor either the propertied or the propertyless. "The economist favors neither side, only efficiency."[99] Clearly, the definition of "efficient" has become more exact and, with that, does a lot more work.

Second, within the Chicago School of economics, the notion of "efficiency" has become inextricably linked with markets.[100] At its core, the Chicago model rests on a few central and simple premises: "the rational pursuit of economic self-interest by economic actors [is] taken as given, competition [is] seen as inherent in and intrinsic to economic life, and market-generated outcomes [are] thought to be superior to those resulting from government interference with the market mechanism."[101] Friedman, Stigler, and other economists at Chicago would build on precisely these premises to demonstrate the "nexus between competitive markets and efficient outcomes," and to argue for "less government intervention, fewer wealth redistribution policies, reliance on voluntary exchange and on the common law for mediating conflicts, and an across-the-board promotion of more private enterprise, which, based on the evidence provided by their empirical research, would facilitate a more efficient allocation of resources."[102]

Third, this refined and central tenet—namely, the efficiency of the market—was picked up in turn by the lawyers in the law-and-economics movement. Here it is important to keep in mind the tight institutional connections leading from the Chicago School of economics to the emergence of law and economics at the University of Chicago Law School. Elaborate treatments of this topic exist already, and I could not do justice without a significant detour—which I would like to avoid at this point.[103] So let me simply telegraph here some connections.

The institutional link began early, in 1939, with the appointment of the first professor of economics at the University of Chicago Law School, Henry Simons. A few years later, in 1945, Friedrich Hayek negotiated the establishment at the law school of the Free Market Study project, a center to promote private enterprise and free market ideas. A Chicago economist, Aaron Director, was hired as project director of the Free Market Study, appointed to the law faculty, and in 1958 founded the *Journal of Law and Economics* at the law school. Meanwhile, in 1950, Hayek joined the Committee on Social Thought, and the ensuing period was marked by intense intellectual collaboration between the Chicago School economists and the growing law-and-economics program at the law school. The economist Ronald Coase was appointed to the University of Chicago Law School in 1964, following the publication in 1960 of "The Problem of Social Cost," and became co-editor, with Aaron Director, of the *Journal.* During this period, the law-and-economics program at the law school brought together, in addition to those already mentioned, Walter Blum, Robert Bork, Harold Demsetz, Edmund Kitch, William Landes, and George Priest. By 1973, Richard Posner, then a young professor at the University of Chicago Law School, had published the first edition of his treatise *Economic Analysis of Law,* which established the movement in the discipline of legal theory. The institutional links continue to the present, with the Posner-Becker blog, joint workshops, and a thriving program in law and economics at the law school—and now, for that matter, at all major law schools in the United States, in part through the financial backing of the John M. Olin Foundation.

The lawyers in this mix would take the Coase Theorem and derive two key corollaries that would ground their economic approach to the law. Recall the core of the Coase Theorem: First, where transaction costs are low or nil, market negotiation will result in the optimally efficient allocation of rights and distribution of resources. In such a situation, there is no need for state intervention, because individuals and firms will negotiate until the efficient outcome is achieved. Or as Richard Posner puts it: "Where market transaction costs are zero, the law's initial assignment of rights is irrelevant to efficiency, since if the assignment is inefficient the parties will rectify it by a corrective transaction."[104] Second, where transaction costs are present, economists should study on a case-by-case basis all of the possible implications of government intervention. As Coase stated in his original 1960 article, however, this tends to be an extremely complex proposition and in most cases should lead us to avoid government regulation since the potential costs generally overwhelm any potential benefits.

In the hands of the lawyer-economists, the Coase Theorem would give rise to two foundational "corollaries" that would come to define the law-and-economics approach. The first is that judges should try to minimize transaction costs in order to facilitate market negotiations (that naturally lead to efficient outcomes). Courts can promote this goal by clearly defining property and contract rights, and by ensuring inexpensive and effective remedies for any breach. Second, where transaction costs are inevitably high, courts should mimic the efficient market outcome in their judicial determinations. In other words, they should follow the central tenet of law and economics that "efficiency generally should be the primary criterion for evaluating legal rules."[105]

It is crucial to recognize here that the "efficient" outcome coincides with the equilibrium position obtained in a perfectly competitive market—or, as Coase would say, in a market with no transaction costs. In this sense, assigning rights to mimic the outcome of the market is not really viewed as government intervention or as "political" by those with a law-and-economics point of view. The process has a certain objectivity to it, an objectivity that reflects the neutrality of the efficient market. It has the neutrality of Pareto outcomes—and who could be opposed to those?

At the same time, when the distributions already match the outcome of the market, there is no need to intervene and reassign legal rights. Indeed, if a judge were to intervene unnecessarily in that type of situation and reassign rights, the judicial decision would be viewed as "activist," "interventionist," or "political." In other words, state interventions that promote perfectly competitive markets (by reducing transaction costs), or that assign rights and liabilities so as to replicate the outcome of perfectly competitive markets, are entirely consistent with the underlying principle of market efficiency. Only those state interventions that go beyond that point violate the principles of a free market.

In this way the law-and-economics movement has tried to sever the efficiency analysis from the political issues of redistribution—assigning the first to judges and the second to legislators.[106] As Mitchell Polinsky, a noted scholar in law and economics at Stanford University, explains: "Efficiency corresponds to 'the size of the pie,' while equity has to do with how it is sliced. Economists traditionally concentrate on how to maximize the size of the pie, leaving to others—such as legislators—the decision how to divide it."[107]

Contesting the Competitiveness of the Market

Now, it would be far too naïve to imagine that the economic analysis of law considers "the market" to be "unregulated." Let me not be misunderstood. The law-and-economics movement has certainly refined and improved on Quesnay's original insight: today it is understood that not all economic activity is naturally ordered; only competitive markets are. The entire force of the modern economic approach is to determine when markets fail and when market regulation is needed to achieve efficient outcomes. Not all market mechanisms are efficient. But here is the point: When there is voluntary, compensated exchange in a space with low transaction costs, an efficient outcome obtains. This point can be illustrated well with an example.

Let us take, for instance, the litigation over excessive management-fee liability in mutual funds that gave rise to the U.S. Supreme Court's 2010 decision in *Jones v. Harris*. The technical issue there was whether a particular statutory provision, section 36(b), added in 1970 to the Investment Company

Act of 1940, created liability for excessive adviser's fees in the absence of a violation of fiduciary duties—or, to put it in another way, whether Congress required just full disclosure and no tricks in the compensation schemes for mutual fund advisers, or whether Congress had mandated a cap on excessive compensation.

In the Seventh Circuit Court of Appeals, the dispute gave rise to a vigorous debate between Chief Judge Frank Easterbrook, who took the more laissez-faire position, and Judge Richard Posner, who took the more regulatory position. According to Easterbrook, who wrote the decision for the unanimous three-judge panel, the statute did not impose a fee cap or independent excessive fee restrictions: "A fiduciary duty differs from rate regulation," Easterbrook wrote. "A fiduciary must make full disclosure and play no tricks but is not subject to a cap on compensation."[108] In the process, Easterbrook departed from a Second Circuit decision on point, the *Gartenberg* case—creating a circuit split, which is what gave rise to the U.S. Supreme Court review— declaring that "we are skeptical about *Gartenberg* because it relies too little on markets."[109]

In a short opinion dissenting from the failure of the Seventh Circuit to rehear the case en banc, Posner made clear his disagreement: the issue was whether the mutual fund market, or more specifically the market for advisers to mutual funds, was sufficiently competitive. If it was, then there would be no need to examine closely the adviser compensation schemes, and no need to regulate the arrangements; but if not, then the fee rates needed to be scrutinized closely. The central issue that divided Posner and Easterbrook—both well versed in the Chicago School law-and-economics approach—was the competitiveness of the mutual fund market, an issue that generated an extensive debate among economists and lawyers in academic journals and in amicus briefs filed with the Supreme Court.[110]

Both agreed that if the mutual fund market was competitive, then regulation of fees was unnecessary. Easterbrook had found that the market was competitive:

> Today thousands of mutual funds compete. The pages of the *Wall Street Journal* teem with listings. People can search for and trade funds over the Internet, with negligible transactions costs. . . . Mutual funds come much closer to the model of atomistic competition than do most other markets. . . . A recent, careful study concludes that thousands of mutual funds are plenty, that investors can and do protect their interests by shopping, and that regulating advisory fees through litigation is unlikely to do more good than harm. . . . It won't do to reply that most in-

> vestors are unsophisticated and don't compare prices. The sophisticated investors who do shop create a competitive pressure that protects the rest.[111]

Easterbrook's conclusion that the market was competitive was bolstered by his assessment of the evidence in the case. Easterbrook had compared the challenged adviser's fees and found them to be similar to market rates; he also had looked at the rate of return for the mutual funds in question and found them to be better than average, suggesting that the adviser had performed well: "the Oakmark funds have grown more than the norm for comparable pools, which implies that Harris Associated [the adviser] has delivered value for money."[112] "Competition rather than litigation determines the fee—and, when judges must set fees, they try to follow the market rather than demand that attorneys' compensation conform to the judges' preferences," Easterbrook concluded.[113]

Posner took the opposite view. In this case, Posner argued, the market was not sufficiently competitive—or at least, the record did not establish that it was sufficiently competitive. "Competition in product and capital markets can't be counted on to solve the problem because the same structure of incentives operates on all large corporations and similar entities, including mutual funds. Mutual funds are a component of the financial services industry, where abuses have been rampant, as is more evident now," Posner wrote.[114] The problem with Easterbrook's reasoning, Posner maintained, was that it relied too heavily on an assumption of competition that was no longer valid: "The panel bases its rejection of *Gartenberg* mainly on an economic analysis that is ripe for reexamination on the basis of growing indications that executive compensation in large publicly traded firms often is excessive because of the feeble incentives of boards of directors to police compensation," Posner added.

Notice that neither Posner nor Easterbrook are simplistically suggesting that markets *tout court* are efficient. There is no naïve Physiocratic claim here that all economic transactions are governed by natural order; nor any automatic or kneejerk reaction against regulation through fiduciary duties or fee caps. There is, in fact, even no automatic opposition to price regulation—here a cap on compensation. All of that would be permissible, or even called for, if the market was not competitive. Everything turns now on the "competition" in the market. But note, once a market has been determined to be a "competitive market," then it is efficient. Efficiency now attaches to competitive markets. In that newly defined space—that more narrowly delineated, more specifically identified space—the logic of natural order reigns. In that space, there is no need for regulation, no need for government intervention—because there the market will regulate itself.

A modern economist might ask whether I am denying the first theorem of welfare economics—namely, that a competitive market equilibrium leads to the efficient allocation of resources. The answer is no. I am not suggesting that there is a mathematical error in the theorem; nor am I merely suggesting that the assumptions are unrealistic (which they certainly are). What I am contesting is the *interpretation* of what the theorem tells us. Most people understand it to mean that free markets are more efficient. But what it tells us, instead, is that massive government intervention (the kind necessary, for instance, to make possible a wheat pit at the Chicago Board of Trade) is necessary to achieve what we call a "free" market; that there are myriad ways to structure those interventions; and that typically they include significant manipulation (such as, for instance, fixing prices at an MCC). The place to focus, then, is not on the simple "free, voluntary, compensated exchange" at the board, but on the complex institutional mechanisms and structures that make such a "free" exchange remotely possible. It is all in the framing.

Efficiency and Natural Order

It is precisely in this sense that the concept of "efficiency" has replaced the term "natural order" or "spontaneous order," and functions in a more powerful way. In the eighteenth century, the Physiocrats maintained that economic markets and exchange were characterized by a "natural order" that autonomously achieved a state of equilibrium that produced a net profit; today, neoliberal writers maintain that competitive markets achieve an equilibrium that is "efficient" and therefore maximizes social welfare without anyone being worse off. On the basis of that efficient outcome—whether factual or hypothetical—the law, we are told, should impose whatever legal regime would have produced those free and autonomous exchanges. In sum, "natural order" has become market "efficiency," and "efficiency" has become entirely neutral.

I want to close this part of the discussion with a reminder of the Coase Theorem, which is at the very heart of law and economics and the economic analysis of crime and punishment. The Coase Theorem states that if transaction costs are low, the state should not intervene because free-market exchange will lead to the efficient outcome; and if transaction costs are high, the state likely should not intervene because the facts are too complex and the government is likely to be inefficient. What is so remarkable about the

Coase Theorem is that it renders scientific and thereby seemingly unimpeachable the basic idea of natural order. This step is, indeed, brilliant. A crowning achievement. It took two hundred years to transform a quasi-religious conception of natural order into a scientific theory of market efficiency.

The Birth of Neoliberal Penality

The function of the criminal sanction in a capitalist market economy, then, is to prevent individuals from bypassing the efficient market because market bypassing—involuntary, uncompensated forms of social interaction—are by their very nature inefficient and reduce social welfare. Criminal activity is best understood as an end run around the market, and criminal law is therefore best understood as that which prevents this kind of market evasion. The central premise of this argument, naturally, is the efficiency of markets: "When transaction costs are low," Posner emphasizes, "the market is, virtually by definition, the most efficient method of allocating resources."[115] The argument also maps perfectly, as well, onto Richard Epstein's conception of the penal sphere. The role of the penal sanction, in Epstein's view, is to prevent fraud and coercion so as to facilitate the proper functioning of the free market. Notice the underlying notion of orderliness and the strong parallel to Quesnay's *ordre naturel.*

This view of the penal sanction has a number of important features. First, punishment is located outside the market and serves to keep compliant individuals within the framework of voluntary, noncoercive, and compensated exchange—that is, within the free market. In this sense, the criminal sanction and the market are demarcated. They are not continuous and do not overlap as they did on the cameralist reading of Beccaria. The relationship between the market and the penal system is binary: there is a market option, which is the space of ordered exchange, and it is marked off from the fraud and coercion option, which is the space of market bypassing, the space outside the market. The two spaces are mutually exclusive and noncontinuous. The criminal sanction delimits the economic sphere, commerce, and trade. It is what makes the economic sphere function properly. Government intervenes outside the market to ensure that everyone is channeled within the market. This duality reiterates the Physiocratic distinction between the zone of natural order in economic exchange and the space of positive penal laws for everyone who is *déréglé*.

Second, all social exchange is modeled on market transactions. In this sense, market rationality influences the penal sphere (but not vice versa). In contrast to an earlier Physiocratic view, economic reasoning reaches into the sphere of disorder. The realm of bargained-for exchanges—what would earlier have been labeled "commerce," "trade," or even "public economy"—has colonized the social and political realm. Whereas for Beccaria there was some way of distinguishing between a social realm and pure commerce, here there is only one conception of human interaction grounded on the model of bargained-for exchanges (excluding, that is, market bypassing). All human relations are analyzed through a transactional lens and can be evaluated in terms of efficiency and utility. This is made clear in Posner's discussion of substantive crimes, parts of which were discussed earlier:

> The dichotomy between acquisitive crimes and crimes of passion is overstated. Acquisitive crimes bypass explicit markets; crimes of passion often bypass implicit markets—for example, in friendship, love, respect—that are the subject of a growing economic literature illustrated by Becker's work on the family. Less obviously, crimes of passion often bypass explicit markets too. . . . Someone who gets his satisfactions in life from beating up other people, without compensating them, rather than from engaging in trade with them is thus bypassing explicit markets.[116]

The distinction between a social realm and economic exchange has been replaced by the dichotomy between the market and market bypassing, in other words, between the market and the penal spheres.

But third, because of the binary nature of the market-penal distinction, rational-choice assumptions seem to operate differently in the two realms. In the ordered sphere of markets, there is little need for government intervention to adjust the rational calculation of individuals: the Coase Theorem tells us that such intervention is entirely unnecessary when transaction costs are low, and likely counterproductive when they are high. By contrast, the penal sphere is dominated by government intervention: human behaviors that bypass voluntary exchange require severe price-fixing and regulation. In other words, the need for government intervention is ratcheted up the minute we cross the line between the market and the penal sphere.

Fourth, there is a clear wealth dimension to these distinctions. The criminal sanction—rather than tort law—is necessary in the case of murder, violent crime, theft, property crimes, and generally street crime because the value at which the deterrence would have to be placed is too high and the defendants are most often unable to pay such a price (Epstein and Posner agree on this). Both for reasons of insolvency and because of the high costs that would be necessary to deter street crime, the tort system is inadequate and the government must intervene. Posner explains: "In cases where tort remedies, including punitive damages, are an adequate deterrent because they do not strain the potential defendant's ability to pay, there is no need to invoke criminal penalties—penalties which . . . are costlier than civil penalties even when just a fine is imposed. In such cases, the misconduct probably will be deterred. . . . This means that the criminal law is designed primarily for the nonaffluent; the affluent are kept in line, for the most part, by tort law."[117]

In sum, the language of "natural order" has been replaced by a more technical and scientific theory of market efficiency, but the parallel to the earlier Physiocrats remains striking. Despite the important differences between Hayekian and Benthamite economic theorists, between the more libertarian Richard Epstein or the more welfarist Gary Becker, the same logic pervades their theories—the logic of neoliberal penality.

Readings, Appropriations, and Self-Presentation

One last thought. Just as there are multiple readings of Beccaria, Quesnay, Smith, and Bentham, there are multiple readings of those who take the Chicago law-and-economics approach. This is particularly true of Richard Posner, who, after many decades of expressly embracing free-market ideology, began to claim in 2009 that he had been a Keynesian all along.

In his *Frontiers of Legal Theory* in 2001, Posner seemed content to embrace the free-market mantle. As he remarked there, the law-and-economics movement "is not merely an ivory-towered enterprise," it seeks to "improve law by pointing out respects in which existing or proposed laws have unintended or undesirable consequences and by proposing practical reforms."[118] Those reforms, Posner acknowledged, have led to deregulation: "The deregulation movement, and the increased respectability of free-market ideology generally, owe something to the law and economics movement."[119] Not long before, in 1995, Posner called himself a classical liberal and explicitly sided with free markets: "By creating a large sphere of inviolate private activity and by facilitating the operation of free markets, liberalism creates the conditions that experience teaches are necessary for personal liberty and economic prosperity."[120]

Times have changed, however, and in his book *A Failure of Capitalism*, published in 2009 on the heels of the subprime mortgage debacle, Posner offered a far more Keynesian self-presentation, writing that "we need a more active and intelligent government to keep our model of a capitalist economy from running off the rails. The movement to deregulate the financial industry went too far by exaggerating the resilience—the self-healing powers—of laissez-faire capitalism."[121] In an accompanying editorial in the *New York Times* in June 2009, Posner added that "our regulatory *culture*" also needs to be addressed. The problem is not just regulatory structure, Posner suggested, but its implementation, which is determined by cultural norms. Our "pathologies of regulation," Posner argued, "are rooted in our regulatory *culture*—the timidity of civil servants, the contamination of public administration by politics and interest groups, and the power of the 'office consensus' to marginalize independent thinkers for not being team players."[122] In other words, we now need not only a regulatory structure, but more high-performing civil-servant regulators. "One possibility," Posner suggested, "would be to rotate career regulators through the different financial agencies to reduce balkanization and make a regulatory career more interesting."[123] Summing up his new position, Posner reflected over the 2009 recession and remarked in *The New Yorker* that Keynesian economics "seems to have more of a grasp of what is going on in the economy."[124] Or, more pithily, "probably the term 'Chicago School' should be retired."[125]

I do not intend here to impose a reading on Richard Posner—especially an earlier, more Chicago School reading. There are, indeed, multiple ways to interpret his writings and his most recent Keynesian turn is just one of many possible readings. I have focused on earlier writings because it is those, I contend, that reflect the dominant public imagination regarding the role of the criminal sanction today—one in which markets are viewed as efficient and the penal sphere is considered the legitimate space for governmental intervention.

7

The Myth of Discipline

François Quesnay's introduction of natural order into economic thought fragmented an earlier, more integrated view of "police" and "public economy." Over the course of the nineteenth and twentieth centuries, the idea of natural order evolved into a scientific theorem about the inherent efficiency of markets and, more generally, into a popular belief in the superiority of free markets. The result is that, today, a vast majority of Americans believe that the free market is "the best system on which to base the future of the world."[1]

This faith in the free market emerged, hand in hand, with a theory of legal despotism according to which the state's most legitimate function, and the one it was best able to carry out, was to police and punish. It is precisely this curious combination of market efficiency and a Big Brother state that has become seemingly obvious today. It is what makes possible the perception of the Parisian *police des grains* as coercive and the Chicago Board of Trade as free. It is what has given birth to neoliberal penality. But it hinges on an illusion: a myth of natural orderliness in the economic realm.

On close inspection, the very categories of "free market" and "discipline" prove chimerical. Our contemporary exchanges and markets are far more regulated than meets the eye. The entire history of the Chicago Board of Trade is, in truth, a series of government interventions and regulatory adjustments that have facilitated a state-sanctioned monopoly and empowered the private practices of a small association of brokers and dealers. Even a cursory glance at the legal framework that surrounds exchanges today reveals a web of intricate rules and oversight that is far from anything that could possibly be described as "free." The fact is, shifts in regulatory mechanisms over the past two centuries have not reduced the amount of regulation, but simply changed its form and style. As John Campbell and Ove Pedersen suggest, "neoliberalism does not so much involve *deregulation* as *re-regulation* of economic activity."[2]

Other ideas from the more distant past also need to be revisited. A closer examination of the police archives reveals that the *police des grains* of eighteenth-century France was far less disciplinary than it has been made out to be. Moreover, the earlier justifications for "police" had far more robust roots in notions of liberty than we tend to attribute today. And by the same token, Physiocratic practices involved far greater regulation of economic exchange than is typically recognized. In fact, Le Mercier's governance of Martinique was highly interventionist, not only in creating a severe police force, but also in the economic domain, all the way down to the grain, bread, and meat markets. Let's pause for a moment, in this and the following chapter, to rethink these categories of "discipline" and "freedom." Let's start here with excess regulation.

Fantastic Disciplinary Inventions

In 1749, Jacques-François Guillauté presented to the king of France, Louis XV, an ambitious plan for reorganizing the urban space of Paris and supervising its inhabitants.[3] Guillauté imagined a perfectly regulated space with minutely numbered and labeled buildings, entryways, floors, stairwells, and doors. Twenty-four neighborhoods would be subdivided into twenty home islands, each placed under the supervision of a new category of watchmen, called "syndics," who would become the "nerves and eyes of the police," producing infinite amounts of perfect information. Further, this information could be accessed instantaneously by means of a remarkable paper-filing machine with large wheels—twelve feet in diameter and thirty-six feet in circumference—that rotated the information at the tap of a foot.[4] Guillauté estimated that any one of the twelve wheels of his paper-filing machine—he called it a "serre-papier," a paper squeeze—could organize 102,400 individual pieces of paper. This whirling paper sifter would realize the dream of perfect knowledge and pure discipline: a faultless system for an all-knowing police.

Guillauté's pitch was originally published in a splendid volume with twenty-eight gorgeous drawings "à la plume" by Gabriel de Saint-Aubin, titled *Mémoire sur la réformation de la police de France*. The original edition from the library of the baron Jérôme Pichon, with Louis XV's coat of arms, was reprinted in 1974 in an elegant large folio edition by a Paris editor. The illustrations are beautifully reproduced and mesmerizing. The text and drawings are a fascinating object of study. To contemporary critical theorists, the *Mémoire* serves as a representation of discipline and regimentation. Foucault referred to it in his 1978 lectures specifically at the point where he defined "discipline."[5] Other theorists today, Eric Heilmann and Olivier Doron, see in contemporary policing practices, such as video surveillance and electronic monitoring, modern avatars of Guillauté's machine.[6] Heilmann in fact traces the birth of modern policing to Guillauté's invention.[7]

Truth be told, though, Guillauté's creative invention fell on deaf ears and his project was essentially lost to history. It stands today as a historical artifact, a completely fanciful idea. A policeman's fantasy. Foucault referred to Guillauté as if he were one of the leading "theoreticians of the *police* in the mid eighteenth century."[8] But in truth, Guillauté was just a simple officer of the *maréchaussée de l'Ile-de-France* (listed in the *Almanach Royal* of 1752 with a slight typographical shift as "Guillotte, rue Mouffetard, près Saint-Médard") and an amateur inventor. He had apparently invented a floating bridge in 1748, the year before his *Mémoire*.[9] Less a theoretician than a dreamer, the policeman would never realize his fantasy, not even come close. As Jean Seznec notes, "The *Mémoire*, in point of fact, remained a dead letter; perhaps the zeal of the author was judged excessive, and his system of surveillance far too exacting. 'The syndics,' baron Pichon noted, 'established a kind of inquisition; and the *ancien regime* wanted none of it.'"[10] It turns out that the true practice of the police was a far less disciplinary enterprise.

Revisiting the *Police des Grains*

Like Guillauté's invention, the picture that Fréminville, Delamare, Duchesne, and the others drew of the *police des grains* was somewhat fantastic. Truth be told, there was far more liberty under the *police des grains* of early eighteenth-century France than the codebooks and manuals might suggest. The regulations, ordinances, and decrees were alphabetized, catalogued, enumerated, and rehearsed extensively in print—especially by those who were ideologically opposed to their very existence—and the rules have come down to us as pure discipline. But in truth, they were not vigorously enforced—or rarely so. Most of the ordinances themselves were trifling administrative regulations, municipal-style minor infractions that involved negligible fines only—if they were even imposed.

Moreover, the police were occupied primarily with enforcing rules about street sanitation, hygiene, minor inconveniences, and late-hour drinking. The extensive formal regulations concerning grain and bread were only truly enforced in times of *disette* (food shortages) to give the impression—or so it seemed—that the monarchy was doing something to address human misery. Today, we look back and see extensive regulatory oversight that shaped the debate over free trade and commerce, but at the time there was far more liberty both in practice and in the discourse of policing. The discrepancy is more than just an inadvertent gap between law on the books and law in action. It is, rather, a question of appropriating history. It is a matter of creating and exploiting categories for political objectives.

The contemporaneous police records from the Châtelet exude the absolutely trivial nature of the daily routine of a *commissaire,* a police commissioner, on his beat. On close inspection of the archives it becomes apparent that his daily routine was dominated by issues related to street cleaning, fecal matter, neglected gravel and stone piles, flowerpots left on windowsills, and, occasionally, late-night drinkers in wine merchants' shops. The police court at the Paris Châtelet—*la chambre de police*—convened on Fridays, and the records maintained today at the National Archives contain the detailed reports that each commissioner filed with the police court at those hearings, detailing their daily activities and the violations, or the *"contraventions,"* that they had observed since the last session.

The cartons for the year 1758 are representative of those at midcentury and extremely relevant for our purposes—recall that 1758 is the year of the publication of Fréminville's *Dictionnaire de la police,* which catalogued and annotated in such detail all the police regulations, as well as the year that François Quesnay developed his *Tableau économique* in reaction against the oppressive enforcement of the police regulations.[11] In the first oversized, black carton, one can review complete sets of the handwritten reports submitted by the commissioners at the court audience, which offer a fascinating view into these commissioners' daily activities. After the sewn thread in the corner of the yellowing papers is unfastened to unfold them—for what seems to be the very first time—these elaborate documents, some neater and more legible than others but all meticulously transcribed, reveal the world of the Paris streets circa 1758. Summaries and tables will be useful, but let me start by giving you a real sense of what these reports are like, how they read. Let me begin with two, chosen at random from different months of the year, that are illustrative of the others.

The first belongs to Commissioner Duruisseau, appointed to the Châtelet in 1751 and assigned to the rue de la Harpe in the neighborhood called Saint André des Arts. The street, located in the fifth arrondissement near the Place Saint-Michel, is still well-known.[12] Duruisseau presented this report at the session of the police chamber held in late April 1758.[13] Like the other manuscripts, it is titled "Report rendered by me [*par nous*] the undersigned *Commissaire* at the audience of the police court held at the Châtelet on Friday, April 21, 1758. These violations [*contraventions*] to the ordinances of the police observed by me [*par nous*] on the following days as duly noted"—whereupon the list begins:

ON APRIL 15, 1758

rue St. Maur

Along the length of the wall of the new house at the corner of the street, and the entrance with the coach doors on the *rue des vieilles Thuilleries,* not swept.

rue du Petit Bacq

A pot on the window of the first floor of the house of the earthen potter on the right-hand side entering from the *rue de Sève.*

One bottle and one pot on the two windows on the second floor of the same house.

The doorway of the coach entrance with the inscription *Lætitiæ Domûs,* and of the connecting cabaret, not swept.

rue messières

A cart full of earth and gravel, manure and other filth, left behind a long while, along the wall of the garden on the right side as you enter from the *rue pot de fer.*

rue du Canivet

Half a cart of earth and gravel, left there a long time, belonging to the new house at the corner of the *rue ferou,* the principal tenant of which is the *Sieur hussard Maréchal* on the said *rue ferou.*

rue de Condé

The doorway in front of the door of the innkeeper, across from the *rue des quatre vents,* not swept.

ON APRIL 17, 1758

No violations.

ON APRIL 18, 1758

rue des Ciseaux

The doorway of the cabaret between the merchant [*de langues fourrées*] and the innkeeper, not swept.

rue des Rosiers

A parakeet cage on the window of the first floor of the second coach door on the right-hand side entering from the *rue de grenelle.*

rue Grenegaud

Four flowerpots on the window of the first floor of the house of the *Sieur Perefius* lemonade-maker.

ON THE 19 OF SAID MONTH

No violations.

ON THE 20TH OF SAID MONTH

rue de Vaugirard

Five cut stones, abandoned a long while, along the length of the wall of the garden of the *hotel de Condé,* that are getting in the way of street cleaning and causing a heap of gravel and garbage.

rue du Regard

A bunch of yard waste and other refuse that has been there for several days at the door of the *hotel de la Guiche.*

rue du Cherche midi

The doorway of the coach door across from the *cabaret du puissant vin,* not swept.

rue du vieu Colombier

A cage on the second window of the first floor of the house of the *Sieur Joyau maitre Charon* across from the *rue Cassette.*

ON APRIL 21, 1758

rue des Cordeliers

A cage on the window of the second floor of the house of the wigmaker between the fountain and the *rue du Paon.*

rue du Bacq

The doorway of the confectioner at the corner of the *rue de grenelle,* not swept.

Reported by us [*par nous*] royal counselor, undersigned commissioner at the audience of the police court held at the Châtelet this day Friday April 21, 1758

[signed] Duruisseau

Here is another report from the end of May by another commissioner, Dubuisson, who was appointed to the Châtelet in 1741 and, at the time, was assigned to the *Marais* area, also known as the Le Temple neighborhood—more specifically to the vieille rue du Temple near the gorgeous Hôtel de Soubise.[14] This report began on May 27 and was filed with the police chamber at the hearing on Friday, June 2, 1758. The report, also in its entirety, reads as follows:

Report made by us [*par nous*], said commissioner at the audience of the police chamber on June 2, 1758, of the violations of the ordinances of the police observed by us [*par nous*] on the following days:

MAY 27, 1758

No violations.

29TH OF THE SAID MONTH

Rue des Coquilles

Water thrown out, in our presence, from the window of the second floor of the house occupied by a cobbler and a peddler next to the locksmith.

Rue des Vieilles garnisons

The door front of the wigmaker at the corner of the said street and of the *Rue de la Tisserandrie*, not swept.

30TH OF THE SAID MONTH

Rue de la Tisserandrie

The sweeper of the door front at the *Hôtel Notre Dame garni*, at fault for improperly sweeping [*faute de Balayage*].

The sweeper of the coach door across from the tile store near the *Rue de la poteris*, at fault for improperly sweeping.

31ST OF SAID MONTH

Rue de la marche

Failure to remove the gravel and earth at the first little green door of the garden with the highest wall at left when you enter from the *rue de poitou*.

Rue neuve St. Laurens

Water thrown daily through every window of the house with large square doors on the left when entering into the said street from the *Rue du temple* next to an alley on which is written *Le Comte Chirurgien*, as the neighbors have said and as the street sweeper has complained about.

A pile of earth neglected and not removed next to a little door, on the right when you enter by the *Rue du temple*, on top of which rests *Notre Dame de Consolation*.

Rue du Vert bois

The mason who works in the alley of the house between the *Josse Le Jeune*, maker of amenities, and the master cobbler, for untidy and encumbering materials and stones on the street and in the gutter.

1ST OF JUNE

Rue de la Mortellerie

The house belonging to the *Dames de l'assomption* and of which the principal tenant is the *sieur Chapes*, master mason, for failure to hang the door that we were obliged to have hung by the *sieur Morles,* tapestry merchant living on the said street, at the expense of the landlords or of the principal tenant of the said house.

Rue Geoffroy Lanier

The little door next to *Langlan,* master glazier, and across from Carton, wigmaker, for failure to have hung the door that we were obliged to have hung by the *sieur Mille,* tapestry merchant living on the same street, at the expense of the principal tenant or of the proprietor of the said house.

Rue Saint Antoine

Four pots in the gutter of the drainpipes of the house at the sign of the *Sauvage D'or* near *La Vieille Rue du temple.*

Certified by me [*par nous*] said commissioner,
[signed] Dubuisson

These are two of the exhaustive manuscripts submitted by the various police commissioners at the Friday hearings. They reflect well the general tenor and character of the other reports—as we can see by comparing them to those others.

One spectacular folder in the March 1758 dossier contains all of the commissioners' reports submitted and considered at the session of the court held on March 3, 1758. By an order of magnitude, the most frequent type of violation observed concerned the failure to sweep or to sweep properly the sidewalk in front of a house or store. More than half of the total violations were problems of "non balayé." The next most frequent violation had to do with fecal matter—apparently human, not animal. On several occasions, the commissioners wrote up offenders for throwing fecal matter onto the sidewalk (we'll come back to that, unfortunately). The next most common violation involved obtrusive objects or piles of stones or rubble that blocked the way and caused a nuisance—things such as a cart of earth and gravel causing an accumulation of other waste, or a pile of garden waste, or a mass of gravel. Next came illicit drinking, mostly late at night in wine merchants' shops that should have been closed at that hour; then people throwing water or other liquids out of their windows; next, flowerpots, earthen pots, bottles, or other objects on the windowsills; and finally other miscellaneous *contraventions* (including traffic violations, refusing to open the door to a night watchman, or playing violin too late at night). In all of the reports, there were only five violations that were in any way related to commerce.

As Table 7.1 shows, the commissioners had their pet peeves. For Commissioner Le Maire, who was in charge of the Mont-Sainte-Geneviève (where

Table 7.1 Count of violations reported by commissioners at the March 3, 1758, hearing in the police chamber of the Paris Châtelet

	Le Maire	Chénon	Dubuisson	Duruisseau	Carlier	Doublon	Demachurin	Thiérion	LeBlanc	Total
Street cleaning	34	19	34	7	1	9	0	0	0	104
Fecal matter	16	9	4	0	0	2	0	0	0	31
Objects that constitute a nuisance	5	2	10	6	0	1	0	0	0	24
Illicit drinking	0	0	0	0	7	3	0	0	5	15
Throwing water out of window	0	0	1	0	0	7	0	0	0	8
Dangerous object in window	0	0	1	0	0	4	0	0	0	5
Traffic violations	0	2	0	0	0	0	0	0	0	2
Illicit gaming	0	0	0	0	0	0	0	1	0	1
Miscellaneous	0	0	1	0	0	0	0	0	0	1
Market or exchange related	0	0	0	1	0	3	1	0	0	5
Total	55	32	51	14	8	29	1	1	5	196

Source: Police records in cartons Y-9495A and Y-9495B at the Archives Nationales de France.

the Panthéon stands today), it was definitely fecal matter. February 21, 1758, seemed to be a particularly bad day, especially on the rue neuve Saint Médard and rue Mouffetard. Le Maire's report for that day reads:

> *Rue neuve saint Médard*
>
> Fecal matter in front of the first house on the left.
>
> Fecal matter on the sidewalk in front of the house of the earthen potter on the left of the widow *Dupré.*
>
> Fecal matter on the sidewalk in front of the house next to the said earthen potter.
>
> Fecal matter on the sidewalk in front of the last house on the right.
>
> Fecal matter on the sidewalk [. . .] of the last house on the left.
>
> *Rue Mouffetard entering on the left*
> *from the rue neuve Saint Médard*
>
> Fecal matter on the sidewalk in front of the house on which it is written *Bruner Le Père Cordonnier,* the said shop being occupied by a [. . .].
>
> Fecal matter on the sidewalk in front of the house next to the alley door on which is written *Colombier Chapentier.*

In addition to noting these *contraventions,* Commissioner Le Maire also reported residents who threw their fecal matter onto the sidewalk. "The tenants of said house" Le Maire cited "for having thrown fecal matter onto the pavement." Similarly, on the next street over, "The tenants of the first house on the left for having thrown fecal matter on the sidewalk." It turns out, though, that Le Maire was not alone. Commissioner Chénon also reported a lot of fecal matter on February 18, 1758, though he preferred simply to note "M.F." on his reports. Chénon also reported that "urine was thrown out of a house in my presence from a floor above the street." (I assume it missed him.)

Commissioner Jean François Joseph Doublon, by contrast, had a real affinity for people throwing water out of their windows. It is almost as if he carried a divining rod. On February 24, 1758, for instance, Doublon personally witnessed, on seven different occasions and at seven different locations, people tossing water out their windows—from the Carré Sainte Geneviève to the Collège de Montaigne, passing through the rue du faubourg St. Jacques. Another commissioner, Thiérry, after having cited someone for throwing water, also wrote him up for "respond[ing] to me that he would always continue to throw water out his window."

Commissioner LeBlanc seemed also to have a dowsing rod, but his led to wine, not water. By a remarkable twist of fate, LeBlanc discovered drinkers, almost by the barrel. He discovered four people drinking illicitly at the wine merchant's shop at ten-thirty at night at the rue Saint Martin, another eight drinking illicitly at another wine merchant's shop at ten-forty-five, six more at the wine merchant's on rue beaubourg, and another eight people drinking *atablées* (sitting at a table no less) at the wine merchant's at the rue du four at one o'clock in the morning. According to the corporal who conducted the night watch, an additional six people had just left the tavern at that late hour. (Each of those incidents is counted only once in Table 7.1 even though they each gave rise to multiple *contraventions* since there were several people at each location.)

Commissioner Carlier similarly had a knack for discovering illicit drinking—again, mostly late at night at wine merchants' shops. On his report for March 3, 1758, on the left-hand side of the yellowing page, in different ink and a slightly different hand—as is true of each of the other reports—there is written a number (and sometimes a livre or sol symbol) that corresponds to the fine imposed by the magistrate at the police hearing. (There is no currency symbol next to the numeral on this page, as there is on most of the other reports, but the arithmetic works perfectly here, with a 2 livres fine per person caught drinking illicitly, the same rate as in the other similar cases of drinking):

4 At the wine merchant with the shop sign *La renommée* . . . *2 Drinkers*
4 At the wine merchant with the shop sign *Le Barril d'Or* [*The Golden Cask*] . . . 2 D.
4 At the wine merchant with the shop sign *L'Étoile d'or* [*The Golden Star*] . . . 2 D.
6 At the wine merchant with the sign of the virgin . . . 3 D.
14 At the wine merchant at the corner of the street of the three pistols . . . 7 D.
6 At the wine merchant at the corner of St. Paul at the sign of the virgin . . . 3 D.

Similarly, in his report for the audience of December 29, 1758, Commissioner LeBlanc discovered more than forty revelers drinking after hours at various wine merchants' shops in the late evening. LeBlanc also had some unique discoveries, such as citing someone for playing violin through the night until five o'clock in the morning. Commissioner Dubuisson had a bit of a fetish for merchants and individuals who neglected to remove excess gravel and earth. And Duruisseau had a knack for observing dangerous objects on windowsills—including bird cages, flowerpots, bottles, and other earthenware sitting precariously on a sill or high in the roof gutters.

These findings are not an artifact of the particular date—March 3, 1758—nor of the hearing, nor of the weather or season. A sampling of other reports from different months reveals very similar distributions of violations, as evidenced in Table 7.2. Similarly, a sampling of the year's reports for two particular commissioners, Dubuisson (Table 7.3) and Duruisseau (Table 7.4), reveal consistency throughout the calendar year. These additional samples of commissioner reports are very similar to the exhaustive March 3 collection and do not reveal any additional market- or commerce-related violations.

The punishments meted out in these *contraventions,* with one single exception, were all limited to minor fines. No one was sent to the Bastille. At the hearings, a police magistrate would swiftly determine a fine for each violation and the amount was listed on the side of each *contravention* on the commissioners' reports themselves, as shown earlier. The amount of the fines tended to be low. The most frequent violation, "non balayé," or not sweeping properly, was also the most consistently measured; it was always assessed at four livres.[15] Fecal matter was fined at the rate of one livre and ten sols, although on occasion it was fined at three, and sometimes at ten livres (especially when there was a lot of it). Obstructive objects that caused a nuisance in the street usually led to fines of four to six livres. Throwing water out the window was assessed at between one livre and ten sols to three, and sometimes four, livres. If it was urine, six livres. Illicit nighttime drinking led consistently to a fine of two livres per person (for instance, when Commissioner LeBlanc caught ten persons drinking, the fine was twenty livres, and when he caught eight, it was sixteen). Dangerous objects on windowsills resulted, generally, in a fine as low as forty sols, but as high as two or four livres. Traffic violations were fined at three livres. To give a sense of these numbers, one of the reports reveals that eggs were selling at market for forty-five livres per thousand, so a fine of one livre and ten sols would have been the equivalent of the cost, at market, of approximately two dozen eggs.

The single exception in the sample of commissioners' reports involved an instance of gaming. On February 3, 1758, Commissioner Thiérion stumbled across a sizeable gaming enterprise at the Hôtel de l'Amerique, on the fashionable rue Saint Honoré in the Palais Royal area: involved were at least fifteen individuals, three hundred and twelve livres in bets left on the table, multiple decks of cards, several rooms, and some debauchery. (It is noted in the report that a certain Bernardine Romain, a thirty-three-year-old native of Valencienne, had slept with one of the culprits "that very evening in the said room.") Ultimately, the money found on the table was confiscated and each of the accused was fined 3,000 livres—the largest fine, by an order of magnitude, seen in these reports.

This brings us, then, to the five violations that were, in any way, related to markets, commercial exchange, or economic transactions—out of the 352

Table 7.2 Sample count of violations reported by other commissioners at hearings in the police chamber of the Paris Châtelet during 1758

	Thiérry June 27, 1758	Chénon August 18, 1758	Le Maire August 11, 1758	LeBlanc December 29, 1758	Total
Street cleaning	3	4	6	0	13
Dangerous object in window	5	0	3	0	8
Illicit drinking	0	0	0	8	8
Traffic violations	0	0	4	0	4
Throwing water out of window	1	0	1	0	2
Objects that constitute a nuisance	0	1	0	0	1
Miscellaneous	0	0	0	3	3
Market or exchange related	0	0	0	0	0
Total	9	5	14	11	39

Source: Police records in cartons Y-9495A and Y-9495B at the Archives Nationales de France.

Table 7.3 Count of violations reported by Commissioner Dubuisson at hearings in the police chamber of the Paris Châtelet during 1758

	March 3, 1758	April 14, 1758	June 2, 1758	October 20, 1758	Total
Street cleaning	34	23	3	24	84
Objects that constitute a nuisance	10	5	3	4	22
Throwing water out of window	1	5	2	2	10
Fecal matter	4	0	0	4	8
Dangerous object in window	1	1	1	0	3
Miscellaneous	1	0	2	0	3
Market or exchange related	0	0	0	0	0
Total	51	34	11	34	130

Source: Police records in cartons Y-9495A and Y-9495B at the Archives Nationales de France.

Table 7.4 Count of violations reported by Commissioner Duruisseau at hearings in the police chamber of the Paris Châtelet during 1758

	March 3, 1758	April 21, 1758	July 7, 1758	October 20, 1758	Total
Street cleaning	7	6	2	10	25
Objects that constitute a nuisance	6	4	0	4	14
Dangerous object in window	0	4	4	2	10
Fecal matter	0	0	0	1	1
Miscellaneous	0	0	0	1	1
Market or exchange related	1	0	0	0	1
Total	14	14	6	18	52

Source: Police records in cartons Y-9495A and Y-9495B at the Archives Nationales de France.

violations observed in the nineteen commissioner reports. The first incident, reported by Commissioner Duruisseau, involved a bunch of peddlers (*"revendeurs et revendeuses"*) who were congregating at the "intersection of *Bussy*" in the Saint-André-des-Arts area between eleven in the morning and two in the afternoon—what is undoubtedly today the little peddlers' market on the rue de Buci. The peddlers were making a lot of noise, blocking traffic, and were generally getting in the way of those who wanted to shop at nearby stores. Duruisseau noted that the number of carts and cars might cause accidents and were a nuisance to the neighbors. Each of the peddlers were fined three livres and ordered not to return.

The next three incidents were reported by Commissioner Doublon, whose beat covered the Saint Benoît neighborhood. One involved a tapestry maker who failed to have his registry audited and was accordingly fined three livres. Another involved a shoemaker who was working in his shop on a Sunday—the prescribed day of rest—and was fined four livres. And the last involved a widow who was letting out rooms to "suspect people of ill repute" (*différentes personnes suspectes et sans avêu*) without a license or permission. She was fined twenty livres.

In contrast to these first four, the fifth *contravention*, involving fraud in the sale of eggs, is truly market related. But it was observed by Commissioner Demachurin whose beat was Les Halles—the central marketplace—and it was the only violation cited by Demachurin in his report submitted at the March 3, 1758, hearing. In contrast to all the other reports, which had multiple citations, Demachurin only presented one incident. According to Demachurin's report, a complaint was filed by Sieur Monge, a fruit seller at Les Halles, that two other merchants had tried to defraud him on the sale of eggs. Monge testified to the police commissioner that the two other merchants—a fruit seller by the name of Vasselle and a *marchand forain*, a traveling merchant by the name of Midy—had tried to trick him into believing that Midy's eggs were especially large and that Vasselle had bought the same type of eggs from Midy at a very high price, namely 60 livres per thousand rather than the going price of 42 to 45 livres per thousand. When Monge asked to see the actual eggs, he determined that they were not as described and he pulled out of the deal. Monge further testified that the two merchants had nevertheless sold the eggs the next day at market at the fraudulently inflated price. Monge's accusation, in essence, was fraud and conspiracy—a charge that would be actionable today as an ordinary fraud in the sale of goods. Ultimately, the magistrate in the case imposed a fine of twenty livres, plus the usual one livre reimbursement to the court for posting the sentence.

Of the 352 incidences of violations reported by the commissioners in this sample—involving far more individuals—only one case involved anyone cited for violating a rule concerning a true market transaction, and it did not involve the *police des grains*. The evidence from these records shows clearly that the daily routine of the police involved predominantly trivial matters, in essence street cleaning, hygiene, and vice control.

This finding is entirely consistent with the history of the founding of the police chamber by Louis XIV. After taking power, the king turned first to finances, but then to justice and police matters. He created two special sessions of his council, one for matters of justice and one for matters of police. The first, the council on justice, he presided over himself on numerous occasions. It produced in 1667 the codification of rules of civil procedure, what was referred to as "ordonnance civile," as well as, in 1670, the codification of criminal procedure—"l'ordonnance criminelle." The second council, which addressed matters of police, we know far less about because it received so much less attention and Louis XIV never presided over any session. It was simply far less important.[16] Louis XIV ultimately carved out the police chamber from within the civil lieutenant's job description and second-seated the *lieutenant de police*. "The *lieutenant de police* will seat ordinarily at the Châtelet in the chamber *dite Chambre civile,* and will dispose of a small office adjacent."[17] The police of the Châtelet was by no means a criminal jurisdiction—there was a separate chamber for those more important matters—it levied only minor fines, if that, and took a second seat to both the criminal chamber and the civil chamber.

The Y-9498 and Y-9499 Cartons

More to the point, a careful review of the more significant sentences meted out by the police chamber of the Châtelet reveals that the *police des grains* constituted a minor function of the chamber's jurisdiction and received far less attention than other salient (and salacious) categories such as vice crimes and derelict servants. This is evident from a qualitative and quantitative review of the collection of 932 sentences and ordinances from the period 1668 to 1787 contained in two cartons at the National Archives, Y-9498 and Y-9499.[18] Of those 932 records, only eighty-six—9.2 percent—are related in any way to the commerce or market in grain, or to bakers, millers, or other activities that have any bearing whatsoever on bread, flour, or grain. Within the category of the highest fines meted out by the police—three thousand livres or more—grain-related offenses represented a tiny fraction of the whole, only one (2.6 percent) of thirty-nine such fines. There were only five sentences that involved any form of detention and none of them had to do with the commerce of grain or the *police des grains:* four of these detention orders involved derelict servants who defrauded their masters in an incident in December 1718, and the fifth involved an eight-year-old vagabond boy who was committed in October 1723 to the "Hôpital" (the mental asylum qua prison, leprosarium, homeless shelter, and hospital) for theft.[19]

This collection of police sentences and ordinances gives a trenchant view of the jurisdiction of the police chamber over the 120 years prior to the Revolution.[20] The cartons contain no fewer than 581 police sentences and 351 police ordinances.[21] These sentences and ordinances show clearly that the most egregious and heavily policed offense was illicit gambling—especially card games, but also skittle and picket games, all with wonderful names like "jeu de pharaon," "jeu de biribi," "jeu de carmagnole," "jeu de pair ou non," and "jeu de siam."[22] A certain François Joseph Martin was even caught in 1746 running, out of his own home, an "académie de jeu de piquet."[23] In fact, a full thirty-eight of the thirty-nine fines of three thousand or more livres involved games of chance, and much of the gambling was associated with debauchery, crimes, and other vices—including, for instance, the assassination in August 1721 of one card player by another at the Hôtel du Mans.[24] The highest fine mentioned is for 7,600 livres imposed on those responsible for organizing an illicit lottery in the Hôtel de Soissons in November 1720—but the fine was ultimately reduced to 100 livres because the lottery was never drawn.[25]

In terms of the *police des grains*, what becomes clear from the record is that enforcement correlated with scarcity—with *la disette*, or grain shortages. The record evidence shows practically a one-to-one correlation between periods of scarcity and sentences related to the *police des grains*. The years of the most pronounced scarcity in France include 1693–1694, 1700, 1709–1710, 1720–1726, 1738–1742, 1747, 1757–1759, and 1765–1775.[26] With the exception of the last two periods, for which there are no sentences covering that period in the collection, every other *disette* corresponds to a spike in the enforcement of grain regulations—and in some cases, to the only time these regulations resulted in disciplinary action. The chronology of the sentences associated with the commerce in grain reflects that the vast majority were entered in years of severe shortage. This trend is reflected in Figure 7.1, which tallies the raw number and percentage of sentences related to the commerce in grain in relation to the total sentences compiled in the collection.

Just as enforcement of the *police des grains* corresponds perfectly to the periods of shortages in grain, so too does the enactment of new ordinances concerning grain and bread. The *police des grains* was an epiphenomenon intended to assuage a hungry crowd—it was by no means a continuous endeavor. This is borne out well by other historical evidence. The nineteenth-century historian Albert Babeau, in his detailed study of village life under the ancien régime, remarked: "It was mostly during times of food shortage that the administration imagined that it could remedy matters by means of restrictive regulations. Tariffs, prohibitions on keeping more than a certain quantity

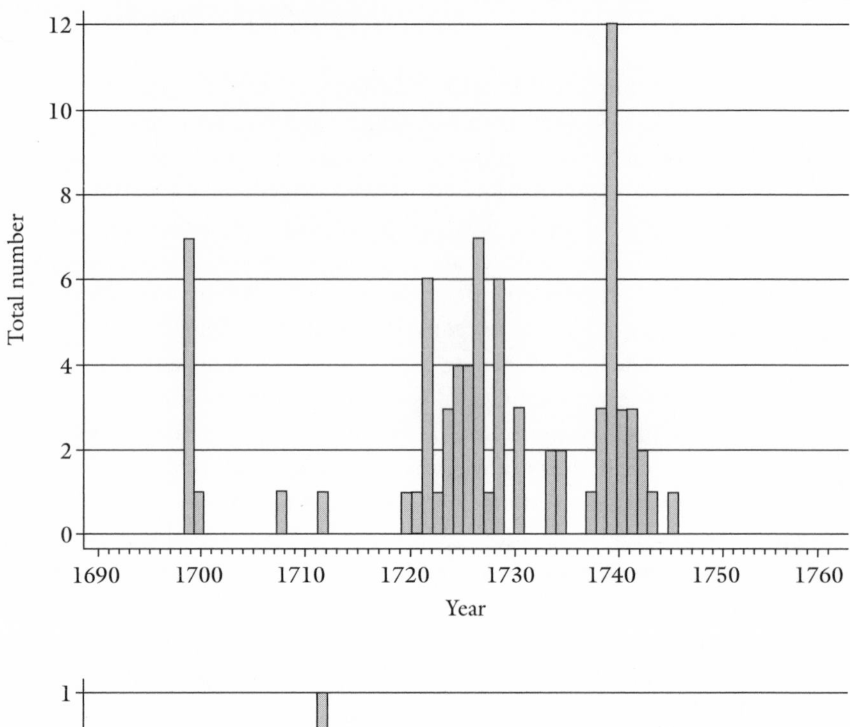

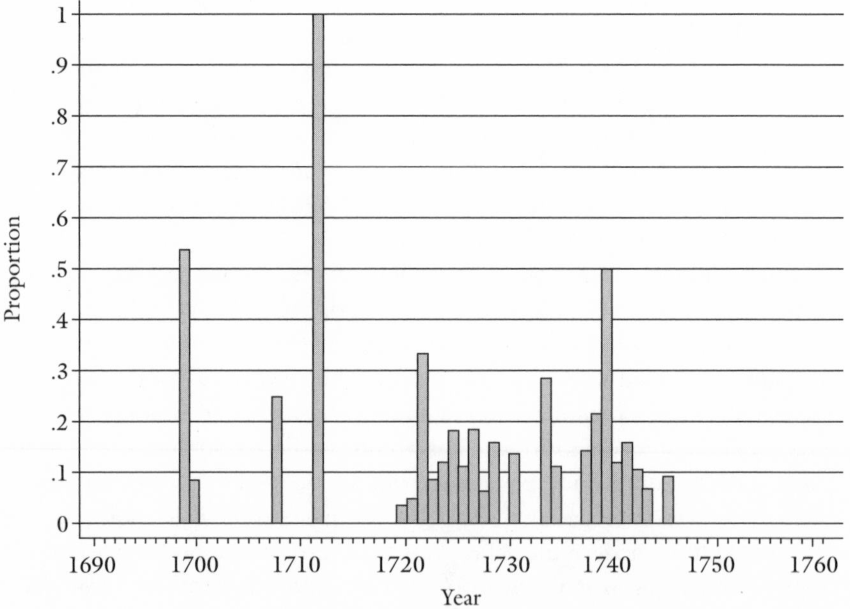

Figure 7.1 *Top:* Total count of grain-related sentences documented in the Y-9498 and Y-9499 cartons at the National Archives. *Bottom:* Proportion of total sentences per year that are grain related among those documented in the Y-9498 and Y-9499 cartons at the National Archives. *Source:* Michèle Bimbenet-Privat, *Ordonnances et sentences de police du Châtelet de Paris, 1668–1787: Inventaire analytique des articles Y 9498 et 9499*. Paris: Archives Nationales, 1992.

of wheat, injunctions to bring the grain and fodder to the nearest market, domiciliary visits, inventories, fines, confiscations, these were the kinds of measures to which they resorted, measures that were imitated during the Terror."[27] In fact, some of the regulations were written in such a way that they would apply only during times of *disette*. For instance, as Duchesne emphasized in his *Code de la police* of 1767, "The police regulation of November 21, 1577, which requires sales to take place in the market, stipulates in fact that it applies in 'times of high prices or uncertainty.'"[28] It was also well recognized, Duchesne explained, that "in the times of high prices, the officers of the *police* should enforce the regulations more rigorously and should focus principally on supplying the markets."[29] The *police des grains* was a political response to crisis moments of unrest and hunger, as Judith Miller demonstrates well in her book *Mastering the Market* (1999).

This conclusion is also borne out in contemporaneous accounts.[30] Commissaire Le Maire wrote one such report on police enforcement for the *lieutenant de police* Sartine at the request of the Empress Marie-Thérèse, who was contemplating reorganizing the Vienna police in the Parisian image.[31] It reflects the sporadic enforcement of these police regulations and that any enforcement coincided with periods of food shortages. The same is true of letters written by the lieutenant De Marville to the minister Maurepas during the period 1742–1747.[32]

Even the most interventionist of policies, the fixing of prices, was haphazardly devised, irregularly enforced, and more of a guideline than a rule. Duschesne noted, for instance, that a tariff had been established in Paris to give an idea of the right price for bread in 1700, but that it never really operated as a fixed price: "Regarding the price of bread, the liberty to sell it by mutual agreement is granted in the big cities because the competition between city bakers and those from outside the city necessarily produces pressure to ease up on pricing in order to increase the volume of sales, which nevertheless does not prevent the magistrates from making sure there are not excesses."[33] Duchesne does report that "there were several attempts in Paris to set a common price," but only mentions the resulting rate basis "because it might serve as a model to other cities, where a bread tariff may be necessary to prevent collusion (which would be so easy among a small number of bakers)."[34]

It turns out that the *police des grains* represented only a small fraction of the business of the *lieutenant de police*, all of which was essentially trivial. The archival records reveal a disproportionate number of terribly minor infractions and a relatively small place for the *police des grains*. The historians of the Parisian grain and bread markets—predominantly liberal opponents of the regulations such as Fréminville and Afanassiev—did a skilled job of picking out the sentences related to the *police des grains* from the haystack of police records. But we should be wary of having so much of our understanding of the *police des grains* filtered through the lens of these opponents, who apparently had a morbid fascination with regimentation. This is not to suggest that enforcement was nonexistent. The police manuals certainly offer evidence to the contrary. Delamare, Fréminville, and Duchesne all catalogued as many of the fines as they could find—desperately tracking and reiterating any proof they had that these ordinances were enforced. But these proceedings were few and far between, and involved only trivial matters.

One last point: the same kind of trivial and unenforced regulations continued in France during the nineteenth century and in some cases, extend to the present. These regulations were and are, in no sense "pre-liberal." Here, for instance, is a "model police code" (*Règelement-Modèle*), based on existing French police regulations, that was printed in 1843. A fascinating document, it lists in numbered provisions under the heading "Section VIII.—Boulangerie":

> 460.—Any person who would like to establish themselves in the community as a baker must make a declaration to that effect at the municipal building [*la mairie*].
>
> 461.—Every baker will be held responsible for keeping in constant reserve the supply demanded by the royal decree regulating this matter.
>
> 462.—Every baker is charged with making bread in the quantities and according to the weight schedule prescribed by the regulations. The bread will be consistently of good quality and properly handled. These requirements, especially regarding weight, are applicable to *specialty breads.*
>
> 465.—Every baker must keep his store continuously stocked with bread.
>
> 467.—Bakers are forbidden from becoming grain sellers, grain measurers, or millers.
>
> 472.—The baker's assistants, when they are kneading bread at night, are forbidden from yelling or singing in such a way as to disturb the neighbors.
>
> 474.—All resale of bread is forbidden.[35]

The rules may be slightly more modern sounding—only slightly—but they betray all the trappings of the disciplinary *police des grains:* minute, intricate, detailed, and most importantly, trivial and underenforced.

Rereading the Tracts

As we have seen, actual reports from long-ago Paris *commissaires* belie the claims of overbearing discipline in eighteenth-century France. But it is equally important to remember that the discourse of liberty at the heart of Beccaria's and Delamare's writings was as strong and robust as that of the Physiocrats. Advocates of the *police des grains* spoke in equally liberatory terms. Regardless of whether we ultimately believe in the sincerity of Beccaria's aspiration to enlightenment and freedom, as the *philosophes* did, or highlight instead the disciplinary nature of the practices he espoused, as Michel Foucault would, it is crucial to acknowledge that Beccaria's text—his text at the very least—favored freedom. "Police" was supposed to protect and promote liberty, not infringe on it.

The logic of freedom permeated Beccaria's discourse of policing. Remember that the argument for governmental intervention and administration that Beccaria developed in his economic writings rested on the central assumption that there was no natural orderliness in human affairs—especially not in commerce—and that, as a result, the only way to achieve an orderly state that provided for the needs of citizens, the only way to protect their freedom, was through the minute regulation of all commercial exchange. Economic entropy—rather than natural order—formed the central premise of Beccaria's thought. Beccaria rested most of his proposed interventions on the underlying claim that self-interested merchants were the ones responsible for unreasonably high prices and resulting shortages of goods—especially grain. These arguments infused the field of public economy and greatly influenced the public discourse on the Continent.

It was precisely to correct these distortions that the pioneers of public economy recommended, and the royal administrators enacted, edicts and ordinances regulating the markets and imposing the regulatory framework that would become known as the *police des grains.* The underlying logic was to rein in merchant self-interest and ultimately reduce the price of commodities. In France, this effort was reflected in numerous royal declarations of the late seventeenth and early eighteenth centuries. As one royal declaration dated October 5, 1693, stated: "We have been informed that the scarcity and high cost of wheat is the product less of the *disette* than of the artifices of merchants and others engaged in the commerce of grain who, sure of sales . . . , horde all the grain they can in granaries and stores, so the markets are not sufficiently supplied."[36]

The discourse of liberty—from merchant avarice—permeated royal interventions in the seventeenth century. Consider this declaration signed July 1, 1694:

> *Royal declaration, given at Versailles on June 22, 1694, that forbids all merchants and other individuals from purchasing, or making any agreements or advance deposits on unripe, standing grain before the harvest, under penalty of confiscation of the aforesaid grain, of its price, and of a thousand-livre fine.*
>
> We have been informed that usurers and other people greedy for illicit gain, after having profited from the food shortage and excessive prices that they themselves brought about because of their stockpiling, are preparing again to deprive the poor of the advantages and relief that they hope to draw from the plentiful harvest, and, taking advantage of the indigence of the laborers and those who work their land with their hands, they purchase unripe, standing grain and make agreements or advance deposits such as were forbidden under severe penalty by the wise decrees of the kings that came before us, in the hope of stockpiling this grain in hidden storehouses and only selling it in times of high prices, and causing, if they could, food shortages, despite the fertility of the year. . . . For these reasons and others, in our sure knowledge, full power and royal authority, we . . . state, statute, and order, desire and please that the decrees of King Louis XI of the year 1462; François I, of 1539; Henry III, of 1577; and Louis XIII, of glorious memory, our most honored lord and father, of the year 1629, regarding the *police des grains*, be executed in form and content. We hereby bar and prohibit most unequivocally all merchants and all our other subjects, whatever their quality and condition may be, from purchasing or making any agreements or advance deposits on unripe, standing grain before the harvest, under penalty of confiscation of the aforesaid grain, of its price, of a thousand-livre fine against each of the offending parties, half going to our own profit and the other half going to the profit of the denouncer, even corporal punishment in the case of a repeat offense . . . Given at Versailles on June 22, the year of our Lord 1694, and of our reign the fifty-second. *Signed*, LOUIS: And below, By the King, PHELYPEAUX. And marked with a seal.
>
> *Registered, heard . . . in Paris, at the Parliament, July 1, 1694.*
>
> Signed, Du Tillet[37]

On its face at the very least, this regulation was fully intended to enhance the liberty and welfare of the ordinary subject. The Russian historian Georges Afanassiev documented this logic throughout the archival records. So, for instance, the "intendant d'Orleans, M. de Bouville" wrote to the "contrôleur général" a letter dated July 17, 1694, urging against any relaxation of these regulations: "I am convinced that prohibitions on selling grain anywhere else than at market would be very useful, because it would increase the quantity at market and thereby make the price go down, given that one could not sell grain elsewhere; if permitted to sell grain in their houses, that is to say, in their castles and more modest farms, the wheat merchants will then be obliged to buy at the sellers' price and will not be able to offer the grain at a lower price at market."[38] Afanassiev summarized the dominant belief at the time: "In very good faith, public opinion imagined that, without the intervention of the *police,* the provisioning of the cities would be seriously compromised. . . . Ample and reasonably priced wheat, that was the sole concern of the administration; except for a very few rare exceptions, it did not seem to think that the interests of the producers also merited attention."[39]

As noted earlier, Nicolas Delamare's *Traité* emphasized this precise link between administration and liberty. Delamare listed in detail all the connivances of merchants and laborers. He describes a *disette* from 1691 and showed how it was made worse by the growers and laborers.[40] Delamare dedicated his *Traité* to the regulation of grain, meats, beverages, fish, and so on, but his goal was freedom—liberty for the consumer from the shenanigans of the merchants. Detailed administration was the only way to ensure *bon marché.* As Duchesne explained, "Experience has demonstrated that the surest way to procure supply is to make sure that all goods are brought to open market. . . . In this way, where an abundant supply is brought to the same location, each person can satisfy themselves at the least risk of being cheated, both in terms of the quality of the goods, because they are subject to the inspection of the officers of the *Police,* and in terms of the price, because everyone is at liberty to speak with several sellers."[41]

The notion of liberty that comes through in these manuals was understood in a different manner than it was by the Physiocrats—or perhaps today. It was the liberty of consumers from the manipulations of the merchants. It was a more paternalistic or protectionist freedom. As Duchesne wrote in his *Code de la police:* "Commerce is the soul of the State since it simultaneously produces public plenty and individual wealth: hence the wise regulations that were made for maintaining the liberty of trade and preserving the good faith, order and discipline necessary to make it flourish."[42] The regulations, we are told, were intended to protect and free the cultivators from the oppression of the merchants. Fréminville wrote, under the entry "WHEAT, *unripe* [*en verd*], purchase of":

> There are greedy and selfish people who know how to profit from the misery of indigent laborers, to whom they offer some small monetary help on the condition that they sell them their wheat, although it is standing and not yet ripe, which often represents the entire harvest that they will have: these greedy people buy it for next to nothing and they make such arrangements in several places: these types of purchases that cause the ruin of impoverished laborers and often reduce them to utter destitution by eating, as the proverb says, *their wheat in the blade:* these types of purchases, I insist, have always been strictly prohibited by a number of decrees.[43]

The discourse was about liberty, and throughout, the objective was to provide for the needs of the many and to protect against the avarice of the few.

In order to more fully grasp the idea of liberty embedded in the *police des grains,* it is also important to remember that this *police* represented, in part, a liberation from seigneurial relations and a substitute to the feudal legal regime. Under the seigneurial system, a coercive regulatory system was enforced by fief-holders to defray the expenses of maintaining the infrastructure—that is, to build roads, mills, presses, and so on. The *tenaciers* (tenants) of the fief-holders were required to use the fiefs' services—their tills for their grain, their mills to make flour, their presses for their wine—for a fee, or in exchange for work (the *corvée*) or an item of value.[44] In addition, a range of seigneurial courts—from lower courts that heard petty criminal cases to higher courts that considered serious cases—meted out justice and would continue in fact until the end of the ancien régime, though their influence waned.[45] As the state, through the monarch, became more robust, it took over these responsibilities. The centralization converted the seigneurial regimen of administration into a *police*—and in this sense, was liberating. In particular, the *police des grains* emerged against this backdrop of feudal relations to provide a more modern, rational, bureaucratic administration of justice. It should come as no surprise that Fréminville wrote both a *Dictionnaire de la police* and, in 1746, a treatise on seigneurial rights. In effect, the regulation of grain and markets has to be understood against the backdrop of feudal property rights prior to the eighteenth century.[46] This perspective not only clarifies the significant liberatory element in the *police;* it also makes sense of the later Physiocratic attempt to replace the *corvée* and other remnants of the feudal order with taxation by a single direct tax.

One final point. The idea that regulation promotes liberty should not be entirely foreign to our modern ears. Karl Polanyi made precisely the same argument in the twentieth century: "The passing of [the] market economy can become the beginning of an era of unprecedented freedom. Juridical and actual freedom can be made wider and more general than ever before; regulation and control can achieve freedom not only for the few, but for all." He continues: "Freedom not as an appurtenance of privilege, tainted at the source, but as a prescriptive right extending far beyond the narrow confines of the political sphere into the intimate organization of society itself. Thus will old freedoms and civic rights be added to the fund of new freedoms generated by the leisure and security that industrial society offers to all. Such a society can afford to be both just and free."[47]

8

The Illusion of Freedom

On the other side of the ledger, there was a lot more discipline in Physiocracy than meets the eye—and there is a lot more constraint in our free markets than we tend to acknowledge today. Here too, an examination of actual practices is revealing. Let's start in the eighteenth century.

Revisiting Le Mercier's *Intendance* in Martinique

We looked earlier at Mercier's style of governing in Martinique and his implementation of a severe police force. But Mercier's autocratic approach was not limited to securing private property or establishing a police presence: it extended to a strict *police des grains* and a highly regimented economic order. Le Mercier de la Rivière, it turns out, was a true believer in the actual policing of markets—despite his economic writings. As *intendant* of Martinique, Mercier passed a wide range of ordinances concerning the strict regulation of commerce, imposing rules regarding butchers, bakers, bread prices, and the like.

A bit of background may be helpful. By a *règlement du roi* issued March 24, 1763, the two highest-ranking officials in the colony were the *gouverneur-général,* who was the head of the colony's military government, and the *intendant,* who led the civil government.[1] Both were charged with governing the colony, but the *intendant* was solely responsible for a number of areas including justice, taxes, markets, commerce, agriculture, and *bon marché*—or, as the edict read, "the ways of making subsistence plentiful and reasonable."[2] By the same order dated March 24, 1763, the king had abolished the local militia in Martinique and conferred the defense of the colony entirely to his regular troops.[3] Also, from as early as 1669, the king had prohibited all foreign commerce in Martinique and the French islands. Only French vessels could trade goods from French ports, and, at first, only French goods. Eventually, during the early eighteenth century, French boats were allowed to bring to the Antilles foreign merchandise as well, but foreign vessels were still prohibited from coming within one league of Martinique.[4]

In a series of ordinances enacted from August 1763 to February 1764, Mercier as *intendant* and the *gouverneur,* Marquis de Fenelon, imposed a range of strict police measures and regulations of commerce that covered both Martinique's social life and its economy. The scope of their regulations is impressive. By order dated September 1, 1763, Mercier and the *gouverneur* imposed strict regulations on all butchers that required them to obtain permission directly from the *intendant* himself or his delegates to acquire a license, and disclose to the police the exact location where animals were being slaughtered. The order also prohibited slaves from being butchers (at the risk of their being sold at profit to the king in case their masters had allowed them to butcher), and set the price of meat. Mercier himself, in fact, fixed the very price of meat:

> We hereby declare, for the present and until further notice, that butchers are authorized to sell beef, veal, and mutton at the rate of 22 sols 6 deniers per pound, and pork at the rate of 15 sols per pound: we forbid them to sell at a higher price, even if they are in agreement with their buyers, nor to mix, in the weighing, the jaws, feet, or entrails of any animal, on the pretext of making up the weight, or for any other reason, all this under penalty of a 500 livres fine.[5]

By separate order dated the same day, September 1, 1763, Mercier and Fenelon also implemented a regulatory scheme for bakers, requiring that all bakers register with the *intendant* himself; that all bakers submit to his subdelegate every fifteen days an accounting of the quantity, quality, and price of flour bought during the intervening period; and that all merchants, ship captains, and sellers of flour do the same every month. Like the order for butchers, it also established the price of bread, officially set at "7 sols 6 deniers la livre."[6]

"The price at which bread is set in this Colony during ordinary times," Mercier declared, "should be considered appropriate for commerce in France and in the Colony."[7] Mercier emphasized that he himself vowed to oversee the just price and make sure it was always set properly: "We have always sought the best means to most conveniently and reliably set the true price of bread in such a way as to be equitable to those who make it and to those who consume it."[8]

Then, by order dated September 24, 1763, Mercier increased the price of bread, from "7 sols 6 deniers la livre, au poids ordinaire de 16 onces" to the same price for only "14 onces."[9] The exact ordinance, reproduced in the Introduction, is striking: when one looks at Mercier's signature on the document fixing bread prices, it is as if the world is upside down. But that is not all. By an order dated October 17, 1763, Mercier and Fenelon required all inhabitants to submit in writing, within eight days, to the *commissaire de la paroisse* (the local police chief) "the exact written declaration, signed by him, of all the goods sold by him since July 29th of the present year, which declaration will contain the quantities sold, the name of the buyer, the price of the sale, and the name of the ship's captain, the merchant, or the agent to whom he has delivered the goods, all of it organized chronologically."[10]

These ordinances complemented a whole set of regulatory interventions that ranged from *bon marché* to public safety, housing construction, and commerce. On September 25, 1763, they prohibited any and all persons from feeding or raising pigs within the limits of any town or *bourg*.[11] By order dated October 14, 1763, Mercier and Fenelon stopped any further construction of buildings in the Bourg de Saint-Pierre "in the interests of commerce."[12] By order dated August 14, 1763, Mercier and Fenelon reduced the number of taverns on the island, regulated consumption at those taverns, fixed their hours of opening and closing, prohibited black people (except domestics with their masters) from being in taverns, and directed who could own taverns.[13] Note that taverns had been highly regulated before, with strict limits on the number of taverns dating to 1758 at least, and that Mercier was only upping the ante.[14] This was true of the butchers as well, who were also highly regulated to begin with; Mercier only increased the number and scope of the regulations they had to follow.[15]

Were the Physiocrats, then, lovers of liberty or were they, instead, enlightened despots who governed economic matters in the same coercive manner that they established a police force? The answer to this question resides in Mercier's practice as *intendant*. Mercier was indeed a Physiocrat when he first arrived in Martinique, and in some respects, he was faithful to Physiocratic principles. He tried to reform the tax system in a manner that was consistent with Physiocratic writings, and during his first tour of duty, he attempted to stimulate free trade with the island, indebting himself personally in the process.[16] He was also faithful to his belief in legal despotism when he created a severe police force. But Mercier departed entirely from his principles with regard to the regulation of markets: somewhat surprisingly, Mercier himself set prices for bread, meat, and other commercial goods.[17]

In this regard, Mercier's practice was entirely at odds with his theory. Now, one might wonder whether Mercier had no other options while *intendant* of Martinique. But that cannot be right. Turgot, more moderate in his writings, would put into practice different regulatory mechanisms only a few years later for all of France. Appointed *contrôleur général des finances* by Louis XVI in 1774—the equivalent of a minister of finance, commerce, and public works—Turgot implemented a number of reforms during his short but notable two years in office. In particular, he eliminated the *corvée* and replaced it with a tax that applied to the privileged classes, and reformed the grain trade, all while supporting government intervention in other domains.[18] Mercier was not locked into creating a *police des grains* in Martinique. He just chose to impose one—freely.

The Genesis of the Chicago Board of Trade

In this respect, Mercier was not alone. The entire history of the Chicago Board of Trade is, in truth, a story of a strict *police des grains* masquerading under free-market rhetoric. Bill Novak demonstrated well in his 1996 book *The People's Welfare* that beneath the façade of laissez-faire, the American states regulated economic and social life extensively in the nineteenth century, using their police powers to control health, safety, and working conditions. The genesis of the Chicago Board of Trade bears this out well. The story of the Chicago Board is one of government-granted monopoly, privileged private interests, and intense regulation of trade, all passing under the guise of free markets. In truth, the invention of boards of trade like the Chicago Board produced a new form of policing in which the state allowed a private association of wealthy merchants to appropriate full regulatory power.

The birth and development of the Chicago Board is a fascinating story of political and social influence.[19] The emergence of the board as a self-regulating, private association that donned the mantle of a public-interest, quasi-governmental agency took many years. After an initial period during which the board failed to achieve self-discipline through self-regulatory mechanisms, there ultimately developed a battle over "bucket shops"—unauthorized markets that allowed trading on the price of commodities and futures—that was transformative and shaped the Chicago Board. The board's efforts at prohibiting bucket shops ended at the U.S. Supreme Court in two famous cases decided in 1905, *Board of Trade v. Christie* and *Kinsey v. Board of Trade*.[20] Justice Oliver Wendell Holmes wrote for the majority and ruled in favor of the board, putting the Supreme Court's stamp of approval on its practices and on its ability to regulate business.

That stamp of approval effectively turned the Chicago Board into a quasi-administrative though still private agency, and ultimately gave it the legitimacy and authority to become a regulatory body. By beating the bucket shops, the Chicago Board became the monopoly for the grain trade. And insofar as there developed what we call today a free exchange, it began as (and remains) a monopolistic club that set commission rates, excluded those it did not want, and closed down its competitors.

How did this come about? And how did it come about without federal intervention, at least until the 1920s? The answer, in essence, is that the Chicago Board of Trade offered policing: The board "provided the market and its participants with the same type of policing activities asked of the federal government. By setting standards of grading, inspection, and weighing, and through the disciplinary control of members, the exchanges regularized and rationalized competition in the marketplace."[21] That assessment still holds true today. The Chicago Board is viewed as a free market; but it is, in truth, a disciplinary mechanism that keeps a market relatively ordered.

Much of the Chicago Board's policing system was put in place in 1859 through the charter that the board received from the Illinois legislature—which remains in place today.[22] The important elements of the charter include, first, judicial authority similar to that of the circuit courts, which is delegated to committees of the Chicago Board to arbitrate disputes; second, administrative authority to appoint "inspectors and weighers of grain" who would issue binding determinations on members of the board; and third, the authority to self-govern through internal rules and management.[23] From its inception, there was no recourse from board arbitration and rule-making, and members, upon joining the Chicago Board, had to promise to abide by its decisions by signing a "solemn compact":

> We . . . hereby mutually agree . . . with each other, and with the said corporation, that we will in our actions and dealings with each other, and the said corporation, be in all respects governed by and respect the Rules, Regulations and By-Laws of the said corporation, as they now exist, or as they may be hereafter modified, altered or amended.[24]

To many of us, this might sound like an oath and a club—with its own rules and self-discipline. But it is the State of Illinois that was sanctioning this society, making it possible, giving it a charter enforceable by law. The State of Illinois essentially delegated its rule-making and adjudicatory authority to a private regulatory agency. The exchange itself was not "unregulated," it was just allowed to be its own "regulator," in a system set up by state sanction, force of law, and formal charter.

Pursuant to the 1859 charter, the board enacted rules regarding who could trade on the exchange, what kind of transactions could take place, and how much people could charge. Because of its charter, the board could ultimately distinguish itself, in the eyes of the courts and public, from the bucket shops and ultimately acquire monopoly power over grain trading. As a result, it came to control the "free" commodities market. Like an administrative agency might, the Chicago Board determines who has access to its trading pits by limiting who is a member of the organization; it also sets specific commission rates and regulates the commercial activities of the dealers in the grain trade.

Regulating Price and Entry

The Chicago Board has fixed the minimum amount of commission that a member could make on a brokered deal since as early as 1878. The board has also served as gatekeeper by means of both admission standards and fees: "By 1882 the initiation fee, once the proposed member had been cleared by a committee and a majority vote of the directorate, stood at $10,000. All these conditions insured that persons of small means would not be involved in speculative ventures on the Chicago Board of Trade, and this was in keeping with the purposes of the Board."[25] In 1900, the board imposed the punishment of expulsion for any member violating the rule about commissions, and, following a trial in 1900, the directors expelled a member for this reason. (The case went to court and the Illinois Appellate Court sided with the board, allowing the regulation and fixing of commissions.)[26]

Regulating Trading Hours

In the early years, the Chicago Board tried to regulate when trading occurred by refusing to enforce trades made before or after regular business hours. But as it became clear that the problem of trading hours was closely linked to the problem of privileged trading (often made outside of approved hours), the directors of the Board persuaded members in 1890 to voluntarily agree to trade only during official hours.[27] In 1895, the directors developed a new method to enforce the rules about trading hours: "As the hour for closing struck, an employee of the Board appeared with a huge Chinese gong and proceeded to drown out all noise in the pits, making it impossible to trade."[28] By 1900, the board had approved a rule tightening the penalties for irregular-hour trading.[29] Two-minute extensions, wheat pit committees, and MCCs (modified closing calls) are all part of today's mechanism to prevent after-hours trading. (Recall, too, that the MCC mechanism embraces a price-fixing component.)

Regulating Options

The Chicago Board enacted a rule in 1865 that required actual delivery in every contract with the purpose of discouraging options trading (what were called "privileges" or "puts and calls").[30] The practice, however, was unaffected. In 1874, the Illinois legislature enacted a criminal provision outlawing options trading—as part of larger legislation that also outlawed corners and attempted corners (more on these later).[31] The prohibition, however, was not enforced vigorously. Two years later, in April 1876, the board passed a resolution providing that any member of the board who engaged in privileged trading on the floor would be suspended from the exchange. This too, however, did not stop privileged trading.[32]

In fact, despite all these rules and prohibitions, trading in privileges continued and was still going strong in 1886. So in 1888, the directors of the board decided to crack down and set up a committee to secretly investigate and suppress the practice. Three board members were accused of privileged trading, tried by the directors, and disciplined. This action, however, created an uproar and further investigation, after which the directors retracted the earlier disciplinary orders, censured about thirty members, and passed a resolution recommending expulsion for any member who engaged in privileged trading in the future.[33]

There were other attempts to get rid of privileged trading. The agrarian movements of the 1890s—populist and progressive—militated for an anti-option statute at the federal level. They believed that options trading had the effect of lowering the price of commodities. An agrarian statute passed the U.S. House and Senate in 1893, but never made it through in conference. As a result, no federal anti-option legislation was adopted.[34] In 1892, the Chicago Board directors tried again to expel members who had engaged in privileged trading, but that led to litigation and backpedaling. At that point, the board gave up entirely and rescinded the rule against puts and calls.[35]

The Grain Futures Act of 1921 is the basis of all federal commodities regulation since that time, and was upheld in 1923 by the U.S. Supreme Court in *Hill v. Wallace*.[36] It involved significant regulation of futures trading: there was to be no futures trading unless the trader owned the property or the contract was made through a board of trade. In the process, the federal legislation put the seal of approval on the board's monopoly. In *Hill v. Wallace* and three years later in *Trusler v. Crooks,* the U.S. Supreme Court struck down provisions of the Grain Futures Act that involved the regulation of corners, of taxes on privileged trades, and of futures not executed on a contract market—but left in place trading of futures on the Chicago Board.[37] Ultimately, in 1974, the Commodity Futures Trading Commission (CFTC) was established to oversee trading in futures and options. In the end, then, options trading became a part of the Chicago Board, overseen by the CFTC over the objection of agrarian interests.

Regulating Corners

In 1868, the Chicago Board stated that it would expel any member who effectuated a corner—which it defined as "the practice of . . . making contracts for the purchase of a commodity, and then taking measures to render it impossible for the seller to fill his contract, for the purpose of extorting money from him."[38] A couple of years later, in the spring of 1874, the Illinois legislature enacted an "anti-corner statute." Corners continued to happen, though, and among board members there developed an accepted practice: members had to abide by the determinations of the board when it set a price to settle a corner. A crisis occurred in 1874 when William Sturges, who had run a corner in corn, defied the board and refused to settle at the agreed price. The board ultimately expelled Sturges, but he fought back, litigating the case for many years. The board ultimately settled and Sturges was reinstated. After that, it adopted "detailed rules for self-regulation" to try to head off such conflicts.[39]

Regulating "Bucket Shops"

Bucket shops tended to trade in smaller quantities for a cheaper commission, which made them more accessible to the small traders. In the early years, many of the brokers on the board floor would "bucket" their trades—take the other side of a transaction and trade at a bucket shop. In 1883, the directors of the Chicago Board passed a rule prohibiting board members from shopping at a bucket. Such conduct was deemed "an unmercantile offense" and would lead to suspension or, for a habitual offender, to expulsion from the board.[40] Then, in 1887, Illinois passed a law against bucket shops as part of a Midwestern movement against gambling. Iowa had passed a similar law in 1884, Ohio in 1885, and Missouri the same year as Illinois.

At about the same time, the Chicago Board began prohibiting its members from disseminating market prices to bucket shops or other exchanges—another way to try to eliminate the buckets. This led to lengthy litigation. In a famous case in 1888, *New York and Chicago Grain and Stock Exchange v. Chicago Board of Trade*, the Illinois Appellate Court sided with the board and allowed it to restrict dissemination of market prices. The court held that the board was a private entity without a public duty to disclose its market prices. On appeal, however, the Illinois Supreme Court ruled against the board. The interest at hand was public, it held, not just private, and there was a general interest in the dissemination of the information.[41]

In response, the board voted to no longer distribute quotations to anyone except board members. The courts blocked that too and after other attempts to restrict the information, the board caved in. Then, in April 1890, the directors of the board voted to stop all transmission of quotations off the trading floor. The directors passed regulations prohibiting communication, had the windows "soaped," barred access to the open board next door, and disciplined any member who shared the information. A year later, the bucket shops were still operating, in part by directly dealing with brokers on the board as a way to get the information about prices. And the policy was creating internal dissent since it had the effect of favoring the larger brokerage houses that had their own private wires as opposed to the smaller firms that did not have their own wire services.[42]

In 1894, the directors tried another approach: they passed a rule requiring members to inform their customers, in writing and on the day of the trade, who was on the other side of a trade. This rule would make it difficult for the member to bucket the transaction himself. The directors then enforced the rule and suspended a member.

There were other initiatives against bucketing in 1895–1899, resulting in a lot of prosecutions, trials, and expulsions. The board began a veritable crusade against bucket shops in the early 1900s, including further litigation to restrict who could receive the quotations. It won a few major legal victories, and pretty soon there were no bucket shops left in Chicago.[43] The board's success in eliminating the bucket shops had a significant effect on the price of a seat on the exchange. In 1898 "the 'high' offer for a seat on the exchange was down to $800. . . . [B]y 1902, with the effective enforcement of the commission rule [against bucket shops], the high offer for a seat reached $4,350."[44]

Futures Trading and Redistribution

It would be tempting to characterize the period before the Chicago Board as a chaotic, standardless state of nature, where merchants and farmers transacted haphazardly at great economic risk: there was no way of knowing that the grain shipment was of high quality, that the farmer was honest and would deliver in nine months, that there were reliable facilities to store the grain in transit, or that the merchant would pay any debts. In this view, the Chicago Board implemented, ensured, and policed standardized grades of grain, monitored the warehouse facilities, enforced futures contracts, and policed its members, creating a more orderly market that would facilitate a larger number of trades in larger quantities, producing efficiencies of scale. But to characterize this transition as one from a state of nature to a free market would be to succumb to an illusion.

What the Chicago Board brought about was not a shift from a state of nature to free exchange, nor the production of order from chaos, but instead the creation of a new order that simply distributed wealth in a different way. Before the board, a farmer could develop a reputation for quality and could charge a premium on the sale of his grain: merchants would know that they would be getting the best quality from that particular farmer and might pay more to him than to others. Farmers and merchants could develop long-standing relationships and build on their dealings with each other. In contrast, the creation and policing of standardized grades of grain eliminated the need for (or at the very least significantly reduced the benefit of) reputational gains: it shifted or lowered the risk in the transaction so that there was less uncertainty for the merchant regarding the quality of the goods, and less uncertainty for the farmer regarding the credit-worthiness of the merchant (guaranteed by the board member). By rendering the farmer fungible, the new order annihilated his individuality: his identity was no longer important. This facilitated the amalgamation of farms, letting loose the benefits of economies of scale. The board member, as middleman, took some of the revenues from the farmer and merchant (in the form of a commission) in exchange for reducing the risk—which had the effect of diverting some profit to the broker. And all this was made possible, in effect, because of the police power that was exercised by the board of trade: policing the grade of grain, ensuring the stability of its members (through wealth criteria for admission), monitoring warehouses, resolving disputes, and closing down the competition.

The power to police is precisely what made the new order possible. It is also what distributed risk, status, and, most important, resources and wealth. It is of crucial importance to see behind the naturalness of the resulting order—behind the idea of free exchange at the Board of Trade—to identify how that order was constructed and who benefited.

Reexamining Contemporary Exchanges

The rhetoric may be about the "free market," but the reality is layers upon layers of complex regulations and intricate rules—the functional equivalent of several *Dictionnaires de la police*—all of which distribute wealth. This is evident the minute we begin to read judicial decisions regarding the regulation of market exchanges, in particular the stock and commodity exchanges and boards of trade. We saw this well in the Introduction with the MCC rules and the minute regimentation of trading on the Chicago Board of Trade. But the same is true throughout the field. Let me offer two illustrative cases.

The first, *Friedman v. Salomon/Smith Barney Inc.*, is a decision rendered by the U.S. Court of Appeals for the Second Circuit on December 20, 2002, involving a challenge to an informal practice by brokerage firms that purportedly discriminated against retail investors.[45] In essence, during the immediate period (thirty to ninety days) following an initial public offering, retail buyers are not allowed to resell in the aftermarket the shares they just purchased in the public offering. This practice of reselling shares in the aftermarket is called "flipping." In the retail investors' view, the limitation on flipping, which did not apply to large institutional investors, only to retail investors, had been sprung on them and was not noted in the prospectus information concerning the original public offerings.[46]

According to the retail investors, the brokerage firms began enforcing a ban on retail flipping in about 1990 and did so informally—they did not strictly forbid the practice, but discouraged it by "blacklisting" both retail investors and their brokerage firms if they engaged in retail flipping. The brokerage firms, according to plaintiffs, "enforce[d] the retail restricted period by denying stock allocations in future public offerings to retail investors who previously flipped stock. [They] also enforce[d] the retail restricted period by denying or restricting stock allocations or commissions to brokers whose retail customers engage in flipping." The retail investors reported that the brokerage firms "monitor[ed] stock sales and flipping on a customer-by-customer basis through the Depository Trust Co., a clearing house for the settlement of securities traded on all major exchanges and the NASDAQ system."[47]

The retail investors argued that these practices distorted the price of shares—to their detriment. The practices allowed institutional investors to sell at an artificially inflated price in the aftermarket because the supply of shares was artificially reduced during the period when retail buyers could not trade; and as a result, the practices forced retail buyers to purchase at an artificially inflated price during the initial offering, without the possibility of gaining from the artificial price hike. In other words, the practices had distributional consequences that disfavored retail buyers.

These practices were patent violations of antitrust principles because they involved coordinated efforts that affected the price of the goods in question. But the question for the Second Circuit was whether they were immune from the antitrust laws because they fell within the ambit of the Securities Exchange Act of 1934. The court's decision in *Friedman* is a technical reading and interpretation of Section 9(a)(6) of the Securities Exchange Act of 1934, 15 U.S.C. § 78i(a)(6), which states:

> It shall be unlawful for any person . . . to effect either alone or with one or more other persons any series of transactions for the purchase and/or sale of any security registered on a national securities exchange for the

> purpose of pegging, fixing, or stabilizing the price of such security in contravention of such rules and regulations as the [Securities and Exchange] Commission [SEC] may prescribe as necessary or appropriate in the public interest or for the protection of investors.

The retail buyers argued that this ordinance made it unlawful to stabilize prices without the approval of the SEC. The brokerage firms, by contrast, argued that this ordinance made it unlawful to price stabilize only if the SEC had a rule against price stabilizing. The Second Circuit sided with the brokerage firms, finding that when Congress passed the Exchange Act, it did not prohibit price stabilization, but instead gave the SEC the authority to regulate it.

The court went over the intricate regulatory history. When Congress passed the Exchange Act, the court found, it did not prohibit pegging, fixing, or stabilizing practices outright, but instead gave the SEC authority to regulate. In 1940, the SEC had acknowledged that stabilization had some "vicious and unsocial aspects," but declined to prohibit the practice. In 1955 and 1963, too, the SEC had revisited the stabilization issue and modified existing regulations—but still did not prohibit the practice. And in its 1963 report to Congress, the SEC had pointed out that various firms combated flipping by depriving salespeople of their commissions "if resales by customers occur within 30 days of the effective date"; by identifying "customers who sold stock in the immediate after-market" and declining to give these customers "allotments of subsequent oversubscribed issues"; and by telling customers "not to sell for varying periods, usually 30 or 60 days." The SEC nonetheless had declined to regulate or prohibit the practices. In 1994, again, the SEC undertook a comprehensive review of its trading-practice rules and posed several questions dealing specifically with flipping in the aftermarket and whether there was a need to regulate the practice. The SEC rule that resulted from this inquiry did not regulate price stabilization in the aftermarket.[48]

Meritorious arguments could be and were made on both sides. The brokerage firms argued that this history showed that the SEC had studied and decided not to disallow a ban on flipping. The retail buyers argued that stabilization was new, it had only existed in its present form since the 1990s, and so all this history was meaningless. But we should take a step back from the advocacy, and look at the controversy as an object of study—rather than on its substantive merits. What is clear is that this debate is a complex regulatory dispute with significant distributional consequences, and that inevitable and important governmental intervention occurs at every juncture of each argument. There is no neutral position, there is no one side that favors liberty.

There are regulations and liberties on both sides of the equation. The dispute involves, in essence, a clearly anticompetitive practice of collusion by brokers to "manipulate" or "stabilize"—pick your term—the price of stocks initially offered in a way that benefits the large institutions and affects the markets. Distributionally, the practice favors the larger investors and facilitates the efforts of companies seeking capital. It represents, at the end of the day, a form of market regulation that is accomplished by the joint actions of broker-dealers: actions that are expressly not regulated by the SEC, nor by the individual exchanges, but that in fact are constantly supervised, studied, and potentially regulated by all of these entities. It is, in effect, a regulatory web—an intricate nest of rules. And its resolution has a tremendous effect on the distribution of wealth.

A second illustration is the Supreme Court's decision *Silver v. New York Stock Exchange,* rendered in 1963—and I will stop after this one because the list of similar cases is far too long.[49] The case involved questions of access to market information and reflects again the intricate and multiple layers of regulatory oversight and rule-making even in the freest of markets—ranging from the self-regulatory rules of the exchanges themselves to the enforcement proceedings of the SEC, to federal court litigation. The case traces well the historical development of overlapping oversight.

The controversy arose as follows. For many years, nonmember over-the-counter municipal and corporate bond dealers had private direct telephone-wire connections between their offices and the offices of members of the NYSE to receive wire information on trades in over-the-counter bonds. In February 1959, however, the NYSE ordered its members to discontinue the telephone lines without giving the nonmembers any notice, any explanation, or any opportunity to be heard. According to the NYSE, the exchange was operating fully within its rights: it had adopted rules to this effect as part of the Exchange Act of 1934, and the SEC had not disapproved of those rules.

The case went to the Supreme Court, which recognized that the change in policy had clear antitrust implications, but observed that matters were far more complicated because the exchange is a self-regulatory institution. "The difficult problem here arises from the need to reconcile pursuit of the antitrust aim of eliminating restraints on competition with the effective operation of a public policy contemplating that securities exchanges will engage in self-regulation which may well have anticompetitive effects in general and in specific applications," the Court noted.[50] The Court then offered praise for self-regulation—for allowing exchanges a free hand in their own governance. Justice Goldberg wrote for the Court:

> Stock exchanges perform an important function in the economic life of this country. . . . The exchanges are by their nature bodies with a limited

> number of members, each of which plays a certain role in the carrying out of an exchange's activities. The limited-entry feature of exchanges led historically to their being treated by the courts as private clubs and to their being given great latitude by the courts in disciplining errant members. As exchanges became a more and more important element in our Nation's economic and financial system, however, the private-club analogy became increasingly inapposite and the ungoverned self-regulation became more and more obviously inadequate, with acceleratingly grave consequences. This impotency ultimately led . . . Congress to enact the Securities Exchange Act of 1934.[51]

The pattern of governmental entry, however, was by no means one of total displacement of the exchanges' traditional process of self-regulation. The intention was rather, as Justice Douglas said while still chairman of the SEC, one of "letting the exchanges take the leadership with Government playing a residual role. Government would keep the shotgun, so to speak, behind the door, loaded, well oiled, cleaned, ready for use but with the hope it would never have to be used."[52]

Thus arose the federally mandated duty of self-policing by exchanges. Instead of giving the SEC the power to curb specific instances of abuse, the act placed in the exchanges a duty to register with the commission, § 5, and decreed that registration could not be granted unless the exchange submitted copies of its rules, § 6 (a)(3), and unless such rules were "just and adequate to insure fair dealing and to protect investors," § 6 (d).

One aspect of the statutorily imposed duty of self-regulation is the obligation to formulate rules governing the conduct of exchange members. The act specifically requires that registration cannot be granted "unless the rules of the exchange include provision for the expulsion, suspension, or disciplining of a member for conduct or proceeding inconsistent with just and equitable principles of trade."[53] In addition, the general requirement of § 6 (d) that an exchange's rules be "just and adequate to insure fair dealing and to protect investors" has obvious relevance to the area of rules regulating the conduct of an exchange's members.[54] The Supreme Court ultimately held that the Exchange Act did not give the SEC jurisdiction to review particular applications of the rules enacted by the exchanges. The SEC could forbid the rule itself, but not any particular application of it.

Again, however, the exact court ruling is beside the point—it may be interesting and important to exchange members, but it is unnecessary for our purposes. The fact is, neither of the possible resolutions of the dispute would amount to a nonregulated outcome. No possible ruling could support the idea of a "free" market. The exchanges are highly self-regulated clubs that restrict entry and exit, and control, in every possible way, the internal dealings of all members and nonmembers; and the regulatory layers on top of that—whether of the SEC, the Exchange Act, or other federal prosecutors—merely add mechanisms for further review and regulation. We have here, once again, the functional equivalent of a disciplinary police of the markets. There is no "natural order," nor is there a realm where efficiency could naturally obtain. The economic domain is tangled in rules and regulations that distribute resources and wealth. There is nothing but layer upon layer of "discipline."

9

The Penitentiary System and Mass Incarceration

A grounding assumption of both early and contemporary liberal thought, then, is a core belief in the duality of free markets versus regulation. But as we have seen, the categories themselves fall apart under close scrutiny. These central notions of "natural order," "market efficiency," and "free markets"—as well as their inverse, "regulation," "discipline," or "heavily regulated markets"—are mere conceptual tropes that serve no useful analytic purpose. They hinder, rather than help. And they have had a devastating effect in the political sphere.

We now come to that price—the price we pay for believing that the economy is the realm of natural orderliness and that the legitimate and competent sphere of government administration lies elsewhere, in policing and punishing. That steep price includes, first, naturalizing the regulatory mechanisms in our contemporary markets and thereby shielding the massive wealth distributions that occur daily; and second, massively expanding the carceral sphere.

Naturalizing Wealth Distributions

First, the rhetoric of neoliberal penality naturalizes the market and thereby shields the massive distribution of wealth that takes place there. It effectively masks the state's role, the state's ties to nonstate actors and associations, and the extensive legal and regulatory framework in which they are embedded. It also hides the freedom that existed before. In other words, it masks both the extent of liberty in the eighteenth century and the amount of regulation today.

There is and there has always been far more constraint in our contemporary markets than we typically acknowledge today. The truth is, every action of the broker, buyer, seller, investment bank, brokerage firm, and exchange member and nonmember is scrutinized and regulated. Rules, oversight committees, advisory letters, investigations, and legal actions abound. The list of do's and don'ts is wide-ranging and pervasive: members of the New York Stock Exchange may get together and fix the commission rate on smaller stock transactions, but freely negotiate commissions for larger stock purchases and sales.[1] Brokerage firms use blacklists to restrict retail buyers from reselling stock during a restriction period, but the same brokerage firms may allow large institutions to dump stock in the aftermarket at any time.[2] The rules and regulations surrounding our modern markets are intricate and often arcane, but they belie the simplistic idea that our markets are "free." The reality is far more complex—as any regulatory lawyer will tell you.

The pervasive regulations—whether they entail permissions or prohibitions—distribute wealth. They affect pricing and in that sense allocate resources to different sectors of the economy. Numerous contemporary scholars and writers have demonstrated well how market regulations, technologies, theories, and even research shape distributions of wealth or, as some suggest, are performative. Donald MacKenzie has explored the practical effects of options theories, Vincent Lépinay the implications of the language and metaphors used to describe complex financial derivative products, Christine Desan the material consequences of currency itself, and Naomi Klein the larger political effects of economic beliefs and institutions such as the Chicago School.[3] There are many well-documented examples and case studies.

Let's look for a moment at a concrete case—options and futures trading and its effect on prices—and try to keep the analysis simple. Historically, futures contracts and especially options contracts were frowned on by the law. Options—what were called "privileged trading"—were specifically prohibited by the boards of trade and by statute until relatively recently. Farmers and producers traditionally opposed futures and options markets—and any expansion in those markets. They argued that trading in futures decreased the mean spot price of commodities and reduced their overall welfare. In contrast, market advocates—including boards of trade, brokerage firms, as well as speculators—tended to favor futures markets and argued that they reduced the risk to the farmers, thereby protecting them from the dangers of market volatility. They suggested that futures would increase the overall liquidity of the markets—including the spot market—thereby reducing the overall variability of prices, and would allow farmers to hedge their risk.

Some commentators argue that the existence of a futures market does not decrease the spot price of commodities—and therefore does not harm the interests of farmers. For instance, in her 1997 article "The Political Dynamics of Derivative Securities Regulation," Roberta Romano summarily dismisses the farmers' arguments regarding the effect of futures markets on commodity prices. "Economic theory and empirical research," Romano writes, "support the analyses of the opponents of the legislation, in that both formal models and empirical studies indicate that the farm groups' assumption that speculation produces artificially low and increasingly volatile cash prices is incorrect."[4] Elsewhere in the same paper, Romano adds, "The economic premise of the farmers' proposal was wrong—restricting futures trading would not raise commodity prices."[5] In sum, Romano argues, futures trading has no significant effect on commodity prices.

Others believe that the existence of a futures market reduces the spot price of commodities, but that there is a countervailing benefit: it transfers the risk premium from the farmer to the speculator, which is why in fact it reduces the spot price of goods. The argument goes as follows. The reason that the farmer needs to hedge his crop is that he is not able to sustain a big loss. He can, of course, sustain a big gain, but he lacks the wherewithal to sustain a major one-year financial shock. The farmer has to be willing to pay something in exchange for not suffering the risk of a downward shock. That something—that premium—is what is reflected in the slightly lower mean price of the commodity. Another way to achieve the same goal would be with insurance: the farmer could pay a premium to be protected or insured against a sharp price drop, but still be the one to recoup any unexpected gains. According to this view, the speculator plays the role of insurer and must be compensated, thus the slightly lower mean price of the commodity.

A close review of the empirical literature suggests, however, that the introduction of futures markets tends to lower the spot price of a commodity. Curiously, the research is split on whether the introduction of futures markets lowers or raises the variability of the spot price. Despite the mixed results regarding variability, there seems to be a general consensus regarding the net effect on the welfare of producers, speculators, and consumers: the introduction of futures decreases the welfare of producers.

Turnovsky and Campbell model and simulate the effect of a futures market in their research and find that the variability in the spot price is always lowered with the introduction of a futures market.[6] According to Turnovsky, lower variability tends to benefit the producer and harm the consumer—but note, this is only one part of the equation, the piece having to do with variability of prices.[7] The reason, in essence, is that lower variability in price results in a net loss in surplus for the consumer: the potential for higher prices associated with greater variability outweighs the possible gains on the other side. Turnovsky and Campbell model the welfare functions of the different market participants and find that, overall, producers' expected profit decreases with the introduction of the futures market, though profits are stabilized.[8] Although the stabilizing effect of futures markets increases farmers' welfare, it is not enough to offset the decrease in welfare from lower profits, and producers' welfare generally decreases; by contrast, consumers and speculators almost always gain from the introduction of the futures market. The overall effect on social welfare is usually positive, though the primary effect is distributional, "favoring speculators and consumers at the expense of producers."[9] When there is high elasticity of demand for a particular commodity, potential gains from a futures market are modest (likely not enough to offset the costs of maintaining such a market), and probably will not justify its existence.[10]

The research literature, then, finds that the introduction of futures (and by implication options) markets reduces the spot price—confirming the suspicions of the growers and agrarian movement. One possible explanation seems to be that the availability of futures markets makes producers more willing to grow commodities because there is less risk and that this increases supply, thus reducing the price. In their simulated welfare function, Turnovsky and Campbell conclude that futures harm the producers: in other words, in the end, the production increases do not offset the reduced mean price.[11] The research literature also suggests that any increased volume in futures trading will have the same effects as has the introduction of futures trading: that is, more trading will further hurt the welfare of the producers.

This logic applies equally to options contracts. Options and futures have the same effect on prices and variability, since they essentially operate in the same way. If this is indeed the case, then the introduction of new options instruments would translate, very simply, into an increase in the volume of market transactions, which would have a similar effect on mean commodity prices.

The bottom line is that the decision whether or not to allow trading in options is going to have distributional consequences. There is no "neutral" or "free" position: the market is regulated one way or the other. And in either case, there will be economic consequences, concrete distributions of wealth. There are also larger political economic consequences associated with the standardization of contracts and of the quality of grains, which create fungibility among farmers and favor large agribusinesses. The question, at the end of the day, is not whether to favor "freedom" or "constraint"—in both cases, we are both freely and coercively imposing a legal regime with or without options. The question instead is to determine exactly who benefits and by how much, and most importantly, to assess politically and normatively the justice of those distributional outcomes.

It is precisely that normative assessment that is prevented by faith in natural order and market efficiency. So long as the distributional consequences are viewed as the natural outcome of a natural order, they become far more normal and necessary. Their assessment becomes practically futile, or at least beside the point, for it makes little sense to challenge the justice or appropriateness of such natural outcomes. It is only when we let go of the illusion of natural order that we truly open the door to a full and robust political assessment of those distributional consequences—as well as of the politically and socially produced norms and rules that regulate markets and shape those outcomes.

An Archeology of Regulation

It is possible to discern at least three different layers of organizational rules in most spheres—whether a market exchange or social interaction. The top level typically receives the most media attention and publicity. This is the area of crime and punishment—of agency enforcement, indictments, federal prosecutions, criminal trials, and media controversy. This is the domain of the SEC, the FTC, the FDA, and the FBI. These criminal interventions result in prosecutions for price fixing, such as those of Archer Daniels Midland, or for insider trading, such as those of Drexel Burnham, Michael Milken, or Martha Stewart.

The bottom layer received critical attention in the early twentieth century, especially by American Legal Realists, most notably Robert Hale, and more recently by scholars such as Stephen Holmes and Cass Sunstein. This is the area of property and contract law—of the fee simple, legal entitlements and privileges, ownership, and contract enforcement. In his 1923 article "Coercion and Distribution in a Supposedly Noncoercive State," Hale argued that property rules distribute coercive power throughout society, simultaneously distributing wealth. "The right of property is much more extensive than the mere right to protection against forcible dispossession," Hale emphasized. "In protecting property, the government is doing something quite apart from merely keeping the peace. It is exerting coercion."[12] And in exerting coercion, Hale emphasized, it is distributing resources: "The income of each person in the community depends on the relative strength of his power of coercion, offensive and defensive."[13] The purpose of Hale's intervention was to demonstrate that there is simply no unregulated space—no free market, no noncoercive transaction—due to the fundamental property regime and legal order that ground society.

But there is also a middle tier that should not be ignored. It often receives less attention because of the technical nature of the rules and the seeming need for these technologies. But it has significant distributional effects. These are the rules about MCCs and market timing, about fixing commission rates and allowing options trading, about warehouse locations and standards of grain in standardized contracts. These are all the rules and regulations that are hidden from view precisely because of our faith in natural order and market efficiency.

Markets are deeply regulated at all three of these levels (Table 9.1). The highest level encompasses explicit criminal rules of market regulation, such as antitrust laws, rules against price fixing and collusion, regulations against corners and insider trading, and explicit government subsidies and interventions (the savings and loans bailout, tax credits, TARP, and so on). The lowest tier, the most basic level of our legal regime, includes property and contract rights and enforcement. The middle layer, equally important, is where we find all the administrative rules that make the system work and operate. This is where the mass of regulatory interventions and privileges—liberties and constraints—are located.

When all these layers of legal entitlements, technical rules, and criminal prohibitions are exposed, it is clear that the notion of natural order or market efficiency is pure fiction. The idea of a self-regulated market is preposterous. It would be like a competitive sporting event without a referee: it would not work, nor has it ever worked. And once we see the rules of the game, it becomes equally clear that those rules and regulations distribute resources. The height of the basketball hoop favors tall people. Allowing tackling in American football favors large people in certain positions. The rules of the game are never neutral. To the contrary, they are outcome determinative. They distribute success, they dole out failure, they allocate scarce resources. This is true in the sports arena just as it is true in the field of market exchange. Markets are not self-sustaining. They do not tend by nature to achieve equilibrium. They require constant intervention and regulation—and it is precisely those regulations that inevitably allocate resources. One of the best examples of this, of course, is the Chicago Board of Trade, which was entirely constructed through government coercion and is pervasively regulated with significant wealth effects. To view the Chicago Board as a "free market" would be the greatest irony of all.

The Expansion of the Penal Sphere

Second, neoliberal penality facilitates the expansion of the penal sphere. It makes it easier to resist government intervention in the marketplace and to embrace criminalizing any and all forms of "disorder." It facilitates passing new criminal statutes and wielding the penal sanction more liberally because that is where government intervention is perceived as legitimate, effective, and necessary.

Any discussion of the expansion of the penal sphere must begin, naturally, with the astounding growth of the American prison population from 1973 to

Table 9.1 The three layers of administration: criminal sanctions, technical regulations, and legal rights

	Trading and dealing	Commercial exchange	Social relations and interaction
Criminal sanctions aimed at prohibiting:	Cornering the market; insider trading; trading off the floor; bucket shops	Restraint of trade; price fixing; collusion; false advertising	Murder; rape; burglary; robbery; theft; arson; embezzlement
Technical regulations aimed at:	Cost and entry; futures and options trading; delivery and warehousing; standardized contracts	FDA approval; health and safety OSHA requirements; labor relations; inspections	School vouchers; daycare licensing; health insurance; coed dorms; harassment policies; immigration
Underlying regime of legal rights covering:	Property rights; contracts law; enforcement of duties; remedies	Property rights; contracts law; enforcement of duties; remedies	Marriage; child custody; privacy; adoption; child support; divorce; trusts and estates

2009—a period marked by the ascendance of market rationality and what has been called neoliberalism.[14] The fact is, the turn to free markets and privatization since the Reagan Revolution has been accompanied by a massive increase and buildup of our prisons. After almost fifty years of relative stability in our prison populations, the inmate population skyrocketed nationwide beginning in the early 1970s, rising from fewer than 200,000 persons to more than 1.3 million in 2002 (or, if inmates held in local jails are included, to more than 2 million persons by 2002). In 2008, the United States reached a new milestone: it incarcerated more than 1 percent of its adult population—the highest rate in the world, five times the rate in England and twelve times the rate in Japan, and the highest raw number in the world as well.

These staggering numbers were even higher within discrete segments of the population. One in thirty men between the ages of 20 and 34 was incarcerated in 2008, and for African-American men in that age group, the number was one in nine: more than 10 percent of black men in that age range were behind bars.[15] America ranks first among all industrialized nations in its rate of imprisonment—by an order of magnitude.[16] Not just that, it also ranks first in raw numbers of persons in prison—even compared to far more populous countries like China (which, with a population more than three times bigger at over 1.3 billion, incarcerated 1.5 million persons in 2008, as compared to our 2.3 million prisoners). These numbers and rates are exponentially higher when we include persons under supervision. According to a report from the PEW Center on the States released in 2008, one in every 31 adults—3.2 percent of the population or about 7.3 million Americans—was in prison, on parole, or on probation.[17]

The length of prison sentences in the United States is also astounding. In 2009, one of every eleven state and federal prisoners was serving a sentence of life imprisonment: 140,610 individuals, or 9.5 percent of the prison population, were serving a life sentence. And of those lifers, 41,095, or 29 percent, were not eligible for parole—that is, they had no possibility of parole release. In five states—Alabama, California, Massachusetts, Nevada, and New York—the rate was even higher, with one in six state prisoners serving a sentence of life imprisonment. In fact, in California, 34,164 persons, or 20 percent of all prisoners, were serving a life sentence, and of those, 10.8 percent are serving life sentences without parole.[18]

The exponential increase in the number and rate of persons incarcerated in state and federal prisons and jails (see Figure 9.1) has led to a huge overall investment in the carceral sphere—an investment that has been growing consistently over the late twentieth and early twenty-first centuries. In 1987, the states spent approximately $10.6 billion of their tax dollars on corrections.[19] By 2001, the number had increased to a combined $38 billion on corrections spending.[20] Believe it or not, those numbers continued to rise sharply during the first decade of the new millennium. California's annual prison budget for 2007–2008 alone reached almost $10 billion—practically the size of the national expenditures in 1987 and nearly twice as large as California's prison budget in 2001.[21] For the country as a whole, the states' investment in the carceral sphere reached a staggering $44 billion in 2007 and $47 billion in 2008.[22] If you include bonds and federal contributions, the states spent more than $49 billion on corrections that same year, up from $12 billion in 1987.[23]

The increase in correctional spending is not just a result of growing budgets—or growing budget deficits—but has outpaced the overall rate of government spending. In fiscal year 2007, states spent on average 6.8 percent of their general fund dollars on corrections, up 1.8 percentage points from 1987 when the states spent on average 5 percent of their general funds on corrections.[24] In some states, such as Oregon, Florida, and Vermont, the government spends about 10 percent of its dollars on corrections—10.9 percent in Oregon, in fact. The result of growing correctional budgets and increasing proportions of the overall state budgets means that other governmental priorities are being crowded out. As the 2008 PEW study reports: "Criminal correction spending is outpacing budget growth in education, transportation and public assistance, based on state and federal data. Only Medicaid spending grew faster than state corrections spending, which quadrupled in the past two decades."[25]

In many states, annual budgets allocate more funding for prisons than for four-year colleges.[26] This is true even in progressive states such as Massachusetts and Connecticut. While the states resist properly funding education for the young, they seem impervious to the costs of juvenile detention, which are far greater. (In California, for instance, the cost for the Department of Juvenile Justice of incarcerating a juvenile for one year averages an astonishing $71,000.)[27] Overall, between 1987 and 2007, state spending on corrections increased by 127 percent, while the increase in higher education spending only increased 21 percent—all this in inflation-adjusted dollars.[28] In five states in 2007—Vermont, Michigan, Oregon, Connecticut, and Delaware—the ratio of corrections to higher education spending exceeded one, meaning that they spent more money on prisons than colleges. Massachusetts, believe it or not, was at 0.98, so it practically spent as much on each. The national average stood at 0.60, meaning that states spent on average 60 cents on corrections for every dollar spent on higher education. That represents a nearly doubling of the 1987 ratio, which was 32 cents on the (higher educational) dollar.[29]

These trends have been accompanied, naturally, by increased correctional employment as a percentage of state employees. In 2006, for instance, state

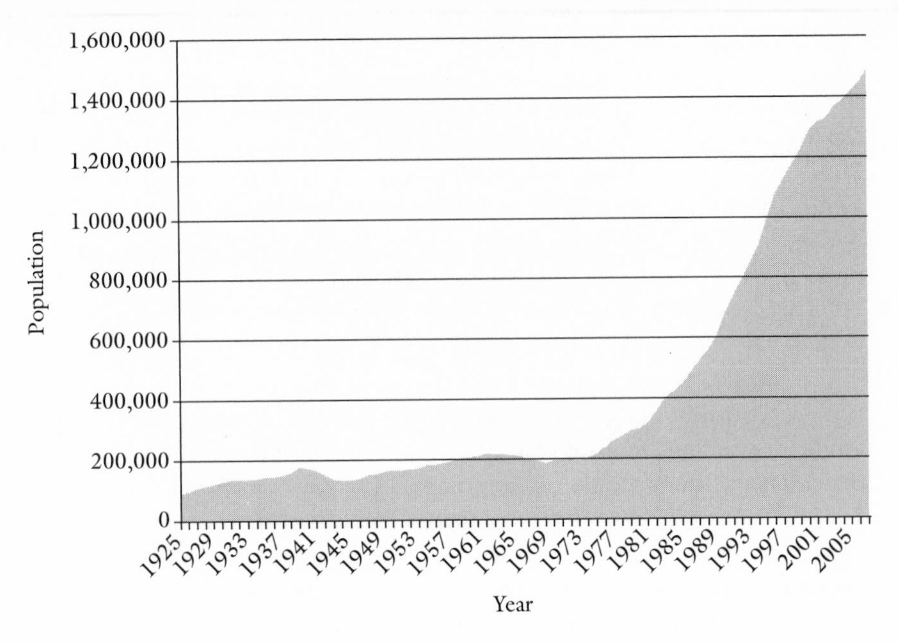

9.1A. State and federal prison population, 1925–2006.

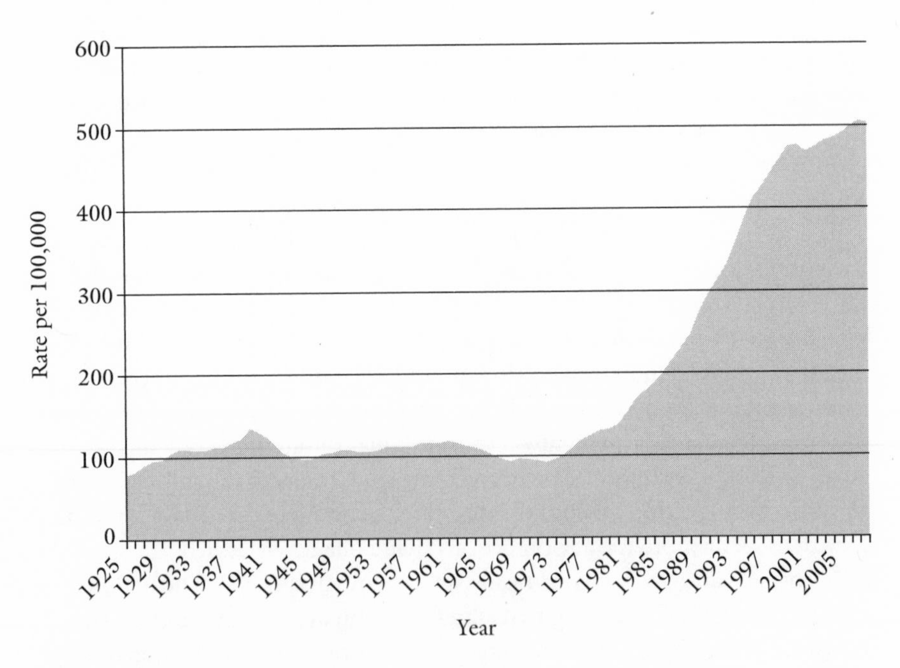

9.1B. State and federal prison rate per 100,000 persons, 1925–2008.

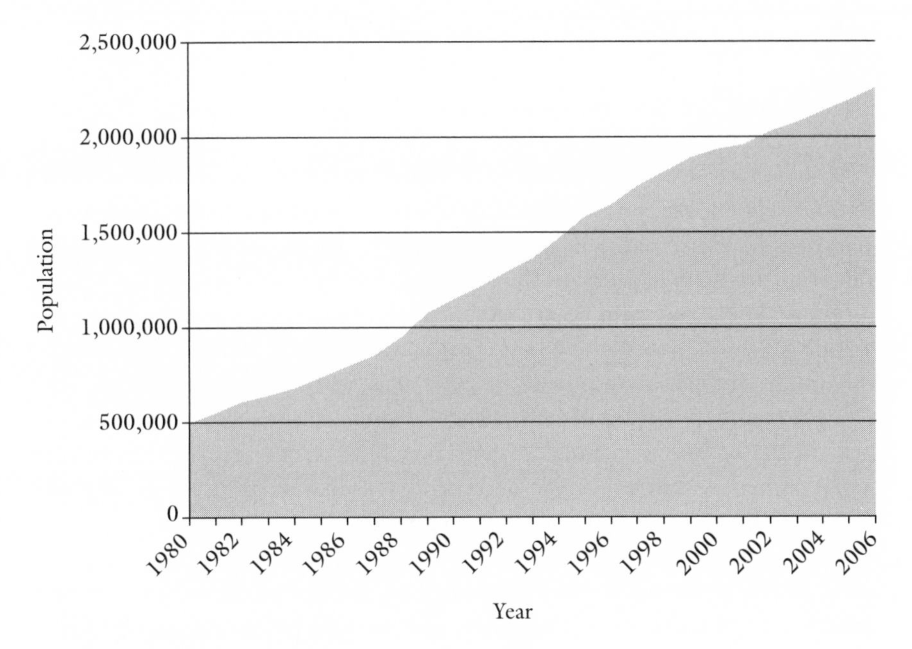

9.1C. Total prison and jail population, 1980–2006.

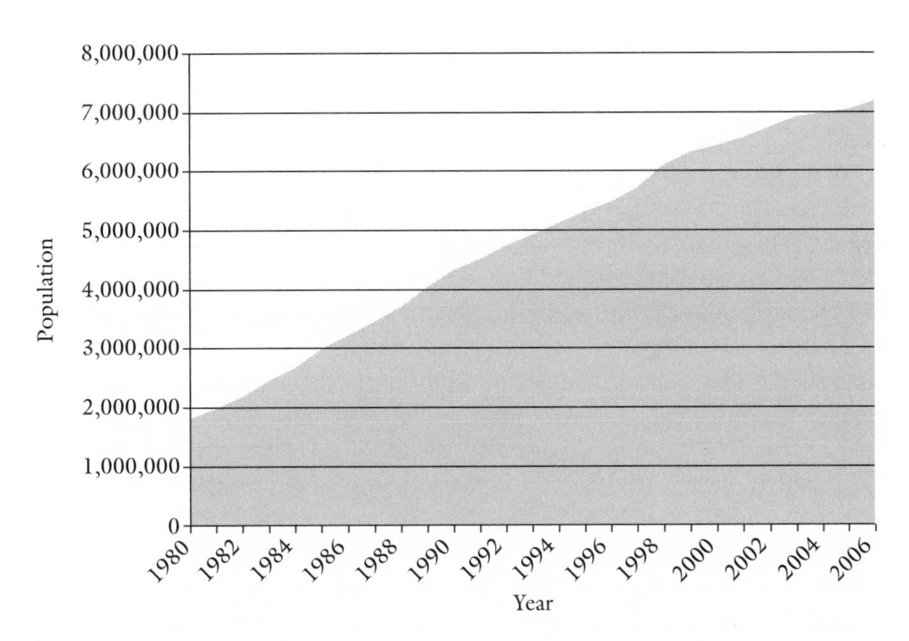

9.1D. Total correctional population (prison, jail, probation, and parole), 1980–2006.

Figure 9.1. Carceral populations in the United States. *Source: Sourcebook of Criminal Justice Statistics 2004,* Bureau of Justice Statistics, U.S. Dept. of Justice, table 6.28.2004, available at: www.albany.edu/sourcebook/pdf/t6282004.pdf, updated with data from *Sourcebook of Criminal Justice Statistics Online,* table 6.13.2008, available at www.albany.edu/sourcebook/csv/t6132008.csv (last visited June 12, 2010).

employees in the corrections workforce accounted for 11 percent of total state workforce at the national level—with highs of 16.9, 15.9, and 15.1 percent in Texas, Georgia, and Florida, respectively. And this is by no means a Southern phenomenon. In the Northeast, state employees in corrections represented 10.2 percent of the workforce.[30] None of these figures includes prison-related employment in the private sector.

The state expenditures on corrections are simply staggering. According to a study released by the Department of Justice in 2004, "The average annual operating cost per state inmate in 2001 was $22,650, or $62.05 per day. Among facilities operated by the Federal Bureau of Prisons, it was $22,632 per inmate, or $62.01 per day."[31] And these figures do not reflect the massive disinvestment in human capital and the abandonment of future generations that accompany such high rates of incarceration.

States only truly began to focus on the exorbitant cost of prisons after the 2008 financial crisis, and since then have begun efforts to reduce their prison populations and expenses. Many states are seeking to reduce prison admissions and length of detention, and to release low-risk offenders. Some states are turning to privatization—an issue I will address later. What the future holds is uncertain—since, like the subprime mortgage market, it too has been built on shaky financial ground. But what is certain is that the United States experienced a truly astounding expansion of its penal sphere during the period 1973 to 2009.

Mass incarceration in the United States—a trend that began in the early 1970s—coincided with a number of other qualitative and quantitative changes in penal administration throughout the country. At about the same time, the United States turned to actuarial methods and risk-assessment tools to predict the success or failure of inmates on parole, to assess the potential for future dangerousness, and to identify violent sexual offenders.[32] It also increased and expanded widely the use of order-maintenance policing strategies, variously called zero tolerance or broken-windows policing, imposed harsher treatment of juvenile offenders, increased use of video surveillance, biometric data collection, data mining, and information gathering, through initiatives such as the "total awareness program" and closed-circuit video surveillance, and implemented harsher sentencing practices—including the adoption of mandatory minimum sentences, "three-strikes laws," drug and gun enhancements, and fixed-sentencing guidelines that recommended longer sentences.[33]

The Condition of Possibility

These carceral developments have been facilitated by—not caused by, but made possible by—the rationality of neoliberal penality: by, on the one hand, the assumption of government legitimacy and competence in the penal arena and, on the other hand, the presumption that the government should not play a role elsewhere. The shocking graph of American incarceration rates—with its exponential curve beginning in 1973—coincides with the enactment of law-and-order measures, of new forms of social control and risk management, and of new forms of race inequality that went hand in hand with the dismantling of the welfare state and the transition, as Loïc Wacquant has demonstrated in *Punishing the Poor,* from welfare to workfare. David Garland has described these fundamental shifts under the rubric of an emerging "culture of control," Malcolm Feeley and Jonathan Simon under the moniker of "new penology" or, for Jonathan Simon, "governing through crime," and Nikolas Rose under the category of "advanced liberal governmental technologies."[34] But traversing all these powerful explanations of the punitive turn is the condition and logic of neoliberal penality.

In both direct and indirect ways, neoliberal penality has facilitated this punitive turn. Directly, it provides politicians with the rhetorical tools and political platforms necessary to get elected. There is a lengthy track record, going back to Barry Goldwater and Richard Nixon at least, of presidential and gubernatorial campaigns that explicitly exploit the neoliberal combination of free-market ideology and tough-on-crime politics—of the need to reduce the size of our "bloated" government at the same time as we increase the punishment sphere and the prison population. This was precisely the theme of Barry Goldwater's acceptance speech at the Republican convention in 1964. Goldwater emphasized the need for security from domestic violence, arguing, "History shows us that nothing prepares the way for tyranny more than the failure of public officials to keep the streets safe from bullies and marauders."[35] At the very same time, Goldwater specifically connected his law-and-order theme with faith in the free markets: "We Republicans seek a government that attends to its fiscal climate, encouraging a free and a competitive economy and enforcing law and order."[36] Notice the explicit conjunction, in the very same phrase, of free markets and law and order. In fact, in much of his political rhetoric, Goldwater would associate the welfare state with criminality as a proximate cause, by tying welfare dependency to crime.[37]

Four years later, in his acceptance speech in 1968, Richard Nixon sounded a similar theme, combining the need for law and order with the goal of limiting governmental intervention elsewhere. Nixon self-consciously deployed the rationality of neoliberal penality, declaring:

> If we are to have respect for law in America, we must have laws that deserve respect. Just as we cannot have progress without order, we cannot have order without progress.
>
> And so as we commit to order tonight, let us commit to progress.

And this brings me to the clearest choice among the issues of this campaign.

For the past five years we have been deluged by Government programs for the unemployed, programs for the cities, programs for the poor, and we have reaped from these programs an ugly harvest of frustrations, violence and failure across the land. And now our opponents will be offering more of the same—more billions for Government jobs, Government housing, Government welfare. I say it's time to quit pouring billions of dollars into programs that have failed in the United States of America.

To put it bluntly, we're on the wrong road and it's time to take a new road to progress.[38]

Notice again how the argument for more severe law and order is joined at the hip with the argument for limited governmental intervention elsewhere: the legitimacy and the competence of government in the field of crime and punishment goes hand in hand with government incompetence when it comes to "Government jobs, Government housing, Government welfare."

Ronald Reagan would exploit this same contrast in the 1980s, effectively arguing that "government's functions had been distorted: the state would be on more legitimate constitutional grounds and would more effectively 'help the poor' by scaling back public assistance programs and expanding the criminal justice system and law enforcement."[39] President Reagan's political strategy embraced neoliberal penality whole cloth. Reagan argued for reducing the size of a "bloated" federal government while simultaneously arguing for increased government intervention in what it does well and legitimately, namely, "public order and law enforcement."[40] Strategically, President Reagan married social conservatism on law and order with fiscal or economic conservatism on deficit spending and opposition to big government—to resounding electoral success. This wedding of free markets and punishment is captured well in his numerous speeches, such as these remarks at an annual convention of the Texas State Bar Association: "Americans object to government intrusion into areas where government is neither competent nor needed, but . . . [they are] also critical of government's failure to perform its legitimate and constitutional duties like providing for the common defense and preserving domestic tranquility."[41] Here is President Reagan's radio address to the nation on his administration's goals in January 1987:

Now is the time for discipline and restraint in the halls of power. You might remember, in the State of the Union I asked Congress for a line-item veto, ratification of a balanced budget amendment, and reform of the budget process. If we're to put our fiscal house in order—and that's essential—it requires fundamental, structural change. . . . One of our priorities, one of the top, continues to be the fight against drug abuse. There've been claims that we've backed off our commitment this year. Nothing could be further from the truth. With all due respect to those who suggest otherwise, our commitment to the battle against drugs is stronger than ever.[42]

President Reagan's law-and-order strategies deliberately fueled prison growth. Edwin Meese III, President Reagan's second attorney general, would expressly embrace the expansion of the carceral sphere as the proper way to advance the agenda of law and order, writing in his book *With Reagan: The Inside Story:* "At the Reagan Justice Department, my predecessor and I carried on a continuing crusade against all these problems, arguing for tougher and more effective sentencing, stressing the protective rather than the 'rehabilitationist' model of penology, and *pushing for construction of additional prison space* so that convicted criminals could be kept away from society."[43]

President George H. W. Bush would similarly deploy these political arguments, stating for instance in his June 1991 radio address to the nation on his administration's domestic agenda:

For the past quarter-century, politicians in Washington have acted as if the Federal Government could solve every problem from chigger bites to earthquakes. No more. We all realize that government has real limits. You can't replace values with regulations. You can't replace parents with caseworkers. And you can't replace the dedication to service with mandates. . . . Several months ago, I challenged the Congress to pass two bills in 100 days. One was a comprehensive crime package. It includes measures to help law enforcement officials defend the peace, to let citizens live without fear of neighborhood terror, to compensate victims, and to punish victimizers swiftly and firmly. The American people are tired of watching hoodlums walk, of seeing criminals mock our justice system with endless technicalities. They want to bring order to streets shaken by chaos and crime.[44]

Lee Atwater, former adviser to Presidents Reagan and George H. W. Bush and former chairman of the Republican National Committee, captured the subtle logic of neoliberal penality well in an elegant statement given at a Republican strategy meeting:

There are always newspaper stories about some millionaire that has five Cadillacs and hasn't paid taxes since 1974. . . . And then they'll have an-

> other set of stories about some guy sitting around in a big den saying so-and-so uses food stamps to fill his den with booze and drugs. So it's which one of these that the public sees as the bad guy that determines who wins.[45]

Crime is on both sides of this equation, naturally—tax fraud in the first case, welfare fraud in the second. But the first has the connotation of free-market capitalism and the second of disorderly street crime. "Who wins" is presented as a choice, but Atwater's vignette instead subtly describes the neoliberal combination of free markets and severe street-crime policing. Who won? Well, mass incarceration answers that question.

Even more important, though, neoliberal penality facilitates the expansion of the carceral sphere indirectly by reducing resistance to these political strategies. It enables punitive policies because most people believe that such policies are the government's proper function. In other words, it reduces any friction or cognitive dissonance associated with witnessing politicians and contemporaries deride government inefficiency while embracing government intervention in the penal sphere. It is precisely the lack of resistance that has fueled our prison populations.

Punishment strategies and policies, it turns out, rarely reflect "democracy at work" and for the most part are not a response to crime trends. As Katherine Beckett has ably demonstrated, political initiatives drive public opinion on crime, and public opinion in turn feeds the political competition over who can appear tougher on crime. This cycle certainly has been true since the 1960s, and it is precisely how neoliberal penality becomes an enabler: by reducing resistance, by resolving cognitive dissonance. In her detailed, statistical analysis of public opinion on crime and drug issues, Beckett shows that the level of public concern on these issues is significantly associated with prior levels of media coverage and political initiatives on crime and drugs, not with prior levels of crime. Political initiative—namely speeches, statements, and policy initiatives made by federal officials on the topic of crime and drugs—leads, rather than lags, popular concern: "The extent to which political elites highlight the crime and drug problems," Beckett found, "is closely linked to subsequent levels of public concern about them."[46] This was true for the issue of crime during the period 1964 to 1973 and for the issue of drugs in the period 1985 to 1992. "Public concern and political initiative move in similar directions and are mutually reinforcing," Beckett concludes, but political initiative comes first.[47] And when it meets no resistance, because the rationality of neoliberal penality has become second nature, it leads directly to the expansion of the penal sphere.

Crime became a political issue in the late 1960s predominantly through the discourse of politicians and officials in an effort to discredit the gains of the civil rights movement. Opponents of the welfare system also used crime as a wedge issue to try to dismantle the poverty programs established under President Lyndon Johnson's Great Society programs.[48] It took several decades, but these strategies culminated under President Bill Clinton with the passage of workfare laws.[49] Race, crime, and welfare—these became a potent mix in presidential, gubernatorial, and local elections, as well as powerful political tools for prosecutors and attorneys general from Robert Kennedy through John Mitchell, Edwin Meese, and John Ashcroft.[50] As David Garland has suggested, the neoliberal turn in the 1970s "produced a new set of class and race relations and a dominant political block that defined itself in opposition to old style 'welfarism' and the social and cultural ideals upon which it was based."[51] Neoliberal penality directly facilitated these developments by providing tough-on-crime politicians with the rhetorical tools they needed, but also by reducing resistance to their political campaigns by making their claims of legitimacy entirely believable.

This is precisely how the seemingly enlightened approach of the economic analysis of crime and punishment doubled back to facilitate mass incarceration. Recall that Gary Becker's intervention in 1968 was attractive to so many readers because of its egalitarian premises—by contrast especially to the therapeutic excesses of penal welfarism and to the strident militancy of law-and-order conservatives. According to the economic view, everyone was a potential criminal; it was only a question of pricing. But when this view was channeled back into the free-market mold and crime became "market bypassing," the underlying logic would serve to justify politicians in packing our prisons. The rationality of neoliberal penality fully legitimated severe government intervention on punishment issues.

It is likely that, in fifty or seventy years, a new generation of historians will ably demonstrate that the period 1970 to 2010 was indeed a period of big government and that the rhetoric of "free markets" was just that, rhetoric—certainly, the government deficits were monumental at points during that period. They will also likely show what those of us who lived through this period know: that the talk of free markets and the influence of the Chicago School dominated. This was reflected in the popularity of President Ronald Reagan in the 1980s, the wave of privatizations that followed, and the rise of Wall Street during the 1990s and early 2000s. With some hubris, but accurately enough, Daniel Yergin and Joseph Stanislaw could write, at the turn of the twenty-first century: "In the postwar years, Keynes' theories of government management of the economy appeared unassailable. But a half-century later, it is Keynes who has been toppled and Hayek, the fierce advocate of free markets, who is preeminent. The Keynesian 'new economics' from

Harvard may have dominated the Kennedy and Johnson administrations in the 1960s, but it is the University of Chicago's free-market school that is globally influential in the 1990s."[52] In dominating the public imagination, though, the illusion of free markets has made possible the growth of our penal Leviathan.

It would be a mistake, though, to suggest that the neoliberal punitive turn was unique in history. The fact is that order maintenance was not invented in 1982 with the article "Broken Windows" by James Q. Wilson and George L. Kelling; order maintenance is a disciplinary practice that traces back at least to the nineteenth century.[53] Actuarial instruments may indeed have exploded in use in the 1970s because of the federal government's use of the Salient Factor Score in parole determinations; but the practice again traces back to positivist criminology and the *défense sociale* movement of nineteenth-century Europe.[54] Biometric-data collection and its use have tragic antecedents in both Europe and North America—with forced sterilization, eugenics, and phrenology.[55] It is important, then, to place the arc of penality in a longer perspective. To relate these modern and admittedly radical manifestations to their earlier kin. To place them within a larger historical framework. To explore other periods when market ideals accompanied expansion of the carceral arena. In other words, to explore not only neoliberal penality, but liberal penality as well. Here, the place to begin is with the very birth of the penitentiary system.

The Market Revolution and the Birth of the Penitentiary

Another formative period in punishment history in the United States—the birth of the penitentiary system beginning in the 1820s—falls squarely during "the Market Revolution," a period spanning from approximately 1815 to the mid-nineteenth century or, for some, slightly later, to the Civil War. This was a period marked by expanding economic opportunities and dominated by an ideal of limited government in commerce—an ideal of "natural and just order" in the words of William Gouge, one of the most popular economic authors of the period.[56]

Historians in the mid-twentieth century, such as Richard Hofstadter, referred to the period as one of laissez-faire ideology: "with some qualifications, it was essentially a movement of laissez-faire, an attempt to divorce government and business," "a phase in the expansion of liberated capitalism."[57] This view underwent some revision, in large part as the result of the work of Oscar and Mary Flug Handlin and, later, Bill Novak and Karen Orren, who unearthed a competing narrative of state interventionism on the ground.[58] Surprisingly, Louis Hartz, who is better known for promoting the influence of liberal individualism in the American context with his 1955 book *The Liberal Tradition in America,* helped launch this reexamination. In his 1948 book, *Economic Policy and Democratic Thought,* Hartz showed how early conceptions of laissez-faire in Pennsylvania actually included a surprising amount of state intervention.

Despite these monographs, what has unified the more recent historical approach to the period is, by and large, agreement on a new rubric: "Market Revolution."[59] As the historian Sean Wilentz observes, "One theme does seem to unite Jacksonian historians of various persuasions and suggest a way of once again viewing the period as a whole: the central importance of the Market Revolution, which, in one way or another, touched the lives of all Americans. As part of that revolution there arose new forms of social life, consciousness, and politics. These, in turn, prepared the way for the Civil War."[60]

The Market Revolution

This new rubric for the period traces to Charles Sellers's important book *The Market Revolution: Jacksonian America, 1815–1846,* published in 1991, and John Lauritz Larson's research that culminated in the 2010 book *The Market Revolution in America: Liberty, Ambition, and the Eclipse of the Common Good.* The term is intended to capture the historical moment when Americans truly began to believe in the market as "the universal arbiter of interests" and "entered an era of capitalist relations."[61] It represents the culmination of a gradual evolution from a land-based political power structure (generally associated with certain forms of early American republicanism) to a system that privileged mobility, capital, and markets. The end of the War of 1812 marks the beginning of what Sellers, Larson, and others refer to as the Market Revolution. As Sellers explains, "Capitalist transformation invaded the southern and western interior when postwar boom galvanized the market culture into market revolution."[62] There were periods of bust—the crisis of 1819, for instance. But according to this view, the Market Revolution exploded in the mid-1820s. "During the jubilee year that peaked on the Fourth of July 1826, returning prosperity set off the decisive phase of market revolution," Sellers writes.[63] "The market fostered individualism and competitive pursuit of wealth by open-ended production of commodity values that could be accumulated as money."[64]

William Gouge captured the dominant ethos with his notion of "natural and just order." A popular economic writer, Gouge published in 1833 his *Short History of Banking and Paper Money in the United States,* which soon became "the bible of the movement" against government control of currency.[65] In that work, Gouge presented a worldview that very much synthesized the idea of natural order and the Market Revolution. Gouge believed that the "natural order of things" would harmoniously produce favorable market results, if it were simply left alone:

> That the operation of the natural and just causes of wealth and poverty, will no longer be inverted, but that each cause will operate in its natural and just order, and produce its natural and just effect—wealth becoming the reward of industry, frugality, skill, prudence, and enterprise, and poverty the punishment of few except the indolent and prodigal.[66]

In this highly influential book, Gouge used the term "natural order" on at least six different occasions, most often referring to the "natural order of things" in money and banking.[67]

Liberal market ideology, naturally, did not spring miraculously into existence in 1820. Adam Smith's writings, as well as those of the Physiocrats, had had an important influence on earlier American political thought. In *Capitalism and a New Social Order: The Republican Vision of the 1790s,* Joyce Appleby highlights how liberal ideals helped pave the way to a new social order based on market principles well before the nineteenth century. Appleby reveals how the republicanism of the Revolutionary period gradually drifted from a notion of classical virtue to an idea of liberal virtue, or how, by the end of the eighteenth century, "virtue more often referred to a private quality, a man's capacity to look out for himself and his dependents—almost the opposite of classical virtue."[68] Similarly, Drew McCoy in his *Elusive Republic: Political Economy in Jeffersonian America,* as well as other historians, have traced the influence of Smith's political economy and of Physiocratic thought on American founding thinkers such as Benjamin Franklin, Thomas Jefferson, and James Madison. McCoy demonstrates that Benjamin Franklin especially was heavily influenced by the French *économistes.* Franklin's personal encounter with the Physiocrats, McCoy has shown, "sharpened many of his economic beliefs and confirmed a basically anti-mercantilist outlook that informed his perception of British colonial policy as well as his broader understanding of England's political economy."[69] Albert Hirschman's 1977 essay "The Passions and the Interests" also highlights the importance of liberal ideas of self-interest at the time.

Appleby, Hirschman, and McCoy's research serves as a slight corrective to the writings of Bernard Bailyn, J. G. A. Pocock, and Gordon Wood, who emphasized the civic republican roots of American Revolutionary ideology. It puts in focus the important role of liberal economic thought in American discourse at the turn of the nineteenth century and the significant influence not only of Adam Smith, but also of the Physiocrats. The combined influence was significant, both on thinkers such as Franklin and George Logan, a prominent Jeffersonian who directly absorbed Physiocratic thought, and on the larger political discourse. As McCoy demonstrates, "the physiocrats articulated most clearly a resonant cluster of fears and concerns that were to find extensive expression among republican thinkers in America."[70] This new discourse translated into ideas of natural order and self-interest: "Locating the ordering mechanism for this system in the consistent drive of individuals to seek their advantage, writers began talking about it as natural, often invoking . . . the natural law of self-preservation."[71]

The influence of liberal economic thought thus predated the 1820s, but was significantly reinforced during the political struggles of the Market Revolution. The debates over government interventionism, free trade, and open markets raged in a number of domains during the period. Following the Panic of 1819 and the enactment of the protectionist Tariff of 1824—which aimed to shield American iron, agricultural products, and some textiles from lower-priced British goods—there was significant controversy over attempts to expand the tariff protections to other manufacturers and to increase them on woolen goods in 1827. In these debates, the Jacksonians towed a moderate line, courting Southern slaveholders who were adamantly opposed to protective measures.[72]

Andrew Jackson and the Second Bank

These and other controversies projected Jacksonian Democrats as anti-interventionists, but perhaps none did so more clearly than the struggle over and ultimate demise of the central bank—the Second Bank of the United States. Andrew Jackson campaigned against the central bank and ultimately broke it, an act that Jackson claimed was his most important achievement in office.[73]

Jackson undoubtedly was opposed to a centralized bank for a mixture of political and strategic reasons—not just on the basis of economic ideology. As the historian Sean Wilentz explains, "Jackson perceived that the bank, by its very design, undermined popular sovereignty and majority rule. As a friend and adviser [wrote] in a key early memorandum to Jackson, the bank had concentrated 'in the hands of a few men, a power over the money of the country.' Unless checked, that power could be 'perverted to the oppression of the people, and in times of public calamity, to the embarrassment of the government.' But even when well administered, the bank was an enormity, which allowed, Jackson wrote, 'a *few Monied Capitalists*' to trade upon the public revenue 'and enjoy the benefit of it, to the exclusion of the many.'"[74] It is crucial to understand here that the Jacksonian political view—which we often associate with workers, farmers, artisans, and yeomen—represented a "hands-off" approach only as opposed to the wealthier financiers who were viewed as trying to capture the state for their economic advantage.[75] The Jacksonian Democrats, in this context, were trying "to keep the hands of established wealth and privilege off the levers of state power, thereby preventing the creation of a new and permanent monied aristocracy."[76] This is why, ultimately, the more populist political faction was the one more closely aligned with quietist economics against the "few Monied Capitalists." Preventing the national bank from being rechartered was crucial, Jackson explained in his own words, to maintain "the great principles of democracy."[77] But regardless of its political origin, Jackson's position favored economic decentralization and greater governmental quietism.

Jackson set out to eviscerate the bank from the moment he took office—in fact, he mentioned this intention in his very first and second messages to Congress. The issue would come to a head by means of a Congressional vote to recharter the bank in 1832. The U.S. government owned only one-fifth of the bank, but the bank's charter gave it the exclusive power to act as the government's fiscal agent, and as a result it issued the majority of all bank notes in circulation, controlled a large portion of all bank lending in the country, and could regulate the entire economy. Pro-bank coalitions pressed Congress successfully to recharter the bank so that its power would have some limits, but Jackson ultimately vetoed the legislation in July 1832, causing what some have described as a "political earthquake."[78]

Jackson's veto message was a carefully crafted and important political document that set forth not only his constitutional views about the responsibilities of the different branches of the government, but also his political views about the role of the state in the economy. Specifically, Jackson portrayed the controversy as one in which big government had to be constrained to avoid capture: in very much the same way that Adam Smith had argued against state monopolies because they were captured by selfish merchants interested only in their wealth and advancement, Jackson argued that a government institution, such as the central bank, had to be eliminated to avoid capture by the financiers bent on promoting their self-interest. "It is to be regretted that the rich and powerful too often bend the acts of government to their selfish purposes," Jackson wrote in his veto message. Distinctions will always exist, he added, "but when the laws undertake to add to these natural and just advantages artificial distinctions, to grant titles, gratuities, and exclusive privileges, to make the rich richer and the potent more powerful, the humble members of society—the farmers, mechanics, and laborers—who have neither the time nor the means of securing like favors to themselves, have a right to complain of the injustice of their Government."[79]

The ensuing presidential campaign against Jackson portrayed him as a French despot in the tradition of Robespierre and the Jacobins precisely because of the bank veto. "The spirit of Jacksonianism is JACOBINISM," the Boston opposition newspaper declared.[80] But in the eyes of most, Jackson had become the protector of the ordinary citizen: "For the most part, the attack on the [bank] captured the public's imagination as proof that Jackson was the intrepid defender of 'the humble members of society'—a phrase Jackson's managers repeated endlessly—against the rich and privileged."[81] The ultimate result was an electoral landslide in 1832, with Jackson receiving 219 electoral college votes against 49 for Henry Clay. Following his election, Jackson then killed the central bank by withdrawing federal deposits from it and depositing them instead at state-chartered banks. There followed an economic crash, but eventually a return to economic normalcy, with the central bank ultimately being simply rechartered in 1836 as a Pennsylvania state bank when its federal charter ran out.[82]

There would be other fronts on the war against government intervention. On the legislative side, popular movements against the granting of monopolies would eventually result in the spread throughout the states of general incorporation acts that would open the process of incorporation to anyone who met the requirements. And on the judicial side, Jackson's appointment in 1836 to the U.S. Supreme Court of Chief Justice Taney—one of his greatest allies in the war against the bank—would reinvigorate the battle against government control of economic matters, such as in the famous Charles River Bridge case.[83]

Naturally, the Jacksonians did not have a lock on the argument for limited government. The position was so popular at the time that even the Whig party—the opposition party to Jackson's Democrats—also tried to present itself as the party of limited government. For instance in 1840 the Whig candidate, William Harrison, campaigned on the idea that it was the Whigs, not the Democrats, who were most faithful to limited government. The Whigs, he argued, were the real followers of Jefferson and Madison. "The old-fashioned Republican rule is to watch the Government," Harrison campaigned. "See that the Government does not acquire too much power. Keep a check on your rulers. Do this, and liberty is safe."[84] As Wilentz explains, "Instead of meddling with the economy and usurping power, the Whigs would undo the Jacksonians' mischief and then leave well enough alone."[85] On both sides, the Jacksonian period represented a moment of market liberalism. While there continues to be some debate over the label "Market Revolution," the rubric is apt.[86]

The Birth of the Penitentiary

The Second Bank of the United States had its headquarters in an imposing Greek Revival building on Chestnut Street in Philadelphia.[87] Only a few blocks away stood another arresting structure: the Walnut Street Jail, birthplace of the American penitentiary. Jackson may well have destroyed the first, but he did absolutely nothing to obstruct the second. During the Market Revolution, the American penitentiary system was born.

In *The Discovery of the Asylum,* David Rothman penned what is still considered the "master narrative" of the history of the American penitentiary. Rothman opened his book with two simple questions: "Why did Americans in the Jacksonian era suddenly begin to construct and support institutions for deviant and dependent members of the community? Why in the decades after 1820 did they all at once erect penitentiaries for the criminal, asylums for the insane, almshouses for the poor, orphan asylums for homeless children, and reformatories for delinquents?"[88] Although historians have offered different answers, "there can be no disputing the fact of the change," Rothman observed. "Here was a revolution in social practice."[89]

To be sure, there were precedents to the penitentiary house.[90] On the Continent, there were penal institutions as far back as the early 1600s, most notably prison workhouses such as the Amsterdam *rasphuys,* the *zuchthaus* in Hamburg, and spinhouses for women—though the management and organization of these workhouses did not evolve significantly between the seventeenth and early nineteenth centuries.[91] There also developed in the mid-seventeenth century in the Netherlands private institutions for the insane and for family outcasts that did not involve forced labor, but instead foreshadowed the later forms of solitary confinement.[92] In France, in 1656, Louis XIV established the Hôpital Général in Paris—that enormous house of confinement for the poor, the unemployed, the homeless, the vagabond, the criminal, and the insane.[93] Once an arsenal, a rest home for war veterans, and several hospitals, the new Hôpital Général served as a prison, in many cases for those who sought assistance from the state and in many more for those sent by royal or judicial decree.[94]

On the young American continent, there were also antecedents. In the immediate post-Revolutionary period, states experimented with houses of repentance and systems of punishment modeled on ideas of Christian penance. The very term "penitentiary" derived its root from those early experiments. The Walnut Street Jail in Philadelphia, built in 1773, would be converted into the country's first penitentiary in 1790—when it acquired an isolation cellblock called "the penitentiary house." The "Pennsylvania system" was invented there, with its all-day isolation and work in single-man cells.

But by the late 1810s, the Pennsylvania system had come into disrepute. It would eventually be replaced by a penitentiary system built instead on the "Auburn model" of collective daytime labor and isolated evenings of penitence—a model that would bring about a massive expansion of the penitentiary system. Construction on Auburn, New York's famous cell house, which began in 1819 and was completed in 1821, led to experiments with different types of solitary confinement, some without labor, and others with congregated daily labor. Ultimately the latter prevailed. Inmates were to engage in daytime labor with others, but in silence; evenings would involve isolation in single-man cells. The Auburn model was based on a proposal developed in 1818 by the governor of New York, De Witt Clinton, in part "to relieve the state treasury of the spiraling costs both of maintaining the penitentiary and suppressing rebellions."[95] The model was successful: "In the age of Jackson," historian Rebecca McLennan explains, the Auburn model "proved far more influential over the everyday life, administrative structures, and official doctrines of the state penal systems."[96]

The Auburn model led to a massive spree of prison construction during the 1820s and 1830s, and created a foundation for the current U.S. prison system. Sing Sing opened in 1825, Connecticut started building Wethersfield in 1827, Massachusetts reorganized its prison at Charlestown in 1829, and Indiana, Wisconsin, and Minnesota followed suit in the 1840s.[97] "Between 1825 and 1850, state prisons of the Auburn type were built in Maine, Maryland, New Hampshire, Vermont, Massachusetts, Connecticut, New York, the District of Columbia, Virginia, Tennessee, Louisiana, Missouri, Illinois, and Ohio," writes McLennan. [98] In addition, Rhode Island, New Jersey, Georgia, and Kentucky built prisons on the solitary labor model, and Pennsylvania, which had invented the system of daytime solitary labor, constructed the Eastern State Penitentiary in the hopes of rejuvenating its model for others to use. Eastern State opened on October 23, 1829, and the construction of the full prison was completed in 1836—just in time for the collapse of the Second Bank of the United States.

"In all, one can properly label the Jacksonian years 'the age of the asylum,'" Rothman observes.[99] On this point, the historians of the penitentiary agree. Adam Hirsch, in his 1992 book *The Rise of the Penitentiary,* similarly states: "The penitentiary had its heyday in the United States in the 1830s. Facilities proliferated, the literature thrived, and visitors traveled great distances to view American prisons in action. In spite of persistent difficulties, the penitentiary became for Jacksonians a symbol of achievement. They brimmed with pride at all the foreign interest their carceral institutions succeeded in attracting."[100] Rebecca McLennan, in her 2008 book on the *Making of the American Penal State,* traces the penitentiary system to "the age of Jackson."[101] Even Pieter Spierenburg, a historian of the early modern period who prefers to rewind the historical clock to the 1600s, admits that in the United States a "relatively condensed transition" to the penitentiary model occurred in the 1820s "due to the particular circumstances of its development."[102] Penal institutions became, in Rothman's words, places of "first resort, the preferred solution to the problems of poverty, crime, delinquency, and insanity."[103]

So why was the "age of the asylum" born during the Market Revolution? Rothman's answer turns on social disorder and the need for moral cohesion—on the perceived need to restore some form of social balance during a time of instability. Rothman's account corroborates fully the Physiocratic idea of liberal penality. The key to America's discovery of the penitentiary, Rothman tells us, was the desire to impose order on a social sphere that appeared to be disordered. "The nation had a new sense of its society," Rothman wrote in *The Discovery of the Asylum*. "Americans now wrote voluminously about the origins of deviant and dependent behavior, insisting that the causes of crime, poverty, and insanity lay in the faulty organization of the community."[104] In his archival research, Rothman reviewed myriad reports by penitentiary inspectors offering biographical sketches and diagnoses of the inmates. These official accounts reveal a dominant story about the causes of crime and delinquency: social and familial disorder. In the penal sphere, the Jacksonian period was haunted by the fear that society "might succumb to chaos."[105] As Rothman explained, "Family disorganization and community corruption, an extreme definition of the powers of vice and an acute sense of the threat of disorder were the standard elements in the discussions. A wide consensus formed on the origins of crime."[106] That consensus revolved around social disorder. Rothman writes: "Jacksonians located both the origins of crime and delinquency within the society, with the inadequacies of the family and the unchecked spread of vice through the community."[107] Far from naturally ordered, society according to this vision was in chaos.

The goal of the penitentiary—like that of the asylum and other institutions—was to create a "new world" that "would correct within its restricted domain the faults of the community."[108] The birth of the penitentiary represented "an effort to insure the cohesion of the community in new and changing circumstances," "to restore a necessary social balance to the new republic, and at the same time eliminate long-standing problems."[109] This correction was to be achieved by constructing institutions, by creating new orderly worlds. By imposing order, rather than letting "natural order" hold sway.

The types of order that the penitentiary imposed were severe. They were, as James Q. Whitman has shown, "harsh justice": "a place of forced labor and corporal punishment," "of 'unrepublican' treatment most strongly associated with slavery in the United States," where "harsh and degrading disciplinary practices began to entrench themselves," including flogging, the iron gag, the ball and chain, and the cold shower.[110] In the quest for stability and social cohesion, the invention of the penitentiary represented an "ordering," through spatial exclusion and corporal punishments, that was necessary (it seemed) to tame the chaos and appease the great apprehension of the unknown.

Rothman's account is masterly and has withstood well the test of time.[111] Moreover, it supports fully the contrast between, on the one hand, an idea of natural order in the economic and commercial realms, and on the other, a notion of a worsening social disorder that called for a punitive, interventionist response. William Gouge's notion of "the natural order of things," which was so important in the economic domain, in the area of money and banking, played no role in social ordering. The Jacksonian efforts to restrain and limit government did not extend to ordering social chaos. And, not surprisingly, the social ordering in the penal sphere was accompanied by a set of anxieties that crystallized around the issues of race, national identity, and immigration. The tilt toward government intervention in the social sphere—as opposed to its laissez-faire counterpart in the economic realm—had a darker side as well, of nativism, fear of foreign radicals, anti-Catholicism, and anti-immigrant sentiment.[112]

Rothman's notion about imposing social order is completely at odds with the Jacksonian efforts in the banking area. The two cannot be reconciled without embracing the Physiocratic opposition between the natural orderliness of the market and the natural disorderliness of the penal sphere. It is precisely that duality of liberal penality that makes sense of the birth of the penitentiary. It resolves the central cognitive dissonance at the heart of the Jacksonian period.

Growth of the Penal Sphere during the Market Revolution

The Market Revolution was accompanied by historic growth in the penal sphere. My purpose here is not to rehearse the history of the penitentiary system through the nineteenth century. Others have written that history well.[113] I will limit myself, instead, to some data on the actual investment in corrections—which, because there have been no systematic studies on the issue, have to be collected from different sources.

We have national prison data only beginning in 1850.[114] Prior to that time, there are just scattered local data, predominantly from the Prison Discipline Society of Boston and the Prison Association of New York, both privately organized associations intended to monitor the growth of prisons. These sources reveal that during the Market Revolution, the percentage of U.S. residents in state prison grew enormously, leading to the high national counts beginning in 1850 and a peak in 1870. From that point on, however, prison rates in the United States would essentially remain relatively stable, with some fluctuations, until the prison explosion in the 1970s. Figure 9.2 charts the growth of the prison population over the period 1850 to 1923.

For a more fine-grained analysis during the Market Revolution, one excellent source of data is the Prison Association of New York, founded in 1844, which began submitting detailed annual reports to the state legislature soon after its founding. Its twenty-eighth annual report, published in 1873, contains detailed budget information about appropriations made by the New York State legislature for the state's prison system from 1848—the time of the adoption of a new management system under the New York Constitution of 1846—and 1872, the last full year before the report. The report reveals a steady increase in appropriations, in expenditures, and in overall deficits for the prison system.

From 1848 to 1872, legislative appropriations increased by more than 920 percent, as seen in Table 9.2. Overall prison expenditures increased consis-

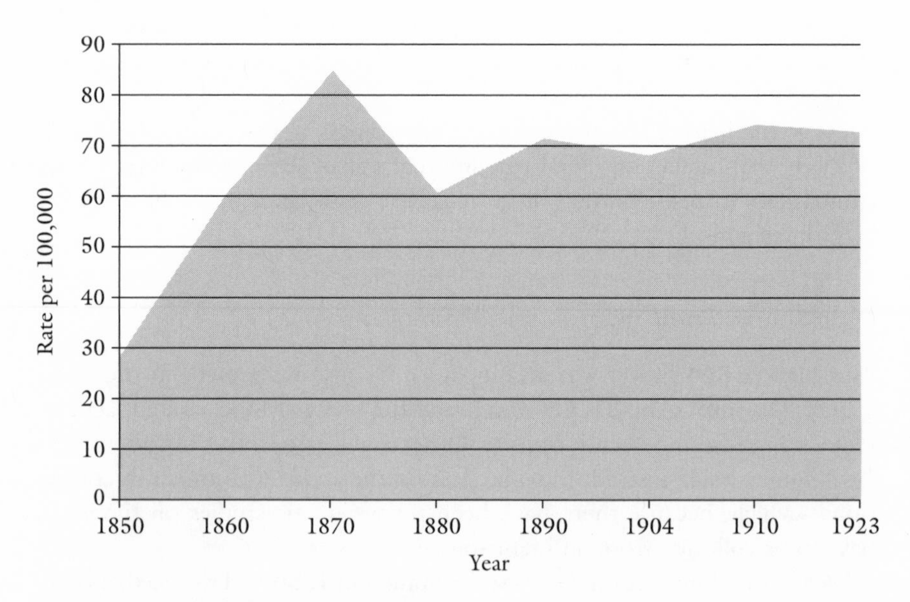

Figure 9.2. Prison rate in state and federal prisons from 1850 to 1923 (per 100,000 persons). *Source:* Data from Cahalan 1986.

Table 9.2 New York State legislative appropriations for prisons, prison system expenditures, and prison system deficits for the period 1848 to 1872 (in U.S. dollars)

Year	Legislative appropriations (in U.S. dollars)	Prison system expenditures (in U.S. dollars)	Prison system deficit (in U.S. dollars)
1848	116,250	204,092	93,433
1849	67,900	188,755	49,469
1850	56,900	208,398	50,975
1851	62,135	206,011	27,097
1852	63,972	211,752	18,449
1853	81,935	250,818	34,708
1854	322,413	272,413	59,235
1855	519,783	233,445	35,215
1856	18,000	222,478	25,373
1857	524,012	212,714	20,931
1858	300,828	250,356	101,182
1859	327,429	279,334	89,497
1860	345,193	295,745	53,117
1861	340,751	288,905	23,352
1862	326,660	294,686	66,204
1863	425,361	291,217	62,886
1864	342,175	342,794	86,837
1865	605,975	414,713	212,207
1866	647,784	463,995	234,582
1867	860,767	779,580	179,566
1868	879,736	844,374	242,735
1869	1,199,498	879,219	225,062
1870	1,146,886	876,612	176,418
1871	849,245	784,567	273,035
1872	1,186,927	not available	not available

Source: Prison Association of New York 1873, 9–12.

tently, rising a total of 284 percent over the period, from $204,092 in 1848 to $784,567 in 1871. Earnings from prison labor also increased, but not sufficiently to cover the rising expenditures, resulting in annual deficits that continually increased over the period, in one accounting by 192 percent. Because of discrepancies in the accounting of the state prison inspectors and the comptroller of the state treasury, the Prison Association ultimately estimated the true deficiencies of the prison system—at least those "to be supplied from the Public Treasury"—as having increased by 1,300 percent from $20,463 in 1848 to $277,099 in 1871.[115] Or, to put it another way, the deficit associated with running the state prison system cumulatively increased over the period, and the prisons, "which had once been self-supporting, or nearly so, had in that period of time, viz., from 1847 to 1869 inclusive, cost the State $6,000,000 at least, over and above all earnings by or at the prisons"—or approximately $100 million in present dollars.[116]

Two final points of comparison are important here. The first, naturally, is the continually rising appropriations and deficits that the State of New York was willing to bear, even during a period marked by the costly Civil War. The deficit associated with this governmental intervention increased over the twenty-three-year period by over 1,300 percent. New York consistently invested increasing amounts of capital into its prison system—at rates greater than one might expect from both the growth in the prison population and overall population growth in the state. From 1848 to 1871, the number of state prisoners in the New York correctional system increased by 116 percent, from 1,342 to 2,904. And over approximately the same period, from 1840 to 1870, the state's overall population grew by 80 percent, from 2,428,921 to 4,382,759. With approximately 2,904 prisoners in the system in 1872, that amounted to an annual appropriation of $409 per inmate (about $7,000 today)—up from $85 per inmate in 1848.

The second point of comparison relates those expenditures to the contemporary investment in corrections. In 1872, the State of New York appropriated $1,186,927.45 to its prison system. In current dollars, that would amount to approximately $20 million.[117] Even that amount, though, is misleadingly high because the prisons generated considerable revenues. In 1871, for instance, the state prison system was operating at a deficit of $277,099—meaning that the penal institutions were costing the state taxpayers approximately $5 million in today's dollars. By contrast, New York spent approximately $2.4 billion for corrections in fiscal year 2009–2010 and maintained a population, in 2008, of approximately 62,000 inmates—for an average per capita spending of about $38,700 per inmate.[118] In terms of appropriations, that represents an increase in the prison budget of more than a hundredfold and more than a quadrupling of expenditures per inmate. There is no question: what we have witnessed in our lifetime is one of the most monumental expansions of the penal sphere that has ever occurred in history.

10

Private Prisons, Drugs, and the Welfare State

Before concluding, let me address some objections to the account offered in this book. The first is that there have been, there may be now, and there are likely to be in the future periods of excessive punishment that are not associated with the rise or dominance of liberal market ideas. How does the analysis presented in this book account for the brutal corporal punishments or the asylums of yesterday, or even repressively punitive regimes elsewhere today? Second, other Western and industrialized countries have embraced liberal market ideas and nevertheless do not incarcerate 1 percent of their adult population. Why does mass incarceration appear to be a uniquely American phenomenon? Third, several Chicago School thinkers, most notably Milton Friedman, opposed the criminalization of drugs and the War on Drugs. In what sense, then, should Chicago School free-market ideas be held responsible for the prison growth associated with today's drug wars? And finally, prisons became increasingly privatized during the latter part of the twentieth century, which suggests that there is a closer relationship between punishment and economy. In what sense is the penal sphere really so distinct from public economy? Let me address each of these important questions in order.

The Crime and Punishment Nexus

First, how does the view presented in this book account for other moments of excessive punishment in other countries? The beastly and tortuous execution in March 1757 of the regicide Robert-François Damiens, which is famously recounted in the opening pages of Michel Foucault's *Discipline and Punish,* was surely a representation of excess. The immediacy and number of executions in China today—some experts report as many as six thousand state executions in 2007—also appear excessive; even more, according to some reports, one out of ten is for a nonviolent, economic crime.[1] What of those examples of excess punishment?

This first objection calls, initially, for clarification. This book focuses on a shift over time from an earlier penal rationality that can be called cameralist to a way of thinking dominated by liberal market ideas. In this sense, this project relates our modern liberal and neoliberal penal practices in the United States to earlier periods. This project does not compare neoliberal penality to other contemporary forms of penal rationality, whether grounded on authoritarian, communist, or religious fundamentalist ideals. I am not arguing here that neoliberal penality leads to worse or more barbarian outcomes than the punishment practices of theistic, communist, or authoritarian regimes. It may well be true that the United States leads the world in its rate of persons behind bars, and even in the raw number of persons in prison. But that tells us nothing of how to compare our mass incarceration rate to several thousand executions, or, in other countries, to summary trials, extrajudicial death squads, or amputation and corporal punishment.

This project does not address those comparisons for several reasons. First, because it would set the bar far too low. But second, because this study is an internal critique of the direction that U.S. penal rationality has taken, arguing that it has come to facilitate the growth of the penal sphere with devastating consequences. It is not an external critique. It does not compare our experience with other contemporary punishment discourses and does not evaluate whether the former is "better" or "worse" in terms of its overall effect on the penal sphere.

Now to the more relevant question: There were other periods of excess in American history. The fact is that the United States institutionalized mental health patients in all sorts of mental facilities in the 1930s, 1940s, and 1950s, at astoundingly high rates.[2] How should we think about those periods—marked, as they were, by greater reliance on Keynesian ideology?

The answer is complex, and my curiosity was piqued originally when I came across a small volume in the library, *Patients in Hospitals for Mental Disease, 1923*. The volume had a humble cover, green soft cardboard, and in small letters, a stamp that a librarian must have pressed on the cover: "Gift of U.S. Govt." The price, marked on the inside cover page, was 35 cents. A modest volume indeed. But inside there was a treasure of numbers, categories, tables, maps, and graphs. This modest volume contained 124 tables, thirteen maps and charts, and eighty-three pages of analysis of the statistics: in short, it was a half-inch-thick compilation of every possible detail regarding the population of mental patients.

Their number, and the attention given to them, it turns out, was remarkable. Everything about this large population was known—the movements, the first admissions, the readmissions, the transfers, the deaths categorized by diagnosis, of every mental patient in every public and private mental institution in every state, including county and city and Veterans Administration

(VA) hospitals. Each institution was listed separately, and all of the patients (including those residents in the hospitals, as well as, separately listed, those on parole or otherwise absent) were catalogued, in raw numbers and with percentage distributions, by gender, race, nationality, psychosis, age, marital status, country of birth, time spent in the hospital, and number of times admitted. Over 250 pages of materials, offering a portrait of a population in minute detail. A mesmerizing wealth of numbers and categories that signaled one thing: this population was important; it needed to be understood, analyzed, and categorized; and it was large. It consisted of 267,617 patients in 1923 (or 245 per 100,000 population), and would double to 513,894 by 1938.

All kinds of different facilities were listed: not just state and county mental hospitals—publicly financed mental hospitals at the state and county level—but also public and private institutions for "mental defectives and epileptics" and for "the mentally retarded," as well as psychiatric wards in general and VA hospitals, "psychopathic hospitals," city hospitals, and private mental hospitals. There was also an entire parole system for persons institutionalized in mental hospitals. In 1933, for instance, the official census reports defined "on parole" as the "temporary absence from an institution of a patient who is being carried on the books," usually "a trial leave of absence preliminary to discharge," but often also an "absence on a visit or for other purposes."[3] The parole numbers were significant: on December 31, 1933, for example, 46,071 mental patients were on parole or otherwise absent, representing almost 10 percent of the total institutionalized patient population of 435,571.

When the patients in these mental health facilities are aggregated with prison and jail populations at the national level, the comparison to our current imprisonment rate is surprising: between 1938 and 1963, the United States consistently institutionalized (in these mental institutions and in prisons and jails) at rates greater than 800 per 100,000 adults—with peaks of 844 in 1948 and 857 in 1955 (see Figure 10.1).

There is no question: the rehabilitative model associated with the welfare state was also large, expensive, and coercive. As Frances Fox Piven and Richard Cloward demonstrate in their classic book *Regulating the Poor: The Functions of Public Welfare* (1971), the welfare state is also a faithful agent of social control. The history of relief programs, in their words, is "a record of periodically expanding and contracting relief rolls as the system performs its two main functions: maintaining civil order and enforcing work."[4] The rise of welfarism and the gradual turn to prudentialism forms a distinct period in penal practice.[5]

But the important point here is that it was founded on a different logic—rehabilitation and treatment—and resulted in different practices and institutions. It represented, at its worst, another kind of punitiveness, but a different kind nonetheless. The type that the United States experienced in the 1820s or the 1970s was distinct. It expressed itself through the criminalization, marginalization, and carceral punishment of a criminal outcast. It rested on the central elements of penality: it used the penal code, the criminal sanction, and the prison. This is different than a rehabilitative program intended to treat individuals—though the resulting regime may well be oppressive. The carceral focus is on criminality, blameworthiness, and punishment, not on madness, nor sickness. And it is here, in the penal domain, that the government is at its "best," fully legitimate and competent, at least according to the neoliberal view.

The research in this book identifies an outcome: the expansion of the carceral sphere, increased investment in prisons, larger populations of criminalized outcasts, expanded government intervention and more tax dollars allocated to corrections departments, more incarcerated and supervised convicts. There is a difference in kind between this outcome and others, in that a certain kind of penal excess is involved. Let me add that there may well be other forms of excess associated with the polar opposite of neoliberal

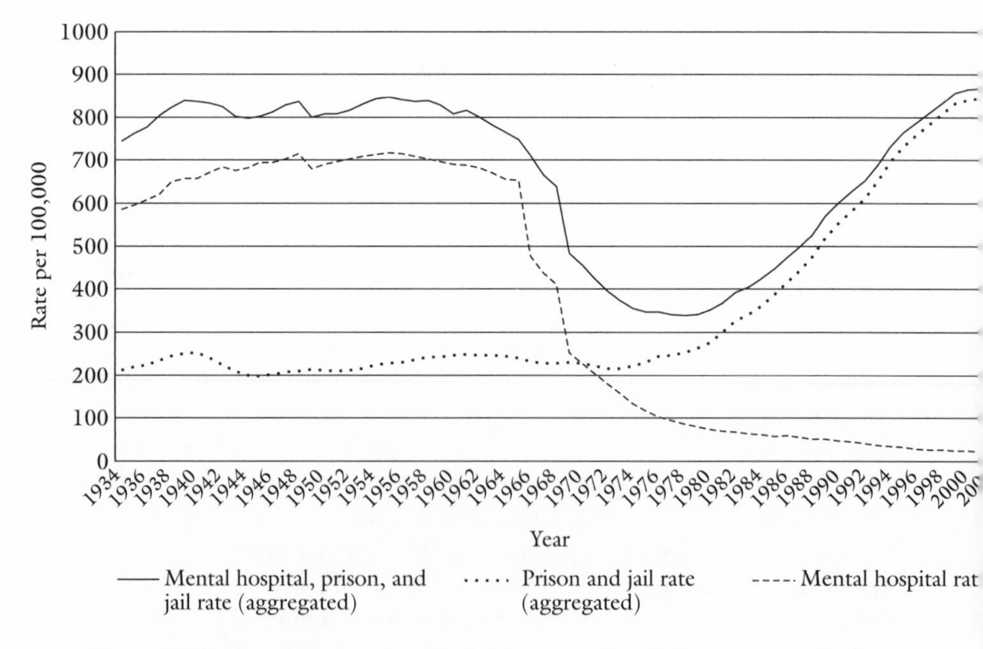

Figure 10.1. Rates of institutionalization in mental hospitals, state and federal prisons, and county jails for the period 1934–2001 (per 100,000 adults). *Source:* Data collected in Harcourt 2011.

penality—with a theory that the government should intervene because it is more efficient than the market. The important point here, though, is that the resulting excess may be different in kind, probably no better, and certainly no worse. This is entirely in keeping with the nominalist foundations of the argument advanced in this book. The problem is not just with the category of "free markets," but also with the category of "regulation." The ultimate goal is to displace both of these categories so that our evaluations and assessments of social and economic forms of organization are no longer determined ex ante. That requires reevaluating periods of regulatory triumph just as it does periods of free-market dominance.

Western Europe and Comparative Penality

A second large question concerns the comparison not to different penal rationalities, but rather to peer countries that equally embrace neoliberal market ideas. This is, in a sense, the flip side of the coin: the first objection was trained on bad outcomes in nonliberal contexts; this objection focuses on better (or less bad) outcomes in other neoliberal spaces. How is it that many European countries, for example, have also taken a neoliberal turn and yet none of them incarcerate 1 percent of their adult population?

Again, let me offer one quick clarification before discussing this equally fascinating question. The genealogy presented in this manuscript is distinctly American, although it begins inevitably on the Continent. The historical periods of the Market Revolution, of the Chicago School, of the Reagan era and the ensuing Washington Consensus are specific to the United States; the timing and influence of the law-and-economics writings are unique to this country. There may be parallels and some overlap with other countries, both in terms of ideas and penal practices. Ronald Reagan and Margaret Thatcher came to power at about the same time, Benjamin Franklin met the Physiocrats in the 1760s, and Alexis de Tocqueville and Gustave de Beaumont introduced the Auburn model quickly to European audiences. Nevertheless, the timing of the American experience is unique in part because of its young history. As the historian of punishment Pieter Spierenburg has emphasized, penal developments in the United States have been, at times, condensed and are peculiar to the circumstances of its youth.[6]

The American penal experience is also unique because of its history of race relations—the oppression of slavery and Jim Crow, the creation of urban ghettos, and the lasting effects of these institutions. Contemporary American politics and punishment have to be understood through the lens of race. Michael Dawson's book *From Katrina to Obama: The Future of Black Politics* (2011) is remarkable in this regard for tying neoliberal transformations to the fragmentation and economic devastation of black communities, which has in turn facilitated the punitive turn. The writings of Angela Davis, Dorothy Roberts, and Loïc Wacquant have also demonstrated the penal exceptionalism associated with the American racial experience.[7] This book may begin with the *commissaire* Emmanuel Nicolas Parisot and journey through Paris with Cesare Beccaria and François Quesnay, but what it explores is the implication of a certain penal rationality on the American carceral sphere.

Nevertheless, it would indeed be crucial to explore whether neoliberal ideas have similarly influenced penality in other Western and industrialized countries. It would be interesting to compare the influence of neoliberal rationality on the carceral experiences of Canada, France, Germany, Italy, Japan, the United Kingdom, or other industrialized "neoliberal" countries. This is, in fact, a topic of great interest to many social theorists and there is some controversy over the basic comparisons themselves.

Some theorists, notably David Garland, highlight similarities in the penal experiences of countries such as the United States and Great Britain, while others, notably James Whitman, emphasize the sharp differences between the American and the European modern experience with punishment.[8] Nicola Lacey is in the latter camp, emphasizing the differences between the United States and countries such as Canada, the Scandinavian states, and other major Western European countries.[9] Lacey specifically focuses on the question of neoliberalism, but proposes an additional set of economic, institutional, and cultural dimensions that mediate neoliberalism to help explain some of the penal differences, including the level of inequality, the composition of labor markets, ethnic diversity and migration patterns, welfare support, educational and vocational systems, as well as other political and institutional factors.[10] Other theorists, such as Alessandro De Giorgi, deploy a more Marxist framework, arguing that penal distinctions can best be understood on the basis of differing labor market needs.[11] Mick Cavadino and James Dignan develop a fourfold typology of political economies (neoliberal, conservative corporatist, social democratic, and oriental corporatist) to help explain some of the differences.[12]

These debates are captivating, though they take me somewhat outside the scope of this project. My impression is that in the modern period the United States may be an outlier in the magnitude of its prison population, but that the larger Western European countries have, to a great extent, mirrored the trends in the United States, with some lag and a lot of attenuation. This suggests—although a more refined analysis and further study is certainly necessary—that the common element of neoliberalism may well remain significant. Let's quickly look at some general trends.

First, like the United States, many European countries institutionalized mental health patients in psychiatric hospitals at higher rates during the mid-twentieth century and, in this sense, may have used mental institutions rather than prisons as a way to control those deemed deviant. The Republic of Ireland, for instance, had much higher rates of institutionalization in a wide range of mental facilities, including psychiatric institutions and homes for unmarried mothers, at midcentury—in fact, eight times higher—than at the turn of the twenty-first century.[13] The same trend of sharply declining institutionalization can be seen in a number of European countries. In Belgium, the number of psychiatric hospital beds per 100,000 inhabitants fell from 275 in 1970 to 162 in 2000; in France, from 242 in 1980 to 111 in 2000; in the United Kingdom, from 250 in 1985 to 100 in 2000; and in Switzerland, from 300 in 1970 to 120 in 2000.[14] These trends are illustrated in Figure 10.2.

Second, many European countries institutionalize individuals at high rates, especially when compared to their rates of incarceration. For instance, among countries in the European Union, the country with the most beds in psychiatric hospitals per 100,000 inhabitants in 2000 was the Netherlands, which had a rate of 188.5. Other highs were posted in Belgium (161.6), Swit-

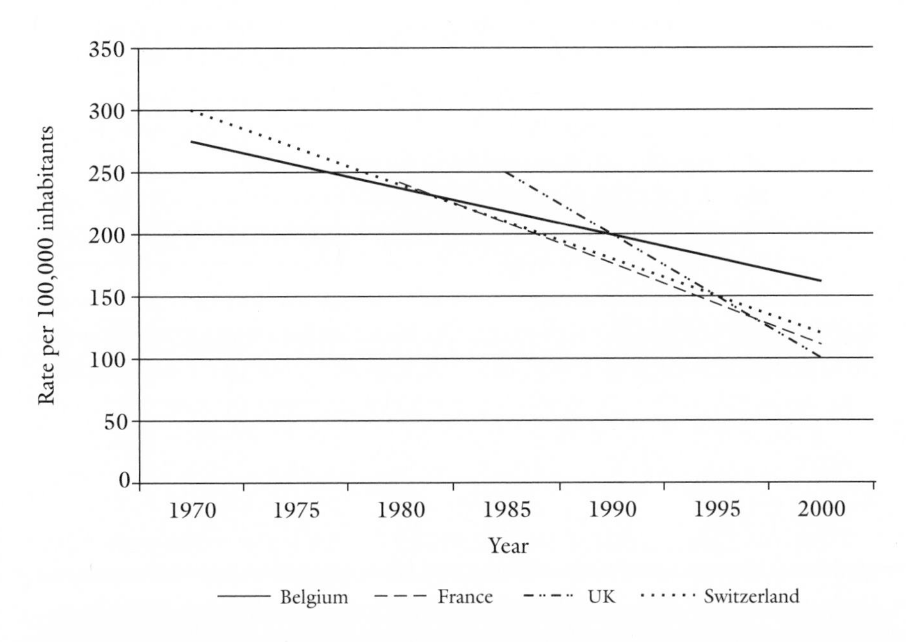

Figure 10.2. Count of psychiatric beds per 100,000 inhabitants in Belgium, France, the United Kingdom, and Switzerland. *Source:* Data from Eurostat 2003, 358, table 6.2.6.

Table 10.1 Mental hospitalization and prison rate comparisons for Netherlands, Belgium, Switzerland, France, Finland, Italy, and the United States

	Number of beds in psychiatric hospitals per 100,000 in 2000	Prison rate per 100,000 in 2006	Combined rate per 100,000
Netherlands	188.5	128	316.5
Belgium	161.6	91	252.6
Switzerland	119.9	83	202.9
France	113	85	198
Finland	102.9	75	177.9
Italy	16	104	120
U.S.A.	25	501	526

Source: Eurostat figures available at http://epp.eurostat.ec.europa.eu; see also *Sourcebook of Criminal Justice Statistics,* available at http://bjs.ojp.usdoj.gov (both last visited June 16, 2010).

zerland (119.9), France (113), and Finland (102.9). The average for the twenty-five European Union countries in 2000 was 90.1, down from 115.5 in 1993.[15] These figures are, indeed, far higher than the corresponding prison rates for the same countries, which stood in 2006 at 128 per 100,000 persons in the Netherlands, 91 in Belgium, 83 in Switzerland, 85 in France, and 75 in Finland. When combined as they are in Table 10.1, the rates of institutionalization appear considerable.[16] The Russian Federation, in fact, has a prison rate of 611 per 100,000, which, when combined with mental health institutionalization, may well be quite high.[17]

Third, like the United States, many European countries increased their rates of incarceration at the turn of the twenty-first century. One recent study has identified positive and statistically significant increases in imprisonment from 1992 to 2001 in Belgium, Germany, Great Britain, Ireland, and the Netherlands.[18] A graphic representation for several of the European states discussed earlier seems to corroborate the upward trends (see Figure 10.3).

When put together, the trends for individual countries are remarkably similar to those in the United States. Italy, for example, experienced sharply declining institutionalization, but sharply increasing incarceration, as shown in Figure 10.4.

Moreover, although the United States has been a leader in the penal field, other Western countries have not been far behind. Canada too has been experimenting with actuarial tools, and the logic of actuarial prediction—though not necessarily the instruments themselves—has penetrated a number of European countries, such as France, which in 2007 warmly embraced preventative detention (*rétention de sûreté*). Canada and many European

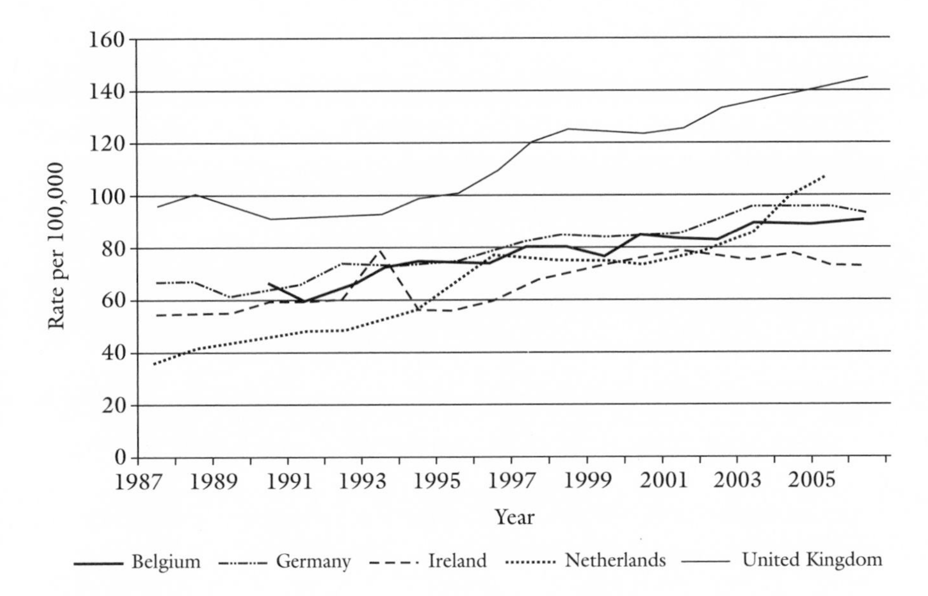

Figure 10.3. Number of prisoners per 100,000 inhabitants in Belgium, Germany, Ireland, Netherlands, and the United Kingdom, 1987–2006. *Source:* Data from Eurostat, available at http://epp.eurostat.ec.europa.eu (last visited June 17, 2010).

countries have also welcomed the increased use of order-maintenance policing strategies, such as zero tolerance and broken-windows policing; harsher treatment of juvenile offenders; increased use of video surveillance, biometric-data collection, data mining, and information gathering through initiatives such as closed-circuit television (CCTV) video surveillance in the United Kingdom and DNA-database collection in England and in France; and harsher sentencing practices, including the adoption of mandatory minimum sentences, "three-strikes laws," and additional prison time, or "enhancements," for crimes involving drugs or the use of a gun.

To be sure, in many of these developments the United States has been an exporter of ideas and technologies, such as broken-windows policing and mandatory minimum sentencing. But not in all. The United Kingdom has been a leader in the use of CCTV video surveillance and the collection of DNA; France was an early innovator in the field of paramilitary antiriot security forces; and Italy has been at the forefront of bunker-style judicial proceedings. The leading actuarial instrument in existence today—the Level of Services Inventory-Revised (LSI-R)—was invented and developed by Canadian researchers, and the same is true of the Hare Psychopathy Checklist-Revised (PCL-R).

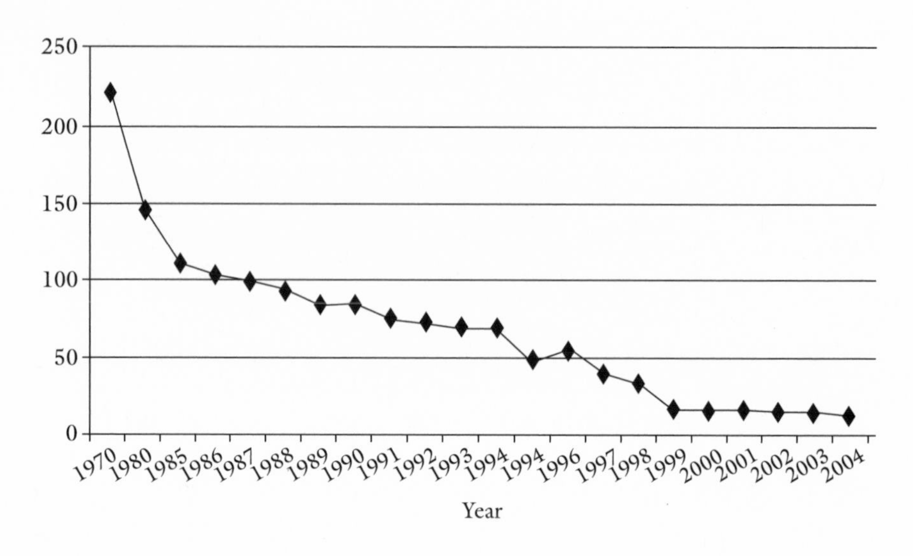

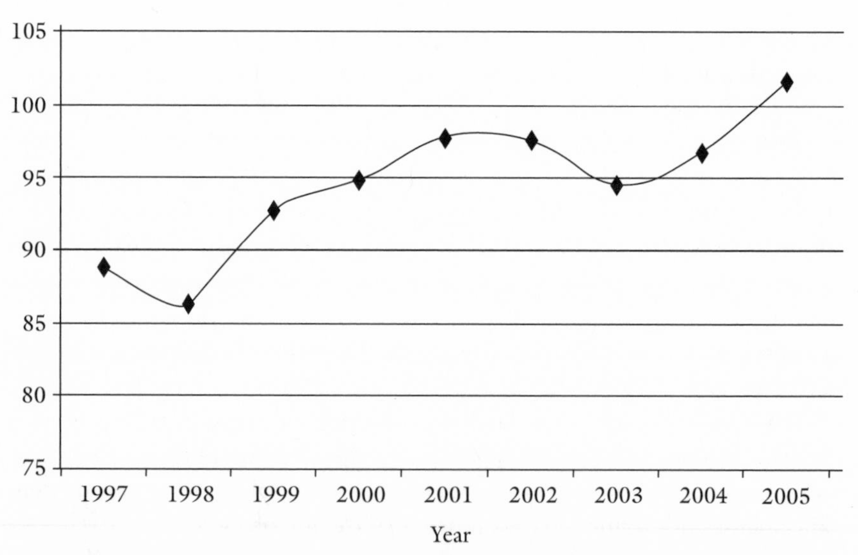

Figure 10.4. *Top:* Psychiatric hospital beds per 100,000 persons in Italy, 1970–2004 (years not to scale). *Bottom:* Number of prisoners per 100,000 persons in Italy, 1997–2005. *Source:* Data from Eurostat, available at http://epp.eurostat.ec .europa.eu (last visited June 17, 2010).

Overall, then, the American penal sphere may be several magnitudes larger than those of other Western liberal democracies, but the trends and developments over the course of the recent past are similar. There is no doubt that the timing, intensity, and effect of these trends will differ among these countries, and that there are unique historical, cultural, and institutional factors that will produce other important variations. The question is whether and how neoliberal ideas may possibly have shaped these trends. To be frank, the answer calls for another book-length treatment. The question to explore there would be whether the degree to which other liberal states embrace neoliberal penality correlates with a change in the size of their penal spheres, which should include not only prisons, jails, and psychiatric hospitals, but also immigration detention centers and other forms of social control.[19]

The Question of Illicit Drugs

Another objection is that the logic of Chicago School economics should not be taken to task for mass incarceration because many in the Chicago School oppose drug criminalization. It is certainly true that several prominent members of the Chicago School, especially Milton Friedman, have opposed the criminalization of illicit drugs. Friedman notoriously opposed the War on Drugs and militated strenuously in favor of legalizing drugs. "The attempt to prohibit drugs is by far the major source of the horrendous growth in the prison population," Friedman wrote in the pages of the *New York Times*. "How many of our citizens do we want to turn into criminals before we yell 'enough'?"[20] Others have also taken a progressive stand on drug legalization, though a more attenuated and nuanced one. Richard Epstein has advocated for a strictly regulated but not criminalized approach to illicit drugs, arguing for instance that "surely if the issue were the legalization of marijuana and other drugs, a respectable argument could be made to allow their sale, subject to a general tax and to prohibitions or restrictions on advertising, which, because of advertising's public visibility, should be reasonably easy to enforce."[21] Richard Posner, too, views illicit drug sales through the prism of efficient market transactions and argues that the criminalization of illicit drugs "is hard for an economist to understand."[22] In his personal capacity, he is opposed to the excesses of the War on Drugs and has written, "If the resources used to wage the war were reallocated to other social projects, such as reducing violent crime, there would probably be a net social gain." He adds that "we normally allow people to engage in such [self-destructive] behavior if they want; it is an aspect of liberty."[23] Moreover, Posner has stated in public that he would favor the legalization of marijuana and perhaps LSD.[24]

This is not to suggest that the issue of drug legalization is a top priority of the Chicago School. If you measure intensity of belief by word count, neither Epstein nor Posner has invested much in the topic (in contrast, perhaps, to Milton Friedman, who did write on the topic more extensively). Epstein and Posner have authored, in combination, well over fifty books on topics ranging from sex to literature to presidential impeachment to pharmaceutical innovation, and yet not one single volume—nor a single article, for that matter—focuses on our modern carceral excess. But still, drug legalization is surely part of the corpus of Chicago School beliefs. And as we all know well, the War on Drugs beginning in the 1980s contributed significantly to the exponential increase in incarceration in the United States.[25]

This objection, however, misconstrues the role of the Chicago School in the account presented in this book. My claim is not that the Chicago School is itself the dominant view in the public imagination. The argument is not that Richard Epstein or Richard Posner's positions are held by the majority of Americans. Not at all. In fact, only a small minority of the American population is familiar with the actual writings of the Chicago School, with their formal reasoning and logic, or with the detail of their positions. Only a tiny fraction of the American population, unfortunately, has read Richard Epstein's *Takings* or Richard Posner's *Economic Analysis of Law*. Even fewer have digested the Coase Theorem, worked through the equations in Gary Becker's economic analysis of crime and punishment, or understand terms such as "Pareto improvement," "Kaldor-Hicks efficiency," or even "transaction costs." Very few have been exposed to Posner's theory that rape constitutes the bypassing of a market in sex and marriage, nor for that matter that illicit drug transactions are efficient because they are voluntary, compensated exchanges that should be viewed in market terms. In other words, the details of the Chicago School positions, including their views on illicit drugs, do not constitute the public imagination or the dominant set of beliefs in this country.

Dominant beliefs operate at a more abstract level. As the polling data show, the American public believes that free markets are the best way to organize society. This book identifies the Chicago School as the most recent technical and scientific expression of this larger set of beliefs. It also reveals how the notion of natural order from the eighteenth century evolved into one of market efficiency at its most sophisticated, erudite, scientific theorization—the version that achieved multiple Nobel prizes, prizes that have validated and confirmed in the public imagination the superiority of the supposedly unfettered free market. The Chicago School writings simultaneously shape and reflect the public imagination, though they themselves do not constitute in all their intricate details American beliefs.

It is important to keep separate the public imagination and the scientific theory. The vast majority of people—the people who are responding to the Gallup polls—do not believe that crime is "inefficient" behavior, but they do believe in the free market. Similarly, they do not believe that drug transactions are "voluntary, compensated exchanges" that should simply be analyzed through a market model. Drug legalization is certainly one area where the more technical law-and-economics models do not mirror the public imagination. And it is, of course, the popular view that facilitates and eases the expansion of the penal sphere.

In the area of drug legalization, there is a larger story about the criminalization of vice behaviors that would need to be fleshed out—behaviors that include not only illicit drugs, but also alcohol, gambling, prostitution, adultery, pornography, tobacco, and other vices. The history of state monopolization, legalization, regulation, criminalization, and penalization in each of these domains is complex, varies from one vice to another, and is highly related to changing conceptions of morality. The administration of vice has its idiosyncrasies that make the field somewhat unique.[26] For this reason, the question of the legalization of drugs is a red herring.

Privatization of Prisons

This leads to a fourth and final question: If there is such a sharp distinction between economy and punishment, how does one explain the privatization of prisons? Hasn't this economic development contributed to the growth of the penal sphere? In a sense, this question is also the flip side of the last objection. The latter viewed economics as liberty enhancing and focused on the issue (legalization of illicit drugs) where free-market economic theories would expand freedom. This objection, in contrast, views economics in somewhat more conspiratorial terms, and questions instead whether economic incentives are taking over the penal sphere and causing more incarceration. Private prisons have indeed played an important role in prison growth since at least the 1980s, and due to severe budgetary problems in the wake of the 2008 economic crisis, some states such as Arizona have begun debating whether to sell their entire corrections operations to private corporations. Many commentators talk about a "prison-industrial complex" that feeds prison growth. Does this reflect a closer relationship between the economic realm and the penal sphere? Isn't mass incarceration all about economics?

This is, again, an opportunity for clarification. The relationship between economy and punishment evolved with each new iteration of liberal and neoliberal penality. Neither Bentham's alchemy, nor the Chicago School theory of market efficiency, represents a pure repetition of Physiocratic legal despotism. In the Physiocratic writings there was, indeed, a sharp demarcation of economy and punishment. Recall that positive law was reserved for punishing severely those who did not abide by the natural order, and punishment was not infused with economic reasoning. Jeremy Bentham, in contrast, conjoined discipline with efficiency in his vision of the panopticon and certainly applied an economic logic of deterrence to the penal code. In Bentham, economic reasoning bled into the punishment field. Gary Becker would push this connection even further by explicitly extending economic rationality to nonmarket behaviors. But again, not vice versa: as the Coase Theorem demonstrates, the realm of competitive markets is precisely where punishment has no role. The criminal sanction is for market bypassing. In other words, since the stark Physiocratic separation of an autonomous economic sphere from "police," economic reasoning gradually has seeped in and infused the penal sphere (though the influence, again, has been unidirectional).

That being said, the historical record bears out that the birth and expansion of the prison is a story driven in part, or at least on occasion, by economic incentives and profit motive. As a historical matter, there is no question that private financial interests have fueled punitive excess in the United States. This was certainly true of American slavery, which must be considered a form of punishment. It was true at the birth of the penitentiary system, which was fostered by contractual penal servitude. It has also been true for private prisons, which have been a significant source of investment, profit, and labor since the early 1980s.

During the Market Revolution, the potential profit associated with contract prison labor certainly fed the penitentiary system. This was an area where the government not only could intervene legitimately, but also, possibly, profitably—a place where, as Georg Rusche and Otto Kirchheimer have shown, the state could achieve "maximum industrial efficiency."[27] Contemporary historians such as Rebecca McLennan have meticulously documented the vital connection between prison growth and profitability through contractual penal servitude. Invented first at the Auburn prison in New York in the early 1820s, "contractual penal servitude went on to become the dominant mode of legal punishment in almost all Northern (and, eventually, all Southern) states" through the late Gilded Age.[28] As McLennan writes, "forced, hard, productive labor was of foundational importance to the penal order that the states erected on the ruins of the old penitential mode of punishment."[29] Alexis de Tocqueville and Gustave de Beaumont would report on the increasing profitability of the Auburn system, noting a steadily increasing surplus for the state treasuries during the Jackson years: "Auburn $25 in 1830 and $1,800 in 1831; Wethersfield $1,000 in 1828, over $3,200 in 1929, and nearly $8,000 in 1831; Baltimore $11,500 in 1828 and nearly $20,000 in 1829."[30]

The Auburn method proved to be both profitable and successful. As McLennan explains, "The contract prison labor system, under which the state sold the labor power of convicts to private interests, quickly became the fiscal and disciplinary foundation of the new system at Auburn; it subsequently proved decisive in the decision of most Northern (and some Southern) states to replace their old penitentiary systems, not with the 'isolation' prison system that Pennsylvania was refining at the Eastern Penitentiary, but with New York's 'Auburn plan.'"[31]

But the success of the Auburn prison system would also, eventually, lead to its downfall.[32] It ultimately triggered protest and opposition during the nineteenth century. The first protests were small-scale and local, involving primarily free workingmen who felt economically threatened by the competition of prison labor. Eventually, however, organized political opposition, labor movements, and large-scale popular campaigns rallied to abolish the practice of penal servitude. McLennan documents this history of mounting protest and opposition, as well as the eventual abolition of the penal methods, in her book *The Crisis of Imprisonment: Protest, Politics, and the Making of the American Penal States, 1776–1941*. In the book she demonstrates ably both the centrality of productive labor to the expansion of the penitentiary system and the role of organized labor in the abolition of penal servitude, as well as the way in which the eventual abolition of contractual prison labor would reshape the penal landscape in the twentieth century. As McLennan writes, the prison crises in the 1880s "constituted the single greatest watershed in the history of American legal punishment since the Jacksonian era and the states' wholesale adoption of prison labor contracting."[33]

The profit motive, however, returned in the 1980s when the privatization of prisons became popular in the United States.[34] In the early 1980s, there were only a handful of private detention facilities housing a small number of inmates. For example, in 1981 the State of Kentucky contracted with a not-for-profit company to manage an eighty-bed minimum-security prison. The privatization of prisons began to grow more rapidly by the mid-1980s when the Corrections Corporation of America, founded in 1983, received two larger contracts: the Houston Processing Center in Houston, Texas, which contained 350 prisoners, and the Silverdale Detention Center in Hamilton County, Tennessee, which held 440 prisoners. By the end of 1988, there were at least twenty privately operated detention facilities operating in nine states at the federal, state, and local levels; by 1990, the number had increased to thirty-five.[35]

By 2008, as many as 8 percent of all prisoners were held in privately run prisons.[36] For federal prisoners, the number of inmates in privately run prisons more than doubled between 2000 and 2008: whereas there were 15,524 such prisoners in 2000, the number reached 33,162 in 2008. State prisoners in privately run prisons also increased between 2000 and 2008 (albeit at a slower rate), from 71,845 in 2000 to 95,362 in 2008. Between 2007 and 2008 alone, the number of federal prisoners in privately run facilities increased by 5.9 percent.[37]

The largest company, the Corrections Corporation of America, employed nearly 17,000 workers nationwide in 2010, not only in security, but also in academic and vocational education, in health services and facility maintenance, and in human resources, management, and administration.[38] A comparison with other large employers in the United States suggests that the Corrections Corporation of America is one of the hundred largest employers in the country.[39] The company is publicly traded on the New York Stock Exchange, and its shares have performed remarkably during the 1990s and 2000s. The value of the company's stock has skyrocketed from its founding in 1983, up from $50 million in 1986 when it first went public on the NASDAQ to $53.5 billion in 1997 when it was selling on the NYSE.[40]

The term "prison-industrial complex" traces to this period in the 1990s and attempts to capture the rapid expansion of the penal system and the way in which prison construction became big business, especially in California where it began to rival agribusiness as a dominant force in rural life.[41] The term gained wider currency with a 1998 article in *The Atlantic* by Eric Schlosser, in which he described it as "a set of bureaucratic, political, and economic interests that encourage increased spending on imprisonment, regardless of the actual need." Schlosser expressly steered away from any conspiracy theory, writing that "the prison-industrial complex is not a conspiracy, guiding the nation's criminal-justice policy behind closed doors. It is a confluence of special interests that has given prison construction in the United States a seemingly unstoppable momentum."[42]

Schlosser dates the origins of the complex to January 3, 1973—the date Nelson Rockefeller, governor of New York, gave a State of the State address demanding that all drug dealers be given a mandatory prison sentence of life without parole. Angela Davis gives a persuasive reading of the prison-industrial complex in her 2003 book *Are Prisons Obsolete?* The term "prison-industrial complex" is somewhat controversial and has been contested by many, especially Loïc Wacquant, for containing too much of a conspiratorial notion and for overstating the size of the effect.[43] But it is nevertheless useful because it highlights the profitability of prison building and the employment boom associated with prison guard labor. There is no question that the prison expansion served the financial interests of large sectors of the economy.

Historically, then, economic incentives have played an important role during moments of penal expansion. In arguing that there is a perceived division between orderliness in the economic realm and state intervention in the punishment field, I am not suggesting that the penal sphere is insulated from economics. I am emphasizing the inverse: that the free market, governed by "natural order," is insulated from punishment. The punishment field is then wide open not only to government intervention, but to profit and economics as well.

What to think of the complex link between punishment and profit, then, is another matter. Keally McBride has a fascinating discussion of the issue of prison labor and profit in her chapter "Hitched to the Post: Prison Labor, Choice, and Citizenship," in her 2007 book *Punishment and Political Order*. McBride identifies there a number of intertwined dimensions to prison labor and profit that run into each other to produce our complex contemporary reality—one marked by oddly inefficient or unproductive prison labor at a time of high unemployment. First, in the liberal imagination, labor is a distinctive and necessary ingredient of citizenship: choosing freely and being able legally to work is a sign of one's capacity to self-govern and of full participation in the political sphere. The flip side of this is that being forced to work is a form of punishment that makes the forced laborer less fit for citizenship. Penal servitude, in this sense, has symbolized civic death, even though—or rather because—it is conjoined with labor. At the same time, labor as a form of punishment has had, historically, both a connotation of rehabilitation and of discipline—and it has also served to defray the costs of imprisonment, to make punishment possible. In addition, in the 1930s, when prison labor became most productive and profitable, labor activism pushed Congress to ban the practice, so that in our current age of foreign outsourcing, prison labor has become essentially unprofitable.

What happens to all these connotations and practices in an era of large-scale unemployment? "In Alabama and Arizona," McBride writes, "wardens have decided to pay for large boulders to be brought to prisons. Convicts break these boulders into gravel with hammers. The gravel, of no practical use, is deposited into pits next to the prison. The prison pays to bring in more boulders to be smashed."[44] McBride argues that prison labor today resolves the tension between liberal ideologies of labor and the reality of contemporary unemployment by creating a form of useless, inefficient, punitive work that merely reinforces the tie between the unemployed and the incarcerated. McBride refers to these practices as "ever more farcical performances of penal labor."[45] In this sense, prison labor reveals the "shifts from late industrial to postindustrial economies."[46]

A host of parallel issues surrounds the private prison, prison guard labor, and prison building. These phenomena, it seems, also reflect our postindustrial condition and especially the "bubble economies" that we have witnessed over the past few decades—the "dot-com bubble" of the late 1990s and the "real estate bubble" of the late 2000s. Prison building (a form of real estate, after all) exploded in the 1990s, generating a remarkable outburst of expenditures, jobs, and debt. It is possible to think of the growth of the prison sector as resembling, in many ways, the growth of the real estate sector: it too was fueled by irresponsible lending or borrowing, growth to levels that exceeded future capacity, and speculative prices.[47]

The Great Recession of 2008 has put severe pressure on the "prison bubble"—if that is a fair term—as many states find themselves challenged to service the debt associated with prison building or carry the expenses associated with massive prison populations. This has been nowhere more clear than in Arizona where, in early 2009, the state legislators began discussing the idea of converting the entire state-run prison system into a privately run corporation to counteract the $3.3 billion revenue shortfall expected in 2009.[48] Some legislators predicted that this change could save the state approximately $40 million annually, whereas others hoped that this could reduce the budget shortfall by $100 million.[49] The plan to privatize the whole sector has gone forward. During the first week of February 2010, the window opened for private companies to submit potential bids for the privatization of nine of the state's ten prisons, which house a total of 40,000 inmates.[50]

If this privatization moves ahead it would represent an important shift, even though it would merely add to Arizona's already significant reliance on private prisons: to date, nearly 30 percent of the state's prisoners are held in privately run facilities.[51] But other states likely would watch the Arizona experience and consider more seriously the idea of privatizing their whole prison sector. It is unclear what will ultimately happen with the prison sector: whether it would ever "pop" as an economic bubble, whether it will be fully privatized, or whether it will gradually shrink. Other trends, some unforeseeable, may emerge that will influence the current situation—recall, for instance, that mental hospitals and asylums were emptied in the 1960s and 1970s due in part to changes in federal reimbursement programs.

One final thought. With the exception of the privatization of prisons and anarcho-capitalist writings on the criminal justice system, there is little sincere reflection among proponents of law and economics about the potential "efficiency" gains of privatizing core criminal-justice institutions such as the criminal courts and the police.[52] There has been little serious attention paid to privatizing domestic security forces or criminal court processes.[53] This is paradoxical from one perspective, and yet entirely consistent with some other paradoxes of neoliberalism. These bastions of government intervention are not unlike those other "unaccountable institutions" like the Federal Reserve and the IMF, which represent, as David Harvey reminds us, such "intense state interventions and government by elites and 'experts' in a world where the state is supposed not to be interventionist."[54]

A Prolegomenon

"The market is the best mechanism ever invented for efficiently allocating resources to maximize production . . . I also think that there is a connection between the freedom of the marketplace and freedom more generally."[1] Surprisingly, these are not the words of Friedrich Hayek. They are also not those of George Stigler or Milton Friedman—though they echo closely Friedman's statement that "economic freedom is also an indispensable means toward the achievement of political freedom."[2] They belong instead to Barack Obama, who at the time, in the summer of 2008—after the collapse of Bear Stearns and of the securitized-mortgage market—was a presidential candidate seeking the Democratic nomination. After the bottom would fall out of the American banking system—after the failure of Lehman Brothers, the bailouts of Fannie Mae, Freddie Mac, and A.I.G., and the passage of a $700 billion TARP rescue package for the financial industry—President Obama's Treasury secretary, Timothy Geithner, would declare: "We have a financial system that is run by private shareholders, managed by private institutions, and we'd like to do our best to preserve that system."[3] Never mind that the American people, as a result of the first $350 billion partial nationalization of the biggest banks, were at that point the largest shareholders of Citigroup, with 7.8 percent of its equity, and the largest holders of Bank of America stock, with 6 percent of its shares.[4]

The persistence of the rhetoric of "free markets" is remarkable. The pervasiveness of both the faith in free markets and the use of its central dichotomy—free versus regulated, private versus government-controlled—is extraordinary. At its heart lies a notion of natural order, of equilibrium, of what we have come to call today "market efficiency." This idea of a natural order in the economic domain evolved from the second half of the eighteenth century onward into one of the most influential rhetorical tropes that has helped shape and fuel our vision of markets and punishment in the twenty-first century. The notion that human interaction could spontaneously and autonomously achieve a stable, orderly, self-sustaining form of equilibrium in the absence of government intervention—what François Quesnay and the first school of *économistes* dubbed *un ordre naturel* in the late 1750s—has facilitated a conception of the market as a self-regulating system that could only prosper by purging itself of the prejudicial meddling of governments and politics. In the face of this new conception of an orderly market, governance would be relegated outside that autonomous space, charged with the responsibility of policing and punishing those who deviate—those who do not see the natural laws or, in more technical jargon, who bypass the market.

It is precisely this form of rationality—this dominant mode of understanding economy and society—that blinds us both to the extent of regulation and discipline in our free markets and to the amount of liberty in earlier systems of market organization. It is this dominant rationality that enables us to look at a situation and see order but not the web of regulatory threads that beget and maintain that order. This bias, this prejudice, this distortion came to us from the Physiocrats and has weaved through liberal writings from Jeremy Bentham to Friedrich Hayek, Milton Friedman, Richard Epstein, and Richard Posner. This rationality has enabled the growth of the penal sphere by naturalizing and legitimating government intervention in criminal matters. It is what both causes friction when the state announces a plan to regulate the economy, and greases the wheels when the state declares a new penal statute or law-enforcement initiative.

The appeal of liberty is indeed a powerful force—especially when it is tied, as it has been since the Physiocrats, to the notion of orderliness. The idea of natural order is itself seductive. As David Harvey suggests, "Concepts of dignity and individual freedom are powerful and appealing in their own right. Such ideals empowered the dissident movements in eastern Europe and the Soviet Union before the end of the Cold War as well as the students in Tiananmen Square."[5] They are precisely what made the Physiocrats sound so revolutionary in their day. It is what gave them so much momentum and influence. And it is what propelled their rationality—that paradoxical alchemy of market liberalism and legal despotism—into the twenty-first century.

In truth, however, the "liberalization" of markets and "privatization" of industries during portions of the nineteenth and twentieth centuries merely substituted one set of regulations, often governmental forms of rule-making, with other regulatory systems that merely favored a different set of actors. There is, to be sure, a sensation of liberation that accompanies the "liberalization" of markets. But it is illusory and serves as a cover that simply renders distributional outcomes more natural. It appears to take the government out of the mix and thereby gives the impression that the outcomes are now based entirely on merit or talent. All the while, the state actually facilitates and makes possible the new order.

The notion of liberty associated with contemporary free markets is a historical artifact, the product of a shift that occurred in the eighteenth century—a shift from an idea of liberty as imposing obligations on the state to ensure *bon marché* or plentiful subsistence markets at low prices, to the more modern idea of liberty from governmental interference in all economic matters. Both of these conceptions of liberty—but for our purposes more importantly the modern idea of liberty—are fundamentally misleading. Modern American economic organization is a system as fully regulated as any previous economic order and it must be evaluated—like any of its variations or alternatives, whether more libertarian or collectivist—on distributional grounds, not on the basis of an illusory metric of liberty.

It is time, well past time, to sever our contemporary assessment of economic organization from the rhetoric of the free market, natural order, and market efficiency. It is time to pull them apart: to purge economic and social analysis of the myth of natural order and the misleading language of liberty. It is time to dispense entirely with terms like "natural order," "spontaneous equilibrium," "free markets," "liberté de commerce"—terms that do no more than obfuscate the real work that needs to be done.

At the end of the day, the notion of a "free market" is a fiction. There simply is no such thing as a nonregulated market—a market that operates without legal, social, and professional regulation. Those forms of regulation—including the criminal sanction—are precisely what distributes wealth and resources, what makes it possible for the Chicago Board of Trade to exclude nonmembers from the trading floor, for the Big Four accounting firms to effectively control accounting standards, and for large commercial banks to essentially coordinate lending practices. All these practices are regulated. The question is thus not *whether* to regulate. Instead the only question is *how* the existing and prospective kinds of regulation distribute wealth. That is the only important question and it is, tragically, masked by our faith in natural order and efficient markets.

A prolegomenon: that is how I introduced this book and it is also how I shall close. The task ahead is to get beyond those timeworn categories of natural order and police, of free markets and excessive regulation, of *sécurité* and *discipline*. We must not merely identify these tropes and locate them within governance, but instead shed them completely. We must do the work that needs to be done—assessing the distributional consequences of different possible forms of social and market organization—without them. This is only a first step. But it is a necessary first step. It will not be possible to break the hold of our excessively punitive carceral state unless we first free ourselves from the very language of "free" markets.

Notes

The Paris *Marais* and the Chicago Board of Trade

1. Fréminville 1758, 78.
2. Ibid., 78–79.
3. Ibid., 79.
4. Ibid.
5. Ibid.
6. Ibid., 73.
7. Ibid.
8. Ibid., 502.
9. Ibid., 501.
10. Ibid., i (cover page).
11. A *bailli* was the functional equivalent of a *lieutenant général de police* or an English sheriff in more rural areas outside of Paris. It was an office that retained important regulatory and administrative functions throughout the ancien régime—including the authority to set market prices. See generally Olivier-Martin 1988b, 66–73. For a biographical entry on Fréminville, see des Essarts 1800, 3:153–154.
12. Fréminville prefaces his work with an acknowledgment to Delamare's famous treatise, all the while signaling the broader reach of his own text and the greater practicality or applicability of his treatise (Fréminville 1758, iii).
13. Ibid., vii.
14. Ibid., vii–viii.
15. Ibid., viii.
16. Ibid., 267.
17. Ibid. (The author of the anonymous text was Claude-Jacques Herbert.)
18. Ibid., 267.
19. Kaplan 1976, 2:680, 682.
20. Weulersse 2003, 1:534.
21. Fréminville 1758, 451.
22. Ibid., 451–452.
23. Ibid., 452.
24. Ibid., 454.
25. *Sentence de la chambre de police du Châtelet, qui déclare valable une saisie d'un*

muid de farine, à la requête du procureur des jurés mesureurs de grain. October 10, 1681. Paris: M. Le Prest.

26. Ibid.
27. Afanassiev 1894, 71 (relying on Delamare 1705–1738, 2:81).
28. Ibid. (relying on *Ordonnance de décembre 1672*).
29. Fréminville 1758, 468.
30. Ibid., 213.
31. Ibid.
32. Ibid.
33. Ibid., 214.
34. Ibid.
35. Ibid., 166.
36. Ibid., 266.
37. Ibid., 367 ("MARCHÉS. *v.* POLICE.").
38. "La guerre du blé au XVIIIe siècle" is the very title of an excellent collection of writings on the topic. See Gauthier and Ikni 1988.
39. *Code Louis XV.*
40. The flow of publications would extend well past the Revolution. See, e.g., Guichard 1792.
41. Smith 1976, 2:48 (book 4, chap. 5), and 2:50.
42. Ibid., 182 (book 4, chap. 9).
43. Foucault 2007, 45 (emphasis added); Foucault 2004b, 46.
44. Nelson 2005b, 1. Leading exponents of this view include Francis Fukuyama (1992), Daniel Yergin and Joseph Stanislaw (1998), and others.
45. Hollingsworth and Boyer 1997a, 1.
46. Nelson 2005b, 1.
47. Ibid.
48. Boyer 1997, 57; see also Lindblom 2001, 10–15.
49. Krugman 2009b; Krugman 2009c.
50. Leonhardt 2008, 31.
51. Epstein 1996, 2.
52. Harvey 2005, 2.
53. See generally, Osborne and Gaebler 1993; Guttman 2000; Kosar 2006; Savas 1999; and Harvey 2005, 2–3.
54. See generally Manta 2008; Guttman 2000, 861.
55. Obama 2006, 156–157; also see generally, Leonhardt 2008, 31.
56. Campbell and Pedersen 2001, 1; Fourcade 2007; Western 2001; and Fligstein 2001.
57. For "hegemonic," see Peck and Tickell 2002, 34; for "new planetary vulgate" see Bourdieu and Wacquant 2001, 2; for "thought virus" see Beck 2000, 122.
58. Comaroff and Comaroff 2001, 43.
59. See The Harris Poll® no. 94, September 27, 2007, available at www.harrisinteractive.com/Insights/HarrisVault8482.aspx (last visited June 18, 2010).
60. See "20-Nation Poll Finds Strong Global Consensus: Support for Free Market System But Also More Regulation of Large Companies" available at www.globescan.com/news_archives/pipa_market.html (last visited June 16, 2010).

61. See Frank Newport, "Americans Leery of Too Much Gov't Regulation of Business: Republicans in Particular Are Worried about Too Much Government Regulation," February 2, 2010, available at www.gallup.com/poll/125468/Americans-Leery-Govt-Regulation-Business.aspx (last visited June 16, 2010).
62. See, e.g., Leonhardt 2007.
63. CFTC 1997, *17 n. 17.
64. Ibid., *9 n. 10.
65. Ibid., *9.
66. Ibid., *12–13 nn. 13 and 15.
67. Ibid., *1.
68. Ibid., *3.
69. Ibid., *4 n. 2.
70. Ibid., *2.
71. Ibid., *3, *4 n. 3, *40, *51, *17 n. 19, and *43 n. 34.
72. Ibid. at *40.
73. Ibid. at *41.
74. Ibid. at *52.
75. Ibid., *48–49.
76. Ibid., *50 n. 45.
77. Ibid., *54. For a fascinating look into (and out of) the pits at the Chicago Board of Trade, see Zaloom 2006.
78. *Friedman* 2002, 798.
79. For an excellent treatment of the relationship between the guild system and the merchant courts, see generally Kessler 2007.
80. Nicolas Delamare (1639–1723) was a *procureur,* then *commissaire* at the Châtelet (May 1673). He was commissioned to codify all the rules of policing and did so in the famous four-volume *Traité de la police*. See the Delamare entry in Olivier Cayla and Jean-Louis Halperin's *Dictionnaire des grandes œuvres juridiques* (Paris: Dalloz, 2008); see also generally Bondois 1935. Incidentally, since there is some confusion on this question, Delamare signed his name in one word and so I will use that form (Olivier-Martin 1988b, 8).
81. Musart 1921, 33–35.
82. Ibid., 35.
83. Delamare died on April 25, 1723, at the age of eighty-four. His collaborator, Leclerc du Brillet, completed and published the fourth volume of the *Traité* in 1738.
84. Delamare 1705–1738, 2:619–620.
85. Smith 1978, 5.
86. Ibid.; see also 331 ["he was to provide for the neteté, surete, and bon marché in the city"]. Smith had in his library Bielfield's *Institutions politiques,* which quotes the chief of police in Paris in 1697: "Le Roi, Monsieur, vous demande sûreté, netteté, bon-marché. En effet ces trois articles comprennent toute la police, qui forme le troisième grand objet de la politique pour l'intérieur de l'Etat" (see generally Cannan 1976, xxv–xxvi).
87. Smith 1978, 333, 398.
88. Ibid., 398, 487.

89. For an excellent early treatment of this issue, see Olivier-Martin 1988b, 13–22. See also Ranum 1968, 272–280; Foucault 2004b, 320–322; Kaplan 1976, 1: 11–14; Pasquino 1991, 109–116; Rancière 1995, chap. 2 on "Politique et Police"; Napoli 2003, 8; Dubber and Valverde 2006, 1–2; Zedner 2006, 82; and Emsley 2007, 61–62. For a wealth of sources on the history and science of policing, see also Le Clère 1991 and 1993; Greer 1936.
90. Olivier-Martin 1988b, 13.
91. Beccaria 1995, 8.
92. Olivier-Martin 1988b, 30.
93. Fréminville 1758, 142 (on charivari); 294 (on flying kites); and 467 (on artichoke leaves).
94. *Collection Officielle,* 3:99 [no. 88, April 3, 1762], 85 [no. 72, October 10, 1742], 84 [no. 70, January 28, 1741], 100 [no. 89, October 14, 1762].
95. On the regulation regarding scythes, see Babeau 1878, 313 [relying on (1) Cahiers du tiers-état de Nemours, *Archives parlementaires,* IV, 205; and (2) Arrêt du 2 juillet 1786—*Anc. Lois,* XXVIII, 211]); on the regulation regarding dogs, see *Collection Officielle* 3:100 (no. 88, April 3, 1762).
96. Duchesne 1767, 96–122 (26 pages on the *police des grains*).
97. Ibid., 7.
98. Olivier-Martin 1988b, 99.
99. See generally, Sallé 1759; Boucher d'Argis 1753; Ranum 1968, 274–280; Bloit and Payen-Appenzeller 1989; Williams 1979, 62–162; Carrot 1992, 80–85; Emsley 2007, 65–66.
100. Emsley 2007, 65.
101. Ibid.
102. Bloit and Payen-Appenzeller 1989, 20.
103. For additional sources describing the police under the ancien régime, see generally Williams 1979; Stead 1983, 12–31; Garrioch 1986, 207–221; Le Taillanter 2001, 19–41; L'Heuillet 2001; and Napoli 2003. For studies of policing in the provinces, see Ruff 1984; and Greenshields 1994.
104. For entertaining reading from the commissioners' *procès-verbaux* from 1789, see generally Bloit and Payen-Appenzeller 1989.
105. One such investigation by Commissioner Picard-Desmarest, which produced verbal interrogations of more than six witnesses, involved the alleged theft of ten bags of flour in October 1789. See ibid., 186–193 (referring to National Archives carton Y-15102B).
106. Quesnay 2005, 570.
107. "Net product" is defined as "a disposable surplus over necessary cost. Anything which increased this net product would cause an expansion in economic activity, and anything which reduced it would cause a contraction in economic activity" (Meek 1962, 19; see also Du Pont de Nemours 1808, 313).
108. Dumont 1977a, 41.
109. Marx 1974, 399.
110. Meyssonnier 1989, 36; see also Morrissey 2010, 57–62; Groenewegen 2002, 62.
111. Schumpeter 1968, 97.

112. Ibid., 223–243; and see generally Beer 1939.
113. In a "Notice" entitled *Sur les économistes,* Du Pont traces Physiocratic thought to three sources or precursors. The first is the duc de Sully, who privileged agriculture. The second is d'Argenson, discussed in the text. The third is Mr. Trudaine le père, who also toiled in these fields. See Du Pont de Nemours 1808, 309; also Du Pont's *Notice sur les Économistes,* reproduced in Turgot 1844 1:258.
114. Rothschild 2004, 4.
115. Ibid.
116. Smith used the term "police" only twelve times in the *Wealth of Nations,* predominantly in a historical manner and, on two occasions, in a descriptive manner. See, e.g., "Such enhancements of the market price may last as long as the regulations of police which give occasion to them" (1976, 1:70); and "sometimes particular accidents, sometimes natural causes, and sometimes particular regulations of police, may, in many commodities, keep up the market price, for a long time together, a good deal above the natural price" (1:67). At no point did Smith use the term as a rubric to expound his political economy, as he had in the *Lectures.*
117. McCoy 1980, 52; see also Faÿ 1929, 342–343.
118. Aldridge 1957, 24–30.
119. Posner 1985, 1195–1196.
120. It would indeed be fascinating to trace the genealogy of the very idea of natural order and to explore its reflections in other domains, such as the family, where the idea of internal and autonomous order shielded the private sphere from governmental intervention, creating separate spaces of public and private. A good place to start would be with John Stuart Mill's *The Subjection of Women* (1988), Martha Nussbaum's chapter on "The Challenge of Gender Justice" (2009), and Fran Olsen's writings (1983; 1985). But that is another project, for another day. This one begins with the emergence of natural order in liberal economic thought in the eighteenth century and focuses on the overlapping spaces of the economic, social, and penal spheres.
121. Nietzsche 1967, 153 (emphasis in original). I thank Bob Gooding-Williams for drawing my attention again to this passage.
122. See Hale 1923, 1935, 1943; also see generally Samuels 1973; Kennedy 1991; Fried 1998; and Ayres 1999. For a more modern expression of similar insights, see Sunstein 1997; Holmes and Sunstein 1999.
123. For an excellent exposition and discussion of this point, see Fried 1998, 46–48.
124. *Friedman* 2002.
125. Gordon 1975.
126. *United States v. National Association of Securities Dealers* 1975.
127. *Finnegan* 1990.
128. *Thill Securities Corp. v. New York Stock Exchange* 1970; Silver 1963.
129. Durand-Molard 1807, 2:253–254.
130. Quesnay 2005, 1017 ("La législation positive ne doit donc pas s'étendre sur le domaine des loix phisiques").
131. Ibid.
132. Ibid.

133. Ibid.
134. Hart 1982, 45.
135. See ibid., 48–52.
136. Quoted in Young 1983, 318; also in Halévy 1955, 21.
137. Bentham 1952, 3:333–334.
138. This definition, which was widely accepted, originated in the hand of Adam Smith (Smith 1976, 2:208–209). The passage has been discussed by many historians and is generally taken to be a fair definition of a moderate (non-purist and non-extreme) version of laissez-faire. See, e.g., Viner 1927, 222–223; Viner 1960, 45; Holmes 1976, 672; and Robbins 1953, 37.
139. Posner 1985, 1195.
140. Kaplan 1974, 155.
141. Foucault 2004a, 258.
142. Becker 1968, 176.
143. Beckett 1997, 51.
144. Ronald Reagan's remarks at a fundraising dinner, quoted in Beckett ibid.
145. See Massey 2007, 5 ("Whereas the largest private fortune in the United States stood at $3.6 billion in 1968, by 1999 it had reached $85 billion, raising the distance between the top and bottom of the social structure by a factor of 24 in just thirty years. Likewise, from 1975 to 2000 wealth inequality increased by 11 percent while income inequality rose by 23 percent. At century's end, the richest 1 percent of Americans controlled 40 percent of the nation's total wealth"); ibid., 31–36.
146. A full discussion would require a separate book-length treatment, and so I will put this more indirect effect aside for now. One interesting place to begin, however, would be with the relationship between social inequality and what has been called "guard labor," defined as the portion of the population involved in policing, prisons, supervisory, and other control functions. See Jayadev and Bowles 2006.
147. For excellent treatments of the expansion of the carceral sphere, see generally, Zimring and Hawkins 2007; Wacquant 1999 and 2009; Parenti 2000; Garland 2001; Mauer, King, and Young 2004; Rhodes 2004; Western 2006; Gilmore 2007; and Simon 2009. For excellent discussions of the collateral consequences of mass incarceration, see generally Mauer and Chesney-Lind 2002; Petersilia 2003; Davis 2003; Braman 2004; Fagan 2004; Meares 2004; Piquero, West, Fagan, and Holland 2006; Comfort 2007; and Manza and Uggen 2008.
148. PEW Center on the States 2008; Moore 2009.
149. For "Market Revolution," see, e.g., Sellers 1991; Wilentz 1997; and Larson 2010. For "laissez-faire," see, e.g., Hofstadter 1973, 55.
150. Larson 2010, 9.
151. See, e.g., Gouge 1968, 84, 85, 115, 117, 132, and 137.
152. Rothman 1971, xiv. In this respect, France experienced similar timing: the period 1815 to 1848 represents, in France, the "era of the triumphant prison." See Perrot 1975, 81; and generally Perrot 1980. This is certainly not always the case and the account I am discussing focuses only on the U.S. experience.
153. See Parenti 2000; Mauer and Chesney-Lind 2002; Petersilia 2003; Davis 2003;

Braman 2004; Fagan 2004; Mauer, King, and Young 2004; Rhodes 2004; Gottschalk 2006; Meares 2004; Piquero, West, Fagan, and Holland 2006; Massey 2007; Zimring and Hawkins 1997; Western 2006; Comfort 2007; Gilmore 2007; and Manza and Uggen 2008. Although my focus here is the United States, our experience with mass incarceration is illuminated by scholarship on similar penal developments abroad, including that by Fabienne Brion, Dan Kaminski, and Philippe Mary in Belgium; Stanley Cohen, Ben Goold, Nicola Lacey, Liora Lazarus, Ian Loader, Richard Sparks, Jock Young, and Lucia Zedner in the United Kingdom; Didier Bigo, Laurent Bonelli, Gilles Chantraine, Eric Heilmann, Fabien Jobard, René Lévy, Christian Mouhanna, Laurent Mucchielli, and Renée Zauberman in France; Adolfo Ceretti, Dario Melossi, Salvatore Palidda, and Federico Rahola in Italy; Rosemary Gartner, Ron Levi, Marion Vacheret, and Mariana Valverde in Canada; Pat O'Malley in Australia; and others.

154. See Campbell and Pedersen 2001, 270; Wedeen 2008, 187; and more generally, Comaroff and Comaroff 2001; Peck and Tickell 2002; Duménil and Lévy 2004; Harvey 2005 and 2009; Laval 2007; Miller and Rose 2008; Mirowski 2009; and Dawson forthcoming 2011 (especially chap. 4).

155. See, e.g., Peck and Tickell 2002, 33, 37; Duménil and Lévy 2004, 1, 205–206, 211; Harvey 2005, 13, 11; and Klein 2007, 59; as well as generally the essays published in Saad-Filho and Johnston 2005.

156. "Late-modern" is a preferred term of David Garland, see Garland 2001, 75 (but see ibid., also using the term "neo-liberalism"); "advanced liberalism" is at times a preferred term of Nikolas Rose, see Miller and Rose 2008, 209; Rose 2007, 3 (but see Miller and Rose 2008, 79–82, using the term "neo-liberalism").

157. On nominalism generally, see Carré 1946; Panaccio 1991, 216; Libera 1996; and Panaccio 1999. Ockham's writings are well presented in Ockham 1992 and 1995; and Spade 1999. For an analysis of Montaigne's nominalism, see Compagnon 1980, 41–42; Starobinski 1985, 40; as well as generally Desan 2008. There are, of course, a number of other contemporary nominalist thinkers and a nominalist tradition in contemporary Anglo-Saxon philosophy. Leading figures in this tradition include Nelson Goodman (who specifically defines nominalism as the refusal to admit any entities other than individual ones; see Goodman 1977, 26), as well as W. V. O. Quine (who co-authored with Goodman, in 1947, *Steps Toward a Constructive Nominalism,* but who later moved away from that position). Important works by Goodman include *The Structure of Appearance,* as well as certain articles such as "A World of Individuals and Predicates without Properties." I do not draw on this Anglo-Saxon tradition in the philosophy of language for purely disciplinary reasons, but it obviously bears important similarities with the nominalist tradition that I do draw on. See generally Gosselin 1990; and Panaccio 1991.

158. I discuss this at greater length in my essay, "*Supposons que la discipline et la sécurité n'existent pas*—Rereading Foucault's Collège de France Lectures (with Paul Veyne)," *Carceral Notebooks* 4 (2008).

159. Foucault 2004a, 5.

160. Veyne 2008, 19.
161. Foucault 1994, 726.
162. Veyne 2008, 63.
163. Foucault 2007, 45 (emphasis added); Foucault 2004b, 46.
164. Foucault 2004b, 111 (substituting *gouvernementalité* for the term *sécurité*).
165. Foucault 2004a, 27 n. 10; "L'économie politique, je crois que c'est fondamentalement ce qui a permis d'assurer l'autolimitation de la raison gouvernementale" (ibid., 15).
166. Foucault 2007, 48; Foucault 2004b, 49.
167. Foucault 2007, 45; Foucault 2004b, 46.
168. Foucault 2007, 45; Foucault 2004b, 47.
169. Foucault 2007, 48–49; Foucault 2004b, 50.
170. This project owes much to the groundbreaking work of Robert Hale, Gunnar Myrdal, Albert Hirschman, Michel Foucault, and other critical theorists and sociologists of markets, all of whom have contributed in important ways to our understanding of late-modern capitalism. I am indebted here, also, to the work of contemporary sociologists of markets, such as Bruce Carruthers, Karin Knorr Cetina, Marion Fourcade, Kieran Healy, Donald Mackenzie, Philip Mirowski, Sarah Babb, and others. See generally, Carruthers 1996; Carruthers and Babb 2000; Fourcade-Gourinchas 2001; Fourcade 2007; Fourcade-Gourinchas and Babb 2002; Cetina and Bruegger 2002; Cetina and Preda 2005; Fourcade and Healy 2007; MacKenzie, Muniesa, and Siu 2007; and Mirowski and Plehwe 2009.
171. See generally Beckett 1997, 33–43; Harcourt 2007, 77–107; Massey 2007, 93–112; and Wacquant 2009.

1. Beccaria on Crime and Punishment

1. Venturi 1971, 102.
2. Morellet 1967, 1:163.
3. Morellet's recollection is slightly different in his letter to Beccaria dated January 3, 1766. In his letter to Beccaria, Morellet writes that d'Alembert had lent Morellet the book in June 1765 and urged Morellet to translate it into French (Beccaria 1910, 116). P. Frisi had originally sent Beccaria's book to d'Alembert or made him aware of it. Beccaria sent d'Alembert additions and revisions of the book (D'Alembert to Beccaria, September 28, 1765, in Beccaria 1910, 108). Incidentally, Beccaria had already met the abbé de Condillac during the latter's visit to Milan, and the two had corresponded after that (Condillac to Beccaria November 29, 1765, and December 20, 1765, in Beccaria 1910, 100, 111). Thus, Condillac may also have played a role in the French reception of Beccaria.
4. "M. Hume, qui a lu avec beaucoup de soin l'original et la traduction, est du même avis [que d'Alembert]." See Morellet to Beccaria, June 3, 1766, in Beccaria 1910, 124.
5. Ibid., 117–118, 119.
6. Morellet 1967, 1:166.

7. "Mr. Trudaine que vous connaissez et que vous avez vu à Paris avant la mort de son père, portant alors le nom de Mr. De Montigny" (Chastellux letter, January 1, 1770, in Beccaria 1910, 169). Beccaria traveled to Paris in October 1766 and was there from approximately October 18 to early December 1766 (see Beccaria's letters in Beccaria 1958, 878–892, esp. 892, where he writes that he was already back in Lyon on December 7, 1766). Immediately upon arriving in Paris, he met D'Alembert, Morellet, Diderot, and the baron d'Holbach (Beccaria to his wife, October 19, 1766, in Beccaria 1958, 882). He also met the Marquis de Chastellux as well as Mr. Trudaine. See Chastellux to Beccaria, January 1, 1770, in Beccaria 1910, 168–169. According to Morellet's *Mémoires,* Beccaria was warmly received by le baron d'Holbach, Helvétius, Mme. Geoffrin, Mme. Necker, and M. de Malesherbes (Morellet 1967, 1:167).
8. According to many commentators, Beccaria was perceived as someone who recoiled from, rather than embraced, intellectual debate, and was considered less interesting in person than his written work might suggest (see Pautrat 2001, 186–187). Morellet wrote of Beccaria in a letter to Pietro Verri dated March 14–15, 1767: "Je crois aussi qu'il est paresseux et qu'il faut le reveiller de son assoupissement: ce seroit bien domage qu'une ame aussi chaude et une tête aussi forte laissat son talent enfoui" (see Morellet 1991, 85). Morellet also wrote, in his *Mémoires,* that Beccaria was dragged to Paris against his will by Verri—struggling against his jealousy regarding a young woman—and that, when he got to Paris, he was taciturn and somber (Morellet 1967, 1:167–168).
9. Venturi 1971, 106–109.
10. Voltaire 1766, section 12: "De la question."
11. Voltaire to Beccaria, May 30, 1768, in Beccaria 1910, 153–154.
12. Venturi 1972, 158.
13. Ibid., 160.
14. Rothman 1971, 59.
15. The success of the book also led to significant recriminations regarding the true author of the manuscript. Pietro Verri claimed that he had written the book and that Beccaria had merely served as a namesake; and several years later, the French publicist and attorney Linguet suggested in his review in *Annales politiques et littéraires* that the French *philosophes* of the *Encyclopédie* were the true authors and masterminds of the little treatise, which was so miserably executed by Beccaria that André Morellet had to essentially rewrite it in translation (Pautrat 2001, 187–188). The first controversy continues today, with the exact contribution of Pietro Verri still undecided.
16. Beccaria 1995, 113.
17. Hart 1982, 40.
18. Ibid.
19. Groenewegen 2002, 40 n. 2; Beccaria 1995 [1764], 129 nn. 1 and 2. The other two chairs in political economy were bestowed on Genovesi in Naples in 1754 and P. N. Christiernin in Uppsala in the 1760s. See Groenewegen 2002, 40 n. 2; Pautrat 2001, 187.
20. Beccaria embraced academia in part because he so feared being pursued for his

writings on punishment. Beccaria in fact was so afraid of being exiled or punished for writing *Dei delliti* that according to Stendhal in 1816 he was traumatized (see Stendhal 1919, 1:119–120).

21. Schumpeter 1968, 179–180.
22. Posner 1985, 1193.
23. Becker 1968, 209.
24. Beccaria 1995, 8.
25. Ibid., 10 (chapter 2); Beccaria 1995, 21 (chapter 6).
26. *Scelestus* is a Latin adjective derived from the noun *scelus* or "evil deed," and means wicked, villainous, or evil-doing. *Homo scelestus* is the criminal man.
27. Beccaria 1995, 21.
28. Ibid., 63, 95.
29. Ibid., 11 (chapter 2).
30. Ibid., 31.
31. Ibid.
32. Ibid., 64.
33. Ibid., 157.
34. It is important to recognize, though, that the relationship between Beccaria's utilitarian theory and the retributive elements in his work is a source of continuing debate and it would be wrong to label him as a pure utilitarian (see, e.g., Young 1983).
35. Venturi 1971, 100; Pautrat 2001, 186.
36. Bellamy 1995, xiv.
37. Beccaria 1995, 7.
38. Bellamy 1995, xix.
39. Beccaria 1995, 141.
40. Ibid.
41. For instance, as of June 2008, the Bibliothèque Nationale de France had a few volumes of the most recent complete edition of Beccaria's writings in Italian, but not the volumes that contain his lectures in public economy or his other economic writings.
42. The most authoritative account of Du Pont's life is M. G. Schelle's *Du Pont de Nemours et l'École physiocratique* (Paris: Librairie Guillaumin, 1888). He was born in Paris on December 18, 1739, and at the young age of twenty-four published his *Reflections on the Wealth of the State* (1763), which draws Quesnay's and Mirabeau's attention and admiration and begins their collaboration. He published *Physiocratie* in 1767—the collection of Quesnay essays that gave birth to the name *Physiocrats*—and *De l'Origine et Progrès d'une Science nouvelle* in 1768. He became the editor of *Éphémérides du citoyen* from 1767 to 1772 (66 volumes). Du Pont was called to Paris and became secretary to Turgot in 1774 under the general controller's administration. He became Turgot's right-hand man throughout the administration until Turgot resigned. After that, he continued to work for the government; he was chosen as deputy for the Third Estate and was known to have opposed the Jacobins. He was imprisoned in La Force with his son. In 1800, at age 55, he moved to the United States. Still in 1803, many years after the death of Quesnay and Turgot, Du Pont self-identified as a

disciple of Quesnay and Turgot. In a letter written from Paris to Thomas Jefferson, then president of the United States, dated 8 Messidor II (June 27, 1803), amid lengthy correspondence with Jefferson, Du Pont referred to these thinkers as "mes illustres maîtres Quesnay et Turgot" and discussed the possibility of returning to the United States to share "les leçons de mes illustres maîtres Quesnay et Turgot" (Du Pont to Jefferson, June 27, 1803, in Chinard 1931, 77).

43. See Vaugelade 2001, 161–163 (Mme. Geoffrin had at her salon Galiani, who was the arch-opponent of the Physiocrats; and Mme. Necker was antiroyalist. As a result, the circles would likely not have included Physiocrats).
44. See ibid., 163–167. Quesnay apparently attended the salon of Madame Suard (Vaugelade 2001, 163).
45. In a letter dated March 17, 1769, the Chevalier de Sainte Croix (secretary at the French embassy at Turin and one of the people behind the *Éphémérides du citoyen,* the journal of the Physiocrats) introduced himself to Beccaria and discussed having read his inaugural lecture. He then proposed translating it into French. (See Sainte Croix to Beccaria, March 17, 1769, in Beccaria 1910, 163.)
46. In a letter dated April 8, 1770, Du Pont seemed to initiate contact and to have never previously met, spoken, or corresponded with Beccaria. "Il y a longtemps que j'ambitionne l'honneur d'enter en correspondance avec vous" (I have aspired, for a long time, to correspond with you), Du Pont writes in the opening sentence of his letter to Beccaria (Beccaria 1910, 175). Du Pont continues: "Il serait très doux pour moi de m'instruire par vos conseils, par vos observations, par les objections même que vous pourriez faire contre la manière dont les *philosophes* français qu'on nomme *économistes* envisagent la science dont vous avez l'honneur précieux d'être le premier professeur établi par les rois" (I would be honored to learn from your counsel, observations, and even criticisms of the way that the French *philosophers* who are called *economists* envisage the very science that you have had the precious honor of being appointed to the first chaired professorship established by a king; 175). Du Pont encloses with his letter a copy of his journal, *Les Éphémérides du citoyen,* and sent under separate cover a copy of his collected edition, *Physiocratie,* which he described as "un recueil que j'ai publié des principaux ouvrages de Mr. Quesnay, auquel nous devons les grandes découvertes qui ont donné à la science de l'économie politique cette précision sévère qui la rend calculable jusque dans ses moindres résultats" (a collection in which I published the principal works of Mr. Quesnay, to whom we owe the great inventions that have given to the science of political economy that very precision that renders it calculable in every minute detail; 176–177).
47. This is apparent from letters by both Du Pont and de Sainte Croix. De Sainte Croix wrote to Beccaria: "La société de nos économistes français semble m'avoir choisi pour son correspondant auprès de vous" (De Sainte Croix to Beccaria, June 22, 1769, in ibid., 165).
48. Beccaria and Adam Smith were not in Paris during the same months in 1766. Smith was in Paris from about November/December 1765 to October 1766 (see Groenewegen 1968, 272). Beccaria was in Paris from October 1766 to

December 1766. The same goes for Turgot. Turgot was in Paris from July to September 1766 (Groenewegen 1968, 272) and thus would not have met Beccaria in person. But it seems from earlier that Turgot would have heard about Beccaria's book at d'Alembert's. Turgot was a member of the circle of *philosophes,* and also wrote entries for the *Encyclopédie.* In terms of other economists, Condorcet and Beccaria only began corresponding in 1771. Beccaria had sent Condorcet his book *Ricerche intorno alla natura dello stile,* and Condorcet replied with comments on it (Condorcet to Beccaria, early 1771, in Beccaria 1910, 178–180).

49. *Éphémérides du citoyen, ou bibliothèque raisonnée des sciences morales et politiques* 1769, 3:159–181.
50. Ibid., 178.
51. Ibid., 178 ("*le droit de propriété* n'est pas *un droit terrible,*") and 179 ("*la contrebande* n'est point *un vol fait au Fisc*") (emphasis added).
52. Beccaria 1995, 88.
53. Ibid.
54. *Éphémérides du citoyen; ou, Bibliothèque raisonnée des sciences morales et politiques* 1769, 3:180–181.
55. Ibid., 6:53–152.
56. Ibid., 66–67 n. 5.
57. Du Pont, in ibid.
58. Ibid., 72 n. 7.
59. Ibid., 79 n. 7.
60. Ibid., 85–90 n. 7; *Éphémérides du citoyen; ou, Bibliothèque raisonnée des sciences morales et politiques* 1770, 1:51.
61. *Éphémérides du citoyen; ou, Bibliothèque raisonnée des sciences morales et politiques* 1769, 1:146–148 n. 23.
62. Beccaria 1995, 8.

2. Policing the Public Economy

1. Schumpeter 1968, 955 and 179.
2. Beccaria 2001, 182.
3. Ibid., 183.
4. Ibid., 182.
5. Ibid., 183.
6. Ibid.
7. Beccaria had published one other short economic tract in 1762, an economic treatment of money in the republic of Milan. Entitled "On the Disorders and the Remedies Regarding Money in the State of Milan in the Year 1762," the manuscript advocated a universal centralized tariff for money as a way to address the chaotic relations of currencies in existence at the time. The essay has not yet been translated into English, but was translated into French in 2001 under the title *Du désordre et des remèdes des monnaies dans l'État de Milan en l'an MDCCLXII* (see Beccaria 2001, 153–177).
8. Groenewegen 2002, 4.

9. These memoranda make up a full volume (along with his correspondence) in the two-volume Italian-language complete works edited by Sergio Romagnoli in 1958 (Beccaria 1958; see also Groenewegen 2002, 19); and a full two volumes of the seven-volume *Edizione Nazionale delle Opere di Cesare Beccaria,* edited by Luigi Firpo and published from 1984 to 1990 (Beccaria 1984–1990).
10. Pasquino 1991, 45.
11. Bellamy 1995, xii.
12. Ibid., 169.
13. Ibid., xlv, 141 (emphasis added).
14. Ibid., 139.
15. Ibid., 138.
16. Ibid., 112.
17. Ibid., 134.
18. Ibid., 132.
19. Ibid., 131.
20. Beccaria 1769, 9.
21. Ibid., 10.
22. Ibid., 7.
23. See Viner 1960, 53 for a discussion of this. Richard Bellamy translated the term as "competition in the prices of goods" (see Beccaria 1995, 131), but that translation distorts the meaning.
24. *Éphémérides du citoyen; ou, Bibliothèque raisonnée des sciences morales et politiques* 1769, 6:68 n. 6.
25. Beccaria 1769, 7.
26. See generally, Olivier-Martin 1988b, 13–22; Ranum 1968, 272–280; Foucault 2004b, 320–322; Pasquino 1991, 109–116; Rancière 1995, chap. 2; Napoli 2003, 8; Dubber 2005, 63–77; Dubber and Valverde 2006; and Emsley 2007, 61–62.
27. "Remontrances du 19 juin 1718," in *Remontrances du Parlement de Paris au XVIIIe siècle, publiées par Jules Flammermont* 1888–1898, 1:71.
28. Olivier-Martin 1988b, 13; Delamare 1705–1738, 1:2.
29. Foucault 2007, 313; 2004b, 321.
30. Von Justi, *Éléments généraux de police* (1769) quoted in Foucault 2007, 314; 2004b, 322; see also Napoli 2003; Valverde 2007.
31. Foucault 2004b, 330–333.
32. Ibid., 333 ("the object of police, in the end, is society in general").
33. See generally Olivier-Martin 1988b, 15–22.
34. Beccaria 1995, 29.
35. Ibid.
36. Olivier-Martin 1988b, 5; Stead 1983, 14.
37. Stead 1983, 15 enumerates these duties; see also Delamare 1705–1738.
38. Bonnassieux 1894, 3.
39. Georg Obrecht's 1608 text, quoted in Pasquino 1991, 49.
40. Ibid., 48.
41. Cannan 1976, xxv.
42. Ibid., xxxiii.

43. Ibid.
44. Afanassiev 1894, 1.
45. Ibid., 71 (relying on *Ordonnance de décembre 1672*).
46. Fréminville 1758, 80–82.
47. Duchesne 1767, 286–288.
48. Afanassiev 1894, 26.
49. Fréminville 1758, 451.
50. Ibid.
51. Duchesne 1767, 103–104.
52. Fréminville 1758, 109–110.
53. Ibid., 456, 470.
54. Ibid., 471.
55. Afanassiev 1894, 4.
56. Ibid., 27.
57. Ibid., 73.
58. See Turgot 1844, 2:216–218.
59. Fréminville 1746, 1:374–375.
60. Afanassiev 1894, 61.
61. Ibid., 69.
62. Fréminville 1758, 71.
63. Afanassiev 1894, 87–88.
64. Beccaria 1995, 20.
65. Ibid., 9.
66. Ibid.
67. Ibid.
68. Ibid.
69. Foucault 2007, 44–45; Foucault 2004b, 46.
70. Foucault 2007, 45; Foucault 2004b, 46.
71. Foucault 2007, 45; Foucault 2004b, 47.
72. Foucault 2007, 46; Foucault 2004b, 47.
73. Foucault 2007, 45 (emphasis added); Foucault 2004b, 46.
74. Foucault 1975, 84.
75. Ibid., 77 and 103; see also ibid., 93, 95–98.

3. The Birth of Natural Order

1. Quesnay 2005, 1010 ("Les loix constitutive des sociétés sont les loix de l'ordre naturel/physique le plus avantageux au genre humain." In the *Éphémérides,* the word "naturel" replaced "physique," which had appeared in the original, handwritten manuscript; see Quesnay 2005, 1010 n. 13. This is the first sentence of the *Préliminaire* of the original handwritten draft, the only section of the essay written entirely by Quesnay, and it was moved for publication to form chapter 8 of the essay by Du Pont de Nemours (see Quesnay 2005, 1006).
2. Le Mercier 2001, 11.
3. Quesnay 2005, 571.
4. See, e.g., Kaplan 1974, 182: "Stripped of its most excessive tendencies (includ-

ing Lemercier de la Riviere's 'legal despotism'. . .), physiocracy was compatible with royal scruples." To a certain extent, this is true of Michel Foucault as well. See Foucault 2004a, 289–290.

5. Smith 1976, 38 (book 4, chap. 9) (emphasis added).
6. Oncken writes, "Dugald Stewart said that he learned from Adam Smith himself that Smith wanted to dedicate *The Wealth of Nations* to Quesnay, and that he had been prevented from doing so only by Quesnay's earlier death." See Oncken 1965, xiv ("Dugald Stewart dit qu'Adam Smith, ainsi qu'il l'a appris de sa propre bouche, a voulu dédier à Quesnay son ouvrage *Wealth of nations,* et qu'il n'a été empêché de le faire que par la mort de Quesnay survenue auparavant"). According to the editors of Smith's correspondence, "[Quesnay] gave a copy of the latter [*Physiocratie,* 2 vols. 1767] to Smith (Bonar 153), and Smith would have returned the compliment by dedicating WN to Quesnay had he lived until 1776. Dugald Stewart had this story from Smith himself: see his 'Account of the Life and Writings of Adam Smith,' *Works of Smith* (1811–12), v. 470" (Smith 1987, 114 n. 1 on Quesnay).
7. It is essentially for this reason that the Physiocrats never attracted a significant following and are essentially forgotten today—because of their emphasis on agriculture and their failure to predict the Industrial Revolution. This was true as early as the mid-nineteenth century. See Du Puynode 1868, 8; Musart 1921, 16.
8. Smith 1976, 38 (book 4, chap. 9).
9. This is not to suggest that Smith and Turgot were not also on friendly relations. Turgot would have been in Paris from July to September 1766 (Groenewegen 1968, 272), and he overlapped with Smith in Paris during those three months. Smith wrote to Hume from Paris on July 6, 1766, during the dispute between Hume and Rousseau, and it is revealing that Turgot is his main discussion partner. See Smith 1987, 113. Morellet writes in his *Mémoires* (1967, 1:244): "J'avais connu Smith dans un voyage qu'il avait fait en France, vers 1762; il parlait fort mal notre langue . . . M. Turgot, qui aimait ainsi que moi la métaphysique, estimait beaucoup son talent. Nous le vîmes plusieurs fois; il fut présenté chez Helvetius: nous parlâmes théorie commerciale, banques, crédit public, et de plusieurs points du grand ouvrage qu'il méditait. Il me fit présent d'un fort joli portefeuille anglais de poche, qui était à son usage, et dont je me suis servi vingt ans." Morellet started to translate *Wealth of Nations,* but another abbé, Blavet, beat him to it, so he stopped (Morellet 1967, 1:244).
10. Turgot, who was famous for implementing free commerce in grain as finance minister for Louis XVI, created careful professional distance from the Physiocrats, and castigated the Physiocrats for taking credit for the argument of *liberté de commerce* when in fact it had been proposed much earlier. See Turgot 1844, 1:163.
11. Groenewegen 1968, 271. "The Turgot myth" is how Edwin Cannan referred to this in 1896 (Cannan 1896, xxiv). Turgot wrote his *Reflections* in 1766, the year that Smith was in Paris, and it "began to appear serially in the *Éphémérides du citoyen* the last two months, in numbers 11 and 12, of 1769; and the first month, number 1, of 1770" (Lundberg 1964, 4). In 1793, out of nowhere,

there appeared in London the first known translation in English, but without an author (4). The rumor developed that Smith may have been the anonymous translator—or that Turgot's book heavily influenced Smith. Lundberg writes that the rumor was respectably laid to sleep "for more than half a century," but argued that "the Smith-Turgot myth is no myth, after all" (8).

12. "The first anonymous translator of Turgot's *Réflexions* into English had of necessity to be Adam Smith, in order that Adam Smith might make use of the many phrases he acquired in translating it, when he came to the writing of his master-work" (Lundberg 1964, 74).
13. Rothschild 1992, 1199. Rothschild seems to want to use Turgot to moderate Smith—but in the process, shows the strong influence of Turgot and Condorcet on Smith. "Turgot and Condorcet show that commitment to free commerce in corn is consistent with support for government intervention in other markets," Rothschild observes (1197). Rothschild then traces numerous parallels in the expressions and writings of Turgot, Condorcet, and Smith (1199). Rothschild writes: "It is unlikely that Smith read either Turgot's *Letters* [1770] or Condorcet's *Reflections,* neither of which was widely known in his lifetime. . . . But Smith . . . described Turgot as 'a person whom I remember with so much veneration,' and wrote of the Reform Edicts [of 1774] that they 'did so much honour to their Author . . . and would have proved so beneficial to his country'" (1205).
14. Campbell and Skinner have suggested that Smith may have derived some of his later ideas on the market from the Physiocrats' systematization of economics. "There is, for example, [in the *Lectures on Jurisprudence*] no clear distinction between factors of production and categories of return, not to mention the macro-economic analysis of the second book of WN with its model of the 'circular flow' and discussion of capital accumulation. While the distinction between rent, wages, and profits may have come from James Oswald, or emerged as the natural consequence of Smith's own reflection on his lectures, the macroeconomic model which finally appeared in the WN may well have owed something, either directly or indirectly, to Smith's contact with the Physiocrats" (the editors' introduction to the Campbell and Skinner edition of the *Wealth of Nations,* 22). Groenewegen also traces Quesnay's influence on Smith to his demonstration of a *unified* economic model. "Quesnay's *Tableau Economique* showed the interconnection between the production, the circulation and the distribution of wealth and the role of three economic classes of society in this process. . . . Above all, this economic model clearly demonstrated the essential unity of economic phenomena, the aspect taken over, and generalised, by Adam Smith" (Groenewegen 2002, 66). And Jean Cartelier writes: "Smith derives the whole terminology productive-unproductive, capital as advances, etc., from Quesnay. More significantly, he borrows Quesnay's definition of production in terms of value (no trace of such a view is to be found in his writings before his trip on the Continent), but adopts a different presentation, opposing productive to unproductive labour" (Cartelier 2003).
15. Cannan 1976, xxxv ("There are some very obvious additions, the most prominent being the account of the French physiocratic or agricultural system which

occupies the last chapter of Book IV"). See also Turgot 1971, xiii, where the translator's introduction notes: "The contribution of Physiocracy to the production of the *Wealth of Nations* was even greater in two other ways,—in raising questions in Adam Smith's mind, which left to himself he would never have put, and in providing him with a phraseology which of himself he would never have hit upon."

16. Cannan 1976, xxxv–xxxvi.
17. Ibid.
18. Oncken 1965, xiv; Smith 1987 114 (n. 1 on Quesnay).
19. Du Pont de Nemours reportedly told J. B. Say that he often encountered Smith in the meetings of the economists (Oncken 1965, xiii). Du Pont de Nemours writes of Smith, "Smith en liberté, Smith dans sa chambre ou dans celle d'un ami, comme je l'ai vu quand nous étions condisciples chez M. Quesnay, se serait bien gardé de le nier" (Du Pont de Nemours 1844, 69). According to Oncken, during his stay in Paris, Smith had close relations with Quesnay and his disciples, and especially with Turgot, whom David Hume had referred to him (Oncken 1965, xiii). Morellet and Turgot saw him many times in France during that period (Oncken 1965, xiii).
20. Although little is known of François Quesnay's early life, it is clear that he was an autodidact. Born in a small town in France to a father variously reported to be a physician, lawyer, or small farmer, Quesnay is reported to have been illiterate until the age of eleven. After having acquired a mostly self-taught classical education, he left his village for Paris to study medicine. There he became successful and was eventually appointed physician to Mme. de Pompadour and lived at Versailles.
21. According to Smith's correspondence with Thomas Miller, the rector of Glasgow University, Adam Smith and the Duke of Buccleugh seem to have first arrived in Paris on February 13, 1764, after Smith resigned his professorship in moral philosophy at Glasgow (Smith 1987, 100–101). Smith spent much of the first year traveling in France with the duke. Smith wrote letters from Toulouse in July 1764 (101), and from his correspondence was still in Toulouse on October 21, 1764, and November 4, 1764 (102, 103). In fact, Smith seems to have still been in Toulouse a year later in August and September 1765 (105, 107), and expected to be in Paris during early November 1765 (105). He wrote from the Hotel du Parc Royale, Paris, on March 13, 1766 (112), and his last known letter from Paris is from October 1766 (121). By the winter of 1766–1767, Smith was back in London. The correspondence suggests, then, that Smith was in Paris from about November 1765 to October 1766—or about eleven months. This is consistent with the best contemporary evidence. Groenewegen writes: "Adam Smith, on the evidence of both Stewart and Rae, was in Paris from December 1765 to October 1766, a period of about ten months" (Groenewegen 1968, 272).
22. Smith 1987, 119–120 (letter dated Oct. 15, 1766, from Paris). "Dr. Gem" was the physician to the British embassy in Paris, a friend of d'Holbach, and later intimate friends with Franklin and Jefferson. In his writings, Smith used a variety of fanciful spellings for "Quesnay."

23. Ibid., 114.
24. Ibid., 114–115 (letter dated Aug. 26, 1766).
25. Ibid., 120 (same letter dated Oct. 15, 1766, from Paris).
26. Ibid., 102 (letter to David Hume dated July 5, 1764).
27. Ibid., 102 n. 6 (editor's note). At the time, Smith complained that Buccleugh was "acquainted with no French man whatever" and therefore was not socializing (Smith 1987, 102). From his correspondence, Smith was still in Toulouse on October 21, 1764, and November 4, 1764 (102, 103). According to Smith's letter to David Hume on October 21, the Duke of Buccleugh was becoming more social: "He begins now to familiarize himself to French company and I flatter myself I shall spend the rest of the Time we are to live together, not only in Peace and contentment but in gayety and amusement" (103). That must not have helped with the writing. Smith seems to have still been in Toulouse in August and September 1765 (105, 107). By August 1765, Hume had been replaced as secretary to the British embassy (105). Smith expected to be in Paris early November 1765 (105).
28. Quesnay's first published contribution to the field of political economy was his 1756 encyclopedia entry on farmers in the French *Encyclopédie* (6:528–540; in the same volume, Quesnay also published an entry on *"Evidence";* see Oncken 1965, 157 n. 1). It is not clear what led to the invitation to contribute in the field of economics—Quesnay was essentially unpublished in that field at the time, though Du Pont de Nemours claims he had been working on these issues for several years before this entry (148). It is especially remarkable because Jean-Jacques Rousseau had written the entry "*Economie* (morale et politique)" the preceding year in volume 5 (1755) and thus seemed responsible for that field (159 n. 1). In his first entry, Quesnay expounds on his signature theory—namely, the idea that agriculture is the unique source of societal wealth: that farmers, not merchants, artisans, or other value-added workers, are the ones who produce wealth in a nation.
29. Smith 1976, 2:194–195.
30. Ibid.
31. Quesnay 1965, 241.
32. Ibid.
33. Meek 1962, 267; Quesnay 2005, 568–569.
34. There was also an important dimension of demographic growth. Promoting the rich farmers was essential to increasing the overall population of France. See Quesnay 2005, 154.
35. Quesnay 1965, 228.
36. Quesnay 2005, 174; 1965, 208.
37. Quoted in Oncken 1965, 150–151.
38. Tocqueville 1988, 249. The Physiocrats also sounded revolutionary because they opposed the corvée as early as the 1760s, notably in Mirabeau's attack in his "Essai sur la voirie, les *corvées* et les ponts et chausses." And there were important connections, later, between the Physiocrats and the Revolution—most notably, the Marquis de Mirabeau's own son, the Comte de Mirabeau, was both an important revolutionary figure and eventually embraced Physiocratic princi-

ples. In fact, in about 1788, the younger Mirabeau would publish a substantial economic text in four volumes called *De la Monarchie prussienne sous Frédéric le Grand*—dedicated to his father in recognition of all the trouble he had caused him—filled with statistics and political economy, and sounding surprisingly Physiocratic.

39. Smith 1976, 2:184 n. 1.
40. Marx 1974, 399.
41. Meek 1962, 266. The "exhaustive study" refers to *Theories of Surplus Value,* (London, 1951), 67–69; the "new *Tableau*" is discussed in *Correspondence of Marx and Engels* (London, 1936), 153–156.
42. Fox-Genovese suggests that Weulersse's work "needs significant revision" (1976, 17). She notes in the margin that "Weulersse exaggerates the interest group approach at the expense of larger intellectual and ideological interpretations, in a manner reminiscent of Charles Beard's work on the American Constitution" (17 n. 7).
43. Dumont 1977a, 5.
44. The idea, very simply, is that in traditional societies—which Dumont defines as premodern "higher civilizations"—relations between men "are more important, more highly valued" than relations between men and things; and that this privileging is reversed in modern societies "in which relations between men are subordinated to relations between men and things" (Dumont 1977a:5).
45. Fox-Genovese 1976, 9.
46. There are several iterations of the *Tableau,* and no one definitive version, for Quesnay formulated several noticeably different versions of it during his life. The more original editions, which seem to be the more explicit and complete versions, were never publicly published during Quesnay's lifetime and were not rediscovered until after the definitive edition of Quesnay's work, edited by Auguste Oncken, was published in the late nineteenth century. For versions of the earlier editions, see Kuczynski and Meek 1972.
47. Schumpeter 1968, 242.
48. For more on *la classe des propriétaires,* see Meek 1962, 20.
49. Cf. Schumpeter 1968, 239–240; Fox-Genovese 1976, 274.
50. Fox-Genovese 1976, 267–268. See also Bourthoumieux 1935, 8 nn.2 and 3 (quoting Mably, *Du commerce des grains*).
51. Bourthoumieux 1935, vii.
52. Ibid., iv.
53. Ibid.
54. Quesnay 1965, 320 (4th observation).
55. Quesnay 1965, 321 n. 1.
56. See, e.g., Quesnay 2005, 1018–1019; ibid., 321 n. 1.
57. Turgot 1971, 111. Du Pont was a secretary for Turgot for many years and had a strong and long relationship with him. Turgot published in the *Éphémérides* because of Du Pont. Du Pont de Nemours, the editor of the *Éphémérides du citoyen,* which was the journal of the Physiocratic party, convinced Turgot to let him publish his *Reflections* in that journal, where they appeared in the November and December 1969 and January 1770 issues (Turgot 1971, viii). There is

considerable back and forth between Turgot and Du Pont de Nemours about minor changes that the editor introduced to the text—and that Turgot was extremely unhappy about.

58. See Turgot 1844, 1:163.
59. Turgot's acquaintance and friend David Hume would take a similar view in a letter addressed to Morellet dated July 10, 1769—though he oddly associated Turgot with the economists. Hume wrote, "I hope in your work you will batter them [your economists], crush them, pound them, reduce them to dust and ashes! The fact is they are the most fanciful and arrogant set of men to be found nowadays, since the destruction of the Sorbonne. . . . I ask myself with amazement what can have induced our friend M. Turgot to join them *(s'associer à eux)*." (Turgot 1971, 112; see also Smith 1987, 114–115 n. 1).
60. For the date of Turgot's writing of *Reflections on the Formation and the Distribution of Riches,* see Lundberg 1964, 4 ("*Reflections* composed in 1766 and began to appear serially in the *Éphémérides du citoyen* the last two months, in numbers 11 and 12, of 1769; and the first month, number 1, of 1770"). Turgot developed a friendship and correspondence with David Hume, who was secretary to the English embassy in Paris from 1763 to 1766 (Turgot 1971, vi). And the *Lettres* are in Schelle 1913–1923, 3:265–354.
61. Rothschild 1992, 1198; quoting Schelle, *Œuvres de Turgot,* 3:326.
62. Turgot 1971, 108.
63. Meyssonnier 1989, 36; see also Morrissey 2010, 57–62; Groenewegen 2002, 62.
64. This work was published in Paris in 1767 by Merlin; see generally Weulersse 1910b, 1:128.
65. De Loménie 1879, 2:175: "Ils se qualifiaient ainsi, en réunissant les deux mots grecs qui signifient: l'un *nature,* et l'autre *pouvoir,* parce qu'ils prétendaient avoir découvert le système de gouvernement et d'administration le plus conforme aux lois de la nature."
66. Referred to in a number of places, e.g., Dubreuil 1908, 72.
67. Fox-Genovese notes that "Quesnay's commitment to free trade has frequently been traced to his medical practice, in which he preferred letting nature take its course to the problematical intervention of ignorant practitioners" (Fox-Genovese 1976, 94). There are, of course, different views on the influence of Quesnay's medical theories on his economics. Some commentators, for example, have focused on the notion of circulation (Meek 1962, 269). Yet others have argued that there is little or no relationship between his medical and economic writings (Steiner 1998, 30).
68. The motto implies that justice, order, and right laws come from nature, whereas caprice, control, and coercion come from man.
69. Quesnay 2005, 570.

4. The Rise of Legal Despotism

1. De Loménie 1879, 2:273 (quoting *J.-J. Rousseau, ses amis et ses ennemis,* vol. 2).
2. Dubreuil 1908, 43; Weulersse 1910, 1:137 and 141. After Diderot read Mer-

cier's book for the censure, he recommended Mercier to Catherine II. He was, in that early phase, a great admirer of Mercier (see Meek 1962, 33). In 1767 he wrote in a letter to the sculptor, Falconet, who was then at the court in Russia: "Lorsque l'impératrice aura cet homme-là, de quoi lui serviraient les Quesnay, les Mirabeau, les de Voltaire, les d'Alembert, les Diderot? A rien, mon ami, à rien. C'est celui-là, qui a découvert le secret, le véritable secret, le secret éternel et immuable de la sécurité, de la durée et du bonheur des empires. C'est celui-là, qui la consolera de la perte de Montesquieu!" (Weulersse 1910b, 1:141; also quoted in Dubreuil 1908, 43–44).

3. Mercier wrote, "Elle ne m'avait appelé à sa Cour que dans l'espoir de me faire servir à organiser, à consolider, le despotisme arbitraire des maîtres de cet empire" (May 1975, 82).
4. Quoted in Morley 1873, vol. 2, p. 153, note 1.
5. De Loménie 1879, 2:336 (quoting from *J.-J. Rousseau, ses amis et ses ennemis,* 2:364).
6. Quesnay 2005, 1017.
7. Ibid.
8. Ibid. ("des voleurs et des méchans").
9. Weulersse 1910b, 1:127.
10. Dubreuil 1908, 41–42.
11. Ibid., 46.
12. See Fox-Genovese 1976, 14.
13. Dubreuil 1908, 9.
14. Ibid., 62.
15. *Maximes du Gouvernement économique d'un royaume agricole,* in Du Pont's *Physiocratie* in 1767.
16. Dubreuil 1908, 64–65 (quoting Mercier, chap. 19, p. 142).
17. Ibid., 66.
18. See Quesnay 2005, 1006.
19. The original manuscript is the text reproduced in Quesnay 2005, 1010–1032. It was the manuscript that was found in the archives of Du Pont de Nemours (which are conserved at the Historical Mills Library at the Hagley Museum). The editors do not indicate a date associated with the manuscript. A revised version of the text was published in the journal of the abbé Badeau, the *Éphémérides du citoyen,* from March to June 1767 (Quesnay 2005, 1006). Du Pont made edits to the manuscript that clearly reflect an attempt to pass censorship—replacing, for instance, "le monarque et la nation" with "le maître et les sujets" (Quesnay 2005, 1011 n. 14).
20. Quesnay 2005, 1017.
21. Ibid., 1016–1017.
22. Dubreuil 1908, 45.
23. Smith 1976, book 5, chap. 2.
24. Le Mercier de La Rivière, 2001, 91.
25. Ibid., 49.
26. Ibid., 115.
27. Ibid., 112.

28. Ibid.
29. Ibid., 116.
30. Ibid., 152.
31. Ibid., 176.
32. See Cayla 2000.
33. Le Mercier de La Rivière, 2001, 86–90.
34. Weulersse 2003, 2:31.
35. Weulersse 1910b, 1:100.
36. May 1975, 16–17.
37. Weulersse 1910b, 1:101–102; May 1932, 13; Fox-Genovese 1976, 46. On his November 1765 review, see Weulersse 1910b, 1:103 n. 4.
38. Although his time in Martinique would precede his 1767 text embracing legal despotism, Mercier had been fully converted to Physiocracy before his departure for Martinique. The exact chronology of Mercier's first encounter with Physiocracy is somewhat unclear. According to Weulersse, Mercier first befriended the circle of *économistes* in 1762 or 1763 (Weulersse 1910b, 1:103 and n. 4). But that claim must be wrong since Quesnay was the link between Mercier and Madame de Pompadour. Another historian, Louis-Philippe May, seems to have a clearer view of the situation. According to May, Mercier had been at Versailles from 1756 to 1759, where he played an important mediating role between the court and the Parlement de Paris (May 1932, 4). It is at that time that he would have encountered and befriended Quesnay. May wrote that "before his departure for America, he was already the friend that Quesnay 'held in highest esteem . . . and regarded as the man of greatest genius,' that Quesnay believed to be 'the only man fit for running the treasury'" (May 1975, 20–21). Du Pont de Nemours similarly suggested that Mercier had been converted to the doctrines of Quesnay before being appointed for the first time as *intendant* to Martinique (De Loménie 1879, 2:211). In fact, according to Louis-Philippe May, Quesnay was the one who recommended Mercier to Madame de Pompadour for the post in Martinique—and Pompadour had him appointed on Quesnay's word (May 1932, 4). What is certain, in any event, is that Mercier was fully converted to Physiocracy by the time of his return to Paris; that is, before his second departure to Martinique in July 1763.
39. May 1932, 16.
40. Ibid.
41. Durand-Molard 1807, 2:235.
42. Ibid., 236.
43. Ibid., 260.
44. Ibid., 262.
45. Ibid., 263.
46. Ibid., 265.
47. Ibid., 279–280.
48. Ibid., 281.
49. Ibid., 289–292.
50. Ibid., 289–290.

51. Le Mercier de La Rivière himself owned black slaves and Mercier "apparently never adhered to the societies of *philantropes* though he did affirm on occasion his aversion to slavery." May 1975, 53.
52. Élisabeth 2003, 53, 52.
53. Quoted in ibid., 55.
54. Ibid., 74.
55. Ibid., 79.
56. May 1975, 53–54 n. 1.
57. See generally Dubreuil 1908, 28–29.
58. Le Mercier de La Rivière 2001, 129.
59. Ibid., 28–29.
60. Ibid., 29.
61. See Dubreuil 1908, 26.

5. Bentham's Strange Alchemy

1. See Foucault 1979, 209 (describing the two images of discipline, the "discipline-blocade" and the "panopticon").
2. Bentham 1995, 45.
3. Foucault 1979, 218.
4. Bentham 1995, 45.
5. Smith 2008, 101.
6. Ibid., 101–102.
7. Marx 1976, vol. 1, chap. 24, sec. 5.
8. Bentham 1952, vol. 1: *The Philosophy of Economic Science,* sec. 28, p. 118.
9. Harrison 1988, xiv.
10. Quoted in Hart 1982, 41.
11. Beccaria 1995:63.
12. Ibid., 53.
13. Bentham 1952, 1:12.
14. Ibid., 14. On Werner Stark and his editorial role regarding Bentham's economic writings, see Schofield 2009.
15. Bentham 1952, 1:14.
16. Ibid., 223.
17. Ibid., 224.
18. Ibid.
19. Viner 1927, 198–199; see also 199–200.
20. Brebner 1948b, 61; see also Holmes 1976, 673.
21. Robbins 1953, 47.
22. Ibid., 48.
23. Ibid., 56.
24. Stigler 1965, 1.
25. Ibid., 2–3.
26. Ibid., 3–4.
27. Stigler 1976, xi–xii.

28. Smith 1976, 1:2.
29. Smith 1937, 2:171.
30. Robbins 1953, 37; see also Holmes 1976, 680; discussed in Paul 1980, para. 3.
31. See Viner 1927; Holmes 1976, 674.
32. Viner 1927, 215.
33. Holmes 1976, 674.
34. Rothschild and Sen 2006, 363; see also "Smith did not particularly esteem the invisible hand and thought of it as an ironic but useful joke" (Rothschild 1994, 319).
35. Smith 1976, 2:171.
36. Rothschild and Sen 2006, 363.
37. Rothschild 1994, 319.
38. Williamson 1994, 323.
39. Grampp 2000.
40. Bentham 1843, 2:501.
41. Viner 1949, 369 and 371 (Bentham's economics "does not have in it, explicitly or implicitly, any trace of a doctrine of natural harmony of interests").
42. Bentham 1952, 1:229.
43. Ibid.
44. Ibid., 231.
45. Ibid.
46. Ibid., 237.
47. Ibid., 248.
48. Bentham 1952, 3:333–334.
49. Ibid., 337.
50. Ibid., 233–235.
51. Ibid., 236.
52. Ibid., 246–248.
53. For an excellent treatment of Bentham's conception of the science of legislation, see Lieberman 1989, 219–256.
54. On Halévy, see Brebner 1948a.
55. Myrdal 1957, 139; see also Myrdal 1990, 48–49. A fuller exploration of this issue would also require delving more deeply into Bentham's *Deontology,* where he discussed a harmony of interests between duty and self-interest. For a critical discussion of Myrdal on Jeremy Bentham, see Hume 1969.
56. Myrdal 1957, 136.
57. For literature reviews of the widely varying readings of Bentham, see Crimmins 1996; Paul 1980; Holmes 1976.
58. Himmelfarb 1969, 190.
59. Keynes 1926; Fay 1920, 48.
60. See Crimmins 1996, 754–755; 766–774.
61. Robbins 1953, 43.
62. Stone 1965, 119.
63. Paul 1980, para. 15.
64. Ibid.
65. Ibid.

66. Holmes 1976, 677.
67. Rowley 1998, 476.
68. Brebner 1948b, 59–60.
69. Ibid., 61. Albert Venn Dicey was a leading British constitutional scholar of his time, professor at Oxford, and author of influential lectures delivered at Harvard in 1898 and published in 1905 as *Lectures on the Relation between Law and Public Opinion in England during the Nineteenth Century.*
70. To varying degrees, naturally. For more extreme positions see, e.g., Roberts 1960; Hume 1967; Holmes 1976; Hume 1981. For a less extreme position, see, e.g., Sigot 1993.
71. Parris 1960, 19.
72. Hart 1965.
73. Bentham, *Defence of a Maxim* (1801), in *The Works of Jeremy Bentham,* ed. J. Bowring (Edinburgh, 1838–1843), 3:257–258; cited in Holmes 1976, 677.
74. Crimmins 1996, 753–754. Christian Laval titles his 1994 study of Bentham in this vein: *The Power of Fictions.*
75. Viner 1949, 362.
76. Paul 1980, para. 27.
77. Dicey 1905, 146, 307.
78. MacDonagh 1958, 65.
79. See, e.g., Cunningham 1917; Knowles 1921; Fay 1928; Lipson 1944; discussed in Paul 1980, n.21.
80. Dicey 1905, 146.
81. See, e.g., Cunningham 1917, 688; Fay 1928, 20; Lipson 1944, 150–164 (though Lipson moves the triumph of laissez-faire to the eighteenth century).
82. Hobsbawm 1968, 197.
83. Brebner 1948b, 61.
84. Ibid., 60.
85. Polanyi 1944, 146, 147.
86. Holmes 1976; Roberts 1960.
87. Nye 2007, xiv.
88. Roberts 1960, vii, 310–319.
89. Paul 1980, para. 36.
90. See, e.g., Taylor 1972, 32–38; Crouch 1967; Paul 1980.
91. Paul 1980, para. 52.
92. Taylor 1972, 64.
93. Spengler 1949, 440.
94. See generally Paul 1980, para. 12.
95. See generally Holmes 1976, 681–682; Semmel 1970, 158–175 (on Cobden and the Manchester School).
96. Paul 1980, para. 18.
97. Cairnes 1873, 244.
98. Sidgwick 1969, 417.
99. Dewey 1987, 16–17; see also Paul 1980, para. 23.
100. Bentham 1952, 3:333–334.

6. The Chicago School

1. For other histories of the law-and-economics movement, see generally Samuels 1976; Reder 1982; Kitch 1983; Kennedy 1998; Rowley 1998; Van Overtveldt 2007; and Horn and Mirowski 2009.
2. Posner 2001, 31.
3. Ibid., 32.
4. Ibid., 34.
5. Ibid.
6. Ibid., 60.
7. See Medema 2007b, 42–45.
8. Posner 2001, 56.
9. As Richard Epstein explained to me, "My economic view comes out of the Coasean/Hayekian tradition. I start with narrow cases and rules, and then generalize to larger phenomena" (personal correspondence).
10. Epstein 1993, 554 n. 6.
11. Ibid., 554.
12. Dube 1990, 71.
13. Hayek 1960, 174.
14. Posner 2001, 6.
15. Epstein 1993, 554.
16. Ibid., 553–554. This is not to suggest that Epstein agrees either with Coase or with Hayek in all respects (personal correspondence and conversations).
17. Regarding the importance of Ronald Coase's article, see generally Medema 1998, 203; Van Overtveldt 2007, 201–202; Kennedy 1998, 466; and Rowley 1998, 474. See also generally Kitch 1983; Reder 1982; and Samuels 1976. I should emphasize that, in personal conversation, Ronald Coase emphatically maintains that he himself was never a member of the Chicago School. Coase stresses that his approach was always "purely empirical," "empirical to the end" (conversation with author, September 7, 2010).
18. Rowley 1998, 479; Kennedy 1998, 466.
19. Medema 2007a.
20. Coase 1991, 11.
21. Ibid. For a contrary argument that Coase's work was far closer to Pigou's, see Hovenkamp 2009.
22. Coase 1991, 11. And on this score, Coase encouraged empirical research, which has led to fruitful studies. See, e.g., *Journal of Law and Economics* 34, no. 2 (October 1991).
23. Coase 1960, 18, 41–42.
24. Ibid., 18.
25. Ibid., 41.
26. Ibid., 18.
27. Ibid.
28. For a critique along these lines, see Kennedy 1981, 397 ("The conclusion seemed to follow that state interference was unnecessary without transaction costs, and technically impracticable with them.")

29. Stigler 1988, 78.
30. Epstein 1993, 556.
31. Ibid., 553.
32. Posner 2001, 6.
33. Quoted in Kitch 1983, 217.
34. Andrew Dilts (2008) identifies another step in Becker's logic that produces a neoliberal tilt, namely that Becker takes preferences as exogenous. By taking the demand for crime as fixed for modeling purposes, Dilts argues, Becker had to focus on punishment rather than on other preference-shaping alternatives.
35. For secondary discussions of this point, see Gray 1986, 27–55; Kukathas 1989, 86–105; Kley 1994, 26–119; Gamble 1996, 36–39; Petsoulas 2001; and Caldwell 2004, 361–369.
36. All of these quotes are from Hayek 1973, 1:37.
37. Ibid.
38. Ibid., 35.
39. Hayek 1967, 72–73, 76.
40. Hayek 1978, 10.
41. Ibid.
42. Ibid., 250; for a discussion of Hayek on Mandeville, see Petsoulas 2001, 78–106.
43. Hayek 1978, 264; for a discussion of Hayek on Hume, see Petsoulas 2001, 107–145.
44. See McNally 1993, 44–45.
45. Hayek 1978, 269.
46. Ibid., 269.
47. Hayek 1973, 2:145.
48. Hayek 1988, 14.
49. See Mirowski 2002, 235–241; also Horn and Mirowski 2009 (and more generally, the essays collected in Mirowski and Plehwe 2009); and Mirowski and Nik-Khah 2007.
50. Mirowski 2002:235–236.
51. Hayek 1967, 160.
52. Ibid., 161.
53. Ibid., 162; see also Hayek 1988, 52; Hayek 1973, 1:22, 95.
54. Paul 1979, 80.
55. For histories of the Chicago School, see Reder 1982; Caldwell 2004; Van Overtveldt 2007; and Horn and Mirowski 2009.
56. Stigler 1988, 140–147; Kitch 1983, 187 (as Milton Friedman recalled, "Hayek indirectly played a crucial role in Aaron [Director] coming to Chicago. Aaron in turn played a crucial role in Hayek's coming to Chicago. . . . Hayek came to Chicago in 1950 in connection with money provided by the Volker Fund, the same foundation that was responsible for the original grant that brought Aaron to Chicago").
57. Stigler 1988, 145.
58. Ibid., 150–151; see also Reder 1982, 10.
59. Milton Friedman, *Schools at Chicago*, Archives of the Communications Depart-

ment of the University of Chicago (1974), p. 2, quoted in Van Overtveldt 2007, 6.

60. Epstein 1995, xii.
61. Epstein 1994, 2159.
62. Epstein 1996, 14–15.
63. Epstein 1994, 2157. In his earlier, more deontological writings (see, e.g., Epstein 1977), Richard Epstein drew the line at fraud and coercion more strictly. In his later, more utilitarian writings (e.g., Epstein 1996), he softens somewhat his aversion to regulation.
64. Quesnay 2005, 1017.
65. Hayek 1978:63.
66. Quoted in Yergin and Stanislaw 1998, 150–151.
67. Posner 2001, 33.
68. Kitch 1983, 173; see also Posner 1985, 1230.
69. Posner 2001, 52.
70. Ibid., 55.
71. Ibid.
72. Ibid., 56; see also Medema 2007b, 31.
73. Becker 1968, 170.
74. Quoted in Beckett 1997, 31.
75. Ibid., 32.
76. Becker 1968, 170.
77. Ibid., 173 (emphasis added).
78. Ibid., 169.
79. Posner 1985, 1195.
80. Ibid., 1196.
81. Ibid., 1197.
82. Ibid., 1198.
83. Ibid., 1197–1198.
84. Ibid., 1199.
85. Ibid., 1199–1200.
86. Ibid., 1200.
87. Ibid.
88. Ibid., 1201.
89. Ibid., 1195.
90. Ibid.
91. Ibid., 1196.
92. Posner 1973, 68. For an even more nuanced analysis of the inefficiency of theft, see Hasen and McAdams 1997.
93. Bentham 1970, 12–13.
94. For a discussion of this, see Bentham 1970, 11, note a, and 14, note d [Additions by the Author, July 1822].
95. That perspective is evident, for instance, in the very first edition of Posner's *Economic Analysis of Law,* where Posner defined efficiency in the following terms: "Efficiency is a technical term: it means exploiting economic resources in such a way that human satisfaction as measured by aggregate consumer willingness to

pay for goods and services is maximized." Posner 1973, 4; see also Reder 1982 (on the Chicago view as "Tight Prior Equilibrium").

96. Rowley 1998, 480–481.
97. Kelman 1987, 121.
98. Posner 2001, 36.
99. Ibid., 37.
100. See Medema 1998, 209.
101. Ibid., 210.
102. Ibid.
103. See generally Reder 1982; Kitch 1983; Rowley 1998, 478–481; Van Overtveldt 2007; Horn and Mirowski 2009.
104. Posner 2001, 6.
105. Polinsky 2003, 158.
106. This distinction is important; see Kennedy 1998, 468.
107. Polinsky 2003, 7.
108. *Jones* 2008a, 632.
109. Ibid.
110. See Morley and Curtis 2009, 2 n. 4.
111. *Jones* 2008a, 633–634.
112. Ibid., 631.
113. Ibid., 633.
114. *Jones* 2008b, 731.
115. Posner 1985, 1195–1196.
116. Ibid., 1197–1198.
117. Ibid., 1204–1205.
118. Posner 2001, 35.
119. Ibid.
120. Posner 1995, 23 ("I take my stand with the John Stuart Mill of *On Liberty* [1859], the classic statement of classical liberalism"); Posner 1995, 24.
121. Posner 2009a, xii.
122. Posner 2009b, A21.
123. Ibid.
124. Quoted in Cassidy 2010, 28.
125. Quoted in ibid., 33.

7. The Myth of Discipline

1. See Chapter 1.
2. Campbell and Pedersen 2001, 3.
3. Guillauté 1974; Foucault 2004b, 348 (discussing Guillauté's proposals for the reform of the *police* and remarking: "Faire de la ville une sorte de quasi-couvent et du royaume une sorte de quasi-ville, c'est bien ça l'espèce de grand rêve disciplinaire qui se trouve à l'arrière-fond de la police").
4. For "nerves and eyes of the police," see Guillauté 1974, 5.
5. Foucault 2004b, 348.
6. See, e.g., Heilmann 2005; Doron 2008.

7. See Heilmann 2005 (the subtitle of which is "La machine de Guillauté et la naissance de la police moderne").
8. Foucault 2004b, 348.
9. Guillauté 1974, 2 (foreword by Jean Seznec).
10. Ibid., 8.
11. All the police records, papers, reports, etc., for the year 1758 are contained in cartons Y-9495A and Y-9495B at the Archives Nationales de France in the *Marais* in Paris.
12. *Almanach Royal, Année M.DCC.LVIII* [1758], 175.
13. Contained in carton Y-9495A at the Archives Nationales de France. For this and the next report, I have retained the street spellings as originally written, even where the official street name was spelled differently. So, for example, the archival record reports *Rue Geoffroy Lanier* and I have retained that spelling, even though the street was officially called *rue Geoffroy-L'Asnier.* See Félix et Louis Lazare, *Dictionnaire administrative et historique des rues et des monuments de Paris* (Paris: Au Bureau de la Revue Municipale, 1855), p. 377.
14. *Almanach Royal, Année M.DCC.LVIII* 1758:175.
15. The currency denominations at the time were livres, sols, and deniers. One livre was the equivalent of 20 sols, and one sol was the equivalent of 12 deniers. The symbol for livres was the number sign, written generally in more curly form. The symbol for sol was an elongated S that resembled the mathematical operator $\int$. The symbol for denier was a curly d, that resembled this: δ.
16. Olivier-Martin 1988b, 103. The police council's sessions began in October 1666, and its eight members met weekly until February 1667. Louis XIV wanted reports and claimed that he was very interested in their deliberations—but did not preside. Colbert was present as well as the maréchal de Villeroy.
17. Ibid., 105.
18. The source data are the 932 sentences and ordinances contained in cartons Y-9498 and Y-9499, as identified in Gerbaud and Bimbenet-Privat 1993. The 932 sentences and ordinances were inventoried and annotated by Michèle Bimbenet-Privat in her 1992 monograph.
19. For the derelict servants, see Records 106, 107, 109 and 110, also Bimbenet-Privat 1992, 25; for the eight-year-old vagabond see Record 203, also in Bimbenet-Privat 1992, 34.
20. The precise manner in which these particular records were compiled remains something of a mystery. The archivist who compiled, inventoried, and catalogued the two cartons in the 1990s, Michèle Bimbenet-Privat—and who, from her 140-page analytic inventory of the archival records, has the greatest familiarity with the documents—speculates that the orders were collected by a *lieutenant général de police* or other magistrate toward the end of the ancien régime to create a documentary record of the police chamber, to conserve the trace of the chamber's jurisdiction and operations, and to create a retrospective dossier of these juridical acts. It is likely that the records were compiled by someone who intended to update the Delamare treatise or Fréminville's dictionary in the last years of the ancien régime, but whose project was derailed by the Revolution. The last recorded juridical act, it turns out, is dated 1787, two years before the

Revolution (telephone conversation with Michèle Bimbenet-Privat on Friday, January 22, 2010; see also ibid., 9).

21. Bimbenet-Privat 1992, 10, mistakenly states that there are 680 sentences and 252 ordinances. A coded dataset of the records tabulates 581 sentences and 351 ordinances.
22. See Records 157, 162, 163, 654, 756, 804, 844, and 856, in Bimbenet-Privat 1992, 30, 78, 88, 93, 97, and 98.
23. Record 856; see Bimbenet-Privat 1992, 98.
24. Record 171; see ibid., 31.
25. Record 145, see ibid., 29.
26. See Meuvret 1946, 646; Kaplan 1974, 126; Miller 1999, 7.
27. Babeau 1878, 313; see also generally Babeau 1885.
28. Duchesne 1767, 119.
29. Ibid., 118–119.
30. See, generally, Le Maire 1879; Bloit and Payen-Appenzeller 1989.
31. Le Maire 1879, 4–6 (foreword by A. Gazier). The report, begun in 1768 and completed in 1771, was not published at the time. It remained in manuscript form until it was finally published in 1879 in a historical review.
32. De Marville 1896–1905.
33. Duchesne 1767:116.
34. Ibid.
35. Miroir and Warville 1843, 433–434.
36. Quoted in Afanassiev 1894, 92–93 (original document at the Archives Nationales de France at Arch Nat. ADXI, 37 and 38).
37. Fréminville 1758, 61–62.
38. Afanassiev 1894, 3 (relying on De Boislisle, *Correspondance des contrôleurs généraux,* vol. 1, no. 1350).
39. Ibid., 25.
40. Delamare 1705–1738, 2:877–878. See also Delamare's theory of the *disette* in Delamare 1705–1738, 2:794–797 and Musart 1921, 88–90.
41. Duchesne 1767, 95.
42. M. D. [Duchesne], *Code de la police* at 245, quoted in Musart 1921, 57.
43. Fréminville 1758, 61–62.
44. This is discussed well in De Loménie 1879 and 1891, 2:17; see also Odier 1862 and Olivier-Martin 1988a.
45. Emsley 2007, 21–22; Stead 1983, 12–14.
46. As De Loménie discusses well in 1879 and 1891, 2:12, it is the rights of fiefholders, not just seigneurs, that need to be explored, given that fief holding was not limited to the nobility.
47. Polanyi 1944:256–258.

8. The Illusion of Freedom

1. Durand-Molard 1807, 2:130–131.
2. Ibid., 161.
3. Ibid., 132.

4. May 1972, 112–113.
5. Durand-Molard 1807, 2:241.
6. Ibid., 242–243.
7. Ibid., 242.
8. Ibid.
9. Ibid., 253–254.
10. Ibid., 274.
11. Ibid., 254.
12. Ibid., 255–256.
13. Ibid., 228–232.
14. May 1972, 248 n. 26, and 248–250; Durand-Molard 1807, 2:102.
15. May 1972, 246–248.
16. On his attempts to reform the tax system in a Physiocratic way, see generally May 1975 and 1978. Denied any funds from Versailles, Mercier indebted himself, taking credit on his own personal account, in order to try to stimulate free trade with the island. He ended up heavily in debt when he had to leave the colony to the British in 1762 (May 1932, 5–14).
17. See generally the memoir that Mercier wrote to Choiseul in May 1978.
18. Rothschild 1992, 1203; Turgot 1844, 1:664–672. Rothschild suggests that the mathematician Condorcet had a similar point of view: although he was a staunch free marketer in the commerce of grain debates, he believed that there should be government intervention in the case of food shortages. (Rothschild 1992, 1202, quoting *Reflections,* 230–231.)
19. This historical account draws primarily from Taylor 1917; Lurie 1979; and Ferris 1988.
20. *Board of Trade v. Christie,* 198 U.S. 236 (1905); *Kinsey v. Board of Trade,* 198 U.S. 236 (1905).
21. Lurie 1979, 203.
22. Taylor 1917, 1:256–260.
23. Lurie 1979, 27.
24. Ibid., 28.
25. Ibid., 75.
26. Ibid., 173.
27. Ibid., 152.
28. Ibid., 161.
29. Ibid., 170.
30. Ibid., 41.
31. Lurie 1979, 56; Taylor 1917, 1:500–508.
32. Lurie 1979, 43.
33. Ibid., 92–93.
34. See, generally, ibid., 107–1230.
35. Ibid., 154.
36. *Hill v. Wallace,* 259 U.S. 44 (1923).
37. *Trusler v. Crooks,* 269 U.S. 475 (1926).
38. *Report on the Grain Trade* 2:110, reported in Lurie 1979, 46.

39. See *Sturges v. Board of Trade,* 86 Ill. 441 (1878) and 91 Ill. 81 (1879); Lurie 1979, 49–50.
40. Ibid., 88.
41. Ibid., 98–99.
42. Ibid., 140–145.
43. Ibid., 157–163; 180–181.
44. Ibid., 200; Ferris 1988, 129–130.
45. *Alan Friedman, Sybil Meisel, and Steven Langsom v. Salomon/Smith Barney Inc., et al.,* 313 F.3d 796 (2nd Cir. 2002), *certiorari denied,* October 6, 2003 (U.S.).
46. Ibid., 797.
47. Ibid., 798.
48. See 17 C.F.R. § 242.104 ("Regulation M"), 1996.
49. *Silver v. New York Stock Exchange,* 373 U.S. 341, U.S. Supreme Court, May 20, 1963.
50. Ibid., 349.
51. Ibid.
52. Ibid.
53. 15 U.S.C. § 78f (b) of the *Securities Exchange Act of 1934.*
54. *Silver v. New York Stock Exchange,* 1963, 349–353.

9. The Penitentiary System and Mass Incarceration

1. *Gordon v. New York Stock Exchange* 1975.
2. *Alan Friedman, Sybil Meisel, and Steven Langsom v. Salomon/Smith Barney Inc. et al.* 2002.
3. See MacKenzie 2007 (exploring options theory and derivatives markets); Lépinay 2007 (exploring linguistic codes of derivative markets); Desan 2005 (denaturalizing the material effect of currency itself); Hénaff 2002 (also exploring money systems); Klein 2007 (exploring the effects of the Chicago School on politics); also Carruthers and Babb 2000. The field of research in science and technology has been greatly influenced by the work of Michel Callon and Bruno Latour, especially Callon's 1998 edited volume *The Laws of the Markets,* and Latour's 2004 book *The Politics of Nature.* Naturally, there is controversy over the implications of performativity theory within the field of science and technology studies; see Mirowski and Nik-Khah 2007; also, more generally, MacKenzie, Muniesa, and Siu 2007. My purpose here is not to resolve these tensions or take sides, but to recognize some affinities with the analysis in this book.
4. Romano 1997, 294.
5. Ibid., 380.
6. Turnovsky and Campbell 1985, 297.
7. Turnovsky 1979.
8. Turnovsky and Campbell 1985, 300.
9. Ibid.
10. Ibid., 301–302.
11. Ibid.

12. Hale 1923, 471–472. See also Sunstein 1997; Holmes and Sunstein 1999.
13. Hale 1923, 477. For an excellent treatment of Hale's thought, see generally Fried 1998.
14. For a discussion of this contested term, see Chapter 1.
15. PEW Center on the States 2008, 3.
16. The rate per resident (not per adult) in the United States was 750 in 2008, compared to 85 in France, 93 in Germany, and 148 in England and Wales. The closest competitor is Russia, at 628. See ibid., 35, table A-7.
17. Moore 2009; ibid.
18. Nellis and King 2009, 3; for earlier statistics, see Mauer, King, and Young 2004.
19. PEW Center on the States 2008, 4.
20. Bureau of Justice Statistics, U.S. Department of Justice, "Special Report: State Prison Expenditures, 2001," June 2004, available at www.ojp.usdoj.gov/bjs/pub/pdf/spe01.pdf (last visited June 16, 2010).
21. California Department of Corrections and Rehabilitation, "2007–08 Budget Overview," available at http://www.cdcr.ca.gov/Budget/Budget_Overview.html (accessed June 16, 2010).
22. PEW Center on the States 2008, 4; Moore 2009.
23. PEW Center on the States 2008, 11.
24. Ibid., 32, table A-4.
25. Moore 2009; PEW Center on the States 2008.
26. Massachusetts Taxpayers Foundation, "Bulletin: State Spending More on Prisons than Higher Education," Nov. 24, 2003, available at www.masstaxpayers.org/data/pdf/bulletins/11–24–03%20Corrections%20Bulletin.PDF (last visited June 16, 2010); see also New York comparisons at www.budget.state.ny.us/archive/fy0506archive/fy0506app1/docs.pdf (last visited June 16, 2010) and compare www.budget.state.ny.us/archive/fy0506archive/fy0506littlebook/higherEd.html (last visited June 16, 2010).
27. See California Department of Corrections and Rehabilitation, Division of Juvenile Justice, "Ward per Capita Cost," fiscal year 2004–2005, available at www.cdcr.ca.gov/Reports_Research/wardcost_0405.html (last visited June 16, 2010).
28. PEW Center on the States 2008, 15.
29. Ibid., 16 and 32, table A-4.
30. Ibid., 33, table A-5.
31. Bureau of Justice Statistics, U.S. Department of Justice, "Special Report: State Prison Expenditures, 2001," June 2004, available at www.ojp.usdoj.gov/bjs/pub/pdf/spe01.pdf (last visited June 16, 2010).
32. Harcourt 2007.
33. On order-maintenance policing strategies, see Harcourt 2001. On the harsher treatment of juvenile defenders, see generally Harcourt 2005. On information-gathering, see Redden 2000; Goold 2004; and Painter and Tilley 1999. And on actuarial methods and harsher sentencing practices, see Harcourt 2007 and Michael Tonry, 1998.
34. Garland 2001; Feeley and Simon 1992; Simon 2007; Rose 2007, 3; and Miller and Rose 2008, 209.

35. Barry Goldwater quoted in "Goldwater's Acceptance Speech to GOP Convention," *New York Times,* July 17, 1964 (also quoted in Beckett 1997, 31).
36. Ibid.
37. See generally Beckett 1997, 34–36.
38. Richard Nixon acceptance speech at the 1968 Republican convention, available at http://www2.vcdh.virginia.edu/PVCC/mbase/docs/nixon.html (last visited June 16, 2010).
39. Beckett 1997, 50–51.
40. Ronald Reagan remarks at a fundraising dinner, quoted in ibid., p. 51.
41. Ronald Reagan remarks at the Annual Convention of the Texas State Bar Association in San Antonio, quoted in ibid., 50.
42. President Reagan, "Radio Address to the Nation of Administration Goals," January 31, 1987, available at www.presidency.ucsb.edu/ws/index.php?pid=34674 (last visited June 16, 2010).
43. Meese 1992, 307 (emphasis added).
44. President George Bush, "Radio Address to the Nation on the Administration's Domestic Agenda," June 22, 1991, available at www.presidency.ucsb.edu/ws/index.php?pid=19721 (last visited June 16, 2010).
45. Lee Atwater, quoted in Beckett 1997, 51.
46. Ibid., 23.
47. Ibid.
48. Ibid., 28; see generally Massey 2007, 93–112.
49. Wacquant 2009, 76–79.
50. Simon 2007, 49–61.
51. Garland 2001, 75.
52. Yergin and Stanislaw 1998, 14–15.
53. Foucault 2004b, 47; Harcourt 2001.
54. Regarding actuarial methods in the United States, see Harcourt 2007; regarding the *défense sociale* movement in Europe, see Prins 1910; Tulkens 1986; and Brion 2008.
55. King 1999.
56. Gouge 1968, 140; Hofstadter 1973, 61 n. 13.
57. Hofstadter 1973, 55.
58. Handlin and Handlin 1947; Orren 1991; Novak 1996. See also Hartz 1948; and more generally, Benedict 1985.
59. Sellers 1991; Wilentz 1997; Larson 2010.
60. Wilentz 1997, 62.
61. Larson 2010, 9.
62. Sellers 1991, 19.
63. Ibid., 237.
64. Ibid., 5.
65. William Gouge's book is referred to as "the bible of the movement" at Gouge 1968, 5; Gouge himself is referred to as the most popular economic writer in Hofstadter 1973, 61 n. 13.
66. Gouge 1968, 140.
67. Ibid., 84, 85, 115, 117, 132, and 137.
68. Appleby 1984, 15; see also Appleby 2010, 19–26.

69. McCoy 1980, 52; see also Aldridge 1957, 23–30; Faÿ 1929, 342–344.
70. McCoy 1980, 46.
71. Appleby 1984, 33.
72. Wilentz 2005, 298–299.
73. See generally ibid., 361–374; and Hofstadter 1973, 56–66.
74. Wilentz 2005, 361.
75. Some historians would argue that the hands-off rhetoric was purely rhetorical and that the Jacksonians were themselves the emergent elite harnessing power to themselves and ultimately engaging in a significant amount of regulation and control. See, e.g., Horwitz 1977; Novak 1996.
76. Wilentz 1997, 77; see also Hofstadter 1973, 56–58.
77. Quoted in Wilentz 2005, 361.
78. Ibid., 369; see generally ibid., 362–374.
79. Quoted in ibid., 370.
80. Qutoed in ibid., 372.
81. Ibid., 373.
82. Ibid., 400–401.
83. See Hofstadter 1973, 63–66. For discussions of the role of private law in the Market Revolution and the Gilded Age, see generally Hurst 1956; Horwitz 1977; Gordon 1984; Kennedy 2006. In the 1837 Charles River Bridge case, the U.S. Supreme Court ruled that the Charles River Bridge Company, which had a charter from the State of Massachusetts to operate a toll bridge, did not have a monopoly agreement with the state.
84. Quoted in Wilentz 2005, 502.
85. Ibid.
86. See, e.g., the essays collected in Stokes and Conway 1996.
87. Wilentz 2005, 364.
88. McLennan 2008, 7 ("master narrative"); Rothman 1971, xiii.
89. Rothman 1971, xiii.
90. This critique is most closely associated with Pieter Spierenburg. See Spierenburg 1991, 3–4 and 2004, 616. But many other historians and theorists before and after have also recognized the continuity of penal institutions. See Foucault 1988, 5 (on lazar houses for lepers on the outskirts of medieval cities and the seventeenth-century Hôpital Général in Paris); Ignatieff 1978, 11–14 (on houses of correction and the Amsterdam Rasphouse); Diederiks 1981, 275–294 (discussing the Amsterdam Rasphouse and eighteenth-century punishments in the Netherlands); Lis and Soly 1984 (discussing the period 1450–1850); and Hirsch 1992, 6–8 (discussing eighteenth-century Massachusetts penal institutions). There is also continuity, of course, at the other end—"from the early republican penitentiary-house, through the great prison factories of the Gilded Age and the penal-social laboratories of the Progressive Era, to the ambitious, penal state-building programs of the New Deal era" to mass incarceration at the turn of the twenty-first century. McLennan 2008, 3; see also generally Rothman 1980.
91. Morris and Rothman 1995, 68 (Spierenburg); see generally Spierenburg 1991, 24.
92. Morris and Rothman 1995, 73 (Spierenburg).

93. Foucault 1988:37.
94. Ibid., 43.
95. McLennan 2008, 56–57.
96. Ibid., 54.
97. Rothman 1971, 81.
98. McLennan 2008, 63; see generally Friedman 1993, 77–82.
99. Rothman 1971, xiv. Interestingly, in this respect, France experienced similar timing: the period 1815 to 1848 represents, in France, the "era of the triumphant prison." Perrot 1975, 81; see also generally Perrot 1980. This is certainly not always the case and the account I am discussing focuses, naturally, on the experience in the United States only.
100. Hirsch 1992, 112.
101. McLennan 2008, 54. Melossi and Pavarini (1981) also trace the invention of the penitentiary to "the Jacksonian Era" (see Melossi and Pavarini 1981, 99–142), as does James Q. Whitman 2008, 173–176.
102. Spierenburg 1991, 3. Spierenburg also recognizes that, overall, not only in the United States but on the Continent more generally, "in Europe the period 1770–1870 was indeed one of crucial transformation," and that it "implied an acceleration of processes" though "processes which had been initiated centuries earlier." Spierenburg 1991, 3. Again, though, my focus in this historical discussion is the United States only.
103. Rothman 1971, xiii.
104. Ibid., xix.
105. Ibid., 69.
106. Ibid., 72.
107. Ibid., 78.
108. Ibid., 133.
109. Ibid., xviii.
110. Whitman 2003, 174–175.
111. Subsequent histories of the penitentiary, naturally, find some faults in Rothman's account. For a synthesis of the critiques, see Hirsch 1992, xiv; McLennan 2008, 7–10. Nevertheless, Rothman's account remains the "master narrative" and has withstood well the test of time. McLennan 2008, 7.
112. See, generally, Hietala 1985; Foner 1995; Higham 2002.
113. For the United States, see Rothman 1971, Hirsch 1992, and McLennan 2008; for the Continent, see Rusche and Kirchheimer 1939, Foucault 1961, 1975, Ignatieff 1978, Melossi and Pavarini 1981, and Spierenburg 1984, 1991.
114. Cahalan 1986, 1–28.
115. Prison Association of New York 1873, 12.
116. Ibid., 9. The present dollar values are calculated using both CPI and GDP deflator measures.
117. Although there are different ways of computing the present value, this seems fair and is based on both the CPI and GDP deflator measures.
118. New York State 2009–2010 Enacted Budget Financial Plan, April 28, 2009, 114 and 132, available at http://publications.budget.state.ny.us/budgetFP/2009-10EnactedBudget-FINAL.pdf (last visited June 16, 2010).

10. Private Prisons, Drugs, and the Welfare State

1. See Chris Hogg, "China Executions Shrouded in Secrecy," *BBC News,* December 29, 2009, available at http://news.bbc.co.uk/2/hi/8432514.stm (last visited June 16, 2010).
2. Harcourt 2006; 2011.
3. U.S. Department of Commerce, Bureau of the Census, *Patients in Hospitals for Mental Disease, 1933: Statistics of Mental Patients in State Hospitals Together with Brief Statistics of Mental Patients in Other Hospitals for Mental Disease* (Washington, D.C.: U.S. Government Printing Office, 1935), 11.
4. Piven and Cloward 1993, xvii.
5. Fabienne Brion and Lucia Zedner demonstrate this well. See Brion 2003; Zedner 2006. For an excellent discussion of a slightly earlier period, 1895 to 1914 in England, see Garland 1985; for a discussion of the underlying turn to risk and welfare, see Ewald 1986.
6. Spierenburg 1991, 3.
7. See generally Davis 1998 and 2005; Roberts 1999; Wacquant 2001 and 2005. See also Gooding-Williams 2009, 248–255.
8. See Garland 2001; Whitman 2003.
9. Lacey 2008.
10. Ibid.
11. De Giorgi 2006.
12. Cavadino and Dignan 2005.
13. O'Sullivan and O'Donnell 2006.
14. Eurostat 2003, 358, table 6.2.6.
15. Eurostat figures, available at http://epp.eurostat.ec.europa.eu/portal/page/portal/eurostat/home (last visited June 16, 2010).
16. The prison numbers are from Walmsley 2006, 5; the psych bed numbers are from Eurostat 2003.
17. See Walmsley 2006, 5 regarding the prison rate in the Russian Republic. Regarding institutionalization, there are troubling reports concerning mental health institutionalization in Russia. See International Helsinki Federation for Human Rights 2006, 2006 Annual Report, Russian Federation report at page 335, available at http://www.unhcr.org/refworld/country,,IHF,,RUS,,4693929859,0.html (last visited June 16, 2010); Kim Murphy, "Speak Out? Are You Crazy? In a Throwback to Soviet Times, Russians Who Cross the Powerful Are Increasingly Hustled into Mental Asylums, Rights Activists Say," *Los Angeles Times,* May 30, 2006.
18. Koster, Waal, Achterberg, and Houtman 2008, 724.
19. On the relationship between immigration policies and criminalization in Europe and beyond, excellent research is being conducted by Salvatore Palidda and his colleagues. See Palidda 2009. I should add that Koster, Waal, Achterberg and Houtman (2008) presents a fascinating challenge and directions for future research on the effects of neoliberal ideology on punishment.
20. Friedman 1998.
21. Epstein 1988, 65–66; see also Epstein 1994, 2175–2176.

22. Posner 1985, 1200.
23. See Richard Posner, *The War on Drugs,* The Becker-Posner Blog (Mar. 20, 2005), available at www.becker-posner-blog.com/archives/2005/03/the_war_on_drug.html (last visited May 1, 2009).
24. See William Grady, "U.S. Judge Expects War on Drugs to Become Small-Scale Skirmish," *Chicago Tribune,* May 26, 1983: "Posner also said during a panel discussion that if it were politically feasible, he would favor the legalization of marijuana and, perhaps, LSD. Though he sees little political support for such legalization, Posner said marijuana is less harmful than alcohol and that LSD 'has never been seriously implicated in anything worse than a psychotic episode.'"
25. See Zimring and Harcourt 2007, 217–221.
26. See Harcourt 2001, 185–214; Zimring and Harcourt 2007.
27. Rusche and Kirchheimer 1939, 130.
28. McLennan 2008, 4.
29. Ibid., 54; see also Melossi and Pavarini 1981, 127–142.
30. Rusche and Kirchheimer 1939, 131 (relying on Beaumont and Tocqueville 1833, 79, 279, and 281).
31. McLennan 2008, 54.
32. Rusche and Kirchheimer 1939, 131–132; ibid., 138.
33. McLennan 2008, 138.
34. Hanson 1991, 4. For excellent treatments of this issue, see generally Parenti 2000; Gilmore 2007; Clear, Cole, and Reisig 2009; and Wacquant 2009.
35. Hanson 1991, 4, 8, and 9.
36. U.S. Department of Justice, Bureau of Justice Statistics, *Prisoners in 2008* 38 (Dec. 2009), available at http://bjs.ojp.usdoj.gov/content/pub/pdf/p08.pdf, p. 38 (last visited June 16, 2010).
37. Ibid.
38. Corrections Corporation of America, *About Us,* http://www.correctionscorp.com/about (last visited Feb. 9, 2010).
39. Forbes.com, *America's Largest Private Companies,* Nov. 3, 2008, available at www.forbes.com/lists/2008/21/privates08_Americas-Largest-Private-Companies_Employees_4.html (last visited June 16, 2010).
40. Parenti 2000.
41. See generally Austin 1990 (using the term "Correctional-Industrial Complex"); and Davis 1995. The use of the term had both theoretical and activist dimensions, leading to the creation of the prison abolitionist organization Critical Resistance; see Braz et al. 2000.
42. Schlosser 1998, 54.
43. Wacquant argues that "the $57 billion that the United States spent on corrections at the local, state, and federal level in 2001 amounted to barely *one-half of 1 percent of the Gross Domestic Product* of $10,128 billion that year. Far from being 'an essential component of the U.S. economy,' corrections remains insignificant on the production side and acts not as an overall stimulus to corporate profits but a gross drain on the public coffers and a meaningless diversion to financial capital." Wacquant 2008, 32; see also Wacquant 2009, xx, 29, and 106.

44. McBride 2007:144.
45. Ibid., 131.
46. Ibid., 127.
47. In conversations with Keally McBride, I sense that we share some of these intuitions.
48. *Private Prisons Offer Potential for State Savings* (May 25, 2009), available at www.yumasun.com/opinion/state-50322-potential-balance.html (last visited June 16, 2010).
49. For the $40 million figure, see ibid.; for $100 million, see Jennifer Steinhauer, "Arizona May Put State Prisons in Private Hands" (Oct. 23, 2009), available at www.nytimes.com/2009/10/24/us/24prison.html (last visited June 16, 2010).
50. Dan Spindle, "Private Companies to Bid in Prisons in Douglas, Safford" (Feb. 2, 2010), available at www.kgun9.com/Global/story.asp?S=11923801 (last visited June 16, 2010); ibid.
51. Steinhauer, "Arizona May Put State Prisons in Private Hands."
52. For an argument supporting the privatization of prisons and collecting the relevant bibliographic sources, see Volokh 2008; for an argument against privatization in this area, see Dolovich 2005. *Anarchy and the Law,* edited by Edward Stringham, provides an in-depth compilation of the philosophy of anarcho-capitalism (2007). Anarcho-capitalism advocates the elimination of the state and the privatization of law enforcement, courts, and other security services. Some of the founders of this school of thought are Murray Rothbard (1926–1995) and David Friedman, the son of Milton Friedman. Interestingly, the first person to advocate leaving police protection to the free market was Gustave de Molinari, a French free-market economist from the nineteenth century (Rothbard 2007). For arguments directly involving the privatization of the criminal justice system, see Rothbard 2007; and Friedman 1973, 1979, and 2007. Friedman 2007 provides a useful summary of the anarcho-capitalist system of private protection in response to a critique by Tyler Cowen.
53. The exception here is Elizabeth Joh's fascinating dissertation on private police and her published works (Joh 2004 and 2005); and again the anarcho-capitalist writings.
54. Harvey 2005, 69.

A Prolegomenon

1. Leonhardt 2008, 32.
2. Friedman 1962, 8.
3. Krugman 2009a.
4. Sanger 2009.
5. Harvey 2005, 5.

Bibliography

Afanassiev, Georges. 1894. *Le commerce des céréales en France au dix-huitième siècle.* Trans. Paul Boyer. Paris: Alphonse Picard et fils, Editeurs.

Aldridge, Alfred Owen. 1957. *Franklin and His French Contemporaries.* New York: New York University Press.

Almanach Royal, Année M.DCC.LVIII [Royal Almanac, 1758]. 1758. Paris: Le Breton.

Appleby, Joyce. 1984. *Capitalism and a New Social Order: The Republican Vision of the 1790s.* New York: New York University Press.

———. 2010. *The Relentless Revolution: A History of Capitalism.* New York: W. W. Norton & Company.

Austin, James. 1990. *America's Growing Correctional-Industrial Complex.* San Francisco: National Council on Crime and Delinquency.

Ayres, Ian. 1999. "Discrediting the Free Market." *University of Chicago Law Review* 66:273–296.

Babeau, Albert. 1878. *Le village sous l'ancien régime.* Paris: Librairie Académique Didier & Cie.

———. 1885. *La vie rurale dans l'ancienne France.* 2d ed., rev. and exp. Paris: Émile Perrin.

Bacot, Guillaume. 2004. *Les Physiocrates et la Révolution française.* Paris: Éditions Picard.

Beaumont, Gustave de, and Alexis de Tocqueville. 1833. *On the Penitentiary System in the United States and Its Application in France.* Trans. Francis Lieber. Philadelphia: Carey, Lea & Blanchard.

Beccaria, Cesare. 1769. *A Discourse on Public Economy and Commerce.* London: Printed for J. Dodsley and J. Murray.

———. 1854. *Le Opere di Cesare Beccaria.* Florence: Felice Le Monnier.

———. 1910. *Scritti e lettere inediti,* ed. Eugenio Landry. Milan: Ulrico Hoepli.

———. 1958. *Opere,* ed. Sergio Romagnoli. 2 vols. Florence: Sansoni.

———. 1984–1990. *Edizione Nazionale delle Opere di Cesare Beccaria,* ed. Luigi Firpo. 7 vols. Milan: Mediobanca.

———. 1995 [1764]. *On Crimes and Punishments and Other Writings,* ed. Richard Bellamy. Cambridge, Eng.: Cambridge University Press.

———. 2001. "Tentative analytique sur les contrebandes." Pp. 179–183 in Beccaria,

Recherches concernant la nature du style, trans. Bernard Pautrat. Paris: Éditions Rue d'Ulm/Presses de l'École normale supérieure.
Beck, Ulrich. 2000. *What Is Globalization?* Cambridge, Eng.: Polity Press.
Becker, Gary. 1968. "Crime and Punishment: An Economic Approach." *Journal of Political Economy* 76:169–217.
Beckett, Katherine. 1997. *Making Crime Pay: Law and Order in Contemporary American Politics.* New York: Oxford University Press.
Beer, M. 1939. *An Inquiry into Physiocracy.* London: Allen & Unwin.
Bellamy, Richard. 1995. "Introduction" to Cesare Beccaria's *On Crimes and Punishments and Other Writings*, ed. Richard Bellamy. Cambridge, Eng.: Cambridge University Press.
Benedict, Michael Les. 1985. "Laissez-faire and Liberty." *Law and History Review* 3:297–331.
Bentham, Jeremy. 1843. *Anarchical Fallacies; Being an Examination of the Declarations of Rights Issued during the French Revolution.* Pp. 489–534 in *The Works of Jeremy Bentham, Published under the Superintendence of His Executor, John Bowring*, ed. John Bowring, 11 vols. Edinburgh: William Tait.
———. 1952. *Jeremy Bentham's Economic Writings*, ed. W. Stark. 3 vols. Leicester, Eng.: Blackfriars Press.
———. 1970. *An Introduction to the Principles of Morals and Legislation*, ed. J. H. Burns and H. L. A. Hart. London: University of London, The Athlone Press.
———. 1988. *A Fragment on Government*, ed. J. H. Burns and H. L. A. Hart. Cambridge, Eng.: Cambridge University Press.
———. 1995. *The Panopticon Writings*, ed. Miran Božovič. New York: Verso.
———. 2007 [1780]. *An Introduction to the Principles of Morals and Legislation.* Mineola, N.Y.: Dover. [This is an unabridged replica of the edition published by Oxford University at the Clarendon Press, Oxford, Eng., in 1907, which was in turn a reprint of "A New Edition, corrected by the Author," published in 1823.]
Béraud, Alain, and Gilbert Faccarello, eds. 2000. *Nouvelle histoire de la pensée économique.* Paris: La Découverte.
Berman, Sheri. 2006. *The Primacy of Politics: Social Democracy and the Making of Europe's Twentieth Century.* New York: Cambridge University Press.
Bimbenet-Privat, Michèle. 1992. *Ordonnances et sentences de police du Châtelet de Paris, 1668–1787: Inventaire analytique des articles Y 9498 et 9499.* Paris: Archives Nationales.
Bloit, Michel, and Pascal Payen-Appenzeller. 1989. *Les mystères de Paris en l'an 1789: Les grandes et petites affaires qui ont marqué l'année, extraites des archives inédites des commissaires de police.* Paris: Sylvie Messinger.
Boltanski, Luc, and Ève Chiapello. 1999. *Le nouvel esprit du capitalisme.* Paris: Gallimard.
Bondois, P.-M. 1935. "Le Commissaire Nicolas Delamare et le traité de la police." *Revue d'histoire moderne* 19:313–351.
Bonnassieux, Pierre. 1883. *Les assemblées représentatives du commerce sous l'ancien régime.* Paris: Berger-Levrault et Cie.
———. 1884. *Examen des Cahiers de 1789 au point de vue commercial et industriel.* Paris: Berger-Levrault et Cie.

———. 1894. *Note sur l'ancienne police de Paris.* Nogent-le-Rotrou, France: De Daupeley-Gouverneur.

Boucher d'Argis. 1753. "Commissaires enquêteurs, examinateurs." Pp. 707–708 in *L'Encyclopédie ou dictionnaire raisonné des sciences, des arts, et des métiers,* ed. Denis Diderot et Jean le Rond D'Alembert, vol. 3. Paris: Briasson.

———. 1765. "Lieutenant de police." Pp. 503–514 in *L'Encyclopédie ou dictionnaire raisonné des sciences, des arts, et des métiers,* ed. Denis Diderot et Jean le Rond D'Alembert, vol. 9.

Bourdieu, Pierre, and Loïc Wacquant. 2001. "NeoLiberalSpeak: Notes on the New Planetary Vulgate." *Radical Philosophy* 105:2–5.

Bourthoumieux, Charles. 1935. *Le Mythe de l'ordre naturel en économie politique depuis Quesnay.* Paris: Marcel Rivière.

Boyer, Robert. 1997. "The Variety and Unequal Performance of Really Existing Markets: Farewell to Doctor Pangloss?" Pp. 55–93 in *Contemporary Capitalism: The Embeddedness of Institutions,* ed. Joseph Rogers Hollingsworth and Robert Boyer. Cambridge, Eng.: Cambridge University Press.

Braman, Donald. 2004. *Doing Time on the Outside: Incarceration and Family Life in Urban America.* Ann Arbor: University of Michigan Press.

Braz, Rose, Bo Brown, Craig Gilmore, Ruthie Gilmore, Donna Hunter, Christian Parenti, Dylan Rodriguez, Cassandra Shaylor, Nancy Stoller, and Julia Sudbury. 2000. "Overview: Critical Resistance to the Prison-Industrial Complex." *Social Justice* 27, no. 3: 1–17.

Brebner, J. Bartlet. 1948a. "Halévy: Diagnostician of Modern Britain." *Thought* 23, no. 88 (March 1948): 101–113.

———. 1948b. "Laissez-faire and State Intervention in Nineteenth-Century Britain." *Journal of Economic History* 8 (supplement: The Tasks of Economic History): 59–73.

Brion, Fabienne. 2003. "Art de la gestion des risques et méthodes de sécurité dans les sociétés libérales avancées." *Recherches sociologiques* 34, no. 2: 109–112.

———. 2008. "Criminalité, extranéité et gouvernementalité." *Carceral Notebooks* 4:23–44.

Cahalan, Margaret Werner. 1986. *Historical Corrections Statistics in the United States, 1850–1984.* Rockville, Md.: Westat.

Cairnes, J. E. 1873. "Political Economy and Laissez-faire." In Cairnes, *Essays on Political Economy.* London: Macmillan.

Caldwell, Bruce. 2004. *Hayek's Challenge: An Intellectual Biography of F. A. Hayek.* Chicago: University of Chicago Press.

Callon, Michel, ed. 1998. *The Laws of the Markets.* Oxford, Eng.: Blackwell.

Campbell, John L., and Ove K. Pedersen, eds. 2001. *The Rise of Neoliberalism and Institutional Analysis.* Princeton, N.J.: Princeton University Press.

Cannan, Edwin. 1896. "Introduction" to Adam Smith, *Lectures on Justice, Police, Revenue and Arms Delivered in the University of Glasgow.* Oxford: Clarendon Press.

———. 1976. "Editor's Introduction" to Adam Smith's *An Inquiry into the Nature and Causes of the Wealth of Nations,* ed. Edwin Cannan. Chicago: University of Chicago Press.

Carré, Meyrick H. 1946. *Realists and Nominalists.* Oxford, Eng.: Oxford University Press.

Carrot, Georges. 1992. *Histoire de la police française.* Paris: Tallandier.

Carruthers, Bruce. 1996. *City of Capital: Politics and Markets in the English Financial Revolution.* Princeton, N.J.: Princeton University Press.

Carruthers, Bruce G., and Sarah L. Babb. 2000. *Economy/Society: Markets, Meanings, and Social Structure.* Thousand Oaks, Calif.: Pine Forge Press.

Cartelier, Jean. 2003. "Productive Activities and the Wealth of Nations: Some Reasons for Quesnay's Failure and Smith's Success." *European Journal of the History of Economic Thought* 10, no. 3 (Autumn 2003): 409–427.

Cassidy, John. 2010. "After the Blowup: Laissez-faire Economists Do Some Soul-Searching—and Finger-Pointing." *New Yorker,* January 11, 2010, pp. 28–33.

Cavadino, Mick, and James Dignan. 2005. *Penal Systems: A Comparative Approach.* London: Sage.

Cayla, Olivier. 2000. "'Si la volonté générale peut errer': À propos de 'l'erreur manifeste d'appréciation' du législateur." *Le temps des savoirs* 2:61–90.

Cetina, Karin Knorr, and Urs Bruegger. 2002. "Global Microstructures: The Virtual Societies of Financial Markets." *American Journal of Sociology* 107, no. 4: 905–950.

Cetina, Karin Knorr, and Alex Preda, eds. 2005. *The Sociology of Financial Markets.* New York: Oxford University Press.

CFTC (Commodity Futures Trading Commission). 1997. *In the Matter of CBOT's Settlement of Disciplinary Charges against Donald W. Scheck, J. Brian Schaer, John C. Bedore, George F. Frey, Jay P. Ieronimo, and Produce Grain, Inc., Related to the March Wheat Expiration on March 20, 1996.* Opinion and Order by the Commodity Futures Trading Commission dated November 6, 1997, 1997 CFTC LEXIS 260.

Cheney, Paul. 2010. *Revolutionary Commerce: Globalization and the French Monarchy.* Cambridge: Harvard University Press.

Chinard, Gilbert. 1931. *The Correspondence of Jefferson and Du Pont de Nemours, with an Introduction on Jefferson and the Physiocrats.* Paris: Les Belles Lettres.

Clear, Todd R., George F. Cole, and Michael D. Reisig. 2009. *American Corrections.* Belmont, Calif.: Thomson.

Clinard, Marshall B. 1952. *The Black Market.* New York: Rinehart.

Coase, Ronald. 1959. "The Federal Communications Commission." *Journal of Law and Economics* 2 (October): 1–40.

———. 1960. "The Problem of Social Cost." *Journal of Law and Economics* 3:1–44.

———. 1991. *Essays on Economics and Economists.* Chicago: University of Chicago Press.

Code Louis XV. 1758–1760. *Code Louis XV: Recueil des principaux édits, déclarations, ordonnances, arrêts, sentences et réglemens concernant la justice, police et finances depuis 1722 jusqu'en 1740.* Paris: Cl. Girard.

Collection officielle des ordonnances de police imprimée par ordre de m. le préfet de police. Vol. 3: *Appendice: 1415–1860.* 1882. Paris: Imprimerie Chaix.

Comaroff, Jean, and John L. Comaroff, eds. 2001. *Millennial Capitalism and the Culture of Neoliberalism.* Durham, N.C.: Duke University Press.

Comfort, Megan. 2007. *Doing Time Together: Love and Family in the Shadow of the Prison.* Chicago: University of Chicago Press.

"Commissaires." 1753. Pp. 707–708 in *L'Encyclopédie ou dictionnaire raisonné des sciences, des arts, et des métiers,* ed. Denis Diderot et Jean le Rond D'Alembert, vol. 3. Paris: Briasson.

Compagnon, Antoine. 1980. *Nous, Michel de Montaigne.* Paris: Éditions du Seuil.

Condorcet, Jean-Antoine-Nicolas de Caritat, Marquis de. 1774. *Lettres sur le commerce des grains. Par M.**.* Paris: Chez Couturier père.

Cressey, Donald R. 1953. *Other People's Money: A Study in the Social Psychology of Embezzlement.* Glencoe, Ill.: Free Press.

Crimmins, James E. 1996. "Contending Interpretations of Bentham's Utilitarianism." *Canadian Journal of Political Science/Revue canadienne de science politique* 29, no. 4 (December): 751–777.

Crosland, C. Anthony. 1956. *The Future of Socialism.* London: Jonathan Cape.

Crouch, R. L. 1967. "Laissez-faire in Nineteenth-Century Britain: Myth or Reality?" *The Manchester School* 35 (September): 199–215.

Cunningham, William. 1917. *The Growth of English Industry and Commerce in Modern Times.* Vol. 2: *Laissez Faire.* Cambridge, Eng.: Cambridge University Press.

Davis, Angela Y. 1998. "Racialized Punishment and Prison Abolition." In *The Angela Y. Davis Reader,* ed. Joy James. Malden, Mass.: Blackwell.

———. 2003. *Are Prisons Obsolete?* Toronto: Open Media.

———. 2005. *Abolition Democracy: Prisons, Democracy, and Empire.* New York: Seven Stories Press.

Davis, Mike. 1995. "Hell Factories in the Field: A Prison-Industrial Complex." *Nation* 260, no. 7: 229–234.

Dawson, Michael. 2011 (forthcoming). *From Katrina to Obama: The Future of Black Politics.* Chicago: University of Chicago Press.

De Giorgi, Alessandro. 2006. *Rethinking the Political Economy of Punishment: Perspectives on Post-Fordism and Penal Politics.* Aldershot: Ashgate.

Delamare, Nicolas. 1705–1738. *Traité de la police,* exp. ed. Paris: J. et P. Cot, M. Brunet, and J.-F. Hérissant.

Deleplace, Ghislain. 1999. *Histoire de la pensée économique: "Du royaume agricole" de Quesnay au "monde à la Arrow-Debreu."* Paris: Dunod.

———. 2002. "The Present Situation of the History of Economic Thought in France." *History of Political Economy* 34 (annual supplement): 110–124.

De Loménie, Louis. 1874. *Mirabeau et son père à la veille de la Révolution: Lu dans la séance publique annuelle des cinq académies le mercredi 28 octobre 1874.* Paris: Typographie de Firmin Didot Frères Fils et Cie.

———. 1879 and 1891. *Les Mirabeau: Nouvelles études sur la société française au XVIIIe siècle.* 5 vols. Paris: E. Dentu.

De Marville. 1896–1905 [1742–1744]. *Lettres de M. de Marville, lieutenant général de police, au ministre Maurepas (1742–1747),* ed. A. De Boislisle. 3 vols. (1896, 1903, and 1905). Reprinted by *Société de l'histoire de Paris: Documents,* vols. 14, 15, and 16. Paris: Chez H. Champion.

Denis, Henri. 2000 [1966]. *Histoire de la pensée économique.* Paris: Presses Universitaires de France.

Desan, Christine. 2005. "The Market as a Matter of Money: Denaturalizing Economic Currency in American Constitutional History." *Law and Social Inquiry* 30, no. 1: 1–60.

Desan, Philippe. 2008. *Montaigne: Les formes du monde et de l'esprit.* Paris: Presses de l'Université Paris-Sorbonne.

Des Essarts, Nicolas. 1786–1791. *Dictionnaire universel de police.* 8 vols. Paris: Moutard.

———. 1800. *Les siècles littéraires de la France, ou Nouveau dictionnaire, historique, critique, et bibliographique, de tous les écrivains français, morts et vivans, jusqu'à la fin du XVIIIe siècle, par N.-L.-M. Desessarts, et plusieurs biographes.* Paris: Desessarts. Available at http://books.google.com/books?id=dTcBAAAAQAAJ (last visited June 16, 2010).

Dewey, John. 1987. *Liberalism and Social Action.* In *John Dewey: The Later Works, 1925–1953,* vol. 11: *1935–1937,* ed. Jo Ann Boydston. Carbondale: Southern Illinois University Press.

Dicey, A. V. 1905. *Lectures on the Relationship between Law and Public Opinion in England during the Nineteenth Century.* London: Macmillan.

Diederiks, Herman. 1981. "Punishment during the Ancien Régime: The Case of the Eighteenth-Century Dutch Republic." Pp. 273–296 in Louis A. Knafla, ed., *Crime and Criminal Justice in Europe and Canada.* Waterloo, Ont.: Wilfrid Laurier University Press.

Dilts, Andrew. 2008. "Michel Foucault Meets Gary Becker: Criminality beyond *Discipline and Punish.*" *Carceral Notebooks* 4:77–100.

Dolovich, Sharon. 2005. "State Punishment and Private Prisons." *Duke Law Review* 55, no. 3: 437–546.

Doron, Claude-Olivier. 2008. "'Une chaîne, qui laisse toute liberté de faire le bien et qui ne permette que très difficilement de commettre le mal': Du système de Guillauté au placement sous surveillance électronique mobile." *Carceral Notebooks* 4:101–130.

Dubber, Markus Dirk. 2005. *The Police Power: Patriarchy and the Foundations of American Government.* New York: Columbia University Press.

Dubber, Markus D., and Mariana Valverde, eds. 2006. *The New Police Science: The Police Power in Domestic and International Governance.* Stanford, Calif.: Stanford University Press.

Dube, Allison. 1990. "Hayek on Bentham." *Utilitas: A Journal of Utilitarian Studies* 2, no. 1 (May): 71–87.

Dubreuil, Paul. 1908. *Le Despotisme légal: Vues politiques des physiocrates.* Paris: Ch. Noblet.

Duchesne, M. 1767. *Code de la police ou analyse des réglemens de police, divisé en douze titres.* Paris: Chez Pierre Prault père.

Duménil, Gérard, and Dominique Lévy. 2004. *Capital Resurgent: Roots of the Neoliberal Revolution,* trans. Derek Jeffers. Cambridge: Harvard University Press.

Dumont, Louis. 1977a. *From Mandeville to Marx: The Genesis and Triumph of Economic Ideology.* Chicago: University of Chicago Press.

———. 1977b. *Homo aequalis: Genèse et épanouissement de l'idéologie économique.* Paris: Gallimard.

Du Pont de Nemours, Pierre Samuel. 1767. *Physiocratie; ou, Constitution naturelle du gouvernement le plus avantageux au genre humain.* Paris: Merlin.

———. 1808. "Sur les économistes." *Œuvres de Mr. Turgot, Ministre d'État, précédées et accompagnées de mémoires et de notes sur sa vie, son administration et ses ouvrages,*" ed. Pierre Samuel Du Pont de Nemours, vol. 3. Paris: Imprimerie de Delance.

———. 1844. "Observations sur les points dans lesquels Adam Smith est d'accord avec la théorie de M. Turgot, et sur ceux dans lesquels il s'en est écarté." Reproduced in vol. 1, pp. 67–71 of *Œuvres de Turgot,* ed. Eugène Daire, 2 vols. Paris: Librairie Guillaumin.

Du Puynode, Gustave. 1868. *Études sur les Principaux Économistes: Turgot, Adam Smith, Ricardo, Malthus, J. B. Say, Rossi.* Paris: Guillaumin et Cie.

Durand-Molard. 1807. *Code de la Martinique.* 5 vols. Saint-Pierre, Martinique: Jean-Baptiste Thounens, fils.

Élisabeth, Léo. 2003. *La société martiniquaise aux XVIIe et XVIIIe siècles, 1664–1789.* Paris: Éditions Karthala.

Emsley, Clive. 2007. *Crime, Police, and Penal Policy: European Experiences, 1750–1940.* New York: Oxford University Press.

Éphémérides du citoyen; ou, Bibliothèque raisonnée des sciences morales et politiques, vol. 3. 1769. Ed. Pierre Samuel Du Pont de Nemours. Paris: Chez Lacombe.

Éphémérides du citoyen; ou, Bibliothèque raisonnée des sciences morales et politiques, vol. 6, 1769. Ed. Pierre Samuel Du Pont de Nemours. Paris: Chez Lacombe.

Éphémérides du citoyen; ou, Bibliothèque raisonnée des sciences morales et politiques, vol. 6. 1770. Ed. Pierre Samuel Du Pont de Nemours. Paris: Chez Lacombe.

Epstein, Richard. 1977. "Crime and Tort: Old Wine in Old Bottles." In *Assessing the Criminal: Restitution, Retribution, and the Legal Process,* ed. R. Barnett and J. Hagel. Pensacola, Fla.: Ballinger.

———. 1985. *Takings: Private Property and the Power of Eminent Domain.* Cambridge: Harvard University Press.

———. 1988. "The Supreme Court 1987 Term: Unconstitutional Conditions, State Power, and the Limits of Consent." *Harvard Law Review* 102:5–104.

———. 1993. "Holdouts, Externalities, and the Single Owner: One More Salute to Ronald Coase." *Journal of Law and Economics* 36, no. 1 (April): 553–586.

———. 1994. "The Moral and Practical Dilemmas of an Underground Economy." *Yale Law Journal* 103:2157–2177.

———. 1995. *Simple Rules for a Complex World.* Cambridge: Harvard University Press.

———. 1996. "The Tort/Crime Distinction: A Generation Later." *Boston University Law Review* 76:1–21.

Eurostat. 2003. *Health Statistics: Key Data on Health, 2002,* European Commission. Available at http://epp.eurostat.ec.europa.eu/cache/ITY_OFFPUB/KS-08-02-002/EN/KS-08-02-002-en.pdf (last visited June 16, 2010).

Ewald, François. 1986. *L'État providence.* Paris: B. Grasset.

Fagan, Jeffrey. 2004. "Crime, Community and Incarceration." Pp. 27–60 of *The Future of Imprisonment in the Twenty-first Century,* ed. Michael Tonry. New York: Oxford University Press.

Farge, Arlette. 1974. *Délinquence et criminalité: Le vol d'aliments à Paris au XVIIIe siècle*. Paris: Plon.

———. 1986. *La vie fragile: Violence, pouvoirs et solidarités à Paris au XVIIIe siècle*. Paris: Hachette.

Faÿ, Bernard. 1929. *Franklin: The Apostle of Modern Times*. Boston: Little, Brown.

Fay, Charles Ryle. 1920. *Life and Labour in the Nineteenth Century*. Cambridge, Eng.: Cambridge University Press.

———. 1928. *Great Britain from Adam Smith to the Present Day: An Economic and Social Survey*. London: Longmans, Green and Co.

Feeley, Malcolm, and Jonathan Simon. 1992. "The New Penology: Notes on the Emerging Strategy of Corrections and Its Implications." *Criminology* 30, no. 4: 449–474.

Feilbogen, Siegmund. 1971. *Smith and Turgot*. New York: Burt Franklin, Publisher.

Ferris, William G. 1988. *The Grain Traders: The Story of the Chicago Board of Trade*. East Lansing: Michigan State University Press.

Finnegan, Michael, v. Campeau Corp., R. H. Macy & Co., Inc., and Macy Acquiring Corp., U.S. Court of Appeals for the Second Circuit, 915 F. 2d 824, decided on October 4, 1990.

Fligstein, Neil. 2001. *The Architecture of Markets*. Princeton, N.J.: Princeton University Press.

Foner, Eric. 1995. *Free Soil, Free Labor, Free Men: The Ideology of the Republican Party before the Civil War*. New York: Oxford University Press.

———, ed. 1997. *The New American History*. Rev. and exp. ed. Philadelphia: Temple University Press.

Foucault, Michel. 1961. *Histoire de la folie à l'âge classique*. Paris: Gallimard.

———. 1975. *Surveiller et punir: Naissance de la prison*. Paris: Gallimard.

———. 1979. *Discipline and Punish: The Birth of the Prison*. Trans. Alan Sheridan. New York: Vintage Books.

———. 1988. *Madness and Civilization*, trans. Richard Howard. New York: Vintage.

———. 1994. *Dits et écrits IV—1980–1988*. Paris: Gallimard.

———. 2004a. *Naissance de la Biopolitique. Cours au Collège de France, 1978–1979*. Paris: Seuil/Gallimard.

———. 2004b. *Sécurité, Territoire, Population. Cours au Collège de France. 1977–1978*. Paris: Seuil/Gallimard.

———. 2007. *Security, Territory, Population: Lectures at the Collège de France*. Hampshire, Eng.: Palgrave Macmillan.

Foucault, Michel, and Arlette Farge. 1982. *Le désordre des familles: Lettres de cachet des archives de la Bastille au XVIIIe siècle*. Paris: Gallimard.

Fourcade, Marion. 2007. "Theories of Markets and Theories of Society." *American Behavioral Scientist* 50, no. 8: 1015–1034.

Fourcade, Marion, and Kieran Healy. 2007. "Moral Views of Market Society." *Annual Review of Sociology* 33:285–311.

Fourcade-Gourinchas, Marion. 2001. "Politics, Institutional Structure, and the Rise of Economics: A Comparative Study." *Theory and Society* 30:397–447.

Fourcade-Gourinchas, Marion, and Sarah L. Babb. 2002. "The Rebirth of the Liberal

Creed: Paths to Neoliberalism in Four Countries." *American Journal of Sociology* 108, no. 3: 533–579.
Fox-Genovese, Elizabeth. 1976. *The Origins of Physiocracy: Economic Revolution and Social Order in Eighteenth-Century France.* Ithaca, N.Y.: Cornell University Press.
Fréminville, Edme de La Poix de. 1746. *La Pratique universelle pour la rénovation des terriers et des droits seigneuriaux.* Paris: Chez Morel l'aîné et Chez Gissey.
———. 1758. *Dictionnaire ou traité de la police générale des villes, bourgs, paroisses et seigneuries de la campagne.* Paris: Chez Gissey.
Fried, Barbara. 1998. *The Progressive Assault on Laissez Faire: Robert Hale and the First Law and Economics Movement.* Cambridge: Harvard University Press.
Friedman, Alan, Sybil Meisel, and Steven Langsom v. Salomon/Smith Barney Inc., et al., 313 F.3d 796, U.S. Court of Appeals for the Second Circuit, December 20, 2002, *certiorari denied,* October 6, 2003 [herein referred to as *Friedman* 2002].
Friedman, David. 1973. *The Machinery of Freedom.* New Rochelle, N.Y.: Arlington House.
———. 1979. "Private Creation and Enforcement of Law: A Historical Case." *Journal of Legal Studies* 8:399–415.
———. 2007 [1994]. "Law as a Private Good: A Response to Tyler Cowen on the Economics of Anarchy." In *Anarchy and the Law: The Political Economy of Choice,* ed. Edward P. Stringham. New Brunswick, N.J.: Transaction Publishers.
Friedman, Lawrence M. 1993. *Crime and Punishment in American History.* New York: Basic Books.
Friedman, Milton. 1962. *Capitalism and Freedom.* Chicago: University of Chicago Press.
———. 1998. "There's No Justice in the War on Drugs." *New York Times,* January 11, 1998. Available at www.hoover.org/publications/digest/3523786.html (last visited June 16, 2010).
Fukuyama, Francis. 1992. *The End of History and the Last Man.* New York: Avon Books.
Gamble, Andrew. 1996. *Hayek: The Iron Cage of Liberty.* Boulder, Colo.: Westview.
Garland, David. 1985. *Punishment and Welfare: A History of Penal Strategies.* Aldershot, Eng.: Gower.
———. 2001. *The Culture of Control: Crime and Social Order in Contemporary Society.* Chicago: The University of Chicago Press.
Garrioch, David. 1986. *Neighbourhood and Community in Paris, 1740–1790.* Cambridge, Eng.: Cambridge University Press.
Gauthier, Florence, and Guy-Robert Ikni, eds. 1988. *La guerre du blé au XVIIIe siècle.* Montreuil: Les Éditions de la Passion.
Gerbaud, Henri, and Michèle Bimbenet-Privat. 1993. *Châtelet de Paris: Répertoire numérique de la série Y. Tome premiers. Les chambres. Y1 à 10718 et 18603 à 18800.* Paris: Archives Nationales.
Gilmore, Ruth Wilson. 2007. *Golden Gulag: Prisons, Surplus, Crisis, and Opposition in Globalizing California.* Berkeley: University of California Press.
Goldstein, Jan, ed. 1994. *Foucault and the Writing of World History.* Cambridge, Eng.: Blackwell.

Gooding-Williams, Robert. 2009. *In the Shadow of Du Bois: Afro-Modern Political Thought in America*. Cambridge: Harvard University Press.

Goodman, Nelson. 1977. *The Structure of Appearance*, 3d ed. Dordrecht, Neth.: Springer.

Goold, Benjamin J. 2004. *CCTV and Policing: Public Area Surveillance and Police Practices in Britain*. New York: Oxford University Press.

Gordon, Robert W. 1984. "Critical Legal Histories." *Stanford Law Review* 36:57–125.

Gordon v. New York Stock Exchange, 422 U.S. 659, U.S. Supreme Court, June 26, 1975.

Gosselin, Mia. 1990. *Nominalism and Contemporary Nominalism: Ontological and Epistemological Implications of the Work of W. V. O. Quine and of N. Goodman*. Dordrecht, Neth.: Kluwer Academic.

Gottschalk, Marie. 2006. *The Prison and the Gallows: The Politics of Mass Incarceration in America*. New York: Cambridge University Press.

Gouge, William M. 1968 [1833]. *A Short History of Paper Money and Banking in the United States, to Which Is Prefixed an Inquiry into the Principles of the System*. New York: Augustus M. Kelley Publishers.

Graham, Lisa Jane. 2000. *If the King Only Knew: Seditious Speech in the Reign of Louis XV*. Charlotte: University of Virginia Press.

Grampp, William D. 2000. "What Did Smith Mean by the Invisible Hand?" *Journal of Political Economy* 108, no. 3: 441–465.

Gray, John. 1986. *Hayek on Liberty*. 2d ed. Oxford, Eng.: Oxford University Press.

Greenshields, Malcolm. 1994. *An Economy of Violence in Early Modern France: Crime and Justice in the Haute Auvergne, 1587–1664*. University Park: Pennsylvania State University Press.

Greer, Sarah. 1936. *A Bibliography of Police Administration and Police Science*. New York: Columbia University.

Groenewegen, Peter D. 1968. "Turgot and Adam Smith." *Scottish Journal of Political Economy* 15, no. 3 (November): 271–287.

———. 2002. *Eighteenth Century Economics: Turgot, Beccaria, Smith, and Their Contemporaries*. Routledge Studies in the History of Economics. London: Routledge.

Guicciardi, Jean-Pierre. 1988. *Mémoires de l'abbé Morellet de l'académie française sur le dix-huitième siècle et sur la Révolution*. Paris: Mercure de France.

Guichard, Auguste-Charles. 1792. *Code de la police*. Paris: N.p.

Guillauté, Jacques-François. 1974 [1749]. *Mémoire sur la réformation de la police de France*. Paris: Hermann, Éditeurs des sciences et des arts.

Guttman, Daniel. 2000. "Public Purpose and Private Service: The Twentieth Century Culture of Contracting Out and the Evolving Law of Diffused Sovereignty." *Administrative Law Review* 52, no. 3: 859–926.

Hale, Robert. 1923. "Coercion and Distribution in a Supposedly Noncoercive State." *Political Science Quarterly* 38:470–494.

———. 1935. "Force and the State." *Columbia Law Review* 35:149–201.

———. 1943. "Bargaining, Duress, and Economic Liberty." *Columbia Law Review* 43:603–628.

Halévy, Élie. 1955 [1901]. *The Growth of Philosophical Radicalism*, trans. M. Morris. Boston: Beacon Press.

Halley, Janet. 2006. *Split Decisions: How and Why to Take a Break from Feminism*. Princeton, N.J.: Princeton University Press.

Hamilton, Alexander. 1965 [1791]. "A Report on Manufactures." Reprinted in *The Reports of Alexander Hamilton*. New York: Harper Torchbooks.

Handlin, Oscar, and Mary Flug Handlin. 1947. *Commonwealth: A Study of the Role of Government in the American Economy; Massachusetts, 1774–1861*. New York: New York University Press.

Hanson, Linda S. Calvert. 1991. "The Privatization of Corrections Movement: A Decade of Change." *Journal of Contemporary Criminal Justice* 7, no. 1 (March 1991): 1–20.

Harcourt, Bernard E. 2001. *Illusion of Order: The False Promise of Broken Windows Policing*. Cambridge: Harvard University Press.

———. 2005. *Language of the Gun: Youth, Crime, and Public Policy*. Chicago: University of Chicago Press.

———. 2006. "From the Asylum to the Prison: Rethinking the Incarceration Revolution." *Texas Law Review* 84:1751–1786.

———. 2007. *Against Prediction: Profiling, Policing, and Punishing in an Actuarial Age*. Chicago: University of Chicago Press.

———. 2011. "An Institutionalization Effect: The Impact of Mental Hospitalization and Imprisonment on Homicide in the United States, 1934–2001." *Journal of Legal Studies* 40 (January).

Harrison, Ross. 1988. "Introduction." In Jeremy Bentham, *A Fragment on Government*. Cambridge, Eng.: Cambridge University Press.

Hart, H. L. A. 1982. "Bentham and Beccaria." In *Essays on Bentham: Jurisprudence and Political Theory*, ed. H. L. A. Hart. Oxford, Eng.: Oxford University Press.

Hart, Jennifer. 1965. "Nineteenth-Century Social Reform: A Tory Interpretation of History." *Past and Present* 31, no. 1 (July): 39–61.

Hartung, Frank E. 1950. "White-Collar Offenses in the Wholesale Meat Industry in Detroit." *American Journal of Sociology* 56:25–32.

Hartz, Louis. 1948. *Economic Policy and Democratic Thought: Pennsylvania, 1776–1860*. Cambridge: Harvard University Press.

———. 1955. *The Liberal Tradition in America: An Interpretation of American Political Thought since the Revolution*. New York: Harcourt, Brace.

Harvey, David. 2005. *A Brief History of Neoliberalism*. Oxford, Eng.: Oxford University Press.

———. 2009. *Cosmopolitanism and the Geographies of Freedom*. New York: Columbia University Press.

Hasen, Richard L., and Richard H. McAdams. 1997. "The Surprisingly Complex Case against Theft." *International Review of Law and Economics* 17:367–378.

Hautefeuille, M. 1811. *Traité de procédure criminelle, correctionnelle et de police; suivi de l'analyse du Code Pénal*. Paris: Hacquart.

Hayek, Friedrich August von. 1960. *The Constitution of Liberty*. Chicago: University of Chicago Press.

———. 1967. *Studies in Philosophy, Politics, and Economics.* Chicago: University of Chicago Press.

———. 1973. *Law, Legislation, and Liberty.* 3 vols. published in 1973, 1976, and 1979, respectively. Chicago: University of Chicago Press.

———. 1978. *New Studies in Philosophy, Politics, Economics, and the History of Ideas.* Chicago: University of Chicago Press.

———. 1988. *The Fatal Conceit: The Errors of Socialism.* Chicago: University of Chicago Press.

———. 2007 [1944]. *The Road to Serfdom: Text and Documents,* ed. Bruce Caldwell. Chicago: University of Chicago Press.

Hazen, Thomas Lee. 1992. "Public Policy: Rational Investments, Speculation, or Gambling?—Derivatives Securities and Financial Futures and Their Effect on the Underlying Capital Markets." *Northwestern University Law Review* 86:987–1037.

Heilmann, Eric. 2005. "Comment surveiller la population à distance? La machine de Guillauté et la naissance de la police moderne." *Séminaire "Distance"* du LISEC. Available at http://archivesic.ccsd.cnrs.fr/docs/00/12/55/74/HTML/index.html (last visited June 16, 2010).

Hénaff, Marcel. 2002. *Le prix de la vérité: Le don, l'argent, la philosophie.* Paris: Seuil.

Hietala, Thomas R. 1985. *Manifest Design: Anxious Aggrandizement in Late Jacksonian America.* Ithaca, N.Y.: Cornell University Press.

Higgs, Henry. 1996. *The Physiocrats: Six Lectures on the French Économistes of the Eighteenth Century.* 1897 ed. London: Continuum International Publishing Group.

Higham, John. 2002. *Strangers in the Land: Patterns of American Nativism, 1860–1925.* New Brunswick, N.J.: Rutgers University Press.

Himmelfarb, Gertrude. 1969. "Bentham Scholarship and the Bentham 'Problem,'" *Journal of Modern History* 41, no. 2: 189–206.

Hirsch, Adam Jay. 1992. *The Rise of the Penitentiary: Prisons and Punishment in Early America.* New Haven: Yale University Press.

Hirschman, Albert. 1977. *The Passions and the Interests: Political Arguments for Capitalism before Its Triumph.* Princeton, N.J.: Princeton University Press.

Hobsbawm, Eric J. 1968. *Industry and Empire: An Economic History of Britain since 1750.* London: Weidenfeld and Nicolson.

Hofstadter, Richard. 1973 [1948]. *The American Political Tradition and the Men Who Made It.* 25th anniversary ed. New York: Alfred A. Knopf.

Hollingsworth, Joseph Rogers, and Robert Boyer, eds. 1997a. *Contemporary Capitalism: The Embeddedness of Institutions.* Cambridge, Eng.: Cambridge University Press.

———. 1997b. "Coordination of Economic Actors and Social Systems of Production." Pp. 1–47 in *Contemporary Capitalism: The Embeddedness of Institutions,* ed. Joseph Rogers Hollingsworth and Robert Boyer. Cambridge, Eng.: Cambridge University Press.

Holmes, Colin J. 1976. "Laissez-faire in Theory and Practice: Britain, 1800–1875." *Journal of European Economic History* 5, no. 3 (Winter): 671–688.

Holmes, Stephen. 1995. *Passion and Constraint: On the Theory of Liberal Democracy.* Chicago: University of Chicago Press.

Holmes, Stephen, and Cass Sunstein. 1999. *The Cost of Rights: Why Liberty Depends on Taxes.* New York: W. W. Norton & Co.

Horn, Rob Van, and Philip Mirowski. 2009. "The Rise of the Chicago School of Economics and the Birth of Neoliberalism." Pp. 139–178 in *The Road from Mont Pèlerin: The Making of the Neoliberal Thought Collective,* ed. Philip Mirowski and Dieter Plehwe. Cambridge: Harvard University Press.

Horwitz, Morton J. 1977. *The Transformation of American Law, 1780–1860.* Cambridge: Harvard University Press.

Hovenkamp, Herbert. 2009. "The Coase Theorem and Arthur Cecil Pigou." *Arizona Law Review* 51:633–649.

Hume, L. J. 1967.. "Jeremy Bentham and the Nineteenth-Century Revolution in Government." *Historical Journal* 10, no. 3: 361–375.

———. 1969. "Myrdal on Jeremy Bentham: Laissez-faire and Harmony of Interests." *Economica* 36, no. 143 (August): 295–303.

———. 1981. *Bentham and Bureaucracy.* Cambridge, Eng.: Cambridge University Press.

Hurst, Willard. 1956. *Law and the Conditions of Freedom in the Nineteenth-Century United States.* Madison: University of Wisconsin Press.

Ignatieff, Michael. 1978. *A Just Measure of Pain: The Penitentiary in the Industrial Revolution, 1750–1850.* New York: Pantheon.

Jackall, Robert. 1988. *Moral Mazes: The World of Corporate Managers.* New York: Oxford University Press.

Jayadev, Arjun, and Samuel Bowles. 2006. "Guard Labor." *Journal of Development Economics* 79, no. 2 (April).

Joh, Elizabeth E. 2004. "The Paradox of Private Policing." *Journal of Criminal Law and Criminology* 9, no. 1: 549–606.

———. 2005. "Conceptualizing the Private Police." *Utah Law Review,* pp. 573–617.

Jones, Jerry N., Mary F. Jones, and Arline Winerman v. Harris Associates, 527 F.3d 627, U.S. Court of Appeals for the Seventh Circuit, May 19, 2008, *rehearing denied* at 537 F.3d 728, *certiorari granted* at 129 S. Ct. 1579 [herein referred to as *Jones* 2008a].

Jones, Jerry N., Mary F. Jones, and Arline Winerman v. Harris Associates, 537 F.3d 728, U.S. Court of Appeals for the Seventh Circuit, August 8, 2008, *certiorari granted* at 129 S. Ct. 1579 [herein referred to as *Jones* 2008b].

Jones, Jerry N., Mary F. Jones, and Arline Winerman v. Harris Associates, 559 U.S. __, U.S. Supreme Court, March 30, 2010 [herein referred to as *Jones* 2010].

Justi, Johann Heinrich Gottlob von. 1760–1761. *Die Grundfeste zu der Macht und Gluckseeligkeit der Staaten; oder, Ausführliche Vorstellung der gesamten Polizey-Wissenschaft* (*Foundations of the power and happiness of states; or, An exhaustive presentation of the science of public police*). Leipzig: N.p.

Kanter, Rosabeth Moss. 1977. *Men and Women of the Corporation.* New York: Basic Books.

Kaplan, Steven L. 1974. "Subsistence, Police, and Political Economy at the End of the Reign of Louis XV." Ph.D. diss., Yale University.

———. 1976. *Bread, Politics and Political Economy in the Reign of Louis XV.* 2 vols. The Hague: Martinus Nijhoff.

Kelman, Mark. 1987. *A Guide to Critical Legal Studies.* Cambridge: Harvard University Press.

Kennedy, Duncan. 1981. "Cost-Benefit Analysis of Entitlement Problems: A Critique." *Stanford Law Review* 33 (February): 387–445.

———. 1991. "The Stakes of Law, or Hale and Foucault!" *Legal Studies Forum* 15, no. 4: 327–366.

———. 1998. "Law and Economics from the Perspective of Critical Legal Studies." Pp. 465–474 in *The New Palgrave Dictionary of Economics and the Law,* ed. Peter Newman. New York: Macmillan Reference Limited.

———. 2006. *The Rise and Fall of Classical Legal Thought: With a New Preface by the Author, "Thirty Years Later."* Frederick, Md.: BeardBooks.

Kessler, Amalia D. 2007. *A Revolution in Commerce.* New Haven: Yale University Press.

Keynes, John Maynard. 1926. *The End of Laissez-faire.* London: L. & V. Woolf.

King, Desmond. 1999. *In the Name of Liberalism: Illiberal Social Policy in the United States and Britain.* Oxford, Eng.: Oxford University Press.

Kitch, Edmund W. 1983. "The Fire of Truth: A Remembrance of Law and Economics at Chicago, 1932–1970." *Journal of Law and Economics* 26:163–233.

Klein, Naomi. 2007. *The Shock Doctrine: The Rise of Disaster Capitalism.* New York: Henry Holt.

Kley, Roland. 1994. *Hayek's Social and Political Thought.* Oxford, Eng.: Oxford University Press.

Knowles, Lilian Charlotte Anne. 1921. *The Industrial and Commercial Revolutions in Great Britain during the Nineteenth Century.* London: G. Routledge & Sons.

Kosar, Kevin R. 2006. *Privatization and the Federal Government: An Introduction.* Congressional Research Service Report for Congress CRS-3, December 28, 2006. Washington, D.C.: Congressional Research Service.

Koster, Willem de, Jeroen van der Waal, Peter Achterberg, and Dick Houtman. 2008. "The Rise of the Penal State: Neo-Liberalization or New Political Culture?" *British Journal of Criminology* 48:720–734.

Krugman, Paul. 2009a. "Bailouts for Bunglers." *New York Times,* February 1, 2009. Available at www.nytimes.com/2009/02/02/opinion/02krugman.html?scp=4&sq=krugman%20&st=cse (last visited June 16, 2010).

———. 2009b. "Banking on the Brink." *New York Times,* February 22, 2009. Available at www.nytimes.com/2009/02/23/opinion/23krugman.html?scp=2&sq=preprivatization&st=cse (last visited June 16, 2010).

———. 2009c. "How Many Banks?" *New York Times,* March 4, 2009. Available at krugman.blogs.nytimes.com/2009/03/04/how-many-banks/?scp=1&sq=preprivatization&st=cse (last visited June 16, 2010).

Kuczynski, Marguerite, and Ronald L. Meek. 1972. *Quesnay's* Tableau Economique. New York: Augustus M. Kelley Publishers.

Kukathas, Chandran. 1989. *Hayek and Modern Liberalism.* Oxford, Eng.: Oxford University Press.

Lacey, Nicola. 2008. *The Prisoners' Dilemma: Political Economy and Punishment in Contemporary Democracies.* Cambridge, Eng.: Cambridge University Press.

L'administration de police à ses concitoyens. 1792–1795. Paris: Imp. de C. F. Patris.

Larson, John Lauritz. 2010. *The Market Revolution in America: Liberty, Ambition, and the Eclipse of the Common Good.* New York: Cambridge University Press.
Latour, Bruno. 2004. *The Politics of Nature.* Cambridge: Harvard University Press.
Laval, Christian. 1994. *Jeremy Bentham: Le pouvoir des fictions.* Paris: Press Universitaires de France.
———. 2007. *L'homme économique: Essai sur les racines du néolibéralisme.* Paris: Gallimard.
Le Clère, Marcel. 1991. *Bibliographie critique de la police: Deuxième édition revue et augmentée.* Paris: Éditions Yzer.
———. 1993. *Bibliographie critique de la police: Supplément à la deuxième édition.* Paris: Éditions Yzer.
Le Maire, Jean-Baptiste-Charles. 1879 [1768–1771]. "Mémoire sur l'administration de la police en France." Pp. 1–131 in *Mémoires de la société de l'histoire de Paris et de l'Ile-de-France,* vol. 5. Paris: H. Champion. (Also referred to as "La police de Paris en 1770: Mémoire inédit compose par ordre de G. de Sartine sur la demande de Marie-Thérèse.")
Le Mercier de La Rivière, Pierre-Paul. 1767. *L'ordre naturel et essentiel des sociétés politiques.* London: Chez J. Nourse.
———. 2001 [1767]. *L'ordre naturel et essentiel des sociétés politiques.* Paris: Librairie Arthème Fayard.
Lence, Sergio H. 2003. "Do Futures Benefit Farmers Who Adopt Them?" ESA Working Paper no. 03–20 (December). Agricultural and Development Economics Division, Food and Agriculture Organization of the United Nations. Available at www.fao.org/es/esa (last visited June 16, 2010).
Leonhardt, David. 2007. "Larry Summers's Evolution: The Former Treasury Secretary Is Having Second Thoughts about How to Make Globalization Work for the Middle Class," *New York Times Magazine,* June 10, 2007, pp. 22–26.
———. 2008. "[Advanced] Obamanomics." *New York Times Magazine,* August 24, 2008, pp. 28–54.
Lépinay, Vincent-Antonin. 2007. "Decoding Finance: Articulation and Liquidity around a Trading Room." Pp. 87–127 in *Do Economists Make Markets? On the Performativity of Economics,* ed. Donald MacKenzie, Fabian Muniesa, and Lucia Siu. Princeton, N.J.: Princeton University Press.
Le Taillanter, Roger. 2001. *36, Quai des orfèvres: Le dossier.* Paris: Grancher.
L'Heuillet, Hélène. 2001. *Basse politique, haute police: Une approche historique et philosophique de la police.* Paris: Fayard.
Libera, Alain de. 1996. *La querelle des universaux: De Platon à la fin du Moyen Age.* Paris: Éditions du Seuil.
Lieberman, David. 1989. *The Province of Legislation Determined: Legal Theory in Eighteenth-Century Britain.* Cambridge, Eng.: Cambridge University Press.
Lindblom, Charles Edward, 1977. *Politics and Markets.* New York: Basic Books.
———. 2001. *The Market System: What It Is, How It Works, and What to Make of It.* New Haven: Yale University Press.
Lipson, Ephraim. 1944. *A Planned Economy or Free Enterprise: The Lessons of History.* London: Adam & Charles Black.
Lis, Catharina, and Hugo Soly. 1984. "Policing the Early Modern Proletariat, 1450–

1850." Pp. 163–228 in *Proletarianization and Family History*, ed. David Levine. Orlando, Fla.: Academic Press.

Lundberg, I. C. 1964. *Turgot's Unknown Translator: The* Réflexions *and Adam Smith*. The Hague: Martinus Nijhoff.

Lurie, Jonathan. 1979. *The Chicago Board of Trade, 1859–1905: The Dynamics of Self-Regulation*. Urbana: University of Illinois Press.

MacDonagh, Oliver. 1958. "The Nineteenth-Century Revolution in Government: A Reappraisal." *Historical Journal* 1, no. 1: 52–67.

MacKenzie, Donald. 2007. "Is Economics Performative? Option Theory and the Construction of Derivatives Markets." Pp. 54–86 in *Do Economists Make Markets? On the Performativity of Economics*, ed. MacKenzie, Fabian Muniesa, and Lucia Siu. Princeton, N.J.: Princeton University Press.

MacKenzie, Donald, Fabian Muniesa, and Lucia Siu, eds. 2007. *Do Economists Make Markets? On the Performativity of Economics*. Princeton, N.J.: Princeton University Press.

Manta, Irina. 2008. "Privatizing Trademarks." Working paper presented at the University of Chicago Law School on September 4.

Manza, Jeff, and Christopher Uggen. 2008. *Locked Out: Felon Disenfranchisement and American Democracy*. New York: Oxford University Press.

Marx, Karl. 1974. *Théories sur la plus-value (Livre IV du "Capital")*, comp. Gilbert Badia. 3 vols. Paris: Éditions Sociales.

———. 1976. *Capital: Volume 1*. Trans. Ben Fowkes. New York: Penguin Books.

Massey, Douglas S. 2007. *Categorically Unequal: The American Stratification System*. New York: Russell Sage Foundation.

Mauer, Marc, and Meda Chesney-Lind. 2002. *Invisible Punishment: The Collateral Consequences of Mass Imprisonment*. New York: New Press.

Mauer, Marc, R. S. King, and M. C. Young. 2004. *The Meaning of Life: Long Prison Sentences in Context*. Washington, D.C.: The Sentencing Project.

May, Louis-Philippe. 1932. *Le Mercier de La Rivière: Intendant des Îles du Vent*. Paris: Marcel Rivière.

———. 1972. *Histoire Économique de la Martinique (1635–1763)*, 2d ed. Fort-de-France, Martinique: Société de distribution et de culture. (Reprint of 1930 text published in Paris at Marcel Riviere.)

———. 1975. *Le Mercier de la Rivière (1719–1801): Aux origines de la science économique*. Aix-Marseille: Éditions du Centre National de la Recherche Scientifique.

———. 1978. *Le Mercier de la Rivière (1719–1801): Mémoires et textes inédits sur le gouvernement économique des Antilles*. Marseille: Éditions du Centre National de la Recherche Scientifique.

McBride, Keally. 2007. *Punishment and Political Order*. Ann Arbor: University of Michigan Press.

McCoy, Drew R. 1980. *The Elusive Republic: Political Economy in Jeffersonian America*. Chapel Hill: University of North Carolina Press.

McLennan, Rebecca M. 2008. *The Crisis of Imprisonment: Protest, Politics, and the Making of the American Penal State, 1776–1941*. Cambridge, Eng.: Cambridge University Press.

McNally, David. 1993. *Against the Market: Political Economy, Market Socialism, and the Marxist Critique*. London: Verso.

Meares, Tracey. 2004. "Mass Incarceration: Who Pays the Price for Criminal Offending?" *Criminology and Public Policy* 3:295–302.

Medema, Steven G. 1998. "Wandering the Road from Pluralism to Posner: The Transformation of Law and Economics in the Twentieth Century." Pp. 202–224 in *The Transformation of American Economics: From Interwar Pluralism to Postwar Neoclassicism: History of Political Economy, Annual Supplement* 30, ed. Mary Morgan and Malcolm Rutherford. Durham, N.C.: Duke University Press.

———. 2007a. "The Hesitant Hand: Mill, Sidgwick, and the Evolution of the Theory of Market Failure." *History of Political Economy* 39, no. 3: 332–358.

———. 2007b. "Sidgwick's Utilitarian Analysis of Law: A Bridge from Bentham to Becker?" *American Law and Economics Review* 9, no. 1: 30–47.

———. 2008. "The Chicago School of Law and Economics." In *The Elgar Companion to the Chicago School*, ed. Ross Emmett. Cheltenham, Eng.: Edward Elgar.

Medlin, Dorothy, Jean-Claude David, and Paul Leclerc. 1991. *Lettres d'André Morellet*, vol. 1: *1759–1785*. Oxford, Eng.: Voltaire Foundation.

Meek, Ronald L. 1962. *The Economics of Physiocracy: Essays and Translations*. London: Allen & Unwin.

Meese, Edwin, III. 1992. *With Reagan: The Inside Story*. Washington, D.C.: Regnery Gateway.

Melossi, Dario, and Massimo Pavarini. 1981. *The Prison and the Factory: Origins of the Penitentiary System*, trans. Glynis Cousin. Totowa, N.J.: Barnes & Noble Books.

Merrick, Jeffrey, and Dorothy Medlin. 1995. *André Morellet (1727–1819) in the Republic of Letters and the French*. New York: Peter Lang.

Meuvret, Jean. 1946. "Les crises de subsistances et la démographie de la France d'ancien régime." *Population* 1, no. 4: 643–650.

Meyssonnier, Simone. 1989. *La Balance et l'horloge: La genèse de la pensée libérale en France au XVIIIe siècle*. Montreuil, France: Les Éditions de la Passion.

MFS Securities Corp. and Marco Savarese v. New York Stock Exchange, 277 F.3d 613, U.S. Court of Appeals for the Second Circuit, January 24, 2002, *certiorari denied*, June 17, 2002.

Mill, John Stuart. 1988 [1869]. *The Subjection of Women*, ed. Susan Okin. Indianapolis: Hackett.

Miller, Judith A. 1999. *Mastering the Market: The State and the Grain Trade in Northern France, 1700–1860*. Cambridge, Eng.: Cambridge University Press.

Miller, Peter, and Nikolas Rose. 2008. *Governing the Present: Administering Economic, Social and Personal Life*. Cambridge, Eng.: Polity Press.

Mirabeau, Victor de Requetti, Marquis de. 1768. *Lettres sur le commerce des grains*. Amsterdam: Chez Desaint.

Mirabeau, Victor de Requetti, Marquis de, and François Quesnay. 1999 [1757–1759]. *Traité de la monarchie*. Paris: L'Harmattan.

Miroir, E. M. M., and E. Brissot de Warville. 1843. *Traité de police municipale et rurale*. Paris: Paul Dupont.

Mirowski, Philip. 2002. *Machine Dreams: Economics Becomes a Cyborg Science*. Cambridge, Eng.: Cambridge University Press.

———. 2009. "Postface: Defining Neoliberalism." Pp. 417–455 in *The Road from Mont Pèlerin: The Making of the Neoliberal Thought Collective*, ed. Philip Mirowski and Dieter Plehwe. Cambridge: Harvard University Press.

Mirowski, Philip, and Edward Nik-Khah. 2007. "Markets Made Flesh: Performativity, and a Problem in Science Studies, Augmented with Consideration of the FCC Auctions." Pp. 190–224 in *Do Economists Make Markets? On the Performativity of Economics*, ed. Donald MacKenzie, Fabian Muniesa, and Lucia Siu. Princeton, N.J.: Princeton University Press.

Mirowski, Philip, and Dieter Plehwe, eds. 2009. *The Road from Mont Pèlerin: The Making of the Neoliberal Thought Collective*. Cambridge: Harvard University Press.

Moore, Solomon. 2009. "Prison Spending Outpaces All but Medicaid." *New York Times*, March 3, 2009.

Morellet, André. 1764. *Fragment d'une lettre sur la police des grains*. Brussels: Chez Musier fils.

———. 1967 [1822, 2d ed.]. *Mémoires inédits de l'abbé Morellet, sur le dix-huitième siècle et sur la Révolution*. 2d ed. in 2 vols. Geneva: Slatkine Reprints.

———. 1991, 1994, and 1996. *Lettres d'André Morellet*, ed. Dorothy Medlin, Jean-Claude David, and Paul Leclerc. 3 vols. Oxford, Eng.: Alden Press.

Morley, John. 1873. *Rousseau*. 2 vols. London: Chapman and Hall.

Morley, John, and Quinn Curtis. 2009. "Voice and Liability in the Shadow of Exit: Voting, Boards and Fee Litigation in Mutual Funds." Working paper dated December 31, 2009, presented at the University of Chicago Law School on January 11, 2010.

Morris, Norval, and David J. Rothman, eds. 1995. *The Oxford History of the Prison: The Practice of Punishment in Western Society*. New York: Oxford University Press.

Morrissey, Robert. 2010. *Napoléon et l'héritage de la gloire*. Paris: Presses Universitaires de France.

Musart, Charles. 1921. *La réglementation du commerce des grains en France au XVIIIe siècle: La théorie de Delamare*. Paris: Champion.

Myrdal, Gunnar. 1957. *Economic Theory and Underdeveloped Regions*. London: Gerald Duckworth & Co.

———. 1990 [1932]. *The Political Element in the Development of Economic Theory*, trans. Paul Streeten. New Brunswick, N.J.: Transaction Publishers.

Napoli, Paulo. 2003. *Naissance de la police moderne: Pouvoir, normes, société*. Paris: Éditions La Découverte.

Nellis, Ashley, and Ryan S. King. 2009. *No Exit: The Expanding Use of Life Sentences in America*. Washington, D.C.: The Sentencing Project.

Nelson, Richard R., ed. 2005a. "Introduction." Pp. 1–24 in Nelson, *The Limits of Market Organization*. New York: Russell Sage Foundation.

———. 2005b. *The Limits of Market Organization*. New York: Russell Sage Foundation.

Nietzsche, Friedrich. 1967. *On the Genealogy of Morals*. Trans. Walter Kaufmann and R. J. Hollingdale. New York: Vintage Books.

Nik-Khah, Edward. 2008. "A Tale of Two Auctions." *Journal of Institutional Economics* 4, no. 1: 73–97.

Novak, William J. 1996. *The People's Welfare: Law and Regulation in Nineteenth-Century America.* Chapel Hill: University of North Carolina Press.

Nussbaum, Martha C. 2000. "'Mutilated and Deformed': Adam Smith on the Material Basis of Human Dignity." Castle Lectures delivered at Yale University.

———. 2009. "The Challenge of Gender Justice." In *Against Injustice: The New Economics of Amartya Sen,* ed. Reiko Gotoh and Paul Dumouchel. New York: Cambridge University Press.

Nye, John V. C. 2007. *War, Wine, and Taxes: The Political Economy of Anglo-French Trade, 1689–1900.* Princeton, N.J.: Princeton University Press.

Obama, Barack. 2006. *The Audacity of Hope: Thoughts on Reclaiming the American Dream.* New York: Random House.

Ockham, William of. 1992 [1334–1347]. *Short Discourse on the Tyrannical Government: Over Things Divine and Human, But Especially over the Empire and Those Subject to the Empire, Usurped by Some Who Are Called Highest Pontiffs,* ed. Arthur Stephen McGrade, trans. John Kilcullen. Cambridge, Eng.: Cambridge University Press.

———. 1995 [1334]. *A Letter to the Friars Minor and Other Writings,* ed. Arthur Stephen McGrade and John Kilcullen, trans. John Kilcullen. Cambridge, Eng.: Cambridge University Press.

Odier, Pierre. 1862. *Esquisse du droit féodal.* Paris: Auguste Durand.

Olivier-Martin, François. 1988a. *Les lois du roi.* Paris: Éditions Loysel.

———. 1988b [1945]. *La police économique de l'Ancien Régime.* Paris: Éditions Loysel.

Olsen, Frances Elisabeth. 1983. "The Family and the Market: A Study of Ideology and Legal Reform." *Harvard Law Review* 96:1497–1578.

———. 1985. "The Myth of State Intervention in the Family." *University of Michigan Journal of Legal Reform* 18:835–864.

Oncken, Auguste. 1965 [1888]. "Introduction" to François Quesnay, *Œuvres économiques et philosophiques,* ed. Auguste Oncken. Darmstadt, Ger.: Scientia Verlag Aalen.

Orren, Karen. 1991. *Belated Feudalism: Labor, the Law, and Liberal Development in the United States.* Cambridge, Eng.: Cambridge University Press.

Osborne, David, and Ted Gaebler. 1993. *Reinventing Government: How the Entrepreneurial Spirit Is Transforming the Public Sector.* New York: Plume.

O'Sullivan, Eoin, and Ian O'Donnell. 2006. "Coercive Confinement in the Republic of Ireland: The Waning of a Culture of Control." *Punishment & Society* 9, no. 1: 27–48.

Painter, Kate, and Nick Tilley, eds. 1999. *Surveillance of Public Space.* Monsey, N.Y.: Criminal Justice Press.

Palidda, Salvatore, ed. 2009. *Criminalisation and Victimisation of Migrants in Europe.* Genoa, Italy: CrimPrev. Available at www.reseau-terra.eu/IMG/pdf/criminalisation.pdf (last visited June 16, 2010).

Panaccio, Claude. 1991. *Les mots, les concepts et les choses: La sémantique de Guillaume d'Occam et le nominalisme d'aujourd'hui.* Paris: Vrin.

———. 1999. *Le discours intérieur de Platon à Guillaume d'Ockham.* Paris: Seuil.

Parenti, Christian. 2000. *Lockdown America: Police and Prisons in the Age of Crisis.* London: Verso.

Parris, Henry. 1960. "The Nineteenth-Century Revolution in Government: A Reappraisal Reappraised." *Historical Journal* 3, no. 1: 17–37.

Pashigian, B. Peter. 1988. "Why Have Some Farmers Opposed Futures Markets?" *Journal of Political Economy* 96, no. 2 (April): 371–382.

Pasquino, Pasquale. 1991. "Theatrum Politicum: The Genealogy of Capital—Police and the State of Prosperity." In *The Foucault Effect: Studies in Governmentality,* ed. Graham Burchell, Colin Gordon, and Peter Miller. Chicago: University of Chicago Press.

Paul, Ellen Frankel. 1979. *Moral Revolution and Economic Science: The Demise of Laissez-faire in Nineteenth-Century British Political Economy.* Westport, Conn.: Greenwood.

———. 1980. "Laissez-faire in Nineteenth-Century Britain: Fact or Myth?" *Literature of Liberty* 3, no. 4: 5–38.

Pautrat, Bernard. 2001. "L'autre Beccaria." Pp. 185–206 in Cesare Beccaria, *Recherches concernant la nature du style,* trans. Bernard Pautrat. Paris: Éditions Rue d'Ulm/Presses de l'École normale supérieure.

Peck, Jamie, and Adam Tickell. 2002. "Neoliberalizing Space." Pp. 33–57 in *Spaces of Neoliberalism: Urban Restructuring in North America and Western Europe,* ed. Neil Brenner and Nik Theodore. Oxford, Eng.: Blackwell.

Perrot, Michelle. 1975. "Délinquance et système pénitentiaire en France au dix-neuvième siècle." *Annales, Économies, Sociétés, Civilisations* 30, no. 1: 67–91.

———, ed. 1980. *L'impossible prison: Recherches sur le système pénitentiaire au dix-neuvième siècle. Débat avec Michel Foucault.* Paris: Seuil.

Petersilia, Joan. 2003. *When Prisoners Come Home: Parole and Prisoner Reentry, Studies in Crime and Public Policy.* New York: Oxford University Press.

Petsoulas, Christina. 2001. *Hayek's Liberalism and Its Origin: His Idea of Spontaneous Order and the Scottish Enlightenment.* London: Routledge.

PEW Center on the States. 2008. *One in 100: Behind Bars in America 2008.* Available at www.pewcenteronthestates.org/uploadedFiles/8015PCTS_Prison08_FINAL_2-1-1_FORWEB.pdf (last visited Jan. 24, 2010).

Piquero, Alex, Valerie West, Jeffrey Fagan, and Jan Holland. 2006. "Neighborhood, Race, and the Economic Consequences of Incarceration in New York City, 1985–1996." Pp. 256–276 in *The Many Colors of Crime: Inequalities of Race, Ethnicity and Crime in America,* ed. Ruth D. Peterson, Lauren J. Krivo, and John Hagan. New York: New York University Press.

Pitts, Jennifer. 2006. *A Turn to Empire: The Rise of Imperial Liberalism in Britain and France.* Princeton, N.J.: Princeton University Press.

Piven, Frances Fox, and Richard A. Cloward. 1993 [1971]. *Regulating the Poor: The Functions of Public Welfare,* rev. ed. New York: Vintage.

Polanyi, Karl. 1944. *The Great Transformation.* Boston: Beacon Press.

"Police." 1765. Entry in *Encyclopédie,* vol. 12, pp. 904–912.

Polinsky, A. Mitchell. 2003. *An Introduction to Law and Economics,* 3d ed. New York: Aspen.

Posner, Richard A. 1973. *Economic Analysis of Law.* Boston: Little, Brown.

———. 1985. "An Economic Theory of the Criminal Law." *Columbia Law Review* 85, no. 6 (October): 1193–1231.

———. 1990. *The Problems of Jurisprudence*. Cambridge: Harvard University Press.

———. 1995. *Overcoming Law*. Cambridge: Harvard University Press.

———. 2001. *Frontiers of Legal Theory*. Cambridge: Harvard University Press.

———. 2009a. *A Failure of Capitalism: The Crisis of '08 and the Descent into Depression*. Cambridge: Harvard University Press.

———. 2009b. "Our Crisis of Regulation." *New York Times*, June 25, 2009, p. A21.

Pressman, Steven. 1994. *Quesnay's Tableau Économique: A Critique and Reassessment*. 1st ed. Fairfield, N.J.: A. M. Kelley.

Prins, Adolphe. 1910. *La défense sociale et les transformations du droit pénal*. Brussels: Misch et Thron.

Prison Association of New York. 1867. *Twenty-second Annual Report of the Executive Committee of the Prison Association of New York*. Albany: C. Van Benthuysen & Sons.

———. 1873. *Twenty-eighth Annual Report of the Executive Committee of the Prison Association of New York, and Accompanying Documents, for the Year 1872*. Albany: The Argus Company.

Quesnay, François. 1965 [1888]. *Œuvres économiques et philosophiques*, ed. Auguste Oncken. Darmstadt, Ger.: Scientia Verlag Aalen.

———. 2005. *Œuvres Économiques Complètes et autres textes*, ed. Christine Théré, Loïc Charles, and Jean-Claude Perrot. 2 vols. Paris: Institut National d'Études Démographiques.

Rancière, Jacques. 1995. *La mésentente. Politique et philosophie*. Paris: Éditions Galilée.

Ranum, Orest. 1968. *Paris in the Age of Absolutism*. Bloomington: Indiana University Press.

Recueil. 1769. *Recueil des principales loix relative au commerce des grains, avec les arrêts, arrêtés et remontrances du Parlement sur cet objet: Et le procès-verbal de l'assemblée générale de police tenue à Paris le 28 Novembre 1768*. N.p.

Redden, Jim. 2000. *Snitch Culture*. Port Townsend, Wash.: Feral House.

Reder, Melvin W. 1982. "Chicago Economics: Permanence and Change." *Journal of Economic Literature* 20, no. 1 (March): 1–38.

Remontrances du Parlement de Paris au XVIIIe Siècle, publiées par Jules Flammermont. 1888–1898. 3 vols. (1715–1753; 1754–1767; 1768–1788). Paris: Imprimerie Nationale.

Rhodes, Lorna A. 2004. *Total Confinement: Madness and Reason in the Maximum Security Prison*. Berkeley: University of California Press.

Robbins, Lionel. 1953. *The Theory of Economic Policy in English Classical Political Economy*. London: Macmillan.

Roberts, David. 1960. *Victorian Origins of the British Welfare State*. New Haven: Yale University Press.

Roberts, Dorothy. 1999. "Foreword: Race, Vagueness, and the Social Meaning of Order-Maintenance Policing." *Journal of Criminal Law and Criminology* 89:775–836.

Romano, Roberta. 1997. "The Political Dynamics of Derivative Securities Regulation." *Yale Journal on Regulation* 4:279–383.

Rosanvallon, Pierre. 1989. *Le libéralisme économique*. Paris: Éditions du Seuil.

Rose, Nikolas. 2007. *The Politics of Life Itself: Biomedicine, Power, and Subjectivity in the Twenty-first Century*. Princeton, N.J.: Princeton University Press.

Rose, Nikolas, Pat O'Malley, and Mariana Valverde. 2006. "Governmentality." *Annual Review of Law and Social Science* 2:83–104.

Ross, Ian Simpson. 1995. *The Life of Adam Smith*. Oxford, Eng.: Clarendon.

Rothbard, Murray. 2007 [1973]. "Police, Law, and the Courts." In *Anarchy and the Law: The Political Economy of Choice*, ed. Edward P. Stringham. New Brunswick, N.J.: Transaction.

Rothman, David J. 1971. *The Discovery of the Asylum: Social Order and Disorder in the New Republic*. Boston: Little, Brown.

———. 1980. *Conscience and Convenience: The Asylum and Its Alternatives in Progressive America*. Boston: Little, Brown.

Rothschild, Emma. 1992. "Commerce and the State: Turgot, Condorcet and Smith." *Economic Journal* 102, no. 414: 1197–1210.

———. 1994. "Adam Smith and the Invisible Hand." *American Economic Review* 84, no. 2 (May): 319–322.

———. 2004. "Global Commerce and the Question of Sovereignty in the Eighteenth-Century Provinces." *Modern Intellectual History* 1, no. 1: 3–25.

Rothschild, Emma, and Amartya Sen. 2006. "Adam Smith's Economics." Pp. 319–365 in *The Cambridge Companion to Adam Smith*, ed. Knud Haakonssen. Cambridge, Eng.: Cambridge University Press.

Rowley, Charles K. 1998. "Law and Economics from the Perspective of Economics." Pp. 474–486 in *The New Palgrave Dictionary of Economics and the Law*, vol. 2, ed. Peter Newman. Hampshire, Eng.: Palgrave Macmillan Limited.

Ruff, Julius R. 1984. *Crime, Justice and Public Order in Old Regime France*. London: Croom Helm.

Rusche, Georg, and Otto Kirchheimer. 1939. *Punishment and Social Structure*. New York: Columbia University Press.

Saad-Filho, Alfredo, and Deborah Johnston. 2005. *Neoliberalism: A Critical Reader*. London: Pluto Press.

Sallé, Jacques-Antoine. 1759. *Traité des fonctions, droits et privilèges des commissaires au Châtelet de Paris*. Paris: P. Alex Le Prieur.

———. 1771. *L'Esprit des ordonnances et des principaux édits déclarations de Louis XV, en matière civile, criminelle et beneficiale*. Paris: Bailly.

Samuels, Warren. 1973. "The Economy as a System of Power and Its Legal Bases: The Legal Economics of Robert Lee Hale." *University of Miami Law Review* 27:261–371.

———, ed. 1976. *The Chicago School of Political Economy*. East Lansing: Michigan State University.

Sanger, David E. 2009. "Nationalization Gets a New, Serious Look." *New York Times*, January 25, 2009. Available at www.nytimes.com/2009/01/26/business/economy/26banks.html (last visited June 16, 2010).

Savas, E. S. 1999. *Privatization and Public-Private Partnerships.* Washington, D.C.: CQ Press.

Schelle, Gustave, ed. *Œuvres de Turgot et documents le concernant,* 5 vols. (Paris: Alcan, 1913–1923).

Schlosser, Eric. 1998. "The Prison-Industrial Complex." *Atlantic Monthly* 282, no. 6: 51–72.

Schofield, Philip. 2009. "Werner Stark and Jeremy Bentham's Economic Writings." *History of European Ideas* 35:475–494.

Schumpeter, Joseph. 1968 [1954]. *History of Economic Analysis.* New York: Oxford University Press.

Sellers, Charles. 1991. *The Market Revolution: Jacksonian America, 1815–1846.* New York: Oxford University Press.

Semmel, Bernard. 1970. *The Rise of Free Trade Imperialism: Classical Political Economy and the Empire of Free Trade and Imperialism, 1750–1850.* Cambridge, Eng.: Cambridge University Press.

Sentence de la Chambre de police du Châtelet. 1681. *Sentence de la Chambre de police du Châtelet, qui déclare valable une saisie d'un muid de farine, à la requête du procureur des jurés mesureurs de grain. 10 octobre 1681.* Paris: M. Le Prest.

Sewell, William. 2005. *Logics of History: Social Theory and Social Transformation.* Chicago: University of Chicago Press.

Sidgwick, Henry. 1969. *The Principles of Political Economy,* 3d ed. New York: Kraus Reprint Co.

Sigot, Nathalie. 1993. "'Be Quiet,' mais modérément: Le rôle de l'état dans la pensée économique de Jeremy Bentham." *Revue économique* 44, no. 1 (January): 23–49.

Silver v. New York Stock Exchange, 373 U.S. 341, U.S. Supreme Court, May 20, 1963.

Simon, Jonathan. 2007. *Governing through Crime.* New York: Oxford University Press.

Smith, Adam. 1853. *The Theory of Moral Sentiments.* London: Henry G. Bohn.

———. 1896. *Lectures on Justice, Police, Revenue and Arms Delivered in the University of Glasgow,* ed. Edwin Cannan. Oxford, Eng.: Clarendon Press.

———. 1937. *The Wealth of Nations.* New York: Modern Library.

———. 1976 [1776]. *An Inquiry into the Nature and Causes of the Wealth of Nations,* ed. Edwin Cannan. Chicago: University of Chicago Press.

———. 1978 [1762–1763; 1766]. *Lectures on Jurisprudence,* ed. R. L. Meek, D. D. Raphael, and P. G. Stein. Oxford, Eng.: Clarendon Press.

———. 1987. *The Correspondence of Adam Smith,* ed. Ernest Campbell Mossner and Ian Simpson Ross. 2d ed. Oxford, Eng.: Clarendon Press.

———. 2002 [1759]. *The Theory of Moral Sentiments.* Cambridge, Eng.: Cambridge University Press.

Smith, Philip. 2008. *Punishment and Culture.* Chicago: University of Chicago Press.

Sonnenfels, Joseph von. 1765–1767. *Grundsätze der Polizei, Handlung und Finanzwissenschaft* (Foundations of the science of police, commerce, and finance). Vienna: N.p.

Spade, Paul Vincent, ed. 1999. *The Cambridge Companion to Ockham.* New York: Cambridge University Press.

Spengler, Joseph A. 1949. "Laissez-faire and Intervention: A Potential Source of Historical Error." *Journal of Political Economy* 57, no. 5 (October): 438–441.

Spierenburg, Pieter. 1984. *The Spectacle of Suffering: Executions and the Evolution of Repression: From a Preindustrial Metropolis to the European Experience.* Cambridge, Eng.: Cambridge University Press.

———. 1991. *The Prison Experience: Disciplinary Institutions and Their Inmates in Early Modern Europe.* New Brunswick, N.J.: Rutgers University Press.

———. 2004. "Punishment, Power, and History." *Social Science History* 28, no. 4 (Winter): 607–636.

Starobinski, Jean. 1985. *Montaigne in Motion.* Chicago: University of Chicago Press.

Stead, Philip John. 1983. *The Police of France.* New York: Macmillan.

Steiner, Philippe. 1998. *La "science nouvelle" de l'économie politique.* Paris: Presses Universitaires de France.

Stendhal. 1919. *Œuvres complètes de Stendhal: Rome, Naples et Florence,* ed. Paul Arbelet and Édouard Champion. 2 vols. Paris: Librairie Ancienne Honoré Champion.

Stigler, George J. 1965. "The Economist and the State." *American Economic Review* 55, nos. 1/2 (March 1): 1–18.

———. 1976. "Preface" to Adam Smith's *An Inquiry into the Nature and Causes of the Wealth of Nations,* ed. Edwin Cannan. Chicago: University of Chicago Press.

———. 1988. *Memoirs of an Unregulated Economist.* New York: Basic Books.

Stokes, Melvyn, and Stephen Conway. 1996. *The Market Revolution in America: Social, Political, and Religious Expressions, 1800–1880.* Charlottesville: University Press of Virginia.

Stone, Julius. 1965. *Human Law and Human Justice.* Stanford, Calif.: Stanford University Press.

Stringham, Edward P. 2007. *Anarchy and the Law: The Political Economy of Choice.* New Brunswick, N.J.: Transaction.

Sunstein, Cass R. 1997. *Free Markets and Social Justice.* New York: Oxford University Press.

Taylor, Arthur J. 1972. *Laissez-faire and State Intervention in Nineteenth-Century Britain.* London: Macmillan.

Taylor, Charles H. 1917. *History of the Board of Trade of the City of Chicago.* 3 vols. Chicago: Robert O. Law Company.

Taylor, Overton H. 1960. *A History of Economic Thought.* New York: McGraw-Hill.

Ten, C. L. 1987. *Crime, Guilt, and Punishment.* Oxford, Eng.: Clarendon Press.

Thill Securities Corp. v. New York Stock Exchange, 433 F. 2d 264, U.S. Court of Appeals for the Seventh Circuit, 1970, *certiorari denied,* 401 U.S. 994 (1971).

Thompson, E. P., et al. 1988. *La guerre du blé au dix-huitième siècle.* Paris: Les Éditions de la Passion.

Tocqueville, Alexis de. 1988. *L'Ancien régime et la Révolution.* Paris: Flammarion.

Tonry, Michael. 1995. *Malign Neglect: Race, Crime, and Punishment in America.* New York: Oxford University Press.

———. 1998. *Sentencing Matters.* New York: Oxford University Press.

Troper, Michel. 2006. *Terminer la Révolution: La Constitution de 1795.* Paris: Éditions Fayard.

Tulkens, Françoise. 1986. "Introduction" to Adolphe Prins, *La défense sociale et les transformations du droit pénal.* Geneva: Éditions Médecine et Hygiène.

———, ed. 1988. *Généalogie de la défense sociale en Belgique (1880–1914).* Brussels: E. Story-Scientia.

Turgot, Anne Robert Jacques. 1808–1811. *Œuvres de Mr. Turgot, ministre d'état, précédées et accompagnées de mémoires et de notes sur sa vie, son administration et ses ouvrages,* ed. Pierre Samuel Du Pont de Nemours. 9 vols. Paris: Imprimerie de A. Belin.

———. 1844. *Œuvres de Turgot,* ed. Eugène Daire. 2 vols. Paris: Librairie Guillaumin.

———. 1971 [1770]. *Reflections on the Formation and the Distribution of Riches,* trans. William J. Ashley. New York: Augustus M. Kelley.

Turnovsky, Stephen J. 1979. "Futures Markets, Private Storage, and Price Stabilization." *Journal of Public Economics* 12 (December): 301–327.

Turnovsky, Stephen J., and Robert B. Campbell. 1985. "The Stabilizing and Welfare Properties of Futures Markets: A Simulation Approach." *International Economic Review* 26, no. 2 (June): 277–303.

United States v. National Association of Securities Dealers, 422 U.S. 694, U.S. Supreme Court, June 26, 1975.

U.S. Commodity Exchange Authority. 1973. "Trading in Commodity Futures Contracts on the Chicago Board of Trade: A Study of the Sources and Distribution of Trading and Commission Income." *Marketing Research Reports.*

U.S. Department of Justice. 1989. *White Collar Crime: A Report to the Public.* Washington, D.C.: Government Printing Office.

Vaggi, Gianni. 1987. *Economics of François Quesnay.* Durham, N.C.: Duke University Press.

Valverde, Mariana. 2007. "Genealogies of European States: Foucauldian Reflections." *Economy and Society* 36, no. 1 (February): 159–178.

Van Overtveldt, Johan. 2007. *The Chicago School.* Canada: Agate.

Vaugelade, Daniel. 2001. *Le salon physiocratique des La Rochefoucauld: Animé par Louise Elisabeth de La Rochefoucauld Duchesse d'Enville (1716–1797).* Paris: Publibook.

Venturi, Franco. 1971. *Utopia and Reform in the Enlightenment.* Cambridge, Eng.: Cambridge University Press.

———. 1972. *Italy and the Enlightenment: Studies in a Cosmopolitan Century.* Great Britain: Longman Group.

———. 1989. *The End of the Old Regime in Europe, 1768–1776: The First Crisis,* trans. R. Burr Litchfield. Princeton, N.J.: Princeton University Press.

Veyne, Paul. 2008. *Foucault: Sa pensée, sa personne.* Paris: Albin Michel.

Villari, Pasquale. 1854. "Vita di Cesare Beccaria." In Cesare Beccaria, *Le Opere di Cesare Beccaria.* Florence: Felice Le Monnier.

Viner, Jacob. 1927. "Adam Smith and Laissez-faire." *Journal of Political Economy* 35, no. 2 (April): 198–232.

———. 1949. "Bentham and J. S. Mill: The Utilitarian Background." *American Economic Review* 39, no. 2 (March): 360–382.

———. 1960. "The Intellectual History of Laissez-faire." *Journal of Law and Economics* 3 (October): 45–69.

Volokh, Alexander. 2008. "Privatization and the Law and Economics of Political Advocacy." *Stanford Law Review* 60:1197–1254.

Voltaire. 1766. *Commentaire sur le livre Des délits et des peines, par un avocat de province.* Geneva: Frères Cramer.

Wacquant, Loïc. 1999. *Les prisons de la misère.* Paris: Raisons d'agir Editions.

———. 2001. "Deadly Symbiosis: When Ghetto and Prison Meet and Mesh." *Punishment & Society* 3:95–133.

———. 2008. "The Place of the Prison in the New Government of Poverty," in *After the War on Crime: Race, Democracy, and a New Reconstruction,* ed. Mary Louise Frampton, Ian Haney López, and Jonathan Simon. New York: New York University Press.

———. 2009. *Punishing the Poor: The Neoliberal Government of Social Insecurity.* Durham, N.C.: Duke University Press.

———. 2011. *Deadly Symbiosis: Race and the Rise of Neoliberal Penality.* Cambridge, Eng.: Polity Press.

Wahnbaeck, Till. 2004. *Luxury and Public Happiness: Political Economy in the Italian Enlightenment.* New York: Oxford University Press.

Wallon, Henri. 1903. *La Chambre de commerce de la province de Normandie (1703–1791).* Rouen, France: Imprimerie Cagniard.

Walmsley, Roy. 2006. *World Prison Population List.* 7th ed. International Center for Prison Studies, King's College, London. Available at www.prisonstudies.org (last visited June 16, 2010).

Wedeen, Lisa. 2008. *Peripheral Visions: Publics, Power, and Performance in Yemen.* Chicago: University of Chicago Press.

Weidemann, Fr., ed. 1832. *Rapports et différences entre les principes de la doctrine du Docteur Quesnay et de celle d'Adam Smith, tirés des œuvres posthumes d'un célèbre savant et publiés par Fr. Weidemann.* Merseburg, Ger.: Librairie de Fr. Weidemann.

Western, Bruce. 2001. "Institutions, Investment, and the Rise of Unemployment." Pp. 71–93 in *The Rise of Neoliberalism and Institutional Analysis,* ed. John L. Campbell and Ove K. Pedersen. Princeton, N.J.: Princeton University Press.

———. 2006. *Punishment and Inequality in America.* New York: Russell Sage Foundation.

Weulersse, Georges. 1910a. *Les manuscrits économiques de François Quesnay et du Marquis de Mirabeau aux Archives Nationales, inventaires, extraits, et notes.* Paris: Geuthner.

———. 1910b. *Le mouvement physiocratique en France de 1756 à 1770.* 2 vols. Paris: Félix Alcan.

———. 2003 [1910]. *Le movement physiocratique en France de 1756 à 1770.* 2 vols. Geneva: Slatkine Reprints.

Whitman, James Q. 2003. *Harsh Justice.* New York: Oxford University Press.

Wilentz, Sean. 1997. "Society, Politics, and the Market Revolution, 1815–1848." Pp. 61–84 in *The New American History,* ed. Eric Foner, rev. and exp. ed. Philadelphia: Temple University Press.

———. 2005. *The Rise of American Democracy: Jefferson to Lincoln.* New York: W. W. Norton.

Williams, Alan. 1979. *The Police of Paris, 1718–1789.* Baton Rouge: Louisiana State University Press.

Williamson, Oliver E. 1994. "Visible and Invisible Governance." *American Economic Review* 84, no. 2 (May): 323–326.

———, ed. 1996. *Liberalism without Illusions: Essays on Liberal Theory and the Political Vision of Judith N. Shklar.* Berkeley: University of California Press.

Yergin, Daniel, and Joseph Stanislaw. 1998. *The Commanding Heights.* New York: Simon & Schuster.

Young, David B. 1983. "Cesare Beccaria: Utilitarian or Retributivist?" *Journal of Criminal Justice* 11:317–326.

Zaloom, Caitlin. 2006. *Out of the Pits: Traders and Technology from Chicago to London.* Chicago: The University of Chicago Press.

Zedner, Lucia. 2006. "Policing before and after the Police: The Historical Antecedents of Contemporary Crime Control." *British Journal of Criminology* 46, no. 1: 78–96.

Zimring, Franklin E., and Bernard E. Harcourt, eds. 2007. *Criminal Law and the Regulation of Vice.* New York: Thompson West.

Zimring, Franklin E., and Gordon Hawkins. 1997. *Incapacitation: Penal Confinement and the Restraint of Crime.* New York: Oxford University Press.

Acknowledgments

This project has benefited immensely from generous conversations and insightful comments from a number of remarkable colleagues, and I am deeply grateful to all of them. First and foremost, I owe a great debt to Ronald Coase, Richard Epstein, and Richard Posner, who graciously read and commented on drafts and sincerely engaged my critique of their work. Special thanks as well go to Fabienne Brion, Josh Cohen, Michael Dawson, Robert Gooding-Williams, Bob Gordon, Duncan Kennedy, Alison LaCroix, Martha Minow, Susan Silbey, Loïc Wacquant, Lindsay Waters, Lisa Wedeen, and two anonymous readers at Harvard University Press for extraordinary comments and guidance. I am also deeply grateful for lengthy discussions and guidance from Andrew Abbott, Pascal Beauvais, Gary Becker, Chris Berk, Olivier Cayla, John Comaroff, Daniel Defert, Andrew Dilts, François Ewald, Joseph Fischel, David Garland, Jan Goldstein, Lisa Jane Graham, Mary Katzenstein, Diana Kim, Patchen Markell, Toni Massaro, Keally McBride, John McCormick, Uday Mehta, Robert Morrissey, Sankar Muthu, Bill Novak, Martha Nussbaum, Turi Palidda, Pasquale Pasquino, Jennifer Pitts, Moishe Postone, Steve Sawyer, Bill Sewell, Jonathan Simon, Carol Steiker, Michel Troper, Mariana Valverde, Michael Welch, Lucia Zedner, and Linda Zerilli. The project has also benefited greatly from comments and conversations with Siva Arumugam, Rosalind Dixon, Don Herzog, Aziz Huq, Amalia Kessler, Jerry Lopez, Jonathan Masur, Richard McAdams, David McBride, Tracey Meares, Tom Miles, Poornima Paidipaty, Joan Petersilia, Randy Picker, Eric Posner, Bill Roy, Adam Samaha, David Strauss, Cass Sunstein, David Weisbach, Noah Zatz, and other colleagues at workshops and conferences at the University of Chicago, Harvard, the University of Michigan, Stanford, and UCLA.

This research has been supported by a Fulbright research grant and by the generous support of my deans, Saul Levmore and Michael Schill, and my chair, Lisa Wedeen, at the University of Chicago. I thank Jan Thomas and Olivier Cayla at the Centre des Normes Juridiques of the École des Hautes

Études en Sciences Sociales and Pascal Beauvais, Florence Bélivier, Elisabeth Fortis, and Pierrette Poncela at the Centre du Droit Pénal at the Université Paris X—Nanterre for their hospitality and intellectual companionship during the Fulbright.

I thank Chris Berk, Elisabeth Geoffroy, and Sam Lim for providing outstanding assistance on the archival and empirical data sets. I am deeply grateful to Lyonette Louis-Jacques, Greg Nimmo, and Margaret Schilt for extraordinary library assistance and guidance. For excellent research on the history of political theory, I am deeply grateful to Jon Jurich, James Johnston, and Brett Reynolds; and for similarly top-notch research on the grain trade, my thanks again go to Matt Johnson, as well as Sam Lim and Dan Montgomery. A special note of appreciation goes to Diana Watral for research and work on the final manuscript, and to Donna Bouvier, Julie Carlson, and Hannah Wong for exceptional assistance at the production stage.

I could not have conducted this research, nor written this book, without the unbending support of my partner, Mia, and my children, Isadora and Léonard. With love, I also dedicate this book to them.

Index